BERLITZ®

DISCOVER
GREECE

We would like to thank Ann Iliokratidou
and Alexandra Vergopoulos, and their
colleagues at the Greek National Tourist
Office, for their cooperation and assistance. We are also very grateful to Miki
Benaki, Beryl Biggins, Aleko Mamiatis,
Nicholas Campbell, Dimitra Fotopolou,
Eileen Harr-Kyburz and Alice Taucher
for their help in preparing this book.

Photographic Acknowledgements

Front cover: Knossos, Crete
(Berlitz Publishing)

Back cover: village of Ia, Santorini
(Daniel Vittet/Berlitz Publishing)

All inside pictures by Luc Chessex
& Jon Davison
© Berlitz Publishing Co Ltd and
Tony Stone Worldwide.

Cartography by Hard Lines, Oxford,
England.

 The Berlitz tick is used to
indicate places or events of
particular interest.

*Although we have made every effort to
ensure the accuracy of all the information in this book, changes do occur. We
cannot therefore take responsibility for
facts, addresses and circumstances in
general that are constantly subject to
alteration.*

*If you have any new information,
suggestions or corrections to contribute
to this guide, we would like to hear from
you. Please write to Berlitz Publishing
at the above address.*

Produced by Fox and Partners, Bath,
England.

Phototypeset, originated and printed by
C.S. Graphics, Singapore.

BERLITZ®

DISCOVER
GREECE

By Jack Altman
Revised by Neil Wilson

Contents

Organising Your Own Personal Odyssey

Travellers planning a visit to Greece are faced with an embarrassment of riches—beautiful beaches, spectacular mountains, secluded islands, ancient cities, Crusader castles. Choosing where to go depends very much on your individual tastes. Students of ancient Greece will want to start with the magnificent archaeological sites concentrated in Athens and the Peloponnese. Hikers and naturalists head for the hills of Crete, Central Greece, and Kephalonia. Sun worshippers will be happiest exploring the beaches of the Cyclades and the Ionian Islands. And history buffs following the footsteps of the Crusaders will be drawn to the islands of the Dodecanese.

Discover Greece is designed to provide a useful and informative guide for several visits over the years, but first-time visitors to Greece can also concoct from its pages an itinerary that provides a

A s dusk falls on the Greek island of Patmos, the village restaurants begin to fill with hungry holiday-makers. Around 10,000,000 tourists visit Greece each year, drawn by the sunshine, clean waters and 15,000 km of unspoilt coast.

good introduction to the country's varied landscapes. It is, of course, impossible to sample all that Greece has to offer in a single visit, but your first trip will undoubtedly whet your appetite to return. Before our detailed description of the various regions, we offer you a **Short List** (p. 72) of what we feel are the essential sights to see in each area. Then, in our **Leisure Routes** chapter (p. 75), you will find itineraries that explore one region or another in pursuit of a particular taste or interest—cultural, sporting or otherwise.

Our eight regional chapters follow a rough loop from Athens and Attica to the Peloponnese, then out to the Cyclades, south to Crete, across to Rhodes and the Dodecanese, up the eastern Aegean to Thessaloniki and the North, through Central Greece and the Sporades, and west across the mainland to the Ionian Islands.

When planning your trip, the first and most obvious choice you have to make is between the mainland and the islands. Try to combine the two. With two or three weeks at your disposal, you should be able to cover quite comfortably a major mainland region like the Peloponnese, or Athens and Central Greece, and still have ample time to get in a little island-hopping too.

However forbidding you may imagine Greece's ancient ruins to be, the great monumental sites like the sanctuary of Delphi, or Agamemnon's palace at Mycenae, exert a mysterious power over even the most blasé imagination. And apart from the mystic attractions of the Byzantine churches and their icons, a quiet moment of meditation spent within their antique walls refreshes body and spirit alike. Taken in small doses before the heat of the day sets in, these inspiring ancient ruins and medieval monuments can act as a tonic when sun-bathing threatens to addle your brain, or the sea begins to shrivel your skin to the texture of a dried apricot. One of the attractions of Mykonos, for instance, is the easy accessibility of the sanctuary of Delos—even the most hardened beach-addict can enjoy the ruins in the morning and be back building sand temples by the afternoon.

If you prefer to avoid the more crowded islands popularized by package tours, you can easily find more secluded spots, but remember that the accommodation and tourist facilities will be correspondingly more modest. The answer here is to rent a house and "go native". But even on the most popular islands like Corfu or Rhodes, it is always possible to get away from the crowd if you are prepared to don your hiking boots and expend a little effort.

You will find detailed practical information in the pages that follow.

When to Go

Greece has a rather short spring, a long, sweltering summer, a slightly cooler autumn, and a winter that is mild by British standards, but sometimes feels much colder than it is—the country is just not designed for cold weather. With only minor regional variations (colder winters in the north), temperatures average from 12°C/53°F in January and February to 33°C/92°F in July and August. But extremes can and do drop winter temperatures to freezing point, and shoot summer highs up over 40°C/104°F—heat waves in Athens are notoriously uncomfortable. Summers are slightly cooler on the coasts and islands, where the sun's heat is tempered by refreshing sea breezes.

In general, the west is moister and greener than the east, true both of Crete and of the Ionian and Aegean seas. Corfu gets the most rain, but even that means only 17 rainy days from May to September (compared with Athens' 14). The months of April and October can both be quite wet.

From time to time in the Aegean (but not on the Ionian islands or the mainland's west coast), the sultry stillness of summer is buffeted between mid-July and the end of August by the notorious *meltemi* wind. Stirred up by a collision of sharply differing atmospheric pressures between the Balkans and North Africa, this north-west breeze begins to blow around 8 a.m. and peters out at sunset. Beach-umbrellas take off, the sand flies in your eyes, and aircraft are sometimes grounded. But yachtsmen say they love it.

Wherever you find yourself in summer, one institution remains sacred, the siesta. From 3 to 5 in the afternoon, all but the most diligent and hard-working Greeks are resting. Don't try to beat them; join them. You'll find that Athens in August, like Rome or Paris, is increasingly closing down all but its most popular tourist attractions.

Mass tourist traffic in the high season makes May, June and September the most attractive months for easy movement around the major destinations; temperatures are more comfortable too, and spring has the added attraction of wild flowers in full bloom.

T he classic colour combination of azure sky and whitewashed walls is enlivened by the reds, pinks and purples of flower baskets and window boxes. Springtime visitors to Greece can also enjoy the magnificent display of wildflowers that carpets the countryside in the months of May and June.

9

What to Take With You

Clothing

Greece's Mediterranean climate encourages lightweight informal clothes. But in the larger cities like Athens and Thessaloniki, people dress appropriately for the occasion; during business hours you see as many suits, ties, smart skirts and blouses as in more temperate climes. Out on the islands, however, dress is decidedly more relaxed. But remember that if you plan to visit any churches or monasteries, long trousers or skirt and a long-sleeved shirt should be worn.

From May to September you won't need an extensive wardrobe—lightweight, drip-dry clothing is the most practical, preferably made of cotton. Laundry service is rare, and light cotton clothes can easily be washed in a hand basin and dried on the balcony. Take along a light sweater or jacket for cool evenings and breezy ferry trips. A good pair of sunglasses and a wide-brimmed sun-hat will come in handy, as will a sturdy pair of walking shoes or boots for hiking and exploring ruins. During the rest of the year it can get chilly, so you'll need a warm jacket and raincoat

Strictly speaking, nude or topless sunbathing is still against the law in Greece, and could result in a fine. But the practice has become generally accepted in many of the more popular resorts—use your common sense and try not to offend the local people.

Useful Extras

A small day pack or "bumbag" is useful for carrying travel documents, money, camera, spare film, sunglasses, maps, reading material, your copy of *Discover Greece* and any other odds and ends. A Swiss Army knife and a small flashlight are worth their weight in gold on anything but the simplest package holiday trip. In summer, insect repellent will come in useful, plus mosquito coils for night time. If you are planning to stay in budget accommodation, soap, towel, toilet tissues and a universal sink plug are recommended. But whatever you do, don't pack too much. There is a lot to be said for the old adage—decide how much money and how much luggage you need, then take twice as much money and half as much gear.

Health and Medical Care

A visit to Greece poses no problems as far as health is concerned. There are no vaccinations required, the tap water is safe to drink, and the food is hygienically prepared. The two main health hazards are sunburn and minor stomach upsets. Treat the sun with respect, and work on your tan gradually—use a high factor sun screen, sunbathe for no more than an hour on the first day, and then build up gradually. Take along sunglasses, a sun hat and a long sleeved shirt to cover up during the middle of the day. Moderation in eating and drinking should help ease you into the change of diet, but any serious stomach problems lasting more than a day should be referred to a doctor—your hotel will be able to recommend one.

Pharmacies are easily recognised by their distinctive sign, a red cross on a white background. A rota system operates for late opening, and a notice on the door will tell you the address of the nearest 24-hour pharmacy. They can give advice on minor problems such as cuts, blisters, sunburn, throat infections and stomach upsets. Travellers taking medication should take an adequate supply of medicines; any prescription drugs should be accompanied by a prescription giving the drug's generic name, not its brand name, which may not be recognised in Greece.

A small **first-aid kit** comes in handy, especially if you're travelling with kids. Keep it small—band-aids, tweezers, a wound dressing, a bandage, antiseptic cream, aspirin, and antihistamine ointment for insect bites and stings, should allow you to cope effectively with minor disasters without having to seek out a doctor or pharmacist.

Insurance

British citizens are entitled to free emergency hospital treatment—you should obtain form E111 from a post office before you leave in order to qualify. You may have to pay part of the price of treatment or medicines; if so, remember to keep receipts so that you can claim a refund when you get home. Full details can be found in the Department of Health's free booklet *Health Advice for Travellers*, available by telephoning the Health Literature Line on 0800 555 777.

However, anything other than basic emergency treatment can be very expensive, and you should not leave home without adequate insurance, preferably including cover for an emergency flight home in the event of serious injury or illness. Your travel agent, bank, building society or insurance broker can provide you with a comprehensive policy which will cover not only your medical costs,

but also theft or loss of money and possessions, delayed or cancelled flights, and so on.

Tourist Information Offices

The Greek National Tourist Organisation (GNTO) can provide information to help you plan your trip before you leave. They supply a wide range of colourful and informative brochures and maps, and extensive listings of hotels and camping sites.

Australia: 51-57 Pitt Street, Sydney, NSW 2000; tel. (02) 241-1663.
Canada: Upper Level, 1300 Bay Street, Toronto, Ontario M5R 3K8; tel. (416) 968-2220.
UK: 4 Conduit Street, London W1R D0J; tel. (0171) 734-5997.
USA: Head Office, Olympic Tower, 645 Fifth Avenue, 5th Floor, New York, NY 10022; tel. (212) 421-5777.
168 N. Michigan Avenue, Chicago, IL60601; tel. (312) 782-1084.
611 W. Sixth Street, Suite 2198, Los Angeles, CA 90017; tel. (213) 626-6696.

The GNTO (known in Greece as EOT— *Ellinikós Organismós Tourismoú*) also operates a network of friendly and helpful tourist information offices throughout the country. Where there is no GNTO office, you can contact the Tourist Police (see below) or one of the many independent information offices.

Athens and Attica
Athens: Head Office (mail and telephone only), Amerikis 2, 10584 Athens;

*S*oldiers in traditional uniform parade near Syntagma Square in Athens.

tel. (01) 32.23.111–9.
Airport information desk, Elliniko Airport East Terminal; tel. (01) 97.99.500. Main information desk, inside the National Bank of Greece, Karageorgi Servias 2 (just off Platia Syntagma); tel. (01) 32.22 25 45. Open 8 a.m. to 6.30 p.m. (closed 2 to 3.30 p.m.) Monday to Thursday, 8 a.m. to 8.30 p.m. (closed 1.30 to 3 p.m.) Friday, 9 a.m. to 2 p.m. Saturday, 9 a.m. to 1 p.m. Sunday and holidays.
Piraeus: Marina Zea; tel: 41.35.716. Open 9 a.m. to 2.30 p.m. Monday to Friday.

Cyclades
Mykonos: Harbour, Mykonos Town; tel. (0289) 23.990/22.201.
Andros: Gavrion; tel. (0282) 71/282.
Tinos: tel. (0283) 23.733/22.234.
Sifnos: Apollonia; tel. (0284) 31.977/31.345.
Paros: Parikia; tel. (0284) 51.220/51.691.
Naxos: Naxos Town; tel. (0285) 24.525.
Ios: Chora; tel. (0286) 91.028.

Crete
Iraklion, Xanthoudidou 1 (opposite Archaeological Museum); tel. (081) 228.203/228.225.
Agios Nikolaos: At bridge over lake, in port police building; tel. (0841) 22.357.
Rethymnon: Venizelou; tel. (0831) 29.148/24.143.
Hania: Kriari 40; tel. (0821) 92.943/92.624

Rhodes and the Dodecanese
Rhodes: GNTO, Makarios 5, Rhodes Town; tel. (0241) 23.655/27.466. Dodecanese Tourism Bureau: A. Makariou & Papagou, Rhodes Town; tel. (0241) 23.655/27.466
Patmos: Skala; tel. (0247) 31.666/31.158.
Kalymnos: Agios Nikolaos (Harbour); tel. (0243) 29.310.
Kos: Akti Maiouli, Kos Town; tel. (0242) 28.724/24.460.

Northern Greece and the Northeast Aegean
Thessaloniki: Mitropoleos 34; tel. (031) 271.889/222.935.
Kavala: Filellinon 5, Pl. Eleftherios, tel. (051) 228.762/231-653.
Lesbos: Novembriou 8, Mytilini; tel. (0251) 42.511.
Chios: Kanari 18, Chios Town; tel. (0271) 24 217.
Samos: Samos Town; tel. (0273) 28.582/92.333.

Central Greece and the Sporades
Delphi: Friderikis 44; tel. (0265) 82.900.
Volos: Pl. Riga Fereou; tel. (0421) 23 500/26.233.

Skopelos: Harbour, Chora; tel: (0424) 23.231.
Skyros: Skyros Town; tel. (0222) 91 123/91.600.

Ionian Islands and Northwest Greece

Corfu: GNTO, Pl. Eleftherios 1, Corfu Town; tel. (0661) 37.520/37.638. Municipal Tourist Office, Customs House, New Port, Corfu Town; tel. (0661) 42.602.
Kephalonia: Harbour, Argostoli; tel. (0671) 22.248/24.466.
Ioannina: Zerva 2, tel. (0651273) 25.086/31.456.

Peloponnese

Sparta: Town Hall; tel. (0731) 24.852
Kalamata: Farou 21; tel. (0721) 22.059/21.959.
Olympia: Praxitelous (near archaeological site); tel. (0624) 23.100/23.125
Patras: Iroon Polytechniou 1; tel. (061) 653.358

Tourist Police

The Tourist Police is a special arm of the police force. They are trained in English and other languages, to assist foreign visitors, and to maintain hotel and restaurant standards. Officers can be recognised by the "Tourist Police" shoulder flash on their uniforms; they may also have a badge showing which languages they can speak. They have branches in many main tourist centres, and can be contacted for information and assistance of any kind. In Athens they are on duty 24 hours a day, and can be reached by telephoning 171. Local numbers are listed in the table below (an asterisk indicates regular police only).

Aegina	22.391
Agios Nikolos (Crete)	26.900
Alonnisos*	65.205
Chios	22.581
Corfu	30.265
Corinth	23.282
Delphi*	82.222
Hania*	71.111
Hydra*	52.205
Ioannina	25.673
Iraklion*	28.224
Kalymnos*	29.301
Kastoria*	22.216
Kavala*	222.905
Kos*	22.222
Larissa*	222.303
Lefkas*	22.346
Lesbos*	22.776
Limnos*	22.200
Missolonghi*	222.222
Mykonos	22.716
Nafplio*	623.061
Naxos*	22.100
Paros*	21.673
Patmos*	31.303
Patras*	623.061
Pieria	23.440
Piraeus*	45.23.670
Poros*	22.256
Rethymnon*	28.156
Rhodes*	27.423
Samos*	27.404
Santorini*	22.649
Sifnos*	31.210
Skiathos*	21.111
Skopelos*	22.235
Skyros*	91.274
Sparta*	28.701
Spetses	73.100
Thessaloniki*	522.589
Tinos*	22.255
Volos*	23.652
Zakynthos*	27.367

Main Duty Free Allowances

Into:	Cigarettes		Cigars (grams)		Tobacco (grams)	Spirits (litres)		Wine (litres)
Greece 1)	800	or	200	or	1000	10	or	90
2)	200	or	50	or	250	1	and	2
3)	400	or	100	or	500	1	and	2
Canada	200	and	50	and	900	1.1	or	1
Ireland	200	or	50	or	250	1	and	2
UK	200	or	50	or	250	1	and	2
USA	200	and	100	and	*	1	and	2

1) Visitors arriving from EU countries with duty and tax paid on items.
2) Visitors arriving from EU countries with duty-free items, or from other European countries.
3) Visitors arriving from outside the EU.
* A reasonable quantity.

Passports and Customs Regulations

For citizens of EU countries, a valid passport or identity card is all that is needed to enter Greece. Other nationalities require a valid passport. For British tourists, a Visitors' Passport is sufficient. Full information on passport and visa regulations is available from the Greek Embassy in London, tel. (0171) 229-3850. Note that tourists who arrive in Greece on charter flights are not permitted to stay overnight in neighbouring countries—this is to prevent you taking advantage of cheap charter flights to Rhodes, for example, and then spending your holiday in Turkey. In effect this means that you can only make day trips to Turkey. You are allowed to remain in Greece for up to three months; to extend your stay, you must apply to the Aliens Bureau, Leoforos Alexandras 173, Athens, tel. (01) 77.05.711, or the local police, at least two weeks before your time runs out.

The chart shows the main duty-free allowances you may take into Greece and, when returning home, into your own country. Prescription drugs must be accompanied by a current prescription. In addition to your personal clothing, you may bring in duty-free a camera, a reasonable amount of film, a pair of binoculars, a typewriter, a radio, a tape recorder, a musical instrument and sporting equipment, including a sailboard, which should be declared when you enter the country.

In 1992 the Greek government began imposing a departure tax of 20 ECUs per person (about £16.00/$24.00) on international flights, and 10 ECUs on domestic flights. This move met great opposition from the Greek tourist industry, who have lobbied hard to have the tax abolished or reduced. So far their efforts have been to no avail, and the tax is still in force.

T he sun sets on the old harbour of Rethymnon on Crete.

How to Get to Greece

By Air

Scheduled flights. Major airlines fly into Athens from all over the world. Although there are some direct services to the islands and outlying regions from European airports, most flights are routed via Athens.

By shopping around the agencies, you will find numerous reduced fares, such as APEX and Standby. This is especially true for British and Australian travellers, but remember that discount fares have a number of restrictions.

APEX tickets must be booked and paid for between seven and 28 days in advance, depending on destination. They also define a minimum and maximum stay, and charge penalties for cancellations or changes in departure date.

If you are travelling from North America you may not find many bargain flights direct to Greece unless you are flying from New York, or perhaps Montreal. You might get a better deal if you hunt around for a cheap flight to one of the major European cities, and then buy another ticket to travel on to Greece from there.

Charter flights and package tours. Charter flights are usually the cheapest way to get to Greece, but these tickets are only available during the main holiday season (April–October), carry many restrictions and offer little flexibility. For instance, you are not allowed to stay overnight in a neighbouring country, and most tickets are for stays of either seven or 14 nights. There is also a legal requirement that accommodation be provided, even on flight-only tickets. This usually takes the form of a hotel voucher, which you may be asked to show on arrival in Greece. Check the conditions carefully before you buy.

There are literally hundreds of package tours available, with flight and accommodation included in the price. These are worth considering if you plan to stay in the one place, though there are also "two-centre" holidays that combine a trip to Athens and Attica with a week in the islands, or a week in Crete followed by a week in Rhodes. There are also many special interest packages available, which cater to the traveller with a particular interest—hiking, learning to sail, natural history or ancient Greece. Your travel agent can provide you with details.

Airports

Ellinikon International Airport lies 10 km/6 miles west of **Athens** city centre. There are two terminals—the West Terminal is for the national carrier Olympic Airways' flights, both domestic and international; and the East Terminal for all other international flights. A free shuttle bus runs between the two (hourly, 8.30 a.m. to 8.30 p.m.). Both terminals have a tourist information desk, currency exchange desk, hotel reservation desk, car hire agencies, duty-free shops, international telephone and fax services, news-stands, bars and restaurants.

A taxi ride into the city centre takes around 25 minutes, or two to three times that during rush hour. There are separate bus services from each terminal. The

Olympic Airways coach runs between the West Terminal and Platia Syntagma, every 20 minutes between 6.30 a.m. and 10.30 p.m. An express coach service runs from the East Terminal to Platia Syntagma and Platia Omonia, every 20 minutes between 6 a.m. and 11 p.m., less frequently through the night.

Thessaloniki has a modern international airport at Mikra, 15 km from the centre of town, with connecting flights to Athens, Limnos, Lesbos, Crete, Rhodes and, in summer, Skiathos. There is a duty-free shop and a tourist information desk. An Olympic Airways coach meets all Olympic flights and drops passengers off at the airline's city terminal, but most travellers choose to take a taxi from the stand outside the terminal. The journey into town takes about 20 to 30 minutes.

By Road

The overland route to Greece runs from Ostend via Brussels, Strasbourg, Munich, Salzburg, Zagreb and Belgrade to Thessaloniki and on to Athens. This road runs right through the former Yugoslavia, and the civil war currently raging there makes the route unsafe. Motorists are advised to take the alternative, and more attractive route to Brindisi in Italy, and take the car ferry from there to Corfu, Igoumenitsa or Patras. The driving distance from London to Athens via Brindisi is about 2400 km (1500 miles).

Motorists planning to take their vehicle abroad need a full driver's licence, an International Motor Insurance Certificate and a Vehicle Registration Document. A Green Card is not a legal requirement, but it is strongly recommended for travel within Greece. An

---

Creative Timetabling

Once you have a rough idea of where you want to go, study Olympic Airways' domestic route-map to see which connections are possible. You must correlate them to the timetable, because not all flights depart daily. Take the trouble to do this yourself as travel agents nowadays don't have the time to work with anything but computers; they will sometimes tell you that your multiple-destination itinerary is impossible, when in fact a little ingenuity can make it work. You'll notice that practically all airports are linked directly to Athens, but there are enough inter-island connections to make island-hopping by air a feasible proposition. Advance reservations (and reconfirmations) are necessary, but be prepared to be flexible in case of sudden flight cancellations due to weather or labour problems. In view of the latter risk, give yourself plenty of leeway to connect with your homeward-bound departure from Athens or wherever.

official GB nationality plate must be displayed near the rear number plate, and head lamp beams must be adjusted for driving on the right. Full details are available from the AA and RAC, or from your insurance company.

By Train

The train journey from London to Athens is long and slow. It is only a little cheaper than a charter flight, but allows more flexibility, especially if you have a Eurail Pass. There are two main routes from Paris. The cheaper route is via the Simplon Pass to Venice, and on through Zagreb and Belgrade to Thessaloniki and then to Athens, but since the advent of civil war in the former Yugoslavia this trip is no longer safe or dependable, and you are advised not to attempt it. The better route is through Italy to Brindisi, then by ferry to Patras, and continuing by rail to Athens.

A way from the cities and coastal resorts, Greek life still moves at a leisurely pace.

By Sea

There are numerous ferry services linking the Italian ports of Venice, Ancona, Bari and Brindisi to Corfu, Igoumenitsa, Patras and Piraeus in Greece. The most popular route is from Brindisi to Patras (17 to 19 hours), with several ferries departing daily from April to October, less frequently in winter; Eurail Passes are also valid on this ferry. Services and timetables are subject to frequent changes and cancellations, and should be checked in advance. The UK agent for the Adriatica line, which runs many Adriatic ferries, is Stena Sealink Ltd, Charter House, Ashford, Kent, TN 24 8EX, tel. (01233) 647 047.

There are also many cruise ships which ply the waters of the Adriatic and the Aegean.

Getting Around in Greece

Air

All domestic flights are provided by the national carrier, Olympic Airways, and are fairly inexpensive by British standards. However, these are only likely to be of interest if you want to see widely separated parts of the country and are pushed for time. Daily services link Athens to the major islands and mainland cities. Flights can be very busy in the high season, so book your seat as far in advance as possible, re-confirm your reservation the day before your flight, and check in at the airport at least an hour before departure. You can get information on fares and schedules from GNTO offices (see TOURIST INFORMATION OFFICES), and buy tickets from any travel agent. Timetables, reservations and tickets are also available from Olympic Airways offices, a few of which are listed here:

London: 164/165 Piccadilly; tel. (0171) 493 3965; reservations (081) 846 9080.
Athens: Syngrou 96; tel. (01) 92.69.111; reservations (01).96.66 666.
Thessaloniki: Komninon 1; tel. (031) 260.121; reservations (031) 230.240.
Crete: Pl. Eleftherios, Iraklion; tel. (081) 229.191; reservations (081) 229 191.
Rhodes: Ierou Lohou 9, Rhodes Town; tel. (0241) 24.571; reservations (0241) 24 555.

Corfu: Kapodistriou 21, Corfu Town; tel. (0661) 38.694; reservations (0661) 38.695.

Ferries

Geography decreed that Greece should be a seafaring nation, and so it has been for thousands of years. Boats are still the most important form of public transport, and provide the most popular and enjoyable way of travelling around the scattered islands. The hub of the Greek ferry system is Piraeus, which has been the port of Athens for nearly 3,000 years. Ferries sail from here to all the Greek islands (except the Ionian Islands, which are served by boats from Patras, Kilini and Igoumenitsa). Details of fares and timetables can be found on the weekly information sheets issued by the GNTO offices in Athens (see TOURIST INFORMATION OFFICES). Fast hydrofoil services sail from Zea to the islands and mainland ports of the Saronic Gulf.

However, the system rarely runs smoothly, and you should be prepared for late (and early!) departures, cancellations due to weather, breakdown, or strikes, and last minute timetable changes. There are over two dozen ferry companies operating over two hundred vessels, but there is no central agency which provides information and tickets for all of them. Prices are controlled by the government, and are pretty cheap compared with the rest of Europe. This means that the harbours are lined with numerous competing ticket agencies all touting their own companies, and unwilling to give the weary traveller any information about competing services. If you plan to make extensive use of the ferry systems, you are strongly advised to get hold of the latest issue of the

Thomas Cook Guide to Greek Island Hopping, which explains the system thoroughly and leads you painlessly through the maze of routes, timetables and ticketing procedures.

Trains

The Greek rail network is not very extensive, and the trains are rather slow, but it is a cheap and often scenic way to cover long distances, and more comfortable than the bus. The trains are run by the Railways Organisation of Greece (OSE), whose offices at Odos Karolou 1, tel. (01) 52.40.674 (near Platia Omonia), and Odos Filellinon 17, tel. 32.36.747 (near Platia Syntagma) sell tickets and provide information on fares and timetables. There are two main railway stations in central Athens, located next to each other on Odos Theodorou Delighiani, northwest of Platia Omonia. The Larissa Station is for trains north to Larissa and Thessaloniki, and onward to Alexandroupoli, with branches to Chalkis, Volos, Kalambaka, and Edessa; the Peloponnese Station, as its name suggests, is for trains west to Corinth, Patras, Pirgos, Kalamata and Argos.

Metro

The Athens Metro provides a good service, with trains running every 5–20 minutes from 5 a.m. to midnight. There is only one line, which runs from the northern suburb of Kifissia, south through Omonia Square, and on to the harbour at Piraeus.

*G*reece *has around 3,000 islands—one fifth of its total land area—although only 169 are permanently inhabited. Ferries form an important part of the transport system, with around 200 vessels plying Greek waters in the high season.*

Buses

Athens has a network of bus and trolleybus routes, with frequent services between 5 a.m. and midnight. Buy a ticket from a news-stand or street kiosk before boarding.

Long-distance buses are cheap, frequent and reliable, and those on the main inter-city routes are often air-conditioned, but can still be uncomfortably crowded. Buses are faster and slightly more expensive than the train over the same route, but the bus network is far more extensive than the railways. The two principal operators are OSE (Railways Organisation of Greece, see above), whose coaches depart from the Larissa and Peloponnese railway terminals in Athens, and the privately-owned KTEL groups (there is a separate group in each province), whose Athens termi-

nals are on the outskirts of the city, at Leoforos Liossion 260, tel. (01) 83.17.059 (for the Peloponnese, Epirus, Macedonia and Thrace), and Leoforos Kifissou 100, tel. (01) 51.48.856 (for Central Greece and Thessaly). Information on fares and timetables is available from GNTO (see TOURIST INFORMATION OFFICES), and advance booking is recommended.

Local buses are the mainstay of public transport in the regions and on the islands. They are often hot, crowded and uncomfortable, and are usually geared to the needs of the local population, travelling from the outlying villages to the main town in the early morning, and returning in the afternoon or early evening. This means they are often not much use for travellers making day trips from the main town, but on the more

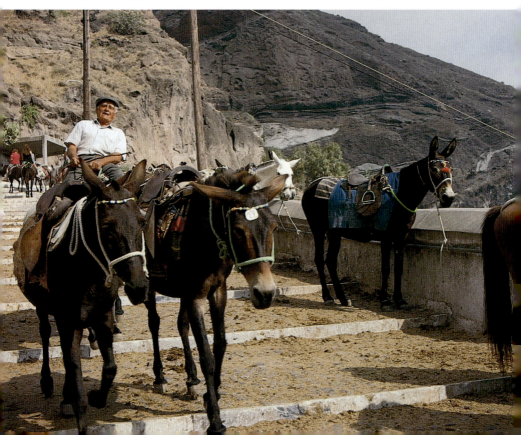

popular islands there are often tourist buses too—check the local tourist information office or travel agent for routes and timetables.

Taxis

In **Athens**, taxis are cheap and supposedly plentiful, but notoriously difficult to find. In theory, you can pick one up at a taxi rank in one of the main squares, or flag one down on the street, but it can be

The Name Game

There is no hard and fast rule for Roman-alphabet transliterations of Greek place-names on signposts and road maps. You should have no problem with Heraklion and Iraklion or Piraeus and Pireéfs, but Greeks prefer Kerkyra to Corfu and Thessaloniki to Salonica. Berlitz has decided to be as flexible as the Greeks, but more consistent, using the most familiar English versions.

Finding your way around towns and cities will be much easier if you learn the Greek alphabet (see p. 39 in the FACTS AND FIGURES section.) All street signs are written in capital letters. The words for street (*odós*), avenue (*leóforos*), and square (*platía*) are used in conversation, but usually omitted from maps and signs.

*O*ne of the more unusual forms of public transport in Greece are the donkey "taxis" of Santorini (Thera). These sturdy beasts ferry passengers up and down the steep trail from the tiny landing stage in the central bay to the town of Fira perched on the rim of the caldera, 330m/1,000ft above.

a frustrating business, especially during rush hours. Probably the best way is to ask your hotel receptionist to order one by telephone. There is an extra charge for this, as there is for each piece of luggage; for pick-up from an airport, harbour, or railway station; for waiting; for travel between midnight and 5 a.m.; and for travel beyond the city limits. If there is room in the cab, the driver can legally pick up extra passengers on the way, if their destination lies in roughly the same direction. Most drivers are honest and helpful, but watch out for cowboys who may try to charge each passenger the full fare. Other tricks include setting the meter to the "double" rate, which should only be used between midnight and 5 a.m., or for trips outside the city limits (check the small window beside the fare display—it should read "1" for normal trips, "2" for double rate), and refusing to use the meter when picking up late in the evening from airport or harbour, demanding instead some extortionate fixed fare. Such practices should be reported to the Tourist Police (see TOURIST INFORMATION OFFICES).

Taxis are relatively cheap and easy to find in the towns of **mainland Greece** and on the **islands** of Crete, Corfu and Rhodes; split between four people, the fare often works out about the same as the bus. But on other islands a taxi ride can cost up to ten times the bus fare. However, if you want to make a day trip to some out-of-the-way place, a taxi is usually much cheaper than a hire car. Meters are not often used in country areas, and a fare should be negotiated beforehand. You can ask your hotel or tourist office for the standard fares, or at least shop around a few different drivers for the best deal.

Car Hire

A rental car gives you the freedom to explore wherever your fancy takes you, independent of bus routes and timetables. But it's not cheap—Greece is one of the most expensive countries in Europe for car hire. The least expensive way to go about it is to book and pay for your rental car before you leave home, through an international hire company or a travel agent, or to buy a fly-drive package from a tour operator. If you plan to explore unsurfaced island back roads, a four-wheel drive vehicle is essential—many island car rental agencies offer jeeps.

The minimum age for drivers is normally 21 years, and you must have held a full driver's licence for at least one year. Make sure the rates quoted include unlimited mileage, local taxes, and full insurance cover. Collision Damage Waiver (CDW) is usually an optional extra that can add up £5 a day to the rate, but you should not consider driving without it; Greece has the worst traffic accident rate in Europe.

Driving in Greece

Greek law requires all vehicles to carry a first-aid kit, a fire extinguisher and a warning triangle; seat belts are compulsory in the front seats, and headlamps must be dipped in built-up areas. Speed limits are 60 kph (37 mph) in built-up areas, 80 or 100 kph (50 or 62 mph) outside built-up areas, and 120 kph (74 mph) on motorways; road signs follow the standard international format used in the UK. Tolls are levied on the two main motorways, from Athens west to Patras, and north to Larissa and Thessaloniki.

You should avoid driving in Athens and Thessaloniki if at all possible, as the cities are plagued with congestion, bad-tempered traffic jams, and a shortage of parking. Police will remove your licence plates if you are caught parking illegally. A restricted access system applies in central Athens (for Greek-registered vehicles only, including rental cars), and is enforced on weekdays from 6 a.m. to 8 p.m.—on days with an even-numbered date, only cars with an even-numbered licence plate are permitted in the restricted zone, and odd-numbered cars on odd-numbered dates.

Driving conditions on the motorways are good, but on other roads you should look out for uneven surfaces, soft shoulders, wandering livestock, and fallen rocks. The minor roads in the mountains and on the islands are often unsurfaced, and like narrow, winding roads everywhere demand caution and concentration.

While service stations are plentiful, the supply of **petrol** may be less than adequate. Fill up whenever possible, even if the tank is still half-full. Unleaded petrol is available only as Super (95 octane), while leaded comes as Regular (91/92 octane) and Super (96/98 octane). Most service stations close at 7 p.m. or earlier, especially on weekends; a few stay open later, on a rota system.

If you are unfortunate enough to suffer a **breakdown**, AA and RAC members can get help from the Automobile & Touring Club of Greece, who operate a 24-hour breakdown service covering all main roads on the mainland, plus the islands of Crete and Corfu—for assistance, telephone 104. Drivers of hire cars should call the emergency number provided by their rental agency. Otherwise it's a matter of seeking out the nearest garage, and hoping that they can help. In the event of an accident, follow the procedure laid down by your insurance policy. You must report the accident to the police if any injury is involved.

Motorbikes, Scooters, and Mopeds

Most major tourist centres, especially in the islands, have agencies which rent out motorised, two-wheeled transport. Mopeds and scooters are ideal for pottering around the back roads over short distances, but for exploring more than a few miles from town, especially in hilly areas like Crete, a motorbike with at least a 50 cc engine is necessary. Bigger bikes of 150 to 200 cc are often available, but you will need a motorcycle licence for these, while an ordinary driving licence is sufficient for bikes up to 50 cc. Helmets are compulsory.

Check that the quoted rates include the compulsory tax and insurance—they usually don't, and it's a hefty extra. Inspect the bike carefully before taking it, as you will be responsible for repairing and returning it if it breaks down. Remember that motorbikes and scooters are potentially very dangerous. Go slowly and keep to quiet back roads until you get the hang of it—every year there are many bad accidents involving tourists on two wheels.

Accommodation

The more popular tourist areas of Greece, such as Athens, Crete, Corfu and Rhodes, offer the traveller a wide range of accommodations, from a simple room in a family house, to luxury international hotels. Away from the big resorts, however, you are likely to find only rooms to let, especially on the islands. Remember too, that outside of Athens many places close down for the winter (November to March), making accommodation more difficult to find.

First-time visitors should be warned about the vagaries of Greek plumbing. If your WC has a waste bin beside it, this is for disposing of used toilet paper. Whatever you do, don't put toilet paper (or anything else) in the loo, or you might block not only your own toilet, but your neighbour's as well!

Hotels are divided into six categories: L (luxury), A (expensive), B (moderate), C (inexpensive), D (cheap) and E (a real bargain—and a real surprise at times, for better or worse!). Room prices are government-controlled, but regulations are not always strictly upheld, and rates can vary unpredictably. However, outside of the luxury category Greek hotel prices are often a bargain by British standards. The base rate must be displayed in each room, along with any extra charges depending on various factors such as the facilities provided (air-conditioning, hot water, telephone, etc.), your length of stay, and of course, seasonal variations. Some places may insist you take full or half board during high season. A government tax is added to the bill. Reductions are sometimes offered for children.

Greek tap water is perfectly safe to drink—indeed the Greeks are connoisseurs of water, eagerly debating the merits of their favourite wells and springs. The electrical supply is 220 V/50 Hz AC, the same as the UK, but sockets are the standard continental two-pin type, which require an adapter (buy one before you leave home).

If you plan to visit Greece in the peak season of July and August, it is advisable to book your accommodation in advance. The GNTO (Greek National Tourist Organization) and most travel agents provide a comprehensive list of hotels and rates (see TOURIST INFORMATION OFFICES). Reservations can also be made through the Hellenic Chamber of Hotels, Stadiou 24, 10564, Athens, tel. (01) 32.33.501 or 32.36.641. If you're in Athens, you can make on-the-spot reservations through the GNTO office at Karageorgi Servias 2, Athens, tel. (01) 32.37.193.

Private accommodation. It's very easy to rent rooms in private homes. Islanders meet the ferries at the harbour with offers of "Rooms"—usually in English—and in every town and village you will see signs proclaiming "Rooms for rent" or "Zimmer frei". Prices are generally negotiable (though with increasing difficulty as the high season

*F*ishermen mend their nets on the quayside in Mykonos. Although tourism is now the major source of income in the Greek islands, the traditional pursuits of fishing and farming still provide a livelihood for many islanders.

but you will probably have to pay much more than usual.

Some of the inexpensive hotels, as well as the island tavernas, offer "roof-space", which is exactly that—a space on the roof where they will usually provide a mattress. For the more adventurous traveller with a sleeping bag, spending the night out under the stars might not be such a bad solution.

Villas. Ranging from small, simple cottages to lavish summer houses, villas can be let for monthly and sometimes weekly rates. When booking, check the facilities provided, which normally, but not always, include refrigerator, hot water and electricity. In low season you can try asking the Tourist Police or the local inhabitants for any possibilities. Otherwise your travel agent or the GNTO will give you names and addresses.

Youth hostels are rather thin on the ground in Greece, but they are simple, clean and comfortable, and you might even be let in without a membership card, if there's room. The doors close at around midnight, and the maximum stay is usually five days. There are hostels in Athens (3), Piraeus, Delphi, Litochoro, Mycenae, Nafplio, Olympia, Patras, Thessaloniki, Corfu (2), Santorini, and Crete (8). Full details can be obtained from the national youth hostel association in your own country.

approaches). In some places, the rooms are run by the local Tourist Police, who have to ensure that the hotels are all filled up first. So in low season, many of the private rooms are closed down to favour the hotel business.

If you have difficulty finding somewhere to stay, contact the GNTO or the local Tourist Police, who will almost always manage to find something for you. When demand is high, certain "informal" arrangements can be made,

Camping is officially permitted only at authorized camp sites, which provide fresh water, toilets and showers, and often have much-needed shade, and access to a beach. In practice, however, unofficial campers are tolerated in many places, especially during the peak season, provided that you use your discretion, ask permission from the landowner, and don't leave a mess. In the islands especially, the shortage of official accommodation has caused the police to turn a blind eye to visitors camping or sleeping out on the beaches and other unauthorized spots. But be warned—it's against the law, and on occasions the law is enforced; you could be fined.

Most campsites are open from April to October. For a full list of camp sites, and further information on camping in Greece, contact the GNTO office in your home country — (see TOURIST INFORMATION OFFICES).

hotel. Banks are generally open from 8 a.m. to 2 p.m. Monday to Thursday, and until 1.30 p.m. on Friday. In Athens, the Platia Syntagma branch of the National Bank of Greece (where there is also a GNTO office—see TOURIST INFORMATION OFFICES) has additional opening hours for currency exchange only: 3.30 to 6.30 p.m. Monday to Thursday, 3.00 to 8.30 p.m. Friday, 9 a.m. to 3 p.m. Saturday, and 9 a.m. to 1 p.m. Sunday.

Traveller's cheques are the safest way to carry your holiday cash, but it's a good idea to buy a small amount of Greek currency before you leave home, especially if you'll be arriving on a weekend. You can exchange them for drachmas—remember to take your passport for identification—but few places accept them as cash. Major **credit cards** are widely accepted in Athens and Thessaloniki and the major tourist resorts, in banks, car hire and travel agencies, and the better hotels, restaurants and shops.

Money

The unit of currency in Greece is the drachma, usually abbreviated to Δρχ in Greek. Coins come in denominations of 1, 2, 5, 10, 20 and 50 drachmas, notes in 50, 100, 500, 1000, and 5000 drachmas.

Exchanging Money

Cash and traveller's cheques can be exchanged in banks, currency exchange booths in airports and railway stations, post offices, major hotels, and occasionally in travel agencies, especially in the islands. **Banks** offer the best rates, but can be busy, and you may feel it's worth your while to pay a little extra for the convenience of changing money at your

Post and Telephone

The **post office** handles letters, stamps, parcels and currency exchange, but not telegrams and telephone calls. They are usually open from 7.30 a.m. to 2.30 p.m. Monday to Friday; the offices on Odos Eolou, Platia Syntagma and Platia Omonia in Athens stay open until 8 p.m. Parcel contents must be checked by staff, so don't seal the wrapping beforehand. You can buy stamps for letters and postcards at news kiosks and souvenir shops too.

From Greece, air mail letters generally take about five to eight days to reach European destinations, and eight to ten days to the USA. Postcards, inexplicably, take slightly longer.

If you want to receive mail **poste restante** while you are in Greece, have your letters sent to you with your surname underlined, c/o Poste Restante, (town name), Greece, and it will be held for you at the town's main post office. In Athens your letters will end up at the head post office on Odos Eolou 100, near Omonia Square, and in Thessaloniki at Odos Tsimiski 43-45. Take along your passport when you go to claim your mail.

Telegrams and telexes can be sent from offices of the Greek Telecommunications Organisation (OTE). There is at least one branch on each island, and in all the principal mainland towns. You can also make long-distance and international telephone calls from these offices. Faxes can be sent from major post offices and from many hotels.

Local **telephone** calls can be made from the red payphones in hotels, cafes and shops, or from the blue telephone booths in the street, both of which currently accept 10-drachma coins. Long-distance/international telephone booths are orange, and take 10 and 20-drachma coins. International calls can also be made at an OTE office, or dialled direct from a hotel or private phone. To call direct first dial 00, then the country code (44 for the UK, 1 for the USA), then the area code (leaving out the initial zero), then the number. To make a British Telecom Chargecard or reverse-charge call, dial 161 for the English-speaking international operator. A three-minute call to the UK will cost roughly £2.

Twenty-four hour OTE offices can be found at Odos Patission 85 in Athens (a few blocks beyond Leoforos Alexandros), and at Odos Ermou 48 (at the corner of Odos Karalou) in Thessaloniki.

Time Differences

Greece is two hours ahead of GMT in winter, and the clock is put forward one hour in summer, making it two hours ahead of British Summer Time too. The clock goes forward on the last Sunday in March, and back on the last Sunday in September. The chart below summarizes the time differences in summer.

Los Angeles	2 a.m.
New York	5 a.m.
London	10 a.m.
Greece	**noon**
Sydney	7 p.m.
Auckland	9 p.m.

Eating Out

You will never discover the adventure of Greek cooking if you stick to your hotel dining room. Pandering as it does to palates intimidated by anything "strange", hotel cooking remains bland and unadventurous. Even when a "local speciality" is offered, like the yoghurt and cucumber appetizer known as *dzadzíki*, the essential garlic is almost imperceptible, on the assumption that it would upset northern European or American guests. The problem posed by hotel restaurants may also be true of many of the tavernas situated in the more popular tourist areas; many find it more profitable to cater to a fairly low common denominator.

Try, whenever possible, to go where the Greeks go. In port towns, for instance, the locals often keep away from the crowded harbourside establishments. In the backstreet tavernas, you will enjoy the zing of a really garlicky *dzadzíki*, often rendered even more refreshing with a touch of mint.

Restaurants are classified into four categories (deluxe, A, B and C), with price ranges controlled by the government (except in deluxe establishments). By law, service charge must be included in the bill. Whether or not you leave a tip is entirely up to you.

The most abundant type of eatery is the **taverna**, where you'll find basic Greek dishes of grilled or roasted meats with salads, though not always a menu. It's common practice to be shown to the kitchen to see what's cooking, and make your choice by simply pointing to what you fancy—handy if your Greek's a little rusty. *Olígo* (meaning "just a little") will get you a half-portion. Ask the prices while you're ordering, if there's no menu.

In a **restaurant** proper *(éstiatório)* the food and service may be a bit more formal than service in a taverna, with a wider range of dishes and Greek specialities. But don't expect elegant, sophisticated dining except in the deluxe establishments.

Look out for three varieties of snack bar. For yoghurt or cheese snacks, try the *galaktopolío* (dairy counter). The *psistariá* (grill) serves different kinds of meat kebab. For a better selection of desserts than most restaurants offer, go to the *zacharoplastío* (pastry shop).

You will also come across the traditional Greek *kafeníon* (café) particularly in the provinces. But this is more of a men's club than a public café, a place to enjoy political debate, a game of backgammon, and small cups of very strong coffee. Strangers are not refused admission, but the place is usually considered something of a haven for the locals, and understandably so in such a tourist-saturated country.

Mealtimes

If you decide to "go Greek" and accept wholeheartedly the institution of the afternoon siesta, you may want to modify your meal times. The Greeks themselves get in a prolonged morning's work and have lunch around 2 p.m.,

siesta until 5, maybe work some more until 8.30 and then dine late around 9.30. Don't be surprised to see diners lingering long after midnight, as most places stay open until 2 a.m. The restaurants will serve you earlier, from midday and early evening, but you will miss the more authentic Greek scene if you keep only to "tourist hours".

Breakfast, a basic affair of coffee with bread and butter for most Greeks, is not usually served in restaurants (though in package tour resorts you can find any number of places offering British-style bacon and eggs). Try looking for a *zacharoplastío* and breakfast on a delicious pastry washed down with coffee.

Greek Cuisine

The basic ingredients of a Greek meal have not changed much since Plato's day. Lamb, goat and veal are charcoal-grilled much as they were by Agamemnon's soldiers at the gates of Troy. Red mullet and octopus, beans and lentils, olives, lemons, basil and oregano, figs and almonds, even the resinous taste of the wine all form a gastronomic link between Greece ancient and modern.

After a pleasant day at the beach or a challenging pilgrimage to an ancient sanctuary, the Greek dinner table offers a spell of total relaxation. Ambience is more important than *haute cuisine*. Greek cooking makes no attempt to emulate the sophistication of the French, or the infinite variety of the Chinese. Yet the people's natural zest for life can always conjure the savoury ingredients

*F*lower stalls line the back streets of Monastiraki in Athens.

of a Mediterranean market into something wholesome, satisfying and not without its own subtlety.

The Menu

The tantalizing thing about the many tasty Greek specialities described here is that only a fraction of them are available at any one time. The menu printed in English often contains them all, but only those items with a price against them are being served that day. Rather than submit to this frustration, do what the Greeks do and go back to the kitchen to see what's being cooked. The cold appetizers are arrayed in glass display-cases. Cuts of meat and the fish catch of the day are lying ready in glass-windowed refrigerators. Hot dishes are simmering on the stove in casseroles—the cook will take off the lid for you to peek in and take a sniff. The management is more than happy for you to point out your choices here and avoid later misunderstandings. Remember fish and meat are usually priced by weight, so that the size you choose there in the kitchen becomes your responsibility when the bill arrives.

Appetizers

It is the Greek custom to eat the appetizers *(mezédes)* with an apéritif of *ouzo* mixed with chilled water, before the rest of the meal is served up. For convenience, they are usually served at resort tavernas along with the main courses, but the essence of the *mezé* remains its leisurely enjoyment—not just something to gulp down while you are waiting for the main dish, but a spread to be savoured in its own right. Besides the garlicky yoghurt-and-cucumber salad called *dzadzíki*, the range is impressive:

A *colourful selection of fresh fruit and vegetables tempts the shoppers in Iraklion's morning market. As a change from restaurant meals, you might like to browse the stalls for a picnic lunch.*

taramá, a creamy paste of cod's roe mixed with bread crumbs, egg yolk, lemon juice, salt, pepper and olive oil; *dolmádes*, little parcels of vine leaves, filled with rice, pine kernels and minced mutton, braised in olive oil and lemon juice and served cold; *melitzanosaláta,* aubergine puréed with onion and garlic; the ubiquitous Greek salad, *saláta choriátiki* (literally "village salad"), a refreshing mixture of tomato, cucumber, feta cheese and black olives; small pieces of fried squid *(kalamarákia tiganitá)* or cold marinated octopus salad *(chtapódi)*; *tirópitakia*, small pastry triangles filled with goat's cheese; marinated mushrooms and white beans; spicy *pastoúrma*, thin peppery, garlicky slices of dried mutton, beef or goat; *loukánika*, spicy sausage, and mussels *(míthia)*; and, of course, dishes of green, black, and brown olives, the best from Thrace and the southern Peloponnese.

Soups

Resort tavernas often do not like to serve soup, because of the temptation to treat these filling dishes as a complete meal. But the best known Greek soup is light enough to appear as an accompaniment—*avgolémono*, chicken broth with egg and lemon, thickened with rice.

At Easter, join the Orthodox Greeks who break the Lenten fast with the traditional *magirítsa*, lamb tripe soup that is spiced and cooked with lettuce, egg and lemon. In Thessaloniki's finer restaurants—and this merchant's city has many—look out for the *patsás* tripe soup that is served all year round. Santorini is particularly reputed for its bean soup *(fassouláta)*, while connoisseurs swear by Sifnos-style chick pea soup *(revíthia soúpa)* with onions, olives and lemon. The best seafood restaurants keep a cauldron of fish soup going and occasionally a spicy squid and tomato soup *(kalamariáki)*.

Fish

One of the great pleasures of the Greek dinner table is its seafood, and the simplest preparation is usually the best. Order your fish grilled—red mullet *(barboúnia)*, swordfish *(xifías)*, often served on the skewer, sole *(glóssa)*, and bream *(lithríni)* are among the most popular, served with garlicky mashed potatoes. In Chios, you can try flying fish or *chelidonópsaro*. The sardines *(sardéles)* are good baked, and whitebait *(marídes)* and mussels are served fried.

If you like your seafood stewed, try the octopus with white wine, tomatoes and potatoes; or prawns *(garídes)* in white wine and feta cheese. Skyros is particularly reputed for its shellfish, notably giant crab *(kaniás)*. Corfu boasts a delicious but sometimes exorbitant *astakós*, a clawless crustacean properly known as crayfish, or spiny lobster or rock lobster, but not just "lobster", as some tourist menus suggest.

Meat

Your first encounter with Greek meat specialities is likely to be at the *psistariá*, a snack bar that serves *souvlákia*, garlic-marinated lamb kebabs with onions, and *gíros*, slices of meat from spit-roasted slabs of pork, veal or lamb (these are also known as *donér kebáb*). This latter is often served with bread and salad. The taverna may also serve *souvlákia* along with *keftédes*, spicy lamb meat balls, minced with mint, onion, eggs and bacon. *Kokorétsi*, lamb tripe sausages, demand a robust stomach. Roast leg of lamb *(arní yiouvetsi)*, served with pasta, is the grand Easter dish. In summer, you are more likely to find lamb chops.

Crete is celebrated for its braised beef with onions *(stiffádo)*, while Corfu does a fine stewed steak *(sofríto)*. A grilled steak *(brizóles)* will generally come well done unless you specify otherwise, and is not usually tender enough to risk less than medium.

Two famous casserole dishes are the test of a restaurant's quality. *Moussaká* has as many variations as there are regions and islands, but basically, it alternates layers of sliced aubergine with chopped lamb, onions, and béchamel sauce, topped with a layer of aubergine skins. The more Italian *pastítsio* uses lamb, mutton or goat's meat in alternating layers with macaroni, mixed variously with seasoned tomatoes, eggs and cheese, topped with a sprinkling of breadcrumbs.

The best wild game is to be found up in Macedonia in September. Try the rabbit *(kounéli)*, sautéed with a lemon sauce. Braised hare with walnuts *(lagós me sáltsa karithiá)* is a dish for the gods, but mere mortals will also appreciate the partridge *(pérdikes)* sautéed and served with pasta.

Cheeses

Greek cheese is made out of ewe's or goat's milk. Feta is the best known of the soft cheeses, popping up in almost every "Greek salad". *Kaséri* is best eaten fresh. On Crete, *anthótyro* and *manoúri* are relatively bland, *graviéra* is harder and sharper. Other hard cheeses are the *agrafáou* and the salty *kefalotíri*. A rare blue cheese to look out for is *kopanistí*.

Desserts

The Greeks eat their after-dinner dessert at the pastry shop *(zacharoplastío)* on the way home. Tavernas rarely have a full selection. Among the most popular desserts are: *baklavá*, a honey-drenched flaky pastry with walnuts and almonds; *loukoúm*, a doughnut-like honey fritter; *kataífi*, a pastry that looks like shredded wheat and is filled with honey or syrup and chopped almonds; and *pítta me méli*, honey cake. *Galaktoboúriko* is a refreshing custard pie. And remember to drop in at the dairy shop *(galaktopolío)* to sample that perfect sour-sweet dish of fresh yoghurt and honey.

The best of the locally produced fruits are the pomegranates, peaches, apricots, grapes and melon.

Bread

One of the sweetest-smelling places in a Greek village is the bakery. If you are shopping for a picnic, get here early for the freshest *kouloúria,* rings of white bread sprinkled with sesame seeds. *Choriátiko* is country bread, flat, off-white and very tasty. And take along a few *moustalevriá,* wine-flavoured sesame biscuits. At the end of the day, the ovens are made available for neighbours' family roasts. If you have rented a house, make friends with the baker and he will do your leg of lamb, too.

Coffee

Unless you prefer bland instant coffee (here known imaginatively as *nes*), order the thick black Levantine brew that the locals drink. *Ellinikó* is what you say for the traditional coffee served, grounds and all, from a long-handled copper or aluminium pot. But be sure of getting it freshly brewed to your liking, correctly served with an accompanying glass of iced water. Ask for *éna varí glikó* (heavy and sweet), *glikí vastró* (sweet but weaker), *éna métrio* (medium), or *éna skéto* (without sugar).

Wines

Greek wine had a much better reputation in the ancient world than it does now. Fermented alcoholic drinks had preceded Greek civilization, but it was the Greeks who turned the growing of vines into an agricultural practice. They were the first to understand the importance of pruning the plants and exploiting dry, stony ground.

Retsína, the unique resinous white wine, was a favourite of the ancient Greeks. Today, pine resin is still added in fermentation as a preservative to pro-

long shelf life in the hot climate. It takes four, at most five minutes to acquire the taste and discover how well it goes with both seafood and lamb. The best, produced in the villages of Messoghia north-east of Athens, comes straight from the barrel—ask for *varéli.* The strongest seems to be the home-brewed stuff in the monasteries.

Non-resinous white wines refined enough for special celebrations are **Robóla** of Kephalonia, **Pallíni** from Attica, and **Château Carras** from Chalkidiki. The Peloponnese produces the best non-resinous whites for everyday consumption, **Deméstica** and **Lac des Roches**.

Go easier on the red wines, which are notoriously full-bodied and rich in alcohol. Among the best are the **Náousa** from Macedonia, Santorini's volcanic **Kaldéra** and the well-known **Mavrodáfni** from Patras. Samos is still famous for its **Sámena**, a muscatel dessert wine.

If you develop a taste for aniseed-flavoured ouzo, neat or with ice and water, one of the finest brands is **Plomári** from Lesbos.

*I*n a country as intimately associated with the sea as Greece, it is little wonder that fish forms an important item on the menu. However, dwindling stocks and soaring demand mean that seafood is no longer an inexpensive treat. But it is well worth paying the price to sample deliciously fresh delicacies like octopus, swordfish and lobster.

Greek or Turkish?

Nothing makes the Greeks more angry than to be told they have no cuisine of their own. Detractors dismiss it as a mishmash of cuisines introduced by their numerous conquerors, pointing to the Turks, for example, as the originators of Greece's strong, thick coffee and honey-drenched pastries. But even these, the Greeks insist, are Greek in origin. We taught the Western world how to cook, they protest. When the Romans conquered Greece, the first things they wanted to take home were our philosophers and our cooks. Our chefs were always held in such high esteem that we had laws protecting their recipes with patents that they could sell at the agora. They took a two-year course at culinary schools in Athens.

Classical Greek cooking had much in common with French nouvelle cuisine: finesse, simplicity, authentic flavours, meats roasted and grilled rather than stewed in rich sauces, using just herbs and a very few basic ingredients.

In Plato's Republic, frugal Socrates proposes an ideal diet that would serve very well for your midday holiday meal: bread, olives, cheese, vegetables and fruit. Epicurus, who held that the highest good is pleasure, but not necessarily self-indulgence, declared: "Simple dishes are as satisfying as sumptuous banquets."

Archestrate, the first gastronomy critic (4th century BC), travelled from his native Gela in Sicily throughout the Mediterranean world, and composed an epic poem on his findings, named Hedypathia (Voluptuousness). Among the few fragments of his work that survive are descriptions of dog's or sow's belly cooked in olive oil and powdered with cumin; eel in Chinese cabbage; and an enthusiastic endorsement of Rhodes sturgeon.

For a short while, it became the fashion to disguise the food and have the guests guess what they were eating. At one banquet, they argued about whether they had eaten chicken, fish or veal and it turned out to be vegetable marrow. Some of the more respectable ancient Greek legacies to world cuisine are fried scampi, turbot with herbs, blood sausage (black pudding), thrush in honey and grilled frogs' legs.

So Roman cuisine was indeed essentially Greek. That is what Constantine and his court brought with them when the Eastern Empire was established in Byzantium. What the Venetians and Genoese brought in also came from the Greco-Roman tradition. And, the Greeks argue, the Turks took over the Byzantine tradition—richer and sweeter perhaps, but still fundamentally Greek.

Shops and Services

Opening Hours

The times given below are a guide to opening hours, though variations do occur, especially in cities, where some banks and post offices open later and at weekends.

Banks

8 a.m. to 2 p.m. Monday to Thursday, and 1 p.m. on Friday.

Post Offices

7.30 a.m. to 2.30 p.m. Monday to Friday.

Shops

Opening times vary, but they are generally from 8 a.m. to 1 or 2 p.m. Monday to Saturday, and from 5 p.m. to 8.30 p.m. Tuesday, Thursday and Friday. Shops in major tourist centres will keep longer hours and may stay open all day.

Museums and Archaeological Sites

It is difficult to generalize, so check with the local GNTO office (see TOURIST IN-FORMATION OFFICES). The **National Archaeological Museum** in Athens opens from 8 a.m. to 7 p.m. Tuesday to Friday, 12.30 a.m. to 7 p.m. Monday, and 8.30 a.m. to 3 p.m. weekends and holidays.

Archaeological sites are usually open morning until evening seven days a week in summer, shorter hours in winter. The **Acropolis** in Athens opens 8 a.m. to 6.30 p.m. Monday to Friday, 8.30 a.m. to 3 p.m. weekends and holidays.

All museums and sites are closed on 1 January, 25 March, Good Friday (until noon), Easter Sunday and Christmas.

Public Holidays

Banks, offices and shops will be closed on the following national holidays.

1 January *Protochronia*
New Year's Day

6 January *ton Theophanion*
Epiphany

25 March *Ikosti Pemti Martiou*
Greek Independence Day

1 May *Protomagia*
May Day

15 August *tis Panagias*
Assumption Day

28 October *Ikosti Ogdoi Oktovriou*
Ochi (No) Day

25 December *Christougenna*
Christmas Day

26 December *Defteri imera ton Christougennon*
St Stephen's Day

Movable dates

Kathari Defteri First day of Lent

Megali Paraskevi Good Friday

Deftera tou Pascha Easter Monday

In addition to these dates, islands and towns will celebrate the feast days of their local patron saints. For example, Athens observes the Feast of St Dionysus the Areopagite on 3 October, a legal holiday in the city.

Note that the dates on which the movable holy days are celebrated are calcu-

lated according to the Orthodox calendar, and often differ from those in Catholic and Protestant countries. In Greece, Easter is a much more important holiday than Christmas.

*O*rthodox icons and images of the saints adorn the domestic shrines in many Greek homes.

Pharmacies
See HEALTH AND MEDICAL CARE, p. 10.

Newspapers and Magazines
Most foreign dailies, including the principal British newspapers and the *International Herald Tribune,* appear on Athens news-stands the day after publication, at a rather stiff price. There is a good selection of foreign magazines from most European countries. On the islands, supply is tailored to demand, and in summer you'll find a good selection of European periodicals and the major American news weeklies. In winter there are few if any foreign publications on sale outside Athens.

There is an English-language daily newspaper, the *Athens News,* and a monthly magazine in English, *The Athenian,* which has a comprehensive listing of the capital's restaurants, nightclubs, cinemas and theatres, and a directory of useful telephone numbers. The GNTO issues *The Week in Athens* free of charge.

Books and Maps

The two main English-language book shops in Athens are Eleftheroudakis, at Odos Nikis 4 (near Platia Syntagma), and Pandelides, at Odos Amerikis 11 (off Leoforos Venizelou). The GNTO provides free maps of the various islands, regions and cities, though these can be frustratingly short of detail. Large scale maps for walkers and climbers are few and far between, and very difficult to get hold of.

More detailed touring and island maps can be bought from book shops in the UK before you leave home. The biggest selection is at Stanford's, 12-14 Longacre, London WC2 9 LP, tel. (0171) 836 1321.

Photography

Major brands of film are widely available, but are not cheap, so it's better to bring an adequate supply with you, and take it home with you for processing. Polaroid film is difficult to find.

There are often restrictions on the use of cameras in museums and archaeological sites—the use of flash and tripod is sometimes banned, so ask permission before you start snapping. For security reasons, it is against the law to take photographs from aircraft over Greek territory.

Beware of the effects of the sun's heat on photographic film—never leave your camera or film in direct sunlight, or in a place that's likely to get hot, like the dashboard shelf or glove compartment of a car left parked in the sun.

Guides and Tours

If you want to hire a personal guide, you should ask at the local GNTO office (see TOURIST INFORMATION OFFICES) or at a travel agency. In Athens you can also hire a licensed, bilingual guide through the Union of Authorized Lecturers/Guides at Odos Apolonos 9a, tel. (01) 32.29.705. Local travel agencies organize excursions ranging from half-day trips to one-week tours

Complaints

The manager or owner of the hotel, restaurant or shop in question, or your holiday company representative (for package tours) should be your first recourse if you want to complain about anything. Otherwise, the local Tourist Police office will be interested to hear of any problems. In most cases, simply mentioning the Tourist Police to the manager should get results.

If you do want to make a complaint, be pleasant about it, and try not to lose your temper. And there's no point in getting angry about mysterious cancellations or last minute postponements of bus or ferry departures in the islands—the schedules should be taken with a large pinch of salt anyway. Just shrug your shoulders and go with the flow—being in a hurry and being in the Greek Islands are mutually incompatible.

Consulates

You should only get in touch with your consulate in the event of a *serious* emergency, such as losing your passport, getting in trouble with the police or being involved in an accident. The consul can issue an emergency passport, give advice on obtaining money from home, and provide you with a list of lawyers, doctors and interpreters. He *cannot* pay your bills, lend you money, fly you home, find you a job or obtain a work permit for you.

Australia: Odos D. Soutsou 37, Athens; tel. (01) 64.47.303.
Canada: Odos I. Gennadiou 4, Athens; tel. (01) 72.54.011.
Ireland: Leoforos Vas. Konstantinou 7, Athens; tel. (01) 72.32.711.
New Zealand: Semitelou 9, Athens; tel. (01) 77.10.011.
UK: Odos Ploutarchou 1, Athens; tel. (01) 72.36.211.
Odos Vodzi 2, Patras; tel. (061) 277.329.
Odos Venizelou 8, Thessaloniki; tel. (031) 278.006.
Odos Thessalonikis 45, Kavala; tel. (051) 233.704.
Odos Alexandras 10, Corfu Town; tel. (0661) 30.055.
Odos 25 Martiou, Rhodes Town; tel. (0241) 27.247.
USA: Leoforos Vass. Sofias 91, Athens; tel. (01) 72.12.951.

Emergencies

Except in out-of-the-way places, you should be able to find someone who speaks English to help you out. But if you're alone and near a telephone, here are some important numbers to remember in an emergency:

Police/emergency	100
Tourist Police	171
Fire	199
Breakdown assistance	104

See also CONSULATES above.

Festivals

Despite the country's rapid modernization, the Greeks are still strongly attached to their old cultural and religious traditions. Some of the festivals are celebrated nationwide, others are regional or local.

1 January: New Year's Day, or *Protochroniá*—St Basil's Day, in whose name you may be offered a sprig of basil, symbol of hospitality.

In the Peloponnese they serve up a "King's Cake" (vasilópitta), with a good-luck coin hidden inside, like the sixpence in a traditional British Christmas pudding.

6 January: at Epiphany, a cross is thrown into the local harbour, lake or river, and the young men of the town dive into the chilly water to retrieve it. The one who recovers it receives a special blessing and a crucifix.

8 January: the women of Monoklisia and Nea Petra in Macedonia, and Strimni in Thrace, continue a tradition of ancient Dionysian fertility rites, and lock their menfolk in the house to do the chores while they go off to carouse in the streets and tavernas.

February: carnival time is celebrated most boisterously in Patras in the Peloponnese, and Iraklion and Rethymnon on Crete. There are costume parties on Rhodes, and bonfires in the hills of Macedonia.

Clean Monday: the first day of Orthodox Lent is marked by general house-cleaning, laundry, and kite-flying, and frugal meals of *lagána* (unleavened bread), *taramá* (salty fish roe) and *halvá* (sesame paste). In Athens, thousands gather to eat fish soup and beans, and dance on Pnyx hill.

Orthodox Easter: festivities are observed with particular enthusiasm in Macedonia and Thrace, and in the southern Peloponnese. Candle-lit processions follow a flower-bedecked funeral bier on Good Friday. On Holy Saturday, at midnight, the priest hands down the sacred flame which is passed from candle to candle to light oil lamps in front of each household' icon. On Easter Sunday, families dine on roast lamb and hard-boiled eggs that have been dyed red. On the following Tuesday, Megara in Attica holds a festival of song, dance and athletics, reminiscent of ancient Greece.

21 May: the anniversary of the Battle of Crete in 1941 is commemorated at Chania with three days of music and dancing. On the same date, at the other end of the country in Lagadas, Macedonia, a fire-walking ceremony celebrates the feast of Saints Constantine and Helen, but this ecstatic ordeal is more reminiscent of ancient Dionysian cults than of Christian ritual—the Orthodox Church disapproves.

June: Athens and Epidaurus begin their summer arts festivals (see p.332). On 24 June, bonfires flare across the country in celebration of John the Baptist. Navy Week is held in Thessaloniki and in ports around the Peloponnese.

July: wine festivals are held in Rethymnon (Crete) and Alexandroupolis (Thrace). 29-30 July sees donkey races for St Soulas Day at Soroni on Rhodes.

August: festivals of classical drama take place at Phillipi and Thasos in the north-east, and there are dance festivals

on Rhodes at Maritsa, Embonas and Kallithea. On 15 August, the Feast of the Assumption is celebrated with dancing and processions in Kremasti and Trianda on Rhodes, and a handicrafts fair, fireworks and dancing at Mochlos on Crete.

8–9 September: regatta at the island of Spetses to celebrate the 1822 naval victory over the Ottoman fleet.

October: the arts festival in Thessaloniki revives an old Byzantine tradition.

7–9 November: a "national holiday" in Crete remembers the 1866 explosion at the Monastery of Arkadi with festivities at the monastery and in Rethymnon.

30 November: St Andrew's Day is celebrated in Patras with a grand procession.

24–31 December: Christmas Eve and New Year's Eve are celebrated with carol-singing in the streets.

T he Greek Orthodox Church is Greece's principal religious denomination, and plays a major unifying role in Greek life, accounting for 97.6% of the population. Significant religious minorities are composed of Muslims (1.4%), mostly in the north-east of the country, and Catholics (0.4%), concentrated in Athens and the Ionian Islands, which were once under Italian rule.

Language

Many Greeks can speak English or German, and some know French as well. In the popular tourist areas you could certainly get by easily without knowing a word of Greek. But it is only polite to learn at least a few basic words of Greek; the locals will appreciate your efforts to speak their language, and it will enrich your own experience of the country.

For the enthusiastic, there are many tape cassette language courses available in the shops. Otherwise, you will find the Berlitz GREEK PHRASE BOOK AND DICTIONARY very useful; it will equip you with the words and phrases you will need in just about any situations you are likely to encounter during your travels in Greece.

Try to learn the Greek alphabet too— it really isn't very difficult, and it makes life much easier if you are able to decipher signposts and street names.

The table on the right lists the Greek letters in their upper and lower case forms, followed by the letters they correspond to in English.

A	α	a	as in bar
B	β	v	
Γ	γ	g	as in go*
Δ	δ	d	**th** in **th**is
E	ε	e	as in get
Z	ζ	z	
H	η	i	**ee** in meet
Θ	θ	th	as in **th**in
I	ι	i	
K	κ	k	
Λ	λ	l	
M	μ	m	
N	ν	n	
Ξ	ξ	x	**ks** in thanks
O	o	o	as in bone
Π	π	p	
P	ρ	r	
Σ	σ	s	as in kiss
T	τ	t	
Y	υ	i	**ee** in meet
Φ	φ	f	
X	χ	ch	as in loch
Ψ	ψ	ps	as in tipsy
Ω	ω	o	
OY	ου	ou	as in soup

*Except before **i-** and **e-** sounds, when it's pronounced like **y** in yes

A Sunburnt Mediterranean Playground Where History Shimmers in the Haze

The two most familiar images of Greece are of sun-drenched holiday islands lapped by an azure Mediterranean, and the architectural splendours of the ruined cities of antiquity. These twin aspects of Greece, modern and ancient, are separated by over two thousand years of turbulent history—a long and often violent journey from the beginnings of democracy in the city-states of ancient Greece, to the emergence of the modern nation which welcomes so many travellers today.

The philosophical doctrines on which the ancient Greeks built the splendid but fragile edifice called western civilization still come in handy during a stay in their country 2,500 years later: stoicism in the crowded airports; hedonism for the beach; Aristotelian logic when attempting to make sense of the ferry timetables; cynicism while haggling over a "genuine" antique; democracy in the queue for a restaurant table; and Socratic irony to win a political discussion. After centuries of tumultuous conquest and civil war, Greece is still a privileged domain of rugged joys and tranquil contemplation.

*G*reeks *ancient and modern—a family poses for a portrait beneath 3,500 year-old frescoes at Knossos, Crete.*

A Land of Mountains

Like many other historically vital nations, Greece stands at a cross-roads of trade and migration routes, with the Slavonic Balkans beyond its northern

41

mountains, Italy to the west across the Ionian Sea, Turkey and Asia on the Aegean's eastern shores, and Egypt and Libya to the south beyond Crete.

The northern mountain barrier guards the valleys of Thrace and the plains of Macedonia. To the west, the long Pindus range thrusts south through Epirus towards the Peloponnese, while the Ionian Islands provide a breakwater for the coast. Mount Olympus dominates the great eastern plain of Thessaly, protected by another mountain barrier leading down to the Gulf of Corinth. Facing the Aegean, the Attica peninsula has Athens at its heart. Corinth is the eastern gateway to the Peloponnese, almost completely mountainous except for narrow lowlands on the west coast, and the plains and valleys of Messenia and Laconia in the south. The circle of islands called the Cyclades, which includes Mykonos, Paros and Naxos, is formed by the mountain tops of a submerged continental plateau. The isles of Kythira and Crete are extensions of the Peloponnese ranges, just as Rhodes is an outlier of Turkey's Taurus Mountains.

In fact, mountains cover three-quarters of the whole country. None of them is very high—Mount Olympus, the tallest, is only 2,917 m (9,570 ft)—but they very frequently present an illusion of great height, with sudden deep valleys and plunging, craggy ravines.

Visitors gain an acute sense of this on the awesome, sinuous drive up Mount Parnassus from the Gulf of Corinth to the sanctuary of Delphi. (They may also make their first encounter with the national obsession with politics when they see partisan slogans that are daubed in blue and white on every available rock face.)

On the mainland, the mountains are largely barren, but Mount Olympus is a haven of shady pines and chestnuts. The bare limestone peaks of Parnassus are snow-covered from winter to early June, but the mountains of some of the southern islands, especially Crete and Rhodes, are much greener, and in some places almost subtropical in their luxuriant vegetation.

The mountains hold a special place in the popular imagination. As the natural redoubt of the heroic *klephts,* the rebellious bandit groups who fought Turkish domination in the 1821 War of Independence, the mountains came to symbolize the spirit of resistance and freedom. It was from the mountains again that the partisans came in World War II to sabotage the German invaders. "May he live as long as the high mountains" is the ritual blessing of well-wishers for a newborn baby. For an invalid, they pray for "the strength of a mountain". And everybody is still pagan enough to sense the aura of Mount Olympus, the abode of the gods; Mount Parnassus, home of the nine Muses; or the childhood home of Zeus on Crete's high peaks, Ida and Dikti.

Cheese, Olives and Wine

Sheep grazing on the greener mountain slopes provide the milk to make traditional Greek feta cheese and rich yoghurt. Goats are gradually disappearing, abandoned by government decree to protect the forests whose young shoots they ravage (though deliberate fire started by building speculators do far more damage).

Greek farmers have always had a tough row to hoe. Cultivation is limited by the arid, stony soil to olive trees and vineyards—apart from some good tobacco plantations in the north. The olive is the perfect tree for the Greek climate: tough, resistant to excessive heat, fierce winds, hail and frost, capable of surviving years of drought. In the Peloponnese, there are trees said to date back to the 17th century, while Attica claims some trees planted in Roman times. Olives of all sorts, green, black, brown, silvery blue, smooth or wrinkled, large and small, play a central role in the Greek diet, while olive oil is used extensively in cooking, and is still the essential fuel for the oil-lamps in churches.

Rather than orderly rows of vines such as those in Burgundy or Chianti, the Greeks often seem to prefer joyously dishevelled vineyards interspersed with wild flowers, fig trees, wild pear or almond trees, which do not always grow there from neglect but are actively encouraged by the peasant, who welcomes their fruit for his refreshment, and their shade for his siesta.

The Cities

Athens plays an overpowering role in Greek life, and it has become an almost obligatory exercise to heap curses on it. A focus for migration from the islands and the rural exodus from the mainland, the national capital has too many people (a population of 4 million, or two out of every five Greeks), too many cars, too much pollution, too much noise. The government might like to call on Heracles' experience of cleaning out the Augean stables in its efforts to decentralize industry, commerce and government itself. Perversely, the city's sprawling concrete, steel and glass makes all the more fascinating the presence in its midst of that perfect symbol of classical Greece – the Acropolis.

In the north, Thessaloniki (the old Turkish name of Salonica is gradually disappearing) presents itself as a brash second city, proud of its gastronomy, its port, and its museum of Macedonian art. But in general, Greece is not too pleased with its modern urban development. After centuries of wars and earthquakes (most recently in 1953 and 1986), the historic city centres have suffered the even more devastating indignity of the building speculators' wrecking-ball. The wine in Patras on the Peloponnese and the great Minoan museum in Crete's capital Iraklion are practically the only reasons not to leave these towns in a hurry—and head for the islands.

The Islands

Geographers argue about just how many islands there are, but agree at something over 3,000, of which only 169 are inhabited. The largest are Euboea (just north-east of Athens) and Crete. The others are mostly grouped together in distinct archipelagos: the Ionian Islands off the west coast; the Sporades north of Euboea; the Cyclades spilling down into the central and southern Aegean; and the 12 isles of the Dodecanese, dominated by Rhodes, stretching along the Turkish coast. The islands have always held a special place in the hearts of this seafaring nation, from the time when Odysseus set out from Ithaca, to the modern era of Greek shipping magnates, bred most frequently on islands like Chios and Andros.

The Ionian Islands of the west coast have something of an Italian air to them, most notable in the Venetian buildings of Corfu and Zakynthos. It is the Aegean Sea that furnishes Greece's popular travel-poster image: dazzling white houses and churches ranged around the harbour, like those of Mykonos or Sifnos in the Cyclades, or up on the cliffs of Santorini, basking in sunshine and circled by an azure sea.

But Greek holidaymakers—Greeks take holidays, too, remember—are often puzzled by the northern European taste for the arid landscape of the southern Cyclades. They prefer to head for the greener islands of Andros, Corfu or Thassos in the north. In the Dodecanese, the charm of Kos is less easy to enjoy during the package-tour high season, and the attractive island of Skiathos in the Sporades is threatened with the same

fate of mass tourism. And while this phenomenon is also creating problems for many of the more popular resorts on the islands of Rhodes, Corfu and Crete, it is still possible to escape from the crowds and enjoy the more secluded spots.

The tourist industry, an essential part of the national economy, has drawn many of the islands' peasants and fishermen into the souvenir shop and restaurant business (or to a new life in the mainland cities). But the natives have remained firmly entrenched in islands like Tinos in the Cyclades, Poros, just off the Peloponnese, and Chios, close to the Turkish coast.

T he glory that was Greece—a view from the Acropolis.

44

Facts and Figures

Geography   Situated at the southern edge of the Balkan peninsula, Greece covers an area of 131,957 sq. km. (50,949 sq. m.) Its immediate neighbours are Albania, the former Yugoslavia and Bulgaria to the north and Turkey across the Aegean Sea to the east. The jagged coastline of deeply incised peninsulas faces the Ionian Sea to the west. The islands, of which the largest are Euboea and Crete, number over 3,000 if all the tiniest islets are included, but only 169 are inhabited. With the Pindus range interrupted on its north-south sweep only by the mouth of the Gulf of Corinth, the country's overwhelmingly mountainous terrain leaves a mere 30% suitable for agriculture. The principal rivers are the Aliakmon winding through Macedonia to the Gulf of Thermaikos, the Acheloos curving south through Epirus to the Ionian Sea, Thessaly's Pinios draining into the Aegean, and the Alfios in the Peloponnese.

Highest mountain   Olympus 2,917 m. (9,570 ft.).

Population   10,089,000, of which only the Turks (0.9%) and Albanians (0.6%) form any measurable minorities.

Capital   Athens, with a population of 1,000,000 in narrow municipal boundaries, 4,000,000 in metropolitan area.

Major cities   Thessaloniki (440,000), Piraeus (210,000), Patras (160,000), Iraklion (115,000), Volos (110,000), Larissa (108,000).

Government   Under the 1975 Constitution voted after the overthrow of the Colonels' dictatorship, the country is a parliamentary democratic republic. The president has a largely symbolic role as head of state elected for a 5-year term, with real power in the hands of the prime minister and his cabinet. Parliament has only one 300-seat chamber where the principal political parties are the Panhellenic Socialist Movement (PASOK), the conservative New Democracy party and the Communist party (KKE). In the process of decentralization, the country is divided into 13 administrative regions.

Religion   Greek Orthodox 97.6%, Roman Catholic 0.4% Protestant 0.1%, Muslim 1.4%, other 0.4%.

How Greek are the Greeks?

After 400 years of domination by the Ottoman Empire, the Turkish influence is still visible. It would be silly to deny it, though it is a point too sensitive to raise in public. Most mosques, and other public buildings of Turkish origin, have been destroyed, and Turkish place-names have been Hellenized. In the cuisine, especially the yoghurt dishes and honeyed desserts, it is not clear how much is truly of Turkish origin or how much was merely appropriated by the conquerors from the Greeks themselves. Greek *ouzo* and Turkish *raki* are close cousins, and though it is not a good idea to order "Turkish" coffee, your *ellinikó* will be the same thing.

So what is a modern Greek? Just as ancient Greece spread its culture throughout the Mediterranean, so the neighbouring nations returned the compliment with invasion or peaceful commerce. Too many Persians, Phoenicians, Egyptians, Serbs, Turks, Albanians and Italians have passed this way and lingered for modern Greeks to bear much resemblance to their ancestors of antiquity. And despite the wealth of sculpture, we have no definite idea of what ancient Greeks looked like. The male and female figures of classical statues reflect an artistic ideal rather than a biological reality.

The swarthy people of today, with flashing eyes and black hair, seem to have the country's dramatic landscape etched in their faces. In temperament, a distinction can be noted between the more volatile and excitable mainlanders, and the calmer and more sombre islanders.

A third group is formed by the returning émigrés, who are regarded with a mixture of envy and admiration. This is an age-old Greek phenomenon—Spartans, Corinthians and Aegean islanders founded colonies all around the Mediterranean, sitting there, in the words of the historian Herodotus, "like frogs around a pond", and returned occasionally to the homeland to show off their new wealth and knowledge. Their return now, in ever-growing numbers since the overthrow of the Colonels in 1974, has brought a welcome fund of

T he village priest is an important local figure, much respected by the members of his congregation.

intellectual and industrial experience—and hard currency. But many return just to retire to the ancestral home town, building large but not always handsome new houses which change the face of the traditional communities.

Whatever differences in temperament may appear, the men—mainlanders, islanders and returning émigrés alike—give free rein to their passions in the all-important café conversations. It is here that you can see how natural it was for this fiercely independent-minded people, always sceptical of authority, to lay down the foundations of democracy—even if it has been a struggle ever since to keep it going. The taste for democracy is tempered, and not necessarily contradicted, by a preference for strong, almost patriarchal leadership. In these endless debates around the café tables, one man always seems to exert a natural authority. He leans back in his chair, speaks in a louder voice, leads—and stops—the laughter, and ignores any remarks that are not affirmations of what he has just said. He can often be recognized by his distinctive hat, his walking stick, and the thick wad of notes with which he ostentatiously pays the bill.

The village's Orthodox priest also plays a prominent role at the café table, smoking, drinking coffee, dispensing advice, listening to local gossip and arbitrating heated arguments. Granted a privileged political position under Turkish rule, the priest remains a revered figure in the community. As he gets on the bus, people will rush to pay his fare or to help him with his bags, even when he is young enough to handle them himself—often younger than his helpful parishioner.

On the rare occasions when they are present, the older women observe their men with an amused detachment. The younger girls are not so very different from their European counterparts, though perhaps a little more demure.

With seemingly the whole of the Western world sooner or later flocking to what they feel to be their cultural roots, the answer to the question of what is a Greek may be, as Shelley once wrote, that we all are. When the Greeks entered the European Community in 1981, a French diplomat greeted them with the comment: "Today we celebrate the fact not that Greece has joined Europe, but that Europe has rejoined Greece."

History

Scarce natural resources left Stone Age Greece sparsely populated until about 4500 BC, when migrants from the Balkans and Asia Minor spread south-from Macedonia. Settlers from Anatolia (modern Turkey) brought bronze arte-

*G*reek seafaring tradition extends back into ancient times.

facts and the plough to Crete, adding a richer diet of olives, figs and vines to the meagre cereal crops they found when they arrived.

Around 1950 BC, a new wave of Eastern European invaders assembled on the mainland, who may be described as the first Greeks as such, in the sense of a people with a certain cultural unity. Regarded by classical Greece as ancestors of the Ionians, the conquerors from the north readily took to the amiable Mediterranean way of life. They brought with them the horse, but they produced no art or luxury comparable to that of their contemporaries in Crete, which was spared invasion for the time being.

Crete and Mycenae

With its rich soil and cattle pastures, the great island enclosing the south of the Aegean enjoyed peace and prosperity.

47

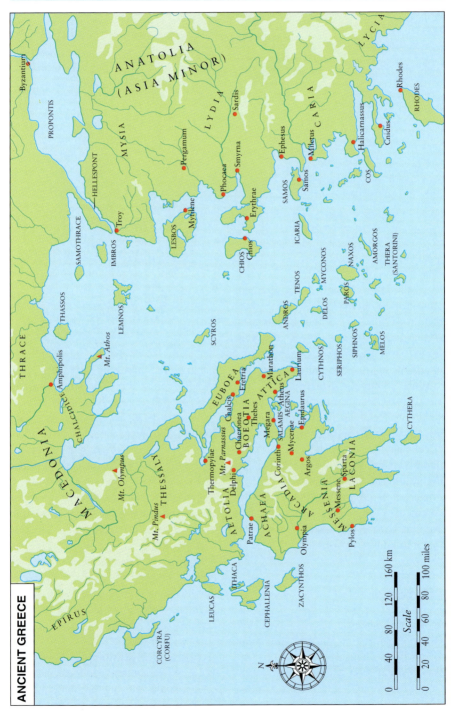

ANCIENT GREECE

Cretans carried on a brisk trade with the Middle East and Egypt, as well as the other Greek islands, with an emphasis on luxury goods: ivory, delicate pottery and finely wrought gold jewellery.

Fearing no enemies, they built their first palaces at Knossos, Phaistos and Malia around 2000 BC without fortifications. It is not clear whether war or earthquake was responsible for the first destruction of the palaces 300 years later, but they were rebuilt even bigger and more splendid. Design was still strictly for pleasure, not defence: decorative entrances, roof terraces facing the beautiful surrounding countryside, ornately frescoed bedrooms, sophisticated plumbing for the bathrooms, and barbecue braziers in the kitchens.

Crete's Minoan civilization, named after the mythical king Minos of Knossos, existed on a very human scale. In small sanctuaries or intimate palace chapels, Cretans worshipped their female deities, the double axe symbolizing the royal power of life and death. Males were subordinate consorts, with the bull as their emblem. The artwork is characterized by a lively sense of colour, movement and humour.

In 1500 BC, a new Balkan invasion of Greece drove the Ionians southwards and this time crossed into Crete. The brilliant Minoan civilization went into decline, and a century later the palace of Knossos was destroyed by earthquake. This was probably simultaneous with the volcanic explosion that devastated the nearby island of Thera (present-day Santorini), the only Aegean island that had developed a civilization comparable to that of Crete.

Through commercial contacts, Cretan civilization infiltrated the Peloponnese,

Theseus and the Minotaur

Many a Greek myth has behind it a hard political fact. Historians believe that the legend of Athens' obligation to sacrifice seven young men and seven maidens to the Minotaur refers back to a time when Crete reigned supreme in the Aegean, and the city had to pay heavy tribute.

The Minotaur was the offspring of a torrid affair between Minos' wife Pasiphaë and a bull. Understandably upset, Minos hid this bull-headed monster in a labyrinth. At nine-year intervals, the powerful king demanded that 14 young men and girls from Athens be surrendered to Crete, and devoured by the Minotaur. The Athenian hero Theseus determined to put an end to this abhorrent practice. He seduced the king's daughter Ariadne, who gave him a ball of thread so that he could find his way back out of the labyrinth, after finding and killing her monstrous half-brother. On his way back to Athens in triumph, Theseus abandoned poor Ariadne, pregnant, on the island of Naxos. Heroes are not always gentlemen.

dominated from 1400 to 1200 BC by the kingdom of Mycenae. But Minoan culture was transformed in the hands of the peninsula's tougher breed of men, and influenced by mercenary warriors returning from Egypt. Tall and bearded, unlike the clean-shaven Cretans, these settlers from north of the Balkans had a taste for hunting, cattle-raiding and pillaging. Such "masculine" themes dominate their otherwise Minoan-style art, and its spirit is epitomized in the massive stone lions over the gates to Mycenae's acropolis. The ceramics were not as sophisticated as Crete's, but their goldsmiths achieved a new level of refinement, as can be seen in the jewellery and death masks now displayed in Athens' National Museum.

Typically, Mycenaeans readily adopted Crete's fertility goddesses, but gave priority to the male deity Zeus they brought from the north—the god of the heavens (his name means "bright sky"), and of rain, thunder and lightning. Henceforth Greek religion was steadfastly male-dominated.

The most famous of the Greeks' raiding expeditions around the eastern Mediterranean ended in the conquest of Troy (on the Turkish coast) around 1230 BC. Scholars argue about whether Homer's Agamemnon is a mythical or historical king, but they agree that the raid actually occurred, and was probably achieved under Mycenaean leadership.

The Archaic Era

Around 1200 BC, fierce Dorians from the Danube valley swept through the western mainland to the Peloponnese, destroying the Mycenaean civilization, and killing or enslaving its people. The invasion bypassed Attica, where the

Ionians had founded Athens a century earlier. Many fled to the Aegean islands and the coast of Asia Minor, while the Dorians occupied Rhodes and the southern Aegean.

At the beginning of what is generally called the Archaic Era, preceding the great exploits of classical Greece, the country entered a cultural Dark Age. The Dorians installed a tough, warrior-oriented society with little apparent interest artistic achievement. It promoted the virtues of strength, valour and loyalty, male camaraderie, the initiation of young warriors by veterans, and nude athletics, all major features of the great kingdom of Sparta founded two centuries later. In religion, Apollo joined Zeus to complete the male take-over of the Greek pantheon. Just as Zeus displaced his wife Hera as the major deity at Olympia, so did Apollo at Delphi.

It was the combination of the Dorians' somewhat rigid austerity with the Ionians' amiable serenity that created the unique strength and grace of Greek civilization.

By the 9th century BC, the country began to awake. The post-invasion exodus across the Aegean opened up new commerce with Asia Minor and North Africa, assisted by the introduction of a written alphabet borrowed from the Phoenicians. In exchange for imported cereals and raw materials—precious metals, tin, copper, amber, ivory, wood

*S*appho (c. 612–580 BC) was one of the most admired Greek poets of the ancient world. This statue of her stands in her home town of Mytilene on Lesbos.

and animal skins—Greek manufacturing talent provided, in addition to wine and olive oil, valued luxury exports such as gold, jewellery, perfumes and textiles, tools, weapons and ships. Athens' refined geometric-patterned vases began to challenge Corinth's commercial supremacy in ceramics. The first temples were built in the northern Peloponnese. Crete and Attica produced the first significant bronze sculpture and Homer composed his great epics, *The Iliad* and *The Odyssey*.

The mountainous country naturally divided the population into independent communities, each constituting a city-state, or *polis*. This was ruled by a powerful aristocracy that had replaced the monarchy everywhere except in conservative Sparta and Thera. The system defied real political unity until it was imposed by Macedonian conquest, but an emerging sense of Greek national identity was fostered by the Olympic Games. From 776 BC, this religious and sporting festival brought the people of the cities and islands together at the great sanctuary of Olympia in the western Peloponnese.

As the population grew, it proved increasingly difficult to eke out a living from the thin and infertile Greek soil, of which the aristocracy appropriated the lion's share. Many looked elsewhere for a living. Traces of Greek settlement at Taranto in southern Italy date back to the 14th century BC, but the major migrations began around 775 BC, from the Peloponnese and the cities of Megara in Attica, and Chalcis and Eretria in Euboea. Agricultural settlements in southern Italy and Sicily were followed by trading posts further west at Marseilles and on the south coast of

Spain. In the northern Aegean they occupied the Chalkidiki peninsula before moving up to the Black Sea. Though retaining religious and cultural attachments to the homeland or *metropolis* (literally "mother city"), the settlements remained resolutely autonomous, not colonies in the modern sense of political dependencies.

Homer and Homer

It is still not clear whether the works attributed to Homer were produced by one man, or by two. Supporters of the "two-authors" theory, for complex textual reasons, suggest that the *Iliad* was composed by a poet from somewhere in Anatolia, perhaps the Izmir of modern Turkey, and the *Odyssey* by an islander, probably from Chios. Those who argue for just one Homer stress the masterly dramatic unity of the poetry, formed out of the patchwork of fantastic adventures. Each epic works towards one end—the satisfaction of Achilles' anger at being cheated of his rights before the battle for Troy; and Odysseus' long journey to wreak revenge on the suitors tormenting his wife Penelope.

All we can surmise of Homer the man, judging from his abundant rustic similes and his sympathy for the common peasant, is that he was probably himself of humble peasant origin. Was he blind, as sculptures often depict him? Greek bards frequently were. It has been suggested that blindness was an asset in memorizing without distraction the long poems they recited at royal courts.

At any rate, Homer, singular or plural was a great crowd-pleaser. Like the tale of Theseus and the Minotaur, the *Iliad* and *Odyssey* may be viewed as pieces of political propaganda. They celebrate the heroism of Greece before the Dorian invasion, as if to warn the conquerors that they were not the only courageous men around.

Rise of Sparta and Athens

Sparta was founded on the Eurotas river in the southern Peloponnese in the late 10th century BC, when four or five villages banded together as one formidable city-state.

A rigid social system with a strict hierarchy of three classes set it apart from other Greek cities. At the top was an élite of Spartan citizens, the Equals *(homoioi),* who alone enjoyed full political rights. Descendants of the Dorian conquerors, they were forbidden to work as farmers, merchants or artisans so as to devote all their energy to military training for the army's officer class. They sat on the councils overseeing their two kings, who jointly commanded the army. Income was derived from the best land of the Eurotas valley, worked by the lowest class, the *helots,* state serfs bound to the land who were probably descended from the indigenous population of the conquered region. For the education and enlightenment of the Equals' children, the *helots* were deliberately oppressed and humiliated—they were forced, for instance, to get drunk, so as to instil in Sparta's future leaders the ideal of sobriety.

The middle rank was held by *perioikoi* ("peripheral dwellers") who farmed the less fertile parts of the Eurotas valley, raised sheep and pigs, and carried on the city's commerce and crafts. They formed more or less autonomous communities, but had no say in political life, and were bound to serve in the Spartan military when required.

Sparta at first tried to dominate the Peloponnese by conquest, but revolts by Argos and Messenia in the 7th century BC forced Sparta to accept more modest alliances recognizing its leadership of a Peloponnesian League. It remained forever reluctant to launch remote expeditions that left the homeland unprotected.

Suddenly, around 550 BC, Sparta mysteriously turned in on itself, banned all travel beyond its borders and refused entry to all foreigners, apparently fearing the "softening" influence of contacts with the outside world.

Sheltered behind its mountains, Athens avoided the rigidly oppressive regimes that the Dorians had imposed elsewhere. Reinforced by Ionian refugees from the Peloponnese, the city developed a more flexible social system that contrasted sharply with that of Sparta. It was governed by an aristocracy of magistrates overseen by a council of elders, and elected by a popular assembly.

In the late 7th century BC, Dracon gave Athens its first code of laws. The law-maker insisted on crimes being punished in court, rather than by clan vendetta with its endless cycle of bloodshed. The adjective "draconian" became a byword for severity when Dracon, asked why he always advocated the death penalty, whatever the crime, blithely replied: "In my opinion, small crimes deserve the death penalty, and I know of no severer punishment for the big crimes."

Athena, protectress of Athens, and goddess of war, handicrafts and practical reason. Most of the magnificent monuments on the Acropolis were raised in her honour.

A Spartan Existence

Life in Sparta was not for the weak. Any new-born sons of the Equals considered too sick or puny were hurled into a ravine on nearby Mount Taygetos.

The rest were taken away from the family home at the age of seven to undergo a gruelling 13-year course of military training under the leadership of the older boys. Summer and winter, they wore the same thin tunic, slept on a rough bed of reeds and lived on a grim diet of black wheat porridge—plus whatever they could steal from neighbouring farms. If they were caught, they were punished—not for stealing, but for getting caught. Physical endurance was the ultimate virtue. Rather than reveal his agony and be caught, one boy ran silently through town with his booty hidden under his tunic—a live fox , chewing away at his stomach.

Boys were educated in physical exercise and the use of arms, and learned to live off the land like savages. Minimal time was spared for reading, writing, arithmetic and some music—as food for the soul, and accompaniment into future battles. Battle training itself was ruthless, with one clan beating another almost to death in a pitched fight for a sacred island in the Eurotas river. Skill and experience of actual killing was acquired by manhunts staged to hunt and slaughter an occasional unfortunate helot.

Once accepted as officer material—the social disgrace of rejection caused many a suicide—the men, married or not, continued until the age of 30 to sleep in all-male dormitories. Anyone wanting to see his wife had to sneak off in the middle of the night. Even when they were living at home, they still had to have one meal a day—that dreadful porridge—in the officers' mess.

And where were the women all this time? Girls were trained to become sturdy child-bearers—lots of gymnastics and wrestling, in dresses that the more prudish Athenians considered so scandalously short that they scornfully referred to Spartan girls as *phenomeridae*, or "thigh-barers". Left to their own devices much of the time, the adult women enjoyed considerable sexual freedom and proved very able managers of the family fortune.

Solon, a champion of social justice, abolished Dracon's more cruel ordinances. The magistrate proposed reforms to protect debt-ridden peasants against arbitrary land-confiscation by the aristocracy. For artisans and merchants, he regulated weights and measures and admitted their guilds to the legislature. But Solon was no democrat. "To the people," he said, "I have given sufficient power without reducing or adding to their rights. For those who had the strength and riches to enforce their power, I have made an effort not to subject them to any indignity."

Paradoxically, it was the advent of a tyrant that set Athens on the road to democracy. In many city-states through-out Greece in the 7th and 6th centuries BC, tyrants (without the negative sense the word later acquired) won the support of oppressed peasants and artisans to seize power from the aristocrats.

In Athens, Peisistratus, a general who had distinguished himself in battle against Megara, came to power in 561 BC on a "platform" of Solon's proposed reforms. Personally wealthy from mine-holdings in Thrace, he redistributed land to impoverished peasants, made state loans to repay their debts, and promoted the growth of olives and vines to replace the poor wheat crops. He toured the country to hear grievances and appease the rich landowners. In Athens itself, Peisistratus organized hugely popular festivals to honour Athena, the city's patron goddess, and Dionysus, the god of wine and the dramatic arts. His ambitious programme of building temples on the Acropolis revealed, particularly in the sculpture, the city's artistic mastery. By 530 BC, Athenian potters were turning out the black- and red-figure ceramics that finally overcame Corinth's domination of the foreign markets.

By arranging the purification of the sanctuary of Apollo on Delos—no births or burials were allowed on the island—Peisistratus imposed the authority of Athens over the Cyclades. This first step towards empire was reinforced by the end of the 6th century BC with victories over neighbouring Boeotia and Chalcis and the establishment in the northern Aegean of Athens' first colonies. An alliance was formed with Sparta's Peloponnesian League.

The 17-year rule of Peisistratus' sons actively encouraged the arts, producing the first written edition of Homer. Sparta supported a brief return to power of the aristocrats until another enlightened tyrant, Cleisthenes, emerged in 508 BC. Himself an aristocrat, he consolidated Athens' growing commitment to democracy by making the governing councils and assembly more representative and abolishing the privileges of aristocratic birth. He also instituted ostracism—banishment without loss of property—as a dignified and bloodless way of dealing with leading citizens who offended the state.

Persian Wars (499–478 BC)

The Greeks' first real awareness of their common Hellenic destiny was spurred by the aggressive presence of the Per-sians in the Aegean. Ionian settlements on the Anatolian coast and neighbouring islands like Samos became Persian provinces after the defeat of Lydia's wealthy king Croesus in 546 BC. Heavy taxes imposed by the Persian military garrisons moved the Ionians to revolt in 499 BC. Fleets from Athens and Eretria provided only token support for their countrymen, but the sacking of Sardis, the Persians' Anatolian capital, incited King Darius to launch an all-out invasion. He crushed the Ionian revolt, but his advance through Thrace and Macedonia was halted when stormy seas wrecked the Persian fleet off the Mount Athos peninsula in 492 BC.

Two years later another fleet crossed the Aegean, spared the sanctuary of Delos, but destroyed Naxos and Eretria. The Persian army landed on the Attica coast only a short march away from Athens. Miltiades forestalled an attack on the vulnerable unwalled city by leading an Athenian army of 10,000 out to the Plain of Marathon. Facing a force six times its own size, the Athenian army outmanoeuvred the Persians and drove them back to their ships, thus winning the famous Battle of Marathon. The Persians lost 6,400 men in the battle, compared with the Athenians' 192, whose burial mound can still be seen at Marathon today.

Before the battle, the revered oracle at the sanctuary of Delphi, always conservative in its inclinations, and playing the safe bet on the apparently stronger side, had predicted Persian victory. Athens' hard-won triumph impressed on its allies the importance of greater Greek solidarity in the face of the Persian foe. (Sparta's contingent of 2,000 men had arrived a day late.)

Darius' son Xerxes raised a new invasion army of 100,000 and this time cut a canal through the neck of the Athos peninsula to avoid the stormy cape. Athens formed a Pan Hellenic league with Sparta in military command over 31 city-states. In 480 BC, while the Persian fleet sailed down to Euboea, the army pushed south through Thessaly to the pass of Thermopylae, the mountain gateway to central Greece and Athens.

Sparta was again unwilling to commit significant forces outside the Peloponnese, concentrating instead on blockading the isthmus of Corinth. The Spartan elders let King Leonidas take only 300 of his royal guard to lead an allied army of at most 7,000. With no hope of victory, the Spartan commander chose to hold Thermopylae long enough for stronger Greek forces to engage the Persian fleet further south. Leonidas and his élite went to their death displaying all the Spartan virtues of courage, discipline and loyalty. The Persians eventually broke through the pass, but their parallel sea engagement against the Athenian fleet at the Battle of Artemisium proved costly.

With Thebes, the capital of Boeotia, deserting the Greek cause to side with the Persians, Athens was left defenceless. The city was evacuated before Xerxes arrived to put it to the torch as a last reprisal for the sack of Sardis 10 years earlier. But the Athenian general Themistocles succeeded in enticing Xerxes into a sea battle in the narrows of Salamis Bay. The hemmed-in Persian fleet suffered crippling losses and Xerxes withdrew to Asia.

Classical Age

The Great Fifty Years of Athenian glory extended from the end of the Persian Wars in 478 BC to the death of Pericles in 429 BC.

Sparta withdrew from the national scene to consolidate its power in the Peloponnese. Athens' naval supremacy and its courageous wartime defence of the Greek cause made it the undisputed leader of a new alliance of Aegean city-states, the Delian League, so named because it kept its treasury on the island sanctuary of Delos. The league had clearly become the basis of the Athenian empire when, in 454 BC, Athens blithely transferred the funds to its own Acropolis.

Besides ensuring a profitable market for its wine, olives and luxury goods, Athens exported its democratic system to city-states whose government had often been a tyranny, not always enlightened. Athens' democracy appealed to an aspect of the citizens' character that remains a constant to this day: a visceral hostility to anyone who grows too big for his boots. An example: Themistocles, military hero of the Persian Wars,

The First Marathon Runners

In the first of two famous runs occasioned by the battle of Marathon, the Athenian courier Pheidippides covered 240 kilometres in two days, carrying a message requesting Spartan support for the Athenian forces. He found the Spartans in the middle of a religious festival, and unwilling to march until after the inauspicious full moon had begun to wane. After the battle, another fellow, evidently not as fit as Pheidippides, ran the 42 kilometres from Marathon back to Athens to announce the historic victory, and dropped dead from exhaustion, thus setting the classic distance for the most gruelling of Olympic races.

became a popular leader both for his timely strengthening of the navy as the backbone of Athenian imperial might, and for constructing fortifications to defend the city itself. But overweening pride and personal greed provoked his ostracism in a vote of 6,000 representative citizens in 472 BC. Like many disgraced Greek heroes, Themistocles went over to the enemy, ending up in the service of the Persian monarch. His successor at the head of the popular party was Ephialtes, a scrupulous democrat of humble origin who fiercely opposed the return to power of the aristocrats. His crusade to prosecute their corruption ended in his assassination in 456.

He in turn was replaced by an equally fervent general, Pericles (495–429 BC). Pericles was born of an aristocratic family, but he was so well-liked by the people of Athens that he remained in power for 11 years. He was wise and rational, and much admired by the historian Thucydides. He brought members of the lower classes onto the council of magis-

trates. His idea of paying public officials a salary meant people other than the rich to exercise authority. Salaries for military service in the navy and army made it less of a burden for the lower classes.

Not all Athenian residents had citizenship rights. Though better treated than elsewhere in Greece, slaves remained, in Aristotle's words, "an animated object of property". Among free men, foreigners were more than welcome in commerce and shipping, as well as the arts and medicine, and even came to dominate the study of philosophy. But although they served in the Athenian army and navy, outsiders could not own land and had no say in the state's political affairs. However, the citizens' political rights entailed, at least for the more wealthy, financial burdens in sponsoring

C lassical sculpture salvaged from the ruins of the Sanctuary of Apollo on the island of Delos, in the Cyclades.

*T*he majority of Greek pilgrims travelling to Delphi did so as a
pious act of national solidarity, gathering at the Sanctuary of Athena
(above) and purifying themselves in the Castalian Spring before visiting the
sacred Oracle. But for politicians and generals seeking advice on military
campaigns and colonial expeditions, the trip was strictly business. To keep
funds rolling in and to protect the sanctuary from acts of vengeance by
disgruntled consultants, the priests who handed down the sacred prophecies
played it very safe, using vague and ambiguous forms of words, and
carefully avoiding saying anything that might upset the touchy Spartans.
Even so they occasionally got it wrong, warning the Athens-led alliance that
it could not defeat the mighty Persians.

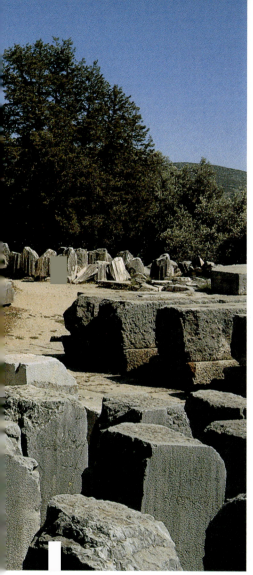

Peloponnesian War (431–404 BC)

Athenian hegemony in the Aegean attracted growing hostility from its rivals. Megara was denied access to the Delian League's markets. Corinth resented Athens' commercial domination and more especially its alliance with the Corinthian colony of Corcyra (Corfu). Thebes was embittered by continuing Athenian hostility ever since it had sided with the Persians, and Sparta feared a challenge to its own supremacy in the Peloponnese.

War broke out in 431 BC. Sparta launched what it regarded as a pre-emptive strike into Attica, burning the olive groves and tearing up the vineyards. The peasants fled in mass exodus to Athens. Plague from Egypt ravaged the over-crowded capital and killed Pericles in 429. The Athenians had to crush an uprising in Lesbos and slave revolt in the Laurium silver mines of southern Attica. With Sparta continuing its land attacks, it was the navy that again turned the tide for Athens with victories on the west Peloponnese coast, and the capture of Sphacteria and Pylos. A precarious peace was negotiated in 421 BC.

Six years later, the Athenians' downward spiral resumed with disastrous intervention in the wars of the Sicilian colonies. The expedition cost them 12,000 men captured or killed, crippling the effort to save the empire. At home, the aristocratic party threatened internal stability. The Aegean islands were in revolt. Sparta allied with Persia, sacrificing the Greek colonies of Asia Minor for financial aid to build a fleet. The Athenians continued to resist for nine more years under Alcibiades' brilliant leadership. But Lysander at last gave

musical and dramatic festivals and paying for warships and their crews.

With the Delian League's funds transferred to the Acropolis in 454 BC, a large portion was spent on rebuilding the city Xerxes had burned down. The monumental reconstruction, not only of Athens' Acropolis, but also of the sanctuaries of Eleusis and Sounion, saw the great explosion of sculptural and architectural talent that gave visual expression to the glory of classical Greece.

Sparta naval superiority in the Aegean with victories from the Hellespont to the port of Piraeus, forcing Athens to capitulate in 404 BC.

Vindictive Thebes wanted the city razed to the ground and reduced to cattle pasture, but Sparta was content with the destruction of Athens' fortifications and the surrender of its fleet and empire.

During the 50-year power struggle that followed the war, Sparta's brutal military garrisons made the Greek city-states nostalgic for Athens' democratic style of imperialism. The islands formed a new, looser confederation under Athens' leadership. In 371 BC, Thebes' general Epaminondas smashed Sparta's army, slaying a third of the kingdom's able-bodied males. He then occupied the Peloponnese and challenged the revitalized Athenian presence in the Aegean. But, lacking a sound political underpinning, Thebes' military supremacy col-

lapsed in 362 BC, leaving Greece leaderless to face a new power rising in the north—Macedonia.

Philip and Alexander

Macedonia's royal house of Dorian horsemen—the king's name Philippus meant horse-lover—ruled over a rough peasant population of Greeks, Illyrians and Thracians.

Philip II (359–336 BC) had acquired his military training in Thebes as a hostage of Epaminondas, and proved a ruthless warrior. This lusty lover of wine and women was totally unscrupulous in politics. He pursued a divide-and-conquer policy of pitting Athens against its Chalcidice colonies, maintaining unrest in Thrace and Thessaly, and exploiting rivalries among Thessaly, Athens and Sparta during the Sacred Wars over the guardianship of Delphi.

Athens' great orator Demosthenes tried to persuade the Greeks to unite against the Macedonian threat. His impassioned appeals to defend liberty and democracy against Philip's monarchy were backed up by a very practical reorganization of state finances and the navy. His eloquence convinced Megara, Euboea, Corinth, Achaea, and even arch-enemy Thebes to join Athens in a confederation. In 338, in one last burst of Pan Hellenic solidarity, they fought bravely at the decisive Battle of Chaeronea in northern Boeotia, but lacked the generals to match Philip's superb military tactics and the ferocious cavalry charges that were led by his son Alexander.

In victory, Philip was both magnanimous and tough. Athens was allowed to retain its autonomy and its fleet, while Sparta had most of its lands in the Pelo-

---

Miracle of the Baked Tablets

One day in June 1952, Michael Ventris announced on BBC radio that the Mycenaeans had used the Greek language. Nobody had known this until the young Cambridge linguist succeeded in deciphering the famous "Linear B" script, his name for the language used in ancient inscriptions that were found at Pylos in the southwestern Peloponnese. A palace fire preserved them for posterity by baking the clay tablets on which accountants had drawn up meticulous invoices. Linear B was derived from stylized forms of hieroglyphics in the more primitive "Linear A" script found on Crete. The inscriptions comprised a series of syllabic signs from which Ventris was able to decipher words like ti-ri-po-de, the Greek plural for "tripod". The rest followed, and Linear B was no longer a mystery.

ponnese laid waste, and was excluded from the new confederation led by Macedonia. While most of the city-states kept their traditional forms of government, Thebes was handed over to an oligarchy under the surveillance of a Macedonian military garrison. Three other garrisons were strategically placed around the country. Philip was planning to cement Greek unity with a national expedition against Darius of Persia when he was assassinated at his daughter's wedding by a royal bodyguard.

The grand adventure of Philip's heir, Alexander the Great, took him far beyond Greece's frontiers only two years after his accession to the throne in 336 BC, on an expedition that established a Macedonian empire stretching from Egypt to India. But Alexander's mission remained always profoundly Greek. From the age of 13, he was tutored by Aristotle, and he took the philosopher's annotated copy of Homer on his journey to Troy and beyond. In his lightning subdual of Greek resistance before setting off for Persia, he destroyed the rebellious city of Thebes—except for its temples, and the house of Pindar the poet.

Alexander combined the cool, analytical talents of his father with the passionate, intuitive powers of his mother, Olympias, and claimed descent from Hercules through the one and Achilles through the other. Like his father, he was a heavy drinker and, like all Macedonians (but contrary to Greek custom), he drank his wine unwatered. His death in Babylon in 323 BC of malarial fever came after a long and riotous bout of drinking.

For a century after Alexander's death, Greece became a pawn in the wars of his successors. Philip V (221–179 BC) made a truly coherent effort to reunite Greece under his Macedonian rule. His initial success provoked the first appearance of Rome on the Greek horizon in 214 BC, with a fleet north of Corfu backing Greek opposition to Macedonian expansion.

Roman Rule

Flaminius, one of a long line of Roman leaders who fervently admired the culture of Greece, defeated Philip's Macedonian forces in 197 BC. During the Isthmian Games near Corinth the following year, he proclaimed "freedom" for the Greeks. Fifty years later, Greece had become a Roman province and Corinth was ignominiously sacked. On the dockside, Roman soldiers used the town's treasured paintings as dice-boards—but no more nonchalantly than the Greek soldiers who carved their names on the sacred statues of Egypt.

In general, the Romans provided a quiet, if not too proud, prosperity. Taxes were efficiently organized and politics remained safely in the hands of the foreign rulers. Besides the usual trade in luxury goods, the Greeks exported to Rome their philosophy, theology, political science, coinage, port construction, domestic, civic and religious architecture, sculpture, literature and the Greek language itself—along with well-paid employment for its experts. There was a neat exchange of Roman pragmatism and Greek taste for beauty and truth. In Latin, it was noted, the names of vegetables were of Latin origin and the names of flowers Greek.

Athens was the most prestigious university town in the Roman Empire. Rhodes was esteemed for its studies in literature and philosophy, and Julius Caesar went there to improve his rhetoric. Wealthy Romans organized sightseeing tours of the great Greek monuments. Among the major attractions were the Olympic Games, by now completely professional, and in Sparta the gruesome spectacle of boys enduring flogging contests in the municipal theatre.

Nero loved Greece. In AD 66, he toured the games and won all the music prizes. He was even declared the winner of a chariot race after falling out of his chariot. He repeated the declaration of Greek freedom and dug out the first clod of earth for the Corinth canal (a project that was not to be realized until 1883), but his plan to follow Alexander's footsteps into Asia was halted by a Jewish insurrection in Judea.

Hadrian was perhaps the sincerest of philhellenic emperors, nicknamed *Graeculus,* "little Greek". On his visits to Athens between AD 125 and 128, he completed the huge Temple of Olympian Zeus, begun 250 years earlier, and built a whole new city quarter, Hadrianopolis, whose main gate still stands today (see p. 106)

In 267, Ostrogoth invaders swept down from the Black Sea, burning and sacking Athens, Corinth, Sparta, Argos and Crete. Thereafter Greece remained a stagnant backwater of the declining Roman Empire until Constantine decided in 324 to move to the east his government of the Balkans, Asia Minor and Greece.

*E*xploring the ruins of ancient cities is one of the great pleasures of a trip to Greece. Wear sturdy shoes, cover up against the sun, and try to visit during the cool of the morning.

The Byzantine Empire

The Eastern Empire's new capital, founded on the site of Byzantium (later Constantinople), was dedicated in 330 with both pagan and Christian ceremonies. In later years, many of the faithful regarded Constantine (306–337) as the first Christian emperor, converted by divine vision on the eve of a battle to control the empire. For Constantine himself, Christianity was a political instrument with which to unite his empire's diverse peoples. In fact, he converted only on his death bed (25 years after the battle) and was given a pagan funeral. Greece itself, especially Athens, remained pagan except for pockets of Christianity in the communities that St Paul had passed through on his missionary travels.

Conversion really got underway with Emperor Theodosius (379–395), a pious Christian who encouraged zealots to destroy Greek temples or appropriate them as churches. He banned all forms of pagan cult and stopped the Olympic Games. In 529, Justinian drove the last nail into the Hellenic coffin by closing the Academy of Platonic Philosophy in Athens.

Meanwhile, after the horrors of plague and invasion, the Greeks left their homeland in droves. They settled around the Mediterranean and above all in Constantinople (regarded by Greeks right into the 20th century as their natural capital). Goths, Visigoths and Slavs poured through the mainland and down as far as Crete, while Arabs raided the Aegean islands.

The many doctrinal conflicts besetting the Orthodox Church did not greatly affect Greece until 726 when, condemning their worship as idolatrous, Emperor Leo the Iconoclast ordered the destruction of all church icons. Leo's opponents, known as Iconodules, saw these holy paintings as emphasizing the true humanity of Jesus and Mary, and refuted the view of them as purely divine. Empress Theodora, a devout Iconodule, negotiated an end to the bitter dispute in 843, after the death of her Iconoclast husband Theophilus. The controversy stimulated Byzantine artists to aim more at spiritual revelation than the naturalistic representation of the holy figures.

The Byzantine Empire reached the peak of its political, economic and cultural power under Basil II (976–1025). But the 11th century also saw the beginning of the Empire's long decline. The Orthodox Church was weakened by its schism with Rome in 1054 (over papal authority). Turks of the Ottoman dynasty began their ascendancy with

Basil the Bulgar-Slayer

This terrible title was earned by the Byzantine emperor after more than 30 years of fighting the Bulgarian army, then the mightiest in Eastern Europe. Bulgarian invasions devastated the Peloponnese, Attica and Boeotia until Basil scored a decisive victory in 996 on the Sperkheios river east of Lamia, near the Gulf of Euboea. Pushing the war back into Bulgaria, he inflicted a final defeat in 1014. Of the 15,000 prisoners taken, he blinded all except one in every hundred, who was left with one eye so that he could lead the others home. Yet this same man had fostered in Greece the greatest achievements of Byzantine art: illuminated manuscripts and silk embroideries, the mosaics of the monastery church at Daphni (near Athens), Sancta Sophia at Thessaloniki, and the monasteries of Mount Athos and Meteora.

conquests of Byzantine territory in Asia Minor. The Crusades to reclaim the Holy Land from the Arabs in the east proved more of a threat than salvation when the Normans tore through Corfu in 1081 on their way to Thessaly. Constantinople called on Venice to come to its aid, but in 1125 Venice helped itself to ports in the Ionian Islands and the Peloponnese.

In 1204, the Crusaders sacked Constantinople itself, and the Greeks became part of a Latin Empire carved up by the French and Italians into the Kingdom of Thessaloniki, the Duchy of Athens and the Principality of Achaea. A Byzantine dynasty held on to Epirus.

In the 14th century, Mistra in the Peloponnese had become a grand capital for the last flowering of Byzantine culture. Constantine XI was crowned there in 1448 in time to meet renewed threats from Turkey. Forces of the Ottoman Empire had occupied the north and were now advancing on the Peloponnese. The emperor called on Rome to help, but his military commander, recalling the Crusaders' barbarity in 1204, said he would "rather see the Muslim turban in the centre of town than the Latin mitre".

After a two-month siege, the Turks took Constantinople on Tuesday, 31 March, 1453, making Tuesday in Greek eyes forever a day of ill omen.

Under Turkish Domination

The Greeks' 400 years of submission to the Ottoman Empire were a bitter experience, but they also toughened the people's fibre in the constant struggle to maintain a national identity.

The sultan's highly centralized system divided Greece into a dozen provinces under military command, but with no civil administration. With a patriarch appointed by the sultan in Constantinople, the Orthodox Church maintained the only direct Greek contact with the Turkish authorities. Although the Church kept alive Greek language and culture through the liturgy and education, its collaboration with the Turks made it suspect when nationalist movements fought for independence.

The Turks' religious tolerance was not disinterested. Heavy taxes on non-Muslims were a source of revenue too attractive to encourage any policy of forcible conversion. Jews settled in major Greek cities—Thessaloniki housed 20,000 expelled from Spain in 1492, joining the Bavarian Jews already there. Orthodox Greeks and Jews were encouraged to engage in commerce, a practice considered undignified for Muslims.

Not that there wasn't any discrimination—some of it minor, like not being allowed to build houses higher than those of Muslims, or to repair their

Unfavourable Report

Despite their shared faith, there was no great love lost between Orthodox Greeks and Russians. Nonetheless, St Petersburg became a focus for Greek exiles' nationalist ideas, and in 1770, Empress Catherine the Great's lover, Alexei Orlov, led a small expeditionary force to support an uprising in the Peloponnese. The Greco-Russian troops were defeated by an Albanian force that ravaged the land for the next ten years. The Greeks had expected a more substantial Russian effort, and Orlov wrote home, like some disgruntled modern tour-operator: "The natives here are sycophantic, deceitful, impudent, fickle and cowardly, completely given over to money and plunder."

churches and ring the bells without official permission. More ambiguous was the 15th-century "tribute of children", by which one in every five sons in a Christian family was taken to serve in the Janissaries (from the Turkish *yenicheri* meaning "new force"), the crack troops of the Ottoman infantry. In fact, this proved a source of considerable pride among the peasants.

During Turkey's power struggles with Venice, it was notable that Orthodox Greeks usually preferred Muslim rule to the proselytizing Roman Catholics who held such places as Tinos, Crete and the Ionian Islands.

Defeat in 1571 by an alliance of Spanish, Venetian and Papal forces at the famous naval Battle of Lepanto (now Nafpaktos) dented the self-confidence of the Ottoman Empire—just five years after the death of its greatest sultan, Suleiman the Magnificent. Not that this was a matter of great concern to the Greeks, who had to man the oars in the galleys of both fleets.

In 1687, the Venetians made one last brutal sally through mainland Greece towards Athens. Their captain, Francesco Morosini, bombarded the Parthenon, and one shell ignited the gunpowder which the Turks had stored in its inner Sanctuary, causing great damage (see p. 102).

Ottoman rule hardened in the 18th century, and the Greeks went once more into mass exile, slowly being replaced by incoming Albanians and Serbs.

The British ambassador wrote: "A man may ride three or four, sometimes six days and not find a village able to feed him and his horse." Evading the tax collectors, farmers and shepherds took to the hills in bands called *klephts*, the

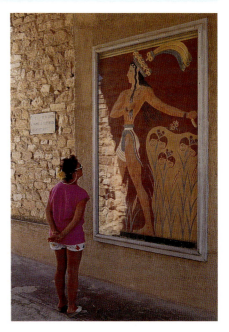

A beautiful example of Minoan art at Knossos.

rebel-brigands who formed the backbone of the subsequent independence movement.

The French Revolution boosted Greek nationalism, and the Napoleonic Wars aroused international interest in Greek independence by diverting the European gentleman's Grand Tour from France and Italy to classical Greece. Most illustrious of this international brigade was Lord Byron, who paid his first visit to Athens in 1809. Less welcome was Lord Elgin, who carved slices off the Parthenon for the British Museum. Greek national identity was largely ignored in the struggles of Russia, Austria, Britain and France over the fate of the Ottoman Empire. Austrian Chancellor Metternich defied anybody even to define the word "Greek".

Pericles, the Great Humanist
The man who dominated Athenian affairs for 27 momentous years came from a family which favoured military toughness and social justice. His father was Xanthippus, a brilliant but ruthless general, and his mother was Agariste, niece of the noble democratic reformer, Cleisthenes. With eloquent and powerful oratory, Pericles championed the weak against the strong, but was not himself a natural democrat. He developed social welfare for the poor, and promoted the public works programme as much for the full employment it provided as for its embellishment of the city. Yet he disdained the common crowd, remaining haughty and unsmiling, and was known to have wept only twice in his life. But his high-minded nature was refined and not insensitive. Of young soldiers lost in battle, he said that they left the city like a "year that has lost its spring".

A friend and pupil of the philosopher Anaxagoras, who emphasized the power of the rational mind, Pericles was an unashamed intellectual. He made Athens a magnet for artists and thinkers from all over the Mediterranean, with a cosmopolitan atmosphere comparable to 20th-century Paris or New York. He avoided politicians and military men, preferring the company of his cultured mistress, Aspasia, a close friend of Socrates. The salon she created for him included the master sculptor Phidias, the urban-planner Hippodamus, the historian Herodotus and the tragedian Sophocles. Typically, Pericles' assistance to the poor included free theatre tickets.

But Pericles was also an energetic military and political leader, asserting Athenian supremacy in the Aegean and outwitting his enemies at home. Unable to impugn Pericles own honesty, they brought trials against his friends on trumped-up charges—his mistress for procuring prostitutes, Anaxagoras for impiety and Phidias for stealing gold allotted to his public statues. The cool Pericles proved ardent in defence of his beloved Aspasia and fiercely loyal to his friends.

Independence

After so many centuries submerged in the Roman, Byzantine and Ottoman Empires, the question of Greek identity was of vital importance. Exiled scholars and diplomats championed the view that a gradual cultural awakening, rather than a violent revolution, was required. Even more vehemently opposed to revolution were the Orthodox Patriarch, fearful for his authority, and the so-called Phanariotes, wealthy Constantinople-based merchants who dreamed of keeping the Ottoman Empire intact with themselves as its leaders.

Far from the Ottoman capital, landowners, local leaders and priests feared for their privileges, and indeed for their lives—they had been dubbed "Turkish Christians".

The most enthusiastic advocates of revolution were of course the *klephts*, who had remained in Greece to carry on the fight: Theodoros Kolokotronis in the Peloponnese (see p. 316), Markos Botsaris in Epirus, and others in the mountains of Macedonia and Crete, as well as merchant-pirates who were operating among the Aegean islands.

With the Turks progressively weakened by war with Russia and the revolt of Ali Pasha, the refractory Turkish governor of Epirus, the revolutionary cause gained the day. On March 25, 1821, now commemorated as a national holiday, uprisings spread from the Peloponnese right across the country. Turkish atrocities aroused the protests of Victor Hugo and the painter Delacroix in France, Byron and Shelley in England, and

Goethe and Schiller in Germany. They saw the Greek freedom fighters as descendants of the warriors of Marathon and Thermopylae. The reality, of course, was less poetic. The Greek forces, however heroic, had also perpetrated brutal massacres. Their various factions were split by bitter political squabbles, assassinations, and civil war. Greece had freed itself of the Turkish yoke, but the price of independence was a monarchy imposed by the great powers. In 1833, a 17-year-old Roman Catholic Bavarian prince was crowned King Otto of Greece. The Turks vacated the Acropolis and Athens became the capital.

It took another 80 years for Greece to retrieve first the Ionian Islands, then its northern territories of Epirus and Macedonia and the key island of Crete. Under Otto's successor, the Danish prince William, crowned George I (again a choice of the great powers), the monarchy grew progressively more democratic, accepting a parliament in 1864. But a Greek parliament was inevitably a quarrelsome affair—provoking nine general elections in its first 16 years, 70 different governments in 50 years. Luckily, an outstanding statesman, Eleftherios Venizelos (1864–1936), arrived on the scene to pull the country together before World War I. The Cretan who had led his island's fight for union (*énosis*) with Greece became prime minister in 1910. He combined personal courage with tough pragmatism and a fiercely patriotic vision, the three qualities that Greeks have always demanded of their leaders.

Wars and Peace

When King Constantine I succeeded his father (assassinated in Thessaloniki in 1913 by a madman), Greece faced the

Saint Paul in Greece

With its many communities of Jewish merchants, Roman Greece was a prime target for the missionary work of Paul of Tarsus. He crossed from Asia Minor into Thrace in AD 49. In Philippi, the first European city to be evangelized, local businessmen had him and his followers thrown into jail as Jewish troublemakers. As the New Testament tells it, they sang God's praises in the night and an earthquake awoke the jailer. Paul baptized him and his family and went off to Thessaloniki. There he was well received by the Greeks, but the Jews created an uproar against "these that have turned the world upside down". In Athens he was upset by a "city wholly given to idolatry", but impressed by the obsessive philosophical curiosity of people who "spent their time in nothing else but either to tell or to hear some new thing". Paul argued with Jews in the synagogue before discussing his "new thing" with the Epicureans and Stoics at the Areopagus. The philosophers mocked his talk of resurrection, so, with only a couple of converts, he left for Corinth. He stayed there 18 months, writing, preaching and establishing a church. He was angered again by his obstreperous fellow Jews and gave them up as a bad cause, vowing: "Henceforth, I will go unto the Gentiles."

onset of World War I in a highly ambiguous position. Venizelos wanted to side with the Western Allies against Germany, Austria and the old enemy, Turkey, but the king, married to the German Kaiser's sister, insisted on neutrality. As commander in chief, he blocked full mobilization and replaced Venizelos with a pro-German prime minister. With the Balkan situation growing critical in 1917, the Allies forced Constantine off the throne and returned Venizelos to power. By the end of the war, Greek

forces marched with the victorious Allies into Constantinople.

But the Greeks' long-cherished "Great Idea" (*Megali Idea*) of retrieving their Byzantine capital had to be abandoned after their disastrous three-year war against the revitalized Turkey of Kemal Atatürk. The 1923 Treaty of Lausanne imposed a massive exchange of Turkish and Greek populations. Simultaneously with the "repatriation" of 800,000 Turks, more than a million Greek refugees moved to Greece. Bringing with them valuable industrial and agricultural skills, they included prosperous and cultivated merchants from Smyrna (now Izmir), future Nobel

*G**reece today – still passionately interested in politics.*

prize-winning poet Georgios Seferiades, and pioneers of the Greek Communist Party who settled in the Athens suburb of Nea Smyrni (New Smyrna).

Greek parliamentary life between the two world wars was again a turmoil of unruly factions. With the anti-democratic era of Mussolini, Stalin, Hitler and Franco, Greece moved inexorably towards dictatorship under the pro-German General Ioannis Metaxas (Constantine's chief of staff in World War I). From 1936 to 1941, he suspended parliament, jailed and tortured Communists and labour leaders, and declared unions and strikes illegal. Following Hitler's example, he burned "subversive" books including Heine and Freud, but also Anatole France and Dostoevsky—and added a ludicrous home-grown touch by censoring Pericles' speeches in Thucydides' history of the Peloponnesian War.

Metaxas partially redeemed himself at the outbreak of World War II with a firm stand against Mussolini, driving the Italian army back over the Albanian border in 1940. But British support arrived too late to stop the German invasion (backed up by its Italian and Bulgarian allies), and Greece was subjected to four years of brutal occupation. It was estimated that 400,000 died in the wartime famine, and 200,000 in resistance fighting. Of Greece's 70,000 Jews, 54,000 were deported and exterminated in concentration camps.

Inspired by the grand symbolic gesture of removing Nazi Germany's swastika from the Acropolis, the Communist underground was the best organized and most ferocious of the many Greek resistance movements. But the endemic factional infighting, provoking even Winston Churchill to come and try to negotiate a compromise, pointed towards inevitable civil war in the wake of the Allied victory. With the Truman Doctrine bolstering the Greek economy against a Soviet take-over, Communists, conservatives and liberals clashed in bloody fighting. The Greek Communists' effort ground to a halt in 1949, after Tito's rift with Stalin stopped the flow of aid across the Yugoslav frontier.

Konstantinos Karamanlis led the most stable of the conservative governments that followed, taking Greece into NATO, haggling with Britain and Turkey over Cyprus, and negotiating entry into the European Economic Community in 1981. Between his two major terms of office came the bitter experience of the Colonels' fascist dictatorship (1967–74). The rule of Colonel Georgios Papadopoulos and police chief Ioannidis suppressed civil liberties and perpetrated vicious torture of imprisoned left-wing leaders. In a supposed defence of "Christian morality", the Colonels banned long hair and miniskirts, deprived film star Melina Mercouri of her citizenship, and forbade the songs of Mikis Theodorakis. He was in good company, as the classical drama of Sophocles, Aeschylus, Euripides and Aristophanes was also censored. The dictatorship aroused considerable anti-American feeling when it became known that Papadopoulos had been trained by the CIA, and that Washington continued to support the regime against the risk of Soviet intervention.

In 1981, Andreas Papandreou's socialist party (PASOK) came to power, but did not act on its election promises to take Greece out of NATO and the Common Market. The economy was "socialized" rather than nationalized, welfare programmes increased, and attempts made to decentralize government bureaucracy. In 1988, a historic reconciliation between Turkey and Greece was broached with two meetings of their prime ministers. By 1989, the flamboyant Papandreou was embroiled in financial and personal scandals, and after indecisive national elections, Greece seemed set for more rounds of factional squabbling. But that's what makes Greek democracy so interesting.

HISTORICAL LANDMARKS

Prehistory	4500 BC	Mainland settled from Balkans and Asia Minor.
	2700	New wave of Anatolians colonizes Crete.
	1950	Ionians invade Greece from Eastern Europe.
Crete and Mycenae	1500–1400	Golden era of Crete's Minoan palaces ending in destruction of Knossos.
	1400–1200	Mycenae dominates Greek mainland.
	13th c.	First buildings on Athens' Acropolis.
	1230–25	Capture of Troy.
Archaic Era	1200	Dark Age after Dorian invasion from Balkans.
	10th c.	Foundation of Sparta.
	c.800–750	Homer composes *Iliad* and *Odyssey*.
	776	First Olympic Games.
	760–700	Greeks colonize southern Italy and Sicily.
Rise of Athens and Sparta	621–593	Dracon and Solon codify Athenian laws.
	6th c.	Sparta dominates Peloponnesian League.
	561–527	Peisistratus, enlightened tyrant of Athens.
	499–487	Persian Wars: Greeks fight off invasions by Darius and his son Xerxes.
	490	Athenians lead victory at Marathon.
	481	Spartans' heroic stand at Thermopylae.
Classical Age	477	League of Delos under Athens' leadership.
	458–456	Aeschylus' *Orestes*, Euripides' first plays.
	447–438	Parthenon built on Acropolis.
	443–429	Pericles ruler of Athenian Empire.
	442	Sophocles' *Antigone*.
	431–404	Peloponnesian War: Sparta and Thebes end Athens' hegemony.
	399	Death of Socrates.
	387	Plato founds his Academy.
	356–336	Philip II, king of Macedonia, launches conquest of Greece.
Macedonian Supremacy	336–323	Alexander completes domination of Greece and founds empire in Asia and North Africa.
	335–322	Aristotle (Alexander's tutor) in Athens.
	323–276	Alexander's successors carve up empire.
	221	Philip V reasserts control of Greece.
Roman Rule	214	Rome intervenes against Philip V.
	196	Roman general Flaminius proclaims Greek "freedom".
	149–146	Greece made a Roman province, Corinth sacked.
	AD 49–52	Saint Paul's missions through Greece.
	128	Emperor Hadrian rebuilds Athens.
	267	Ostrogoth invasions devastate Greece.
Byzantine Empire	324	Constantine makes Byzantium (later called Constantinople) capital of Eastern Empire.
	391–393	Emperor Theodosius bans pagan cults, closes Greek temples, stops Olympic Games.

	529	Justinian closes Athens' Platonic Academy.
	6th–8th c.	Slavs invade and dominate Greek mainland.
	726–843	Doctrinal conflicts, iconoclasm launched by Em peror Leo III destroys churches' holy images.
	826	Arabs occupy Crete.
	976–1025	Byzantine art flourishes under Basil the BulgarSlayer.
	1054	Schism between Orthodox and Roman churches.
	1081–83	Norman Crusaders rampage through Ionian Is lands and Thessaly.
	1204–61	Crusaders sack Constantinople: Greeks under Latin Empire (French and Venetians).
	14th c.	Mistra is cultural centre of Byzantine Empire.
Turkish	1453	Turks seize Constantinople, rule Greece through
Domination		approved Orthodox patriarch.
	1517	Defeat at Lepanto (Nafpaktos) heralds long de cline of Ottoman Empire.
	1687	Venetians sweep through Peloponnese to Athens, devastate Parthenon.
	1714	Greeks go into mass exile as Turks bring in Al banians and Serbs.
	1789–1815	French Revolution and Napoleon stimulate Greek nationalism.
Independence	1821	Rebellion in Peloponnese launches Greek War of Independence.
	1832	European powers recognize Greek state.
	1833–62	Otto of Bavaria king of Greece.
	1912–13	Victory in Balkan Wars retrieves Epirus and Macedonia.
	1913	Prime minister Venizelos wins *énosis* (union with Greece) for his native Crete.
Wars and Peace	1914–18	Initially neutral in World War I, Greece joins Western allies.
	1919–22	War with Turkey ends "Great Idea" of regaining Constantinople as Byzantine capital.
	1923	Exchange of 1,500,000 Greeks and Turks.
	1936–41	Dictatorship of General Metaxas.
	1941–44	German occupation with Italian and Bulgarian allies. Communists lead resistance.
	1944–49	Bloody civil war against Communists.
	1955–63	Conservative Karamanlis takes Greece into NATO, long dispute with Turkey over Cyprus.
Dictatorship and	1967–74	Colonels' coup d'état installs dictatorship.
Democracy	1974–80	Karamanlis returns to establish republic.
	1981	Papandreou's socialist party PASOK reluctantly takes Greece into Common Market.
	1989	Indecisive national elections after political and personal scandals.

Just the Essentials

You will never get to—or want to—see everything. But for a first trip to each region, here is our list of the major landmarks of Greek sight-seeing. It will help you to establish your priorities.

Athens
Acropolis: hilltop sanctuary of the
  gods
National Archaeological Museum:
  the nation's ancient treasures
Plaka: renovated historic
  neighbourhood
(2–3 days)

Attica
Piraeus: ancient and modern port
Cape Sounion: Poseidon's temple
  with superb view
Daphni: superb Byzantine mosaics
(1–2 days)

Peloponnese
Mycenae: palace of Agamemnon
Nafplio: charming resort town
Epidaurus: classical Greek threatre
Monemvasia: fine Venetian town
Mistra: Byzantine monasteries and
  mansions
The Mani: wild and windswept
  peninsula
Olympia: sanctuary of Zeus and
  Olympic Games
(8–10 days)

Saronic Islands
Hydra: artist's home from home
Spetses: relaxed family resort
(1–2 days)

Cyclades
Mykonos: archetypal holiday island
Delos: Apollo's sanctuary
Paros: superb beaches and water
  sports
Santorini: impressive volcanic
  scenery
(8 days minimum)

Crete
Knossos: famous Minoan palace
Iraklion: archaeological museum
Agios Nikolaos: most popular resort
Samaria Gorge: spectacular hike
(6 days)

Rhodes
Rhodes Town: Knights' Quarter and
  bazaar
Lindos: ancient port city and
  acropolis   *(4 days)*

Dodecanese
Patmos: arid beauty, grand monastery
Astypalaea: haven of peace
(3–4 days)

North
Thessaloniki: good restaurants and
  archaeological museum
Sithonia: best Chalkidiki beach
  resorts
Mount Athos: remote monastic
  peninsula   *(8 days)*

North-east Aegean Islands
Lesbos: pine-covered home of
  Sappho
Chios: dramatic lunar landscapes
(4–5 days)

Central Greece
Delphi: most beautiful of sanctuaries
Mount Pilion: mountain scenery
Meteora: monasteries perched on
rock pinnacles
(4 days minimum)

Sporades
Skiathos: great beaches
Skyros: fine handicrafts   *(4 days)*

Ionian Islands
Corfu: family resorts, lovely scenery
Zakynthos: Venetian charm, beautiful
beaches   *(5–6 days)*

North-west Mainland
Ioannina: lakeside bazaar town
Dodona: ancients' oldest oracle
Metsovo: handsome mountain village
(2 days)

Going Places with Something Special In Mind

If you are planning a trip to Greece with specific interests in mind, a better idea than taking an off-the-shelf package tour is to design a holiday plan to fit in with your own tastes. Below we offer a selection of routes and themes, some following a specific itinerary, others presenting a list of destinations with a unifying theme. Others list locations where you can pursue particular activities.

The Attic Peninsula

This attractive peninsula is a popular destination for day trips from Athens, and offers beaches, historical sites, and mountain slopes.

1 GLIFADA
Busy beach resort within easy reach of Athens, with many seafood restaurants.

2 VOULIAGMENI
Attractive, upmarket resort with beautiful beach.

3 CAPE SOUNION
Magnificent headland with Temple of Poseidon, a splendid vantage point for sunset and sunrise.

4 VRAVRONA
Sanctuary of Artemis and museum with fine marble sculpture.

5 RAFINA
Alternative port for ferries to the Cyclades and southern Euboea.

6 PLAIN OF MARATHON
Site of the famous battle between the Athenians and the Persians.

7 RAMNOUS
Ruins of ancient city in romantic, isolated site overlooking the sea.

8 MONI KAISARIANI
Abandoned 11th-century monastery in peaceful setting among wooded hills.

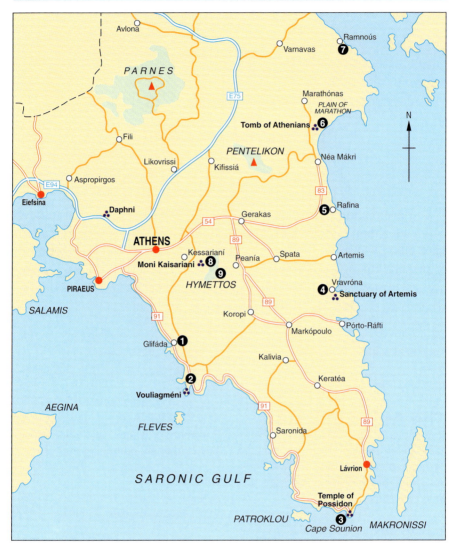

Gulf of Corinth Circuit

*T*he Attic Peninsula, a day-trip from Athens offering beaches, mountains and historical sites.

This is a five to seven-day circular route from Athens, which takes in a number of important historical sites, and offers the chance to cool off at the beach.

9 MOUNT HYMETTOS
Hilltop viewpoint overlooking Athens, with vistas extending west to the Peloponnese and east to Euboea.

1 DAPHNI
Byzantine monastery renowned for its magnificent mosaics.

*T*he Gulf of Corinth, a week's round-trip from Athens.

2 ELEUSIS
Sanctuary dedicated to the Earth-goddess, Demeter.

3 OSIOS LOUKAS
Beautiful monastery with magnificent 11th-century Byzantine mosaics.

4 DELPHI
Apollo's shrine, navel of the universe and site of the famous Delphic oracle.

5 NAFPAKTOS
Port where Venetian citadel overlooks site of famous naval battle of Lepanto.

6 ANDIRIO
Car ferry across Gulf of Patras to Rio.

7 LOUTRA KILLINIS
Attractive beach resort. Ferry service to Zakynthos and Kephalonia from Killini.

8 OLYMPIA
Sanctuary of Zeus and Hera, birthplace of the Olympic Games.

9 MANTINEA
Excellent example of 4th-century BC fortifications.

10 TIRYNS
13th-century BC citadel, with Cyclo-pean ramparts and underground cisterns.

11 EPIDAURUS
The country's best-preserved ancient Greek theatre.

12 MYCENAE
Ancient city with Lion Gate, and tombs of Agamemnon and Clytemnestra.

13 CORINTH
Temple of Apollo is one of the oldest temples in Greece.

14 CORINTH CANAL
Impressive channel cut through narrow neck of land.

Southern Peloponnese Circuit

A multi-day tour from Nafplio.

T he Southern Peloponnese Circuit takes in historic sites, delightful towns and villages and pretty beaches.

1 LEONIDIO
Charming little town at end of a spectacular coast road.

2 GERAKI CASTLE
13th-century Frankish castle with fine views.

3 MONEMVASIA
Fortified Venetian town.

4 GITHIO
Delightful fishing village with pretty beaches.

5 MISTRA
Great mediaeval Byzantine city set in an enchanting wilderness.

6 MANI PENINSULA
Windswept peninsula of castles, ghost towns, and wild, unspoiled landscapes.

7 MESSENE
Grand Arcadia Gate leads to ruined city in lovely pastoral setting.

8 METHONI
Town with great Venetian citadel, and pleasant sandy beach.

9 PYLOS
Harbour town with Turkish fortress and pleasant waterfront square.

10 PALACE OF NESTOR
Palace of Agamemnon's adviser, where the famous Linear B clay tablets were discovered.

11 OLYMPIA
Sanctuary of Zeus and Hera, birthplace of the Olympic Games.

12 BASSAE
Magnificent 5th-century BC Temple of Apollo.

The Mani Peninsula
A circular day-tour from Githio of the fortified towns, castles, towers and churches of this wild and barren peninsula.

1 PASSAVA CASTLE
13th-century Frankish fortifications.

2 KELEFA CASTLE
Side road leads to huge 17th-century Turkish fortress.

3 AREOPOLI
Main village of the Mani Peninsula, with characteristic tower houses.

4 DIROU CAVES
Road leads down from Pirgos Dirou to cave with boat trip on underground lake.

5 NOMIA
Fortified village with splendid views over the tower houses below.

6 GEROLIMIN
Attractive fishing village tucked under soaring cliffs.

7 VATHIA
Ghost town of tower houses and ruins.

*T*he Mani Peninsula circuit offers historic fortifications and ruins, and includes an underground lake boat trip and a creek where you can cool off at the end of the day.

8 CAPE MATAPAN
This is the southernmost point of the Greek mainland, and is reached by a one-hour walk from Porto Kagio.

9 KOKKALA
A tiny village beside an attractive sheltered creek where you can swim.

Mount Pilion

*M ount Pilion offers tra-
dition and beauty among its pines
and rushing streams.*

The lush mountain haunt of the centaur
Cheiron. A delightful excursion from
Volos in Central Greece.

1 PORTARIA
Beautiful mountain resort. Chapel with
16th-century frescoes.

2 MAKRINITSA
Side road to traditional village, with
views of Gulf of Volos.

3 CHANIA
Winter sports centre at summit of road.

4 ZAGORA
Pilion's largest village, set amongst lush
orchards, with grand sea views.

5 CHOREFTO
The port of Zagora, with lovely beach.

6 TSANGARADA
Enchanting summer resort, decked in
flowers, with 1,000-year-old plane tree
in square, and terrific view of Skiathos.

7 MILOPOTAMOS
Side road leads down to beautiful beach.

8 MILIES
Charming village with folk museum and
important historical library. Good walks
along abandoned narrow-gauge railway.

9 VIZITSA
Restored village of traditional mansions
and tower houses, many offering
accommodation.

Vineyards

No neat, tailored Chianti country here—
Greek vineyards are a colourful tangle
of vines dotted with fruit trees that provide welcome shade and refreshment.

1 KEPHALONIA
Potamiana region north-east of Argostoli produces Robola white wine.

2 PATRAS
Production and distribution centre at the
heart of the Peloponnesian vineyards.

3 NEMEA (PELOPONNESE)
Famous for its its full-bodied red wines
known locally as "blood of Hercules".

*A taste of local produc-
tion, from well-known Greek wines
to French-style reds and whites.*

4 CORINTH
Vines best known for table grapes and
currants, named after the town.

5 MESSOGHIA
Attica's best centre for *retsina* wines.

6 PORTO CARRAS
Sithonia's French-style vineyards produce quite sophisticated reds and whites.

7 TINOS
Picturesque vineyards surrounded by
dovecotes.

8 SAMOS
Fertile interior produces rich sweet muscatel wines.

9 SANTORINI
Heady red wines from the volcanic soil.

10 MAROUSSI
Wine factories in Athens suburb.

Pottery

This ancient Greek tradition continues on the islands and the mainland. You can find reproductions of Geometric and Classical patterns and modern designs. Ask at the local GNTO office for the whereabouts of the workshops.

1 AEGINA
Manufacturer of two-handled water jars.

2 NAFPLIO
Green-glazed Peloponnesian style.

3 IOANNINA
Barter for colourful Epirote ceramics in the old bazaar.

4 METSOVO
Cottage industry survives in this mountain village.

5 SIFNOS
At Vathi, potters model their wares right on the beach.

6 CRETE
Iraklion workshops reproduce Minoan ceramics.

7 RHODES
Famous Lindos pottery now produced in Rhodes Town factories.

*R*eproductions of Classical designs mix with pottery of today (above), and for a taste of Corfu as experienced by writer Gerald Durrell, a tour takes in his old haunts, including favourite picnic spots and beaches.

Gerald Durrell's Corfu

The author of the much-loved book *My Family and Other Animals* lived on Corfu with his family for a number of years, exploring its nooks and crannies and observing its wildlife.

1 KALAMI
The beautiful bay where the Durrells' "white house" stands. The house is now a taverna.

2 CORFU TOWN
Where the reluctant Gerry was sent for lessons.

3 KANONI
The "strawberry pink villa" was situated on the hillside above the island monastery of Vlacherna.

4 ANTINIOTISSA
Lake beside little Agios Spiridon beach that was one of the family's favourite picnic haunts.

5 MIRTIOTISSA
Beach described by Lawrence Durrell as "...perhaps the loveliest in the world...".

Classic Walks of Crete

Crete offers many attractions for keen hikers—dramatic coastlines, deep gorges, rugged mountains, and plains covered in wild flowers. You will need to wear good walking boots, as the terrain is often rocky, and you should carry enough water to last the day. Remember to take a hat and sunscreen—there is little or no shade on some of the walks.

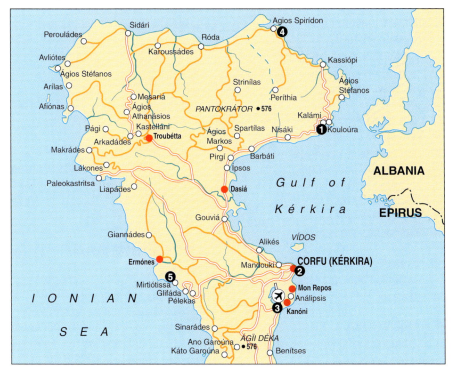

1 SAMARIA GORGE

The classic walk of Crete through a spectacular narrow gorge. 5 to 6 hours.

2 IMBROS GORGE

A shorter, easier and more solitary hike than Samaria, from the village of Imbros to Komitades. 3 to 4 hours.

3 MOUNT GINGILOS
(2,080 M, 6,824 FT)

A rugged climb from Xiloskala through spectacular rock scenery. Experienced walkers only. 4 to 5 hours round trip.

4 AGIA ROUMELI–CHORA SFAKION

Hike along a steep, beautiful stretch of the south coast. 7 to 8 hours.

5 PSILORITIS (MOUNT IDA)
(2,456 M, 8,058 FT)

The summit of Crete's highest mountain is reached by a long but straightforward hike from the Idaian Cave. Experienced, well-equipped climbers only. Snow well into summer. 7 to 8 hours round trip.

6 CAPE VOUXA

A rough track leads out to the end of the Gramvoussa peninsula, where there are

*C*rete is a haven for walkers of all levels of experience.

secluded beaches and little islands. 2 hours from end of track.

7 LASITHI PLAIN

Easy walk across flat plain dotted with wind-pumps, and carpeted with wild flowers in spring. 1 to 2 hours.

8 BUTTERFLY GORGE

Beautiful, pine-fringed gorge–full of red butterflies in summer. 2 to 3 hours.

9 KATO ZAKROS

Lovely hike through a gorge from Zakros village to Minoan ruins at Kato Zakros. 2 to 3 hours.

Snorkelling and Diving

Scuba diving is restricted by law in many parts of Greece to protect underwater archaeological sites. But here are some of the places where you can explore the world beneath the waves.

1 PALEOKASTRITSA (CORFU)
Good training facilities, and good diving in a superb setting.

2 PAXI AND ANTIPAXI
Take a boat to the caves on Paxi's west coast or to Antipaxi's Vrika and Voutomi beaches for the best diving.

3 ALONNISOS
Marine conservation park. The best diving off Kokkinokastro peninsula.

4 PAROS
Divers head for Langeri, Agia Maria and Platis Ammos beaches.

5 TELENDOS (KALYMNOS)
Explore this ancient submerged town.

6 OLOUS (CRETE)
From the resort of Elounda you can explore a submerged ancient city.

*G*reece offers superb diving and underwater exploration.

7 MOCHLOS (CRETE)
Swim around the underwater remains of a Minoan village.

The Iliad

The events of the Trojan War recounted in Homer's ancient classic.

1 MOUNT PILION
Where Achilles was reared by the centaur Cheiron and fed on the heart, lungs and liver of lions and wild boars, and the marrow of bears, to give him courage.

2 SKYROS
Where Achilles hid disguised as girl, but

*F*ollow the story of
The Iliad, Homer's ancient classic.

Odysseus tricked him into revealing himself by sounding a trumpet-blast and the clash of arms.

3 AULIS
Where the Greek fleet gathered before sailing for Troy, and Agamemnon sacrificed his beautiful daughter Iphigenia to the goddess Artemis.

4 LESBOS
Where Odysseus wrestled with King Philomeleides.

5 MYCENAE
The Palace of Agamemnon.

6 PYLOS
Where the palace of wise king Nestor,

Agamemnon's trusted counsellor, sat on Englianos hill.

7 TROY
The city of King Priam, where Odysseus and his warriors entered the besieged citadel in the belly of a wooden horse.

8 SAMOTHRACE
Where Poseidon watched the Trojan war from the peak of Mount Fengari.

The Odyssey

Scholars have traced the route of Odysseus' legendary journey home to Ithaca after the Trojan War, but the final leg, beyond Crete, is largely conjecture. Some place the episode of Scylla and Charybdis in Italy or even further away —ours is a popularly accepted itinerary through Greek waters.

The Departure From Troy

1 TROY
The battle site was discovered by Heinrich Schliemann on the Turkish coast, and it is still being excavated by American archaeologists.

2 MARONIA
Odysseus sacks "Ismarus", the Thracian city of Cicones.

3 SKYROS
The fleet of 12 ships stops over for three days of repairs after hitting storms off Mount Athos.

4 CAPE MALEA
After a smooth crossing via Cape Sounion, a fierce *meltemi* wind drives the fleet south via Kythira, and beyond Crete to Cyrenaica (Libya).

5 PALEOCHORA
The peninsula (which was originally an island) where the men hunted goats while Odysseus fought the Cyclops in his cave on the south-west coast of Crete.

*T*race Odysseus' journey home to Ithaca after the Trojan War.

Homecoming to Ithaca

6 GRAMVOUSSA
Isle of Aeolus off north Crete, where the ships awaited a favourable wind to sail.

7 MESAPOS
Home of Laestrygonians who destroyed the fleet except for Odysseus' ship.

8 PAXI
Island where Circe seduced the hero into staying for a year.

9 NEKYOMANTEION OF EPHYRA
Near Parga, the oracle of the Dead at the Halls of Hades, visited by Odysseus.

10 LEFKAS CHANNEL
Passage between Charybdis and cave of man-eating Scylla on Mount Lamia.

11 PALEOKASTRITSA, CORFU
Where lovely Princess Nausicaa finds Odysseus washed up on the beach.

S t Paul's travelled to Greece for missionary work, as recorded in the New Testament's Acts of the Apostles.

12 ITHACA
Our hero finally rescues Penelope from her suitors.

Saint Paul in Greece

The Hellenistic education of Paul the Apostle made Greece a natural first target for his missionary work in Europe.

1 PHILIPPI
5th-century church ruins mark the site of Paul's first conversion *(Acts 16:14)*.

2 THESSALONIKI
Paul took the Egnatia Road to preach to Jews in the synagogue *(Acts 17:1)*.

3 ATHENS
He harangued sages on the hill of Areopagus, and debated in the Agora. *(Acts 17:15–34).*

4 CORINTH
Paul was judged by the Roman proconsul in the ancient agora. *(Acts 18:11).*

Byzantine Monasteries

If arranged in advance, certain monasteries will receive you as a guest—those on Mount Athos, for example. You can visit others provided you are dressed in long-sleeves and long trousers or skirt.

1 MOUNT ATHOS
An autonomous theocracy within the Greek state—there are 20 monasteries on its peninsula.

2 METEORA
The monks here have built their refuges on rock pinnacles in Thessaly.

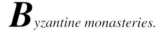

Byzantine monasteries.

3 DAPHNI
West of Athens, renowned for its magnificent mosaics.

4 KAISARIANI (NEAR ATHENS)
Abandoned 11th-century monastery in delightful setting, with mill, bakery, bath-house and refectory.

5 MISTRA
Beautiful monastery churches amid ruins of Byzantine city in the Peloponnese.

6 PATMOS
Built where St John the Divine recorded his Revelations—rich museum of Byzantine art.

The Crusaders in Rhodes

The Normans, Italians, Spanish, Germans and English all left their mark in

Akrotírio Koúmbournou • ❶ **RHODES TOWN**

Kólpos *Rodíni Park*
Triánda
Triánda
Kremastí Asgouroú
Koskinoú
❼ ✝ **Filérimos**
Paradísion Thérme
Kallithéas
Theológos
(Thólos) Maritsá
Soroní Dipótama Kallithié Faliráki
Fáne
Kámiros Kalamón Psínthos
Petaloudes Afándou
Psínthos
Loutáni
Eleoússa Archípolis Kolímbia
Platánia
Mandríkon
N. Alimniá Kámiros Skala ✝ **Tsambiki**
N. Mákri Apóllona Archángelos
❻ Kritiniá ❷ *Akr. Archangélou*
Malóna
N. Strongilí Embonas
Amartos Makkáris **Feraklós**
N. Tragoússia *Attáviros* Assourí Charáki
Gadourás
Akr. Laérma
Armenistís Ag. Issídoros Kálathos
Siánna *Akrotírio Milanós*
Inko
❺ Monólithos Istrios Lárdos ❸ **Líndos**
Profília
Asklipiíon Kontári *Akr. Mirtiás*
❹ Kólpos
Kólpos Lárdou
Apolakkiás
Apolakkiá Vátion
Koukouliári Gennádion
✝ Messanagrós
Skiádi
N. Kténia
Lachaniá
Kattaviá
Chóchlakas
Agios Pávlos Plimíri
N. Karavólas *Akr. Víglos*

Akrotírio Prassonísi

Aegéon Pélagos

*L*andmarks of the Crusades in Rhodes (left), and the Chalkidiki
Peninsula (above), rich in history and beautiful scenery.

90

Greece on their way to and from the Holy Land. In Rhodes, The Knights of St John fortified not only the capital, but the whole island, with castles along the cliffs and hilltops.

1 KNIGHTS' QUARTER
Capital's headquarters for main garrison, with palaces, hospital and churches.

2 ARCHANGELOS
East coast 15th-century fortress.

3 LINDOS
Commander's Palace built on the ancient acropolis.

4 ASKLIPIIO
Fortress built inland in centre of hilltop village.

5 MONOLITHOS
15th-century castle on rocky crag.

6 KAMIROS KASTELLO
Ruined fortress near site of ancient Greek port town.

7 FILERIMOS
Plateau where the Knights launched their attack to capture the island in 1309.

Chalkidiki Peninsula

The three headlands of Kassandra, Sithonia and Athos thrust into the Aegean like the prongs of Poseidon's trident. This makes a good tour from Thessaloniki.

1 AGIA TRIADA
Pleasant beach resort and fishing village.

2 OLYNTHOS
Important city of 4th-5th century BC.

91

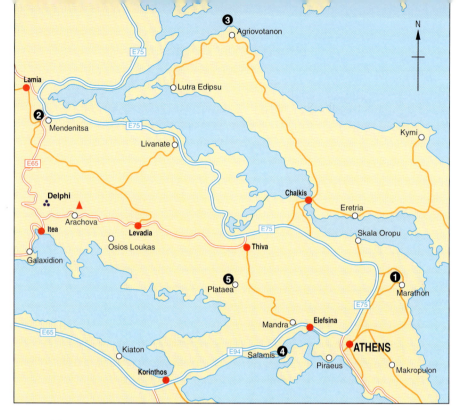

3 KASSANDRA PENINSULA

Many excellent beaches and resort towns, mainly for package tours.

4 GERAKINI

Lovely beach resort set among olive groves, lawns and flower gardens.

5 SITHONIA

Peninsula of beautiful coastal scenery.

6 PORTO CARRAS

Upmarket resort with good facilities for watersports.

7 XERXES' CANAL

Traces of the canal cut in the 5th century BC by the Persian king.

8 MOUNT ATHOS

Mountainous religious retreat of remote monasteries – no women allowed.

9 OURANOPOLIS

Departure point for sightseeing boat trip around Mount Athos.

10 NEA APOLONIA

Hot springs resort by attractive lake.

The Persian Wars

The great battles of ancient times were those that symbolized the unity of the Greek kingdoms and city-states. Two waves of Persian invaders brought the Greek nation together on land and sea under the leadership of Athens and Sparta.

1 MARATHON

A burial mound on the Attica plain marks the victory of Greek armies under Athenian Miltiades against the Persians in 491 BC.

2 THERMOPYLAE

Mountain pass in Thessaly where Leonidas led heroic the Spartan resistance to the armies of Persian emperor Xerxes in 480 BC.

3 CAPE ARTEMISIUM

While the Spartans battled at Thermopylae, the Athenians held the Persian navy off the north coast of Euboea.

4 STRAITS OF SALAMIS

Themistocles' decisive naval victory to the west of Athens drove Xerxes' fleet back across the Aegean in 479 BC.

5 PLATAEA

Greek forces under Pausanius defeated the Persians, though outnumbered, and settled the outcome of the Persian Wars.

*T*he Persian Wars (left) and Philip and Alexander (below).

Philip and Alexander

Trace the beginnings of these two great conquerors, father and son, in the kingdom of Macedonia.

1 THESSALONIKI

Archaeological museum has Philip's bones, armour and gold funeral casket, and an ivory portrait of Alexander.

2 PELLA

Philip's capital, birthplace of Alexander.

3 LEFKADIA

Tomb of one of Alexander's officers.

4 VERGINA

The royal tombs, where Philip's grave was discovered.

5 DION

The garrison town from which Alexander launched his imperial conquest.

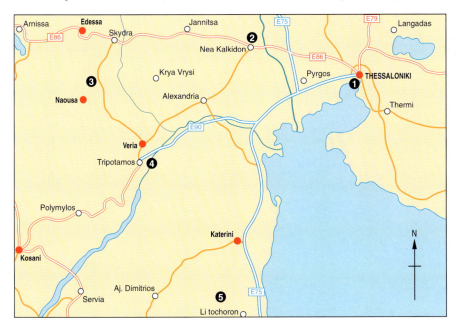

"Athens, the Eye of Greece, Mother of Arts and Eloquence"

Milton's description of the Greek capital could hardly be bettered. Athens was the original focal point of Hellenic culture, the window through which the ancient Greeks looked out upon their world, and the showcase for their achievements in the fields of art, philosophy and politics. After centuries of drowsy stagnation, the city once again pulses with vitality, the industrial, cultural and intellectual heart of modern Greece. Attica is the hinterland of this sprawling capital, a pretty peninsula of beach resorts, historical sites and rolling wooded hills.

Attica's particularity owes much to its self-contained geography. The peninsula thrusts out into the Aegean, bounded on the south by Cape Sounion (with its splendid temple) and on the north by a mountain barrier stretching from the Saronic Gulf to the Euboea Channel. In ancient times, this barrier separated Attica from Boeotia and kept it off the track of most of the invaders pouring down from the north to the Peloponnese. The fierce Dorians passed it by, allowing a gentler, more democratic Ionian civilization to evolve. And if the Athenians could not finally keep out the Persians, they did at least gain time to evacuate the city after the Spartans' courageous effort at Thermopylae, and their own navy's holding action at Artemisium. Attica's own vestige of the great Persian Wars can be visited on the Plain of Marathon.

*T*he urban sprawl of modern Athens spreads across the lower slopes of Mount Lycabettus.

Today, despite the radar stations that disfigure their summits, the historic mountains of Parnes, Pentelikon and Hymettos are popular with summer hikers and winter skiers. Pentelikon is still rich in the magnificent white marble that graces Athens' Acropolis, and Hymettos welcomes pilgrims to its Kaisariani monastery.

Another fine Byzantine monastery church is at Daphni, north-west of Athens. Further west, mysticism of a more ancient era pervades the sanctuary of Eleusis. South-east of Athens, you can flee the jumbo jets' flight paths to the smart seaside resort of Vouliagmeni. As lively as ever, Piraeus is the major starting-point for island-hopping, while quiet little Rafina over on the east coast has ferries going out to the Cyclades.

Athens

The miracle is undeniable. The architectural splendours of the ancient city valiantly resist the stranglehold of the Greek capital's modern sprawl. The amphitheatre of hills to the north, east and south that provided such a harmonious setting in classical times now forms a monstrous atmospheric repository for industrial and traffic pollution eating away at the monumental marble. More than 4,000,000 people (40% of the national population) are crammed into the metropolitan area. Meanwhile, the monuments, outside on the Acropolis and the Agora, or sheltered under glass in the museums, seem to retain in their stone enough of their ancient power to make a visit here as magical as ever.

But thanks to the verve of the Athenians themselves, the modern city, too, has its attractions. Not in its gruesome contemporary architecture, but in the old neighbourhood of the Plaka, refurbished and revitalized in the 1980s. A few august buildings of King Otto's 19th-century capital survive, and café life everywhere, from broad, bustling Platia Syntagma to the tiniest back street, retains all its old charm. Don't even think of driving around the city centre. Leave the hassle to the taxi-drivers or just walk, preferably on the shady side of the street. Visit archaeological sites as early in the morning as possible, and save your museum-trips for the heat of the afternoon.

The Acropolis

The historical heart of the ancient city is the logical starting point of your visit.

The most direct approach is by the 230 bus from Platia Syntagma, reaching the entrance from the south. Hardy walkers can take a more interesting route from the back of Syntagma through the old Plaka neighbourhood via Mnissikleous Street to view the dramatic north face of the Acropolis. The best times of day—especially for photography—are early morning and late afternoon.

Literally the "upper city", the Acropolis is a great table of grey limestone rock veined with rust-coloured schist, rising some 90 m (300 ft) above the Attic plain. Inhabited since the Stone Age, it became a fortified citadel in the Mycenaean period (13th century BC). Seven hundred years later, the tyrant Peisistratus built his palace there, but Athenian democracy made it the exclusive home of the gods. In 480 BC, the Persians destroyed its temples—and Athena's sacred olive tree—but Pericles restored them all, and made them even more splendid than before.

96

ATHENS & ATTICA

EUBOEA

N

Halkoutsi
Oropou
Agii Apostoli
Paralia Vamava
Avlona
Varnavas

PARNES

Marathonas
Plain of Marathon
Tombs of Athenians

Fili
PENTELIKON
N. Makri

Likovrissi
Kifissia

Aspropirgos
Eiefsina
Daphni
83
Rafina

Gerakas
54
Spata
ATHENS
89
Kessariani
Peania
Artemis
Moni Kessarianis
HYMETTOS
PIRAEUS
Sanctury of Artemis
SALAMIS
89
91
Koropi
Markopoulo
Porto-Rafti
AEGINA
Kalivia
Keratea
Vouliagmenti
FLEVES
91
Saronida
89
SARONIC GULF
Lavrion
Temple of Possidon
PATROKLOU
Cape Sounion
MAKRONISSOS

Sites of historic interest
Mountains
High land
0   5   10 km
0   2   4   6 miles

97

ATHENS

Despite the ravages of the Roman, Byzantine, Turkish and Venetian invaders, and the "enlightened" thievery of Lord Elgin, what you see today is essentially Pericles' noble 2,500-year-old conception of a sanctuary for the Greek nation.

Quite apart from the damage caused by air pollution, and well-meaning but misguided 19th-century restoration work, a major threat to the sanctuary has been the wear caused by millions of tourists' feet. During the current prolonged period of restoration, moonlight tours have been discontinued and access is limited to boardwalks and special paths which take you around, but not

into, the temples. Food must not be taken inside the Acropolis limits.

Entrance is through the **Beulé Gate**, named after the French archaeologist who discovered the Roman construction of the 3rd century AD. Its zigzag path replaces a broad straight processional ramp built by Pericles. During the Panathenaic Festival for Athena's birthday, the night of the midsummer full moon, a wheeled ship bearing a sacred, embroidered saffron robe for the goddess was escorted up the ramp by garlanded priests and priestesses, flute players, cavalrymen and maidens. She-goats, ewes and heifers brought up the rear— female sacrifices to the virgin goddess.

To the left of the present path is a marble plinth 10 m (30 ft) high, which at various times supported a monument of chariots and statues of Anthony and Cleopatra. Behind the pedestal is a fine view across to the Temple of Hephaistos on the Agora (see p. 107).

The **Propylaea**, a monumental gatehouse, is the grandest of all surviving secular edifices of ancient Greece. The luxury of its white Pentelic marble aroused protests from Athens' allies when Pericles started to delve into their Delian League defence funds to cover costs. Begun in 437 BC, it was left unfinished six years later at the outbreak of the Peloponnesian War.

The central building's portico of six Doric columns is flanked by two wings serving as reception halls for visitors to the Parthenon. The north wing became known as the Pinacotheca for paintings described there by Pausanias, a Greek guidebook author of the 2nd century AD The sturdy, unadorned Doric porch leads to a vestibule of more slender Ionic columns with their characteristic scrolled capitals. Restorers have retrieved a fragment of the coffered marble ceiling, originally painted blue with gold stars.

On a terrace over to the right is the graceful Ionic-porticoed **Temple of Athena Nike**. Dedicated to the goddess in her role as "bringer of victory", this work by Callicrates points towards his masterpiece, the Parthenon. During the Venetian invasion of 1687, the little temple was dismantled by the Turks to make way for an artillery position on

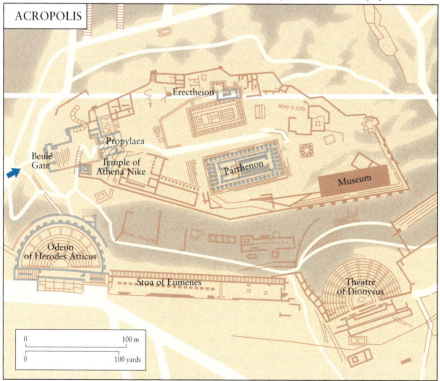

ACROPOLIS

Erectheion

Propylaea

Beulé Gate

Temple of Athena Nike

Parthenon

Museum

Odeon of Herodes Atticus

Stoa of Eumenes

Theatre of Dionysus

| 0 | 100 m |
| 0 | 100 yards |

*T*he Acropolis, the symbol and centre of Pericles' Athenian empire, continues to dominate his capital city. The most blasé of visitors, contemptuous of the urban pollution and the unsightly modern buildings sprawling around it, cannot but admire its awesome nobility. Above the traffic-clogged streets and choking exhaust fumes, the gods still sit in grandiose residence.

The sloping plateau leading up to the Parthenon was originally dominated by a bronze statue of Athena Promachos (the Champion) celebrating Athens' victory at the Battle of Marathon. Her helmet and spear point glinting in the sun served as a welcome landmark for sailors approaching Piraeus after rounding Cape Zoster. Her greatest monument, the **Parthenon** (Home of the Virgin) still stands, battered but unbowed by centuries of bombardment and plunder. The wonderment of a first approach to this most revered of ancient monuments is undimmed by any amount of picture-postcard familiarity.

Inaugurated for the Panathenaic Festival of 438 BC, the centrepiece of Pericles' new Athens was the supreme architectural achievement of classical Greece. Both shrine and state treasury, it guarded the defence funds of Athens and its allies in the Delian League. The temple's mastermind was Phidias, the greatest artistic genius of Athens' golden era. He laid out the overall concept for its construction, executed by Callicrates and Ictinus, and designed the temple's sculptural decoration. He may himself have sculpted part of the frieze between the columns and the roof, but his most important personal contribution was a gigantic wooden statue of Athena coated in gold and ivory. She reigned in the temple's inner sanctum, forbidden to ordinary mortals, until she was carried off by an unknown plunderer, probably in the 5th century AD.

A hundred years later, under Emperor Justinian, the Parthenon became the Church of Saint Sophia, with galleries added for female worshippers and underground vaults for the bishops' tombs. It was a Catholic cathedral for

this strategic south-west corner of the bastion. The masonry was later gathered up by 19th- and 20th-century archaeologists and painstakingly reassembled, using drawings of another Callicrates temple of similar proportions as a guide.

Except for cement casts from four panels which are now in the British Museum, the sculpted friezes of Athena's exploits and Athenian battle scenes have been rendered indistinct by years of weathering.

13th-century French barons. The Turks used it first as a mosque and then, as Venetian artillery made clear with one well-aimed shell in 1687, a powder-magazine that exploded and burned for 48 hours.

View the temple from the south to take in the peristyle (oblong colonnade) of 46 Doric pillars. The long-gone roof was of marble-tiled wood, but the rest is entirely of Pentelic marble weathering from white to its present honey colour. Sculpture on the pediment gables at either end was largely destroyed by Byzantine church-builders and the Venetian bombardment, but from ancient accounts and surviving fragments both in London and in the Acropolis Museum (see p. 103), we know that they portrayed the birth of Athena and her contest with Poseidon for control of Athens.

Of 92 sculpted metope panels on the entablature topping the columns, only the **western frieze** is still intact and in place. Depicting mythical fights between giants, Thessalian hunters and brutal centaurs, the friezes were an allegorical celebration of Greek valour against the Persians.

The **Erechtheion** is the last and most complex of the four great monuments on the Acropolis. Dedicated to three deities—Erechtheus, one of the city's mythical snake-man monarchs; Poseidon, with whom Erechtheus is closely associated; and Athena—it is built on two levels over on the north side of the plateau. The Peloponnesian Wars were raging throughout its 15-year construction. It suffered the usual indignities from the barbarians who followed, among them a Turkish military commander who used it as a harem, and Lord Elgin, who shipped parts of it back to the British Museum in London.

The temple marks the site of Athena's mythical contest with Poseidon for the patronage of the city (see p. 103). A new, but suitably old-looking olive tree has been planted outside the west wall, where Athena's original sacred tree once sprouted, and Poseidon's trident has left its marks on a rock hidden in a hole in a corner of the north porch.

The **north porch** is greatly admired for the elegant moulding of its Ionic columns—one of which was carried off by Lord Elgin, along with part of the marble beam above. Note, too, the doorway's fine moulding, a blue marble frieze and panelled ceiling (all much renovated under the Romans). The sanctuary housed a venerated olive wood statue of Athena, definitely fallen from heaven because, it was said, no Greek artist would have carved anything so primitive.

Most celebrated feature of the Erechtheion is, of course, the southern **Porch of the Caryatids**. Gracefully doing the work of four columns at the front and two at the sides, six maidens unflinchingly hold up the roof, with baskets of fruit protecting their pretty heads from the marble beams. They take their name from the girls of the Spartan village of Caryai, admired for their proud upright posture. But the Athenians gave them long stately Ionian robes rather than the shameless miniskirts favoured by the Spartans.

Today's statues are in fact replicas, as five of the originals had to be rescued from the ravages of modern pollution and taken indoors to the Acropolis Museum. The sixth, part of Lord Elgin's booty, is in London.

T<i>he famous Caryatid Porch is only a small part of the Erechtheion sanctuary, completed in 405 BC just before the final defeat of Athens in the Peloponnesian Wars. It stands on the south side, above an earlier temple to Athena.*

Save the **Acropolis Museum** for last. In nine galleries, its collection of sculpture covering the whole history of the sacred hill will make more sense after you have visited the sites from which the pieces have been recovered. Just as important for your well-being, its refreshingly cool interior offers welcome respite from that blistering sun.

Galleries 1, **2** and **3** are devoted to pre-classical works of the 6th century BC, prior to the great building pro-

The City of Athena

The Athenians have always claimed their city was founded not by invaders but by an aboriginal population known as the Pelasgians. This was underlined by the primeval form, half-man, half-serpent, of their first king, Cecrops, a son of Mother Earth. He acted as judge in the contest between Poseidon and Athena for divine patronage of the city. The sea-god laid his claim by thrusting his trident into the rock of the Acropolis and causing a spring to gush forth sea water. It's still there today, they say, near the site of the Erechtheion temple. The more practical-minded Athena tapped her spear on the rock and an olive tree sprouted. Judging Athena to have given the land a better gift, the city became hers and was named after her.

gramme of Pericles. You will notice that many of the sculptures have traces of the paint that originally provided bright

The Elgin Marbles
In 1801, Thomas Bruce, Lord Elgin, British ambassador to the Sublime Porte, as the Ottoman court at Constantinople was then known, obtained from the Turks a *carte blanche* to plunder the Acropolis. His permit authorized excavation of the ruins, the making of casts and drawings of the sculpture, and gave him the right to carry away sculpted figures and inscriptions. At the time, the British envoy argued, much of the monumental masonry was being dismantled by the Athenians themselves for use in their own houses.

With an Italian art-scholar to help him pick out the choicest pieces, Elgin took back to London large parts of the Parthenon frieze, attributed to the great sculptor Phidias, and one of the huge Caryatids supporting the Erechtheion temple.

Lord Elgin's defenders argue that the British Museum has preserved the artworks from nearly two centuries of war and pollution. Greeks feel that their sovereignty in the matter has been too long ignored, and that the very name of the Elgin Marbles betrays an arrogant scorn for the Greeks' rights to the treasures of their own Acropolis. The actress-turned-politician Melina Mercouri has waged a long campaign for the return of the marbles to Greece, now that their own museums are perfectly well equipped to care for them.

highlights to costume, face and limbs. Working mainly in limestone, the sculptors were clearly more comfortable with animals, lithe and vigorous creatures from nature or myth, than with human figures, stiff and stylized. Outstanding promise of things to come is the Moschophoros (No. 624), a statue of a man purposefully carrying a calf on his shoulders as a gift to the gods. Marble from Mount Hymettos permits better treatment of detail in the man's hair, and more tension and life in the limbs of the man and his animal offering.

Galleries 4 and **5** are given over principally to statues of girls *(kore)*, posted in the temples as handmaidens to the gods. The works here take you to the end of the Archaic period. The somewhat cumbersome Doric robe is gradually replaced by a lighter, more feminine Ionic linen tunic. And you can follow the evolution of the celebrated "Archaic Smile", which dominated pre-classical statues as an artistic convention rather than a psychological observation. This becomes clear when you look at Kore 674, dated around 500 BC; the girl's smile is already vanishing, replaced by an expression more intriguingly wistful. Largest of the maidens is the imposing marble Kore of Antenor (681).

Gallery 6 demonstrates a major leap forward in technique expressing a bolder energy. The Kritios Ephebe (698) is an athletic military cadet, agile and confident, released from the heavy archaic posture. No sign of a smile on the melancholy Blond Ephebe (689), so called because of the yellow tints discernible in his hair, or the girl aptly known now as *"La Boudeuse"* (609)— French for "The Sulker".

Galleries 7 and **8** give excellent close-ups of sculptural fragments from the Parthenon and Erechtheion pediments and friezes. They depict Poseidon, Athena and the Panathenaic procession.

Gallery 9 provides a suitable climax to the museum tour with the originals of the Erechtheion Caryatids. Protected now by air-conditioning, special lighting and a glass screen, they are at last safe, but inevitably less exhilarating to behold than in their original setting.

Ancient Athens

West of the Acropolis are three hills that played a vital role in the city's history. The **Areopagus** *(Ários Págos)* was the hill of Ares, a war god unpopular with the Greeks because he invariably sided with their enemies, notably the Trojans. The hill affords a fine view over the Agora and across to the Propylaea on the Acropolis. The Areopagus was synonymous with the aristocracy's supreme court on the north side of the hill which judged capital crimes of murder and treason. It was here that tragedian Aeschylus set the trial (and acquittal) of Orestes for the murder of his mother. The court became a governing council, a sort of self-perpetuating Senate or House of Lords opposed by Pericles in his fight for democratic government. On the north side of the hill, where St Paul harangued the Athenian sages, are traces of a 16th-century church. It was dedicated to Dionysius the Areopagite, the one council elder who followed Paul back to Rome, where he was converted to Christianity and became Athens' patron saint.

Across the street rises the **Pnyx** *(Pníka),* the democratic counterpart to the Areopagus. The terrace of the semi-circular space where the citizens'

M asterpieces of Greek sculpture are preserved in the Acropolis Museum.

assembly *(ecclesia)* was held was on a higher level so that nosy nobles could not look down on its deliberations. The very impressive **Acropolis Sound and Light show** is held on the Pnyx with an English-language commentary (enquire at the tourist information office in the National Bank building, Karagiorgi Servias 2, just off Platia Syntagma, for times of the show).

The tree-covered **Mousion**, hill of the Muses, is also known as *Lófos Filopáppou,* after the Syrian prince Antiochos Philopappos, Roman consul and benefactor of Athens in the 2nd century AD. His tomb is marked by a marble monument. Always important strategically for artillery, it provided the Venetian commander Morosini with a clear shot at the Parthenon in 1687. In World War I, Greek royalists manned the hill to fire on Allied forces, and in 1967 it was a key position in the Colonels' coup d'état. The best shots today are made with a camera, zooming in on the Acropolis or over the city to the Bay of Phaleron and Piraeus harbour.

The **Theatre of Dionysus** (*Théatro Dionísou*) stands almost directly below the Parthenon. It was built in the 5th century BC to stage the tragedies of Aeschylus, Sophocles and Euripides and the comedies of Aristophanes. Apart from a front row of 67 marble "thrones" for VIPs, the Greeks of classical times—17,000 in a full house—had to content themselves with ledges of beaten earth. It was the Romans who installed the curving terraced seating of marble and limestone.

The carved relief of scenes from Dionysius's life forms the façade of a raised stage. Next to the auditorium, the double-tiered colonnade of the **Stoa of Eumenes** (*Stoá Evménous*—2nd century BC) was a sheltered promenade for theatre-goers before and after the performance, which always took place in the daytime. The original Stoa linked up with a smaller theatre seating 5,000, the **Odeon of Herodes Atticus** (*Odíon Iródou Attikoú*). Herodes was a wealthy Athenian elected to the Roman senate. He dedicated the theatre to his deceased wife in AD 161. The huge triple-tiered arched façade is typical of Roman theatres. Modern restoration has covered the limestone seating with white Pentelic marble for modern audiences enjoying operas and concerts during the Athens Summer Festival (see p. 332).

At a bend in the main road between the Acropolis and Syntagma, **Hadrian's Arch** (*Píli Adrianoú*—AD 132) marked the border between old Athens and the Roman emperor's new city, Hadrianopolis. On the side facing the Acropolis is the inscription: "This is Athens, ancient city of Theseus." The almost petulant vanity of the emperor becomes apparent on the other façade with its inscription:

"This is the city of Hadrian and not of Theseus." But he did deserve the ancients' gratitude for completing the great **Temple of Olympian Zeus** (*Stíles Olimpíou Diós*), of which only 15 of its 104 majestic Corinthian columns remain. It measured 205 by 129 m (672 by 423 ft), the largest temple in Greece, though there were bigger ones in the colonies of Sicily and Asia Minor. Construction of the Temple of Olympian Zeus had begun under the tyrant Peisistratus in the 6th century BC It was conceived as a purely Doric edifice; the Corinthian columns were added by Antiochus IV Epiphanes 400 years later. Hadrian's finishing touches included a gigantic statue of Zeus that was modelled on Phidias' work for Olympia (see p. 152), and one only slightly less colossal of himself.

At first glance, the **Agora** (bus No. 230 to Tission terminus) looks like an indecipherable mess of rubble, of which only the most hardened archaeology buff could hope to make sense. But with an effort of the imagination, it is not impossible to recall that the area sprawling below the northern ramparts of the Acropolis was "downtown", the throbbing heart of the ancient city and unmistakable ancestor of every city centre and village square in Greece.

From the entrance on Odos Adrianou, you look down on broken pillars, walls and paving stones that once were shops, banks, market, mint, council chamber, schools, libraries, gymnasium, concert hall, dance hall, temples, the courthouse where Socrates was said to have been tried, and the prison in which he committed suicide. A panoramic pictorial reconstruction helps you to visualize and situate the original buildings.

Over in the south-west corner is the Horos, marked with the inscription "I am the boundary stone of the Agora". Entering at this point, all were expected to be ritually purified, for the Agora was the sacred centre of the city. Strolling among the ruins, you may catch a distant echo of the ancient voices that used to ring out across the Agora.

Near the boundary stone, Socrates held court at the shop of Simon the cobbler, a literate fellow who, long before Plato, began writing down the sage's dialogues. St Paul wandered around arguing with all and sundry, while the Stoics grimly endured the exhortations of the man they called "the babbler".

To the Epicureans, of course, conversation was a great pleasure. Aristotle's opinion was that "Man is by nature a political animal". And Pericles defined perfectly the rules of the Agora game: "We do not say that a man who takes no interest in politics is a man who minds his own business; we say that he has no business here at all."

The long porticoed gallery closing off the east side of the Agora is a reconstitution of the 2nd century BC **Stoa of Attalos** (*Stoá Attálou*) which served as a shady promenade and pavilion from which to watch the Panathenaic Festival procession. It was made into a **museum** in the 1950s by the American School of Classical Studies in Athens, which has carried out excavations of the Agora since 1931. The museum exhibits the major archaeological finds from the site: vases, coins, household utensils and an enormous bronze shield captured from the Spartans.

On a small hill above the Agora is the beautiful Doric-columned **Temple of Hephaistos** (*Naós Iféstou*), first of the major temples built by Pericles after the Persian wars. Although it is more popularly known as the **Theseion** (*Thisío*), because of the scenes of Theseus' exploits portrayed on its frieze (along with those of Hercules), it was in fact dedicated to Hephaistos, god of fire, Olympian blacksmith, and patron of all metalworkers. Archaeologists have uncovered traces of iron foundries and workshops near the temple, and 2,500 years later, metalworkers are still sweating away in shops just the other side of the railway tracks.

This is the best preserved of Athens' temples, more slender than the Parthenon with its graceful 34-column peristyle. Not the least of the temple's charming features is its garden with myrtle, pomegranates, olives and cypresses, all trees that graced the garden in Roman times.

To the west of the Agora (along Odos Ermou) is the **Keramikos** where the ancient Athenians buried their dead—most notably those fallen in battle—in elaborately sculpted tombs. It was here that Pericles made his famous funeral oration for soldiers that were killed in the first battles of the Peloponnesian War. His exaltation of the democratic values for which they had died became his own political testament (he died a year later): "I declare that our city is an education to Greece. In my opinion each single one of our citizens, in all the manifold aspects of his life, is able to show himself the rightful lord and owner of his own person, and to do this with exceptional grace and exceptional versatility."

Some of the best of the sculpture, along with fine funeral vases, are displayed in the cemetery's museum.

Mathematical Genius

The marvel of the Parthenon's power and beauty was not achieved simply through some intuitive whim. Brilliantly applied mathematics was the subtle servant of architectural harmony, breathing life into the abstract concept of classical equilibrium. The Parthenon is no cold rectangular box of straight drawing-board lines—its subtle curves and intricate variations in horizontals and verticals achieve an inspiring vision of symmetry. The temple's arrangement of 8 columns at either end and 17 along the sides conforms to what was felt to be an ideal width-to-length ratio of 4 to 9—roughly 30 m (101 ft) wide to 70 m (228 ft) long. Similarly, 4:9 is the ratio between the diameter of each column and the space between any two of them. These spaces vary to accord with the thicker corner columns. Formed by a dozen fluted drums rising to a height of 10.4 m (34 ft), all the columns lean slightly inward and start to swell out a third of the way up (otherwise, an optical illusion would make them look concave). The temple's paved floor rises gently towards the centre to create a deliberately convex surface.

Plaka

After a few disastrous years as a tawdry tourist-trap in the 1960s and 70s, the city's most ancient residential area, just north-east of the Acropolis, has recovered its old authentic charm. A sleepy haven of tranquillity by day, it livens up at sunset, but without the blare of amplified bouzouki music that rather spoiled the atmosphere in former years.

Ancient ruins, Byzantine churches and folk museums recall the neighbourhood's history, but its main charm is the unique atmosphere of the streets themselves, narrow winding lanes that often climb steep stairways to follow the original paths of ancient Athens. Amid all the charted wonders of the city, Plaka is a place of serendipity, the chance discovery of concealed beauties: vines curling around a pink, ochre, or whitewashed villa with blue or green shutters, a garden of hibiscus, jasmine, roses and a fragrant pot of holy basil. Early morning is the best time to explore. In the evening, you can return to enjoy the open-air cafés and restaurants and souvenir shops.

Lacking formally defined boundaries, Plaka roughly covers the area south of the Odos Ermou shopping street. But the heart is closer to the Acropolis. You

may well prefer your own adventurous itinerary through the Plaka maze. If not, we suggest the following: starting out from Syntagma, head down Odos Filellinon and turn right into Kidathineon. The houses here were built in the earliest years of the Bavarian monarchy. At No. 17, now the **Museum of Greek Folk Art** *(Mousío Laïkís Ellinikís Téchnis)*, you can admire the fine display of Byzantine gold, silver and jewellery and embroidery from the islands.

Further down Kidathineon, turn left into Farmaki to visit the 12th-century **church of St Catherine** *(Agia Ekatéríni)* set in a sunken palm-shaded

It is once more respectable, even chic, to live in the Plaka. The noise of its once notorious bars and nightclubs has been eliminated or subdued to create a pleasant residential neighbourhood.

courtyard. In front, two Ionic columns, believed to be the remains of a Roman bath, were incorporated in an earlier church on the site.

Nearby is the **Monument of Lysicrates** *(Mnimíon Lisikrátous)*, erected to commemorate a prize won in 334 BC by a boys' chorus. Lysicrates was their

An Urban Oasis

In Athens' chequered modern history, the Plaka neighbourhood is a rare success story of urban conservation. For centuries, it was the nucleus of the village to which the city had dwindled following the departure of the Romans. (The name Plaka is variously interpreted as "flat place", as opposed to the rugged Acropolis, or just "old place" from the Albanian word *pliaka*.)

Patrician villas with handsome garden courtyards appeared in the building boom after King Otto re-established Athens as Greece's capital in 1834. Miraculously, they survived the next building boom that razed most of the 19th-century city after World War II. But a third boom, of mass tourism, nearly proved fatal, with the invasion of rowdy bars and tacky night-clubs. An alliance between wealthy businessmen and the socialist government of the 1980s turfed out the riff-raff and renovated the houses, which now provide chic residences for the successors of the 19th-century patricians, for whom not even the Greeks have found a word more attractive than yuppies.

sponsor. It is celebrated in classical architecture as the first building to make exterior use of Corinthian columns. The six columns support a dome formed from a single marble block carved to imitate fish-scale tiling. On top stood the prize, a three-legged bronze cauldron known as a tripod. A frieze shows Etruscan pirates being turned into dolphins by Dionysus, at whose festival the prize was won.

Several such monuments once lined the Street of Tripods (Odos Tripodon). This one was incorporated in a monastery (later burned down) where Lord Byron stayed in 1810, sitting among the columns while he worked on *Childe Harold*.

Follow Epicharmou off to the left from Tripodon towards **Anafiotika**, a remarkable whitewashed village within the city. To cope with Athens' severe housing shortage after Greek independence, a law granted occupancy to anyone who built a house—or at least managed to get the roof up—between sunset and sunrise. First to occupy the site were two stonemasons from the little Aegean island of Anafi (east of Santorini). Other Anafiot masons followed, building and restoring houses and churches in their native style. Today, Anafiots living here on the heights of Plaka outnumber the 300-odd residents back on their home island.

One of the churches, at the top of the village, **Agios Simeon**, is guarded by a stately cypress and offers a splendid view of Athens.

Further west, Odos Klepsidras takes you to the **Roman Agora** (*Romaïkí Agorá*). Over to your right is Plaka's best-known landmark, the **Tower of the Winds** (*Aérides*), built by astronomer Andronicus in the 1st century BC. It once housed an elaborate water clock fed by a spring on the Acropolis and was topped by a triton—half man, half fish—that served as a weather vane. Bas-reliefs on each side of the octagonal marble tower represent the eight points of the compass and their corresponding winds: Notos, the rainy south wind, pours water from an urn; Zephyr, the west wind, heralding spring, scatters flowers; and, all too familiar to summer visitors, Sciron, the searing north-west *meltemi* wind of July and August, carries a bronze brazier of charcoal.

In the marketplace north of the tower, the **Turkish Mosque** was built to celebrate the Ottoman capture of Athens in

1456. Minus its minaret, it now houses an archaeology workshop.

Just four Doric columns remain of the original entrance to the Roman Agora, the **Gate of Athena Archegetis**, built in the 1st century BC. One of the door supports, protected by a rusty iron grille, is inscribed with Emperor Hadrian's edict taxing olive oil, which casts doubt on just how much of a Graecophile he really was.

North of the old Roman marketplace, a colourful modern **flea market** flour-

T *he Roman-era Tower of the Winds was in reality a water clock. This Plaka district landmark measured the passage of time by the rising and falling of the water level in a cylinder housed inside the white marble tower.*

ishes on Platia Monastiraki and along Odos Pandrosou, site of the old Turkish bazaar. It is most active on Sunday mornings when the hurdy-gurdy music offers a welcome change from the ubiquitous taped bouzouki renderings of *Zorba the Greek*. Even if you are not in the market for antiques or old brass, embroidery, rugs or leather ware, the stalls of fresh drinks and cool coconut should be very welcome.

The square's monastery church dates back to the 10th century but suffers from its modern restoration. More interesting is the 18th-century **Tzistarakis Mosque**, built with the marble of one of the massive Corinthian columns from the Olympic Zeus temple. After the usual retaliatory removal of its minaret in 1821, it was commandeered first as a prison and then as a **Folk Art Museum** *(Mousío Laïkís Ellinikís Téchnis)*. Climb up to the open loggia for a good view over the Plaka neighbourhood.

On your way back to Syntagma along Pandrosou, you will pass the 19th-century **Mitropolis**, the cathedral of the Greek Orthodox Church after the split with Constantinople. This hybrid curiosity, its interior allegedly inspired by Venice's Basilica of St Mark, was built from parts of 70 other demolished churches. If you return to Syntagma by way of Odos Ermou, you'll see the **Kapnikarea**, a Byzantine church in the middle of the busy street.

Modern Athens

Get your bearings on the modern city from the fine panoramic viewpoint on the 277 m (908 ft) summit of **Mount Lycabettus** *(Likavittós)*. Take the cable-car from Odos Ploutarchou in Kolonaki. Planted there in the Attic plain, the conical peak was supposedly created from a rock dropped by the goddess Athena, frightened by an owl on her way to building the Acropolis.

At the very top is a 19th-century chapel dedicated to St George. This is the scene of a candlelight procession on the eve of the Orthodox Easter. Just below it, a visitors' pavilion provides refreshments and an unbeatable view (at least early in the morning, before the traffic smog rises) of the Acropolis and the city over to Piraeus harbour. On the terraces, you can consult the orientation maps in marble which indicate all the important sights.

Cannons on the western slopes are fired on Greek Independence Day (March 25).

The Origin of Ostracism

The most unprepossessing but nonetheless intriguing exhibits in the Agora museum are the shards of pottery *(ostraka)* on which Athenians wrote the name of any prominent citizens who had become unpopular enough to warrant ostracism. A majority vote among at least 6000 citizens resulted in the ostracized man being given 10 days to leave the country for a period of 10 years, after which time he could return to Athens and recover his citizenship, property and honour. Among the most famous figures to be ostracized were Pericles' father, Xanthippus, discredited as a politician but amnestied as a general to fight against the Persians; Themistocles, the creator of Athens' naval power who was felt to have grown too big for his boots; and Thucydides, who profited from his exile (for losing a battle) to write his historical masterpiece, *The Peloponnesian War*. One important candidate for ostracism, deservedly named Aristides the Just, was asked by an illiterate citizen to help him write down the name "Aristides" on his pottery shard. The statesman obliged, but asked why the fellow wished to ostracize him. "Because," he replied, "I'm tired of hearing him called 'the Just'."

*C*rowds gather to attend a political rally in Platia Omonia, in the heart of modern Athens. Greece, which in 1991 celebrated the 2,500th anniversary of the birth of democracy, is a nation which is still passionately interested in politics. There are few things a Greek enjoys more than a good old political argument around the café table.

The hub of the modern city is **Platia Syntagma** (*Platía Sintàgmatos*). Its name refers to the charter of Greek statehood proclaimed in 1843. Airlines, travel agencies, and other international businesses have their offices here, the airlines their agencies. Miraculously, orange trees, palms and cypresses manage to survive the exhaust fumes from the eight busy streets that converge on Syntagma. On the square's smart cafe terraces, Athens' wheeler-dealers and decision-makers hide behind their dark glasses. They take a solitary coffee with their morning newspaper, then rendezvous with their business partners or lovers at midday, disappear for the after-noon siesta, and return to argue politics and divorce settlements in the evening. The square boasts the city's grandest hotel, the **Grande Bretagne**, a monument in its own right, and a noble example of the city's 19th-century neo-classicism. Treat yourself to a drink in the plush bar of what was originally the home of Danish architect Theophil von Hansen, designer of Athens' University, Library and Academy.

Across the east side of the square is the national **Parliament** (*Voulí*), which was the royal palace until 1935. Sentries (*évzones*) in traditional white uniform guard a memorial to the nation's unknown soldier. The changing of the

113

Caught Red-Handed
With the decline of Athenian democracy, citizens had to be paid to ensure their attendance at the assembly on the Pnyx ("crowded place"). People passed through a narrow entrance hemmed in by ropes daubed with wet red paint. Thus anyone trying to duck out of his civic duty bore a tell-tale mark which disqualified him from collecting his attendance fee.

Republican Guard is held on Sundays at 11 a.m. Engraved on the monument are texts from Pericles' funeral oration in 430 BC, honouring the Athenians who were killed in the first year of the Peloponnesian War.

Beyond the flower stalls and the members' entrance to the Parliament building, you can take refuge from the downtown traffic with the ducks and peacocks in the **National Garden** *(Ethniko Kípos)*. You will find blessedly cool shade in this quiet oasis of flowers, greenery and ornamental ponds. The busts are of modern Greek poets and political heroes. Open-air concerts and plays are performed at the Zappion exhibition halls.

Nestling in the hollow of Arditos Hill is the marble **Olympic Stadium**, where the first modern Olympics were staged in 1896. It stands on the site of an ancient stadium built in 330 BC for the games of the Panathenaic Festival. It has the traditional U-shaped plan to be seen at Olympia and Delphi, with a length of 184 m (about 604 ft), the ancient Greek measure of one *stade*.

North-west from Syntagma, take the broad avenue, **Panepistimiou**, past the most imposing of the city's surviving 19th-century neoclassical buildings, all devoted to the nation's higher education. These piles of Pentelic marble pay

rather heavy-handed tribute to ancient Greece, jolting modern taste with their façades painted and gilded in the classical tradition. A distant echo of the Acropolis's Erechtheion, the Ionic-columned Academy *(Akadimía)* has statues of Plato and Socrates sitting rather uncomfortably at the entrance. It stands next to the University *(Panepistímio)*, where British visitors will recognize a statue of Gladstone, and Greeks point out their own great statesman, Ionannis Kapodistrias, assassinated by Greek rivals in the fight for Independence. Beyond is the National Library *(Vivliothíki)*, with nearly a million books and manuscripts, among which are beautifully hand-illuminated Gospels of the 10th and 11th centuries.

Opposite the University, take Odos Korai over to Platia Klafthmonos, or Sobbing Square, so named because citizens came here to register their complaints with King Otto. His modest two-storey palace with a balcony on the south-east side of the square is now the **Museum of the City of Athens**, whose exhibits illustrate his reign (1832–62). But the more important attraction here is the 12th-century church of **Agii Theodori**, the finest of Athens' few Byzantine monuments.

Stadiou's broad avenue of shops takes you on to **Platia Omonia**, linking the capital to its mainland provinces. Its radiating streets run north to Thebes, Macedonia and Thrace; south to Piraeus; east to Marathon; and west to Corinth and the Peloponnese. Here too is the central station of the municipal subway, where thousands of Greeks pour in each day from the countryside and mill around the subterranean shopping centre.

*J*uicy strawberries piled high on a stall in an Athens street market. Greek agriculture has been hampered in the past by poor investment and an inheritance system that split land into ever smaller holdings. Now it produces much of the EC's fruit and vegetables, half its tobacco, and is the only European grower of cotton.

South of Omonia are the bustling **city markets**. You can explore the fruit, vegetable and herb markets on Sophocles and Euripides Streets; poultry, rabbits and other wild game are to be found on Armodiou. Liveliest of all are the fish and meat markets along Eolou and Athinas. The counters of these covered refrigerated halls are of course made of the finest marble.

Amid the city's largely unimaginative, and occasionally downright hideous, 20th-century buildings, two modern edifices are worthy of your attention. East of the National Garden on Vasilissis Sofias Street, the white-façade of the **Hilton Hotel** is a handsome work by Greek architect Vassiliadis. Notice the "graffiti" painted by Iannis Moralis to symbolize Greek culture. Even more distinguished is the **United States Embassy** (1961), one of the last designs of Bauhaus master Walter Gropius. His thoroughly modern structure pays homage to classical Greece with a peristyle of marble-faced columns surrounding a two-storey rectangular steel-and-glass core.

National Archaeological Museum *(Archeologikó Mousío)*

This great treasury of ancient Greek art is at Odos Patision 44, not far from Platia Omonia. Though the exterior is understandably neoclassical, the museum's interior provides an admirably modern setting, easy of access, displaying works from all over the ancient Greek world.

With the exceptions of those discovered in Crete, Delphi, Olympia and Thessaloniki, all Greek archaeological finds were originally brought here. But an increasingly decentralized cultural policy will in future leave works in regional museums close to their original sites. Thus, the frescoes of Thera (see p. 178) are due to be removed one day to a museum on Santorini.

Ranging from prehistoric times to the era of Roman rule, the exhibits span some 7,000 years. Give yourself at least half a day to see the highlights.

Mycenaean Room (No. 4). Of all the treasures recovered in 1876 from the royal chamber tombs at Mycenae, the most famous is Agamemnon's gold death mask (16th century BC). Scholars insist there is no proof (or even historical likelihood) that this is the facial imprint of the man who led the Greeks to Troy. But look at that kingly brow, the haughty mouth with moustache and beard, and you may share with its finder, German archaeologist Heinrich Schliemann, the conviction that here indeed is Homer's sad and stubborn hero.

Look, too, for the grand silver bull's head with golden horns and rosette, showing it to be prepared and ready for sacrifice. And the two gold Vaphio cups (15th century BC) from a tomb near Sparta, portraying a wild bull being captured in a net, after being lured into ambush by a cow.

Room 9. Among the marble sculpture of the Archaic era is the exquisite Attic maiden Phrasikleia (540 BC)—her name is on the base, along with the sculptor's signature, Aristion of Paros.

Room 13. Here, the Kroisos tomb statue of 525 BC is a more sturdy and fleshy figure than earlier Archaic work.

Room 15. One of the museum's proudest possessions is the towering bronze Poseidon (460 BC), poised to hurl his trident. Probably looted 2,000 years ago, the god accompanied a wrecked Roman ship down into his watery realm, and was found on the sea bed off Artemision (at the northern tip of Euboea) in 1928.

A fine sculpted Eleusian frieze shows the goddess Demeter giving a youth ears of corn, to initiate him and all mankind into the mysteries of cultivation.

Room 21. Found at the same time as Poseidon, the bronze Jockey of Artemision (2nd century BC) is urging on his steed with all the excitement of the race. Pedantic art-scholars might suggest that the boy is much too small relative to his horse, and was originally part of another sculpture.

Room 28. Another piece stolen by the Romans during the infamous plundering of Corinth (see p. 130), the Youth of Antikythira (340 BC) is a superb study in grace and balance, left arm swinging free and right leg lightly poised. He is thought to represent the young Paris offering the prize apple to Aphrodite.

Room 30. Later Hellenistic bronzes here show a keenly observed psychology, notably the head of a philosopher (3rd century BC) with his furrowed brow and piercing gaze framed by unruly hair and beard. From Olympia comes the bronze head of a boxer, complete with cauliflower ears, flattened nose and championship laurels.

Room 48 (upper floor). Excavations at Akrotiri on Santorini delivered the Thera frescoes from 3,500 years of burial under the volcanic ash that shrouded the island's Minoan civilization. With neighbouring Crete's own treasures kept in the museum at Iraklion (see p. 190.), Athens has here a rare opportunity to admire the life and grace of that culture. Scenes include a naval expedition, a naked fisherman carrying strings of fish, boys boxing, and a spring landscape with clumps of lilies growing in the ravines. Also on the upper floor, the **Vase Collection** traces Greek ceramics from the first painted pottery of the Bronze Age (2000 BC) through the stylized Geometric patterns (10th to 7th centuries BC) and Attica's rather stiff black-figure vases (6th century BC) to the triumph of classical Athens' lively red-figure vases of the 5th century BC.

Other Museums

The **Benaki Museum** (*Mousío Benáki,* corner of Vasilissis Sofias and Koumbari streets) was installed in the mansion of a wealthy Greek art lover. His eclectic collections include Mediterranean art of prehistoric times, Byzantine art, traditional Greek costume and jewellery, and historical memorabilia, particularly from the war of Independence.

The nearby **Museum of Cycladic Art**, (*Nyofitou 4, Kononaki*) is a superb museum opened in the late 1980's, displaying some beautiful artifacts from the Cyclades, many dating back to prehistoric times. The museum is spacious so the exhibits can be fully appreciated.

The **Byzantine Museum** (*Vizantinó Mousío,* Vas. Sofias 22), in an elegant villa, houses a vast collection of sacred sculpture, panel paintings and jewellery from the 9th to the 15th centuries, and icons from the great revival of the 14th and 15th centuries. Three rooms present reproductions of churches from the earliest (5th century), middle and post-Byzantine eras.

The **National Gallery of Painting** (*Ethnikí Pinakothíki,* Vas. Konstantinou 50) presents Greek art of the 19th and 20th centuries, much influenced by the classical, Byzantine and folk art traditions. France has donated a series of paintings by Picasso, Utrillo and Picabia to honour Greece's liberation in 1945.

The **War Museum** (corner of Vas. Sofias and Rizari) is the cultural contribution of the Colonels' military dictatorship from 1967 to 1974. Models of ships and aircraft, weapons, uniforms, flags and medals trace Greek warfare from Mycenae to World War II.

Piraeus *(Pireéfs)*

Three superb natural harbours, for commerce, fishing and leisure, sustain the town's position as the Mediterranean's third most active port city (after Marseilles and Genoa). Piraeus has a population of half a million when considered independently of metropolitan Athens. And that is the way it has always preferred to be considered. Founded in prehistoric times by Minyan warriors, it built its strength in classical times on its cosmopolitan population—Egyptian, Phoenician and Jewish merchants, as well as the boldest entrepreneurs from Greek overseas colonies. Their descendants sit today in gleaming marble banks and shipping offices, eclipsing the

world of sailors' taverns and golden-hearted tarts made famous by Melina Mercouri's film *Never On Sunday*.

But the town remains a delight for anyone lured by the romance of ships big and small. Built on a peninsula thrusting into the Saronic Gulf, the town's chequerboard street plan was laid out by Pericles' town planner Hippodamus (behind the railway station, Platia Ippodamias pays him tribute). On the peninsula's west shore, where the town hall clock provides a traditional meeting-place, the bustling **Great Harbour** serves international freighters, cruise liners and inter-island vessels. Behind the town hall, the colourful **bazaar** draws a crowd of islanders stocking up with vegetables, fruit and spices.

Across the peninsula on the east shore, **Zea Harbour** is a haven for luxury yachts and fishermen. The **Nautical Museum** (on Akti Themistokleous) traces Greece's maritime history from models of ancient Athenian triremes to 20th-century submarine conning towers and torpedoes. Graphic displays provide detailed explanations of the great naval battles of Salamis (480 BC), where the Athenians smashed the Persian fleet, and Lepanto (1571), where a combined Christian fleet was victorious over the Turks. Incorporated in the museum building is part of the Long Wall fortifications built by Themistocles to protect Piraeus and Athens against Persian and Spartan attack.

Further east is the most attractive of the harbours, **Tourkolimano** (Turkish Harbour, now officially called Mikrolimano, or Little Harbour) where the sleekest Mediterranean racing yachts have their berths. Its basin describes an almost perfect circle with only the narrowest of outlets. Many of the region's best seafood restaurants line the quay and provide delightful vantage points from which to watch the bobbing masts and brightly coloured sails.

Ancient shipwrecks around the harbours have yielded some surprising art treasures, which stock the **Archaeological Museum** (Charilaou Trikoupi 31). Try to visit the upper floor for the three magnificent bronzes found in 1959: a graceful Apollo (530 BC); Athena (350 BC) with Athenian owls and griffins on her helmet; and the huntress Artemis with a quiver on her shoulder.

Drive up the **Kastela Hill** cliff-road for a superb view over the peninsula and out to the Saronic Islands (see p. 156).

Attica

Each of the region's main attractions makes an easy day excursion from Athens. Some of them can be combined in one long tour—for example, visiting the temple at Cape Sounion in the morning, and then relaxing on the beach at Vouliagmeni in the afternoon. Or reverse that with a swim in the morning, a siesta after lunch, and then a trip down to the cape for a magnificent sunset.

However you plan your trips, start out as early as possible. Except for the mountain resorts, it's only going to get

*T*he bustling port of Piraeus has been the port of Athens for nearly 3,000 years. Today it is the hub of the ferry network linking the capital to the scattered islands.

119

hotter as the day goes on, and the archaeological sites have little shade.

Athenians spend their weekends at the seaside resorts down the coast, beyond the international airport. Weekday traffic is much easier. Elegan Vouliagmeni, just 22 km (14 miles) from the capital, has some beautiful bathing beaches around its peninsula, with the added advantage of shady pines. At the marina, you can take lessons in water-skiing.

Go down to the southern tip of the coast at **Cape Sounion**. On a promontory overlooking the Aegean, stand by the marble columns of **Poseidon's Temple** (c. 440 BC) to watch the sun set beyond the islands. Only 16 of the temple's original 34 Doric columns still stand. The Ionic friezes have been largely obliterated by time but are believed to have depicted battles of the giants and the exploits of Theseus (like Athens' Temple of Hephaistos, and probably the work of the same architect). Some 60 m (197 ft) above the sea, the precipice looks out over seven islands, with Milos visible on the clearest days.

Lord Byron couldn't resist carving his name on one of the pillars. He was rather more inspired when he wrote:

Place me on Sunium's marbled steep,
Where nothing, save the waves and I,
May hear our mutual murmurs
sweep;
There, swan like, let me sing and die.

North-east of the cape, across rolling wooded hills, lies **Lavrion** (Laurium in ancient times), an industrial town no less grimy than in ancient times when tyrant Peisistratus developed its silver mines. Slave-labourers here furnished Pericles with finances for the Athenian fleet until they revolted during the Pelo-ponnesian War. Today, French companies extract cadmium and manganese from the mines and lead from the ancient slag heaps.

If you are sailing to the Cyclades islands from the east coast port of Rafina, spare some time to drive down to **Brauron** *(Vravróna)*. There, amid attractive pine trees and marshland, is the mysterious **Sanctuary of Artemis**, lying in ruins below a 15th-century Byzantine chapel. According to local belief, the goddess rescued Iphigenia, daughter of Agamemnon, from sacrifice here by substituting a bear. Little girls disguised as bears danced in the sanctuary's ritual. In the **museum**, they are portrayed by exquisite marble sculptures of the 4th century BC.

If you prefer to stick strictly to historical fact, head for the **Plain of Marathon**, battlefield of the Athenians' most famous victory over the Persians in 490 BC (see p. 55). Buses to the site leave from Odos Mavromateon. A pleasant ride takes you through the pines and plane trees of the smart residential suburb of Kifissia, at the foot of Mount Pentelikon. (The mountain's heights are disfigured by quarries where the marble for many of Athens ancient monuments was excavated.) Named after the fragrant fennel *(márathos)* gathered there, the crescent-shaped **battlefield** curves 10 km (3 miles) around the bay of Marathon from Cape Kavo up

*P*oseidon's temple on the promontory of Cape Sounion remains a handsome landmark for sailors rounding the Attic peninsula on their way to or from Piraeus.

to the Kynosura promontory. At night, imaginative souls have heard the phantom clank of swords and the neighing of horses—very imaginative indeed, as there was no cavalry present. Signposted inland is the monument of the **Tomb of the Athenians**, the burial mound of the 192 Greek soldiers who fell in battle. Near the mound, a marble memorial to the "Warrior of Marathon" is a copy of a bas-relief in the National Archaeological Museum, which was in fact made before the battle took place. A **museum** displays prehistoric pottery and funeral vases from the battle tombs. On the outskirts of Marathon village, flags around a marble platform mark the start of the battle messenger's brave and foolhardy run back to Athens with news of the victory—the statutory 42.195 km (26.219 miles) of the modern marathon.

Daphni and Eleusis

These two celebrated sanctuaries, one Byzantine and one pagan, are unfortunately now surrounded by a dismal industrial environment of oil refineries and shipyards. The **monastery of Daphni** protects its celebrated mosaics behind battlements that date back in part to the earliest Christian settlement of the 6th century. The walls, and the church of 1080, include masonry from a sanctuary of Apollo destroyed in AD 395—the god's sacred laurels (*dáfni*) grew here in abundance. The temple columns offer a fascinating contrast with the Gothic arches of the Cistercian monks, installed in the 13th century by the Crusaders.

Two cypresses and an olive tree mark the church's south entrance. Inside, you will be transfixed by the piercing gaze of the **Christ Pantocrator mosaic** in the central dome. He is surrounded on the vaulted ceiling by the 16 prophets of the Old Testament. The best preserved of the other mosaics, on the south side of the narthex (vestibule), portray the *Presentation of the Virgin Mary* and the *Prayers of Joachim and Anna* (her apocryphal parents).

To penetrate the most sacred mysteries of ancient **Eleusis**, you must leave the westbound highway after Aspropyrgos and take the old Corinth road to Elefsina. Priests of old and their initiates walked in their annual September processions from the Athenian cemetery of Keramikos, along the Sacred Way, or *Ierá Odós* as it is still named. Today, only classical historians could make detailed sense of the sanctuary, destroyed by the barbarians after the pagan cult was banned by Emperor Theodosius in AD 395. But visitors can at least feel something of its mystical aura. A little **museum** with a model of the original site, ceramic paintings and

---

The Tragedy of King Aegeus

On rare smog-free days, the terrace of the Athena Nike temple affords the sea view that King Aegeus gazed upon while watching for the return of his son Theseus. He was waiting for the great hero to return from Crete, where he had gone to slay the dreaded Minotaur (see p. 49). The ship carrying the Athenian youths to their ritual sacrifice had put to sea with black sails—if Theseus escaped alive, he was supposed to hoist the white sails of victory as a signal of his triumphant return. But Theseus forgot to change the sails. His father spotted the black sails of death and jumped off the rock in despair. Another version of the story says he threw himself into the sea, which was thenceforth named the Aegean Sea, after the unfortunate king.

marble reliefs, illustrates the focus of the cult: humanity's blessed gift of corn from the goddess Demeter. Indeed, more knowledge would be sacrilegious since the shrine's rituals were shrouded in secrecy.

Tragedian Aeschylus and military commander Alcibiades were severely condemned on suspicion of having respectively revealed or ridiculed aspects of the holy rites. All we know, from Roman initiates like Cicero, Hadrian and Marcus Aurelius, is that the experience was spiritually exalting.

Mounts Hymettos and Parnes

These two mountains close to Athens offer welcome escapes from the heat.

Approached via the eastern suburb of Kaisariani, Mount Hymettos (*Ímettós*) is treeless, but its slopes are fragrant with lavender, juniper, thyme, sage and mint, and popular with bees whose honey has been appreciated since ancient times. The mountain takes on a bewitching mauve colour at sunset. Moni Kaisariani is a fine 11th-century monastery standing at the source of the Ilissos river at the end of a ravine shaded by planes, pines and cypresses. Water from a spring above the monastery is said to cure sterility. The monks are long gone, but the monastery is maintained as a national monument. You can visit the monks' mill, bakery, bath house and refectory, with its imposing vaulted kitchen. The church has some noteworthy 17th-century frescoes, and a dome supported by Roman columns.

North of Athens, pine and oak forests and rocky ravines make **Mount Parnes**, 1,413 m (4,635 ft), a popular spot for summer hiking. As well as a casino, night-club and cinema, the mountain's smart resort hotel offers swimming and tennis, and a cable-car for trips higher up the mountain (the actual summit is an off-limits military zone).

Aphrodite's Golden Apple

Throwing down a golden apple inscribed "For the fairest", the gods chose Paris to arbitrate in the subsequent squabble among Hera, Athena and Aphrodite about which of them was entitled to the prize. So the young Trojan herdsman told them to undress. Aphrodite was first to strip off, but Hera complained that she had kept on her magic girdle, which made everyone fall in love with her. Aphrodite agreed to remove it, "as long as Hera takes off her helmet. She looks ghastly without it."

To avoid any bitchiness, Paris asked to see each goddess separately. Hera was first, slowly turning around to show off her splendid figure. She promised he would rule all Asia and be the richest man alive if he gave her the prize.

He refused her bribe and called Athena. In her pragmatic, soldierly manner, she told him it was only common sense to declare her the winner, and promised him victory in all his battles if he did so. But Paris told her he was only a mere herdsman, and not very keen on war, but he would not hold that against her.

Last and determined not to be least, Aphrodite moved so very, very close to Paris that they almost touched. "What's a handsome young fellow like you doing tending cattle?" she whispered. "Go and seek out Helen of Sparta. She is as beautiful and passionate as I am, and yours for the asking, even though she is married to Menelaus, brother of Agamemnon. I have the power to make her fall in love with you. If, of course..."

Aphrodite won the golden apple, Paris won Helen, and Troy suffered the vengeance of the Greeks.

Three Wise Men

In the Western world, the Greeks were pioneers in formulating ideas about truth independent of a theological creed. They sought the meaning of life not through magic or superstition but in the patient application of man's own reason. The process had begun around 600 BC over on the coast of Asia Minor, among the philosophers of Miletus who speculated on the nature of the universe, probably inspired by contact with Babylon and Egypt. Philosophical methods became more refined in Athens during the classical age. Three great thinkers stood out.

Socrates (c.470–399 BC)

According to traditional accounts, his father was an Athenian sculptor and his mother a midwife. As fashioners of life in both its ideal and actual forms, they were appropriate parents for the man the Greeks acknowledged as the "father" of philosophy. It might also be said that Socrates' notoriously cantankerous wife, Xanthippe, was an admirable test of the patience necessary for his reasoning.

Socrates

He is believed to have practised as a sculptor for a time. He also served as an infantry-man. His principal activity was as an unpaid teacher of aristocratic youths in the Agora. In a society where duplicity was an instrument of success, Socrates' integrity won their unstinting admiration. His pupil Plato depicts him as ugly but physically powerful, with considerable personal charm. More than any brilliant insight into the meaning of existence, his great philosophical legacy, set out in Plato's Socratic Dialogues, was his scrupulous method of intellectual inquiry, a perpetual questioning of all certainties. With his young disciples, he explored various avenues towards truth using his famous technique of "Socratic irony". By confessing his own ignorance and constantly cross-questioning his antagonists, he exposed their inconsistencies and faults of logic.

The 30 Tyrants who seized power after the collapse of Athenian democracy brought Socrates to trial in 399 BC. He was charged with having introduced alien gods and corrupting the youth of Athens. According to Plato's account, Socrates gave a self-mocking testimony of the Delphic oracle's statement that he, Socrates, was the wisest of all men. This was true, he said, since the Delphic oracle never lies, but only in the sense that Socrates, unlike other more prominent men, had the wisdom to recognize how little he knew, if anything at all. When found guilty, he chose the option of taking poisonous hemlock. He said he faced death with the serenity of a man who "has sought the pleasures of knowledge and has arrayed the soul not in some strange attire but in its own proper jewels—temperance, justice, courage, nobility and truth".

Plato (c.428–347 BC)

The son of a distinguished Athenian family, Plato had a more aristocratic turn of mind than his master Socrates. The latter's death and the rule of the 30 Tyrants turned him away from a career in politics. He was convinced no state could thrive until philosophers became kings, or kings philosophers. He spent some time in Syracuse, Sicily, hoping to convert its tyrant Dionysius II into his ideal philosopher-king. But court intrigue made his task impossible.

In about 387 BC, he founded a school near the grove of Academe on the outskirts of Athens. Here he hoped to teach young men science and philosophy. How this might work was set out in his utopian work *The Republic*. Convinced that democracy could only engender disorder, he divided society into three classes: workers, soldiers and rulers. For the rulers, he conceived a rigorous educational system: gymnastics from 17 to 20; mathematics from 20 to 30; and the study of ideas from 30 to 35. The best pupils were to become active leaders from 35 to 50, and then return to study. *The Republic* was one of the Dialogues Plato wrote to expound the master's dialectic method, but principally to test his own theories. Man's senses, he argued, are an obstacle to understanding ideal beauty and truth. Ordinary man lived in a state of ignorance, chained in a dim cave world of shadows. The philosopher casts off his chains and progresses through dialectics towards the light of day—knowledge.

Plato's Academy continued for nine centuries after his death, and Platonic theories of universal ideas have had continuing influence on the thinking of Judaism, Christianity, Islam and Renaissance Humanism.

Aristotle (384–322 BC)

Born in Macedonian Chalkidiki, Plato's star pupil at the Academy was the son of a doctor. Bald and thin-legged, Aristotle had a taste for fine clothes and jewellery. He spoke with a lisp, and his small beady eyes had a formidable mocking expression.

Though he never became a statesman himself, he did use what he learned at Plato's school for the élite in preparing Alexander to rule an empire. He taught Greek drama and some elements of political science to the 13-year-old boy Homer.

Aristotle was more interested in the practical sciences than abstract theory. Just as Socrates and Plato had developed dialectics for philosophical inquiry, so Aristotle laid down ground rules for scientific method. He travelled through the northern Aegean in search of specimens for the study of zoology, his favourite science. Alexander financed a museum and sent him specimens gathered by his hunters and fishermen from all over the empire. Paying tribute to his classification system, Charles Darwin said: "Linnaeus and Cuvier [zoologists of the 18th and 19th centuries] have been my two gods, but they were mere schoolboys to old Aristotle."

At his school and library in Athens, Aristotle organized research into music, theology and the other sciences. He extended his passion for classification from animals to constitutional history, listing all the various state-forms of Greek cities. More realistic than Plato, he saw political systems as subject to the selfishness of the rulers: monarchy becomes tyranny, aristocratic rule deteriorates into unscrupulous oligarchy, and democracy into vicious demagogy. He was a man who preferred common sense to dogma and extremism.

The Ancient Spartan Stronghold Where Helen Lived and Loved

The Peloponnese contains a magnificent concentration of important historical sites—Mycenae, legendary home of the cursed House of Atreus, where Orestes murdered his mother and Agamemnon died at the hands of his wife; Olympia, where the first Olympic Games were held in the 8th century BC; Epidaurus, where the followers of Asclepius perfected the arts of medicine; and Mistra, a jewel of Byzantine culture set in the steep hills of Sparta.

For the visitor keen to explore the spirit of ancient Greece, this predominantly mountainous southern peninsula offers a vigorous but always rewarding challenge. The secret of enjoying the great sites of antiquity, here as in other parts of the country, is to choose a comfortable resort in the vicinity of the ruins as a "base camp" for your explorations.

*T*he Byzantine ruins of *Mistra straggle up a steep hillside in the Taygetos Mountains. This and other historic sites in the beautiful Peloponnese peninsula lie within easy reach of Athens.*

This is particularly true in the Peloponnese where so many of the archaeological sites are perched on hilltops, and involve a fair amount of hiking and climbing. Even at sites such as Olympia, which is situated on a plain, there is a lot of ground to cover, so plan your trips carefully, and take it easy. To enjoy the sites to the full, you should be well rested, make an early start (to make the most of the cool of the morning) and take the opportunity to relax or have a swim afterwards. Some conveniently located base camps are Nafplio in the north-east (for Epidaurus and Mycenae), Githio in the south (for Mistra and the castles of Mani), and Killini in the west (for Olympia and Bassae).

PELOPONNESE

LAMIA

E951

Nafpaktos E65 Itia LIVADIA

MESSOLONGI E962

THIVA

PATRAS Diakofto

E65 Vouraikos E65 ATHENS

† Kalavrita
Ag. Lavra Corinth E94
33 Canal

Killini KORINTHOS

Loutra Corinth & AEGINA
Killinis Acrocorinth

PYRGOS E65 Mycenae Aegina

Olympia 74 Tirkyns

ARGOS 7 NAFPLIO Poros

76 TRIPOLI 70 Epidaurus

Andritsena Bassae E65

Astros Paralio Astros Vlihos Idra

7 HYDRA

E961 Paralia Tirou SPETSES

Tiros Spetses

Messene Leonidio Sabatiki

PARNON

Mistra Kosmas

Nestor's Palace E65

Messini SPARTI

82 KALAMATA Evrotas Geraki

TAIGETOS

Pylos Kardamili

Methoni Areopoli Githio

SAPIENDZA Pirgos Dirou Géfira Monemvasia

SCHIZA Kotrona

Kokala

Gerolimenas Vathia

Agia Pelagia

Milopotamos

KYTHIRA

Chora

♣ Sites of historic interest
Land over 900 metres

0   25   50 km
0   10   20   30 miles

128

The most comfortable time of year to visit the Peloponnese is in spring and autumn. Nearly all the archaeological sites are located well inland and do not enjoy the sea breezes that temper the summer's heat out in the islands. Which brings us to the peninsula's little bonus, the offshore islands of the Saronic Gulf—Aegina, Poros, Hydra and Spetses, any of which could serve as a comfortable base for exploring the Argolid, should you decide to visit in summer. They are also described in this chapter. And off the west coast, the Ionian islands of Zakynthos, Kephalonia and Ithaca (see p. 308) all have ferry services to Killini or Patras.

To the ancients, the Peloponnese itself, despite the narrow isthmus joining it to Attica, was considered an island. Its name means the "island of Pelops", a legendary king who dominated the region after winning a chariot race against his rival. Today, the peninsula is truly an island, separated from the mainland by the deep cutting of the Corinth Canal. That is where we begin our tour.

Corinth

What remains of that ancient city of luxury and sin that St Paul used as his missionary base in Greece? Precious little. **New Corinth** (*Korinthos*) is a dreary city of modern buildings, rebuilt several times after the successive earthquakes of 1858 and 1928. Its only reasonable cafés are on the waterfront, and the closest beach is 10 minutes drive to the west at **Lechaion**, site of its ancient port.

Corinth's strategic position commanding all traffic from the Adriatic through the Gulf of Corinth to the Aegean has lost its commercial importance now that most freighters are too wide to use the 19th-century canal. But it is a natural fuel and refreshment stop for drivers bound from Athens to the Peloponnese. So take a closer look at the canal, visit the site of ancient Corinth and its museum and, if it is not too hot, climb up to the hilltop citadel.

The Corinth Canal

This impressive waterway cuts a neat slice through the narrow neck of land linking Athens to the peninsula's north coast. The canal is almost 6.5 km (4 miles) long but only 25 m (82 ft) wide and 8 m (26 ft) deep. The modern canal, begun by the French in 1882, and completed by the Greeks in 1893, was the accomplishment of an ancient dream. Periander, the enlightened Tyrant of Corinth, made an abortive attempt to chop through the isthmus at the end of the 7th century BC. The Roman Emperor Nero made a more determined effort in AD 67, breaking ground himself with a golden shovel before 6,000 Jewish slaves from Palestine continued the work—which was interrupted by the insurrection in Gaul. Meanwhile, merchants were content to have their ships hauled on trolleys across the narrow neck of land, rather than negotiate the longer and more dangerous sea route around the peninsula. Traces of their slipway, the *diolkos*, can still be seen cutting diagonally across the western end of the canal.

Ancient Corinth

South-west of the modern city, the archaeological site occupies a plateau overlooking the Gulf of Corinth at the foot of what was once an almost impregnable citadel, Acrocorinth. It was, until the rise of Athens, the most prosperous and populous of Greek cities. It led Greek colonization of the Mediterranean with settlements in Sicilian Syracuse and the island of Corfu. The city's ceramics industry, textiles and fine bronzeware made its fortune throughout the Mediterranean and beyond. The birthplace of the trireme, a galley with three tiers of oars, its shipbuilders won orders from all over the Aegean. Even after Athens' ceramics and other fancy goods had captured overseas markets, Corinth remained a synonym for luxury, elegance and sin— sailors sang the praises of its exceptional brothels.

The town's most celebrated contribution to Greek art was the decorative Corinthian column, with gracefully carved acanthus leaves decorating the capital. The Romans plundered and destroyed the city in 146 BC, but when St Paul arrived 200 years later, after Julius Caesar had rebuilt the town, the apostle still found it necessary to rail against the "filthiness of flesh and spirit" he found there.

Just outside the archaeological site proper are the ruins of a small **Roman theatre** and a larger **arena** for gladiators or, when filled with water, for mock sea battles. Inside the enclosure, the **museum** houses fine Corinthian ceramics of the 7th century BC, gaily decorated with warriors, cockerels and swans. Other exhibits come from the town's Roman era, mosaics and statuary of the 2nd century AD.

Step down to the **Temple of Apollo** (6th century BC), of which seven monolithic limestone columns remain—

Doric, not Corinthian. The rest of the site is mostly Roman. Below the temple, the vast **Agora** (marketplace) has a long portico closing off the south side. The double colonnade originally had 71 Doric columns along the façade and 34 Ionic columns in the interior. At the rear, archaeologists identified 33 taverns and "night-clubs". Night quarters were upstairs.

Across the centre of the Agora is another row of shops in the midst, of which are the remains of a **Bema**, or judge's tribune, where the Roman proconsul acquitted Paul of improper preaching in AD 51.

The paved **Lechaion Road** running north from the Agora led to the old port. Down a stairway off to the right is the **Peirene Fountain**, a Roman structure of colonnades and arched chambers surrounding a rectangular basin. Its waters were released from the earth by a hoof-kick from the winged horse Pegasus.

*T*he spectacular defile of the Corinth Canal.

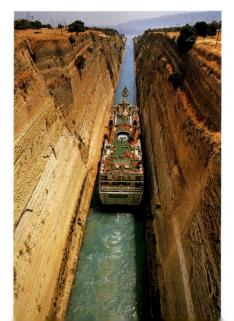

The Origins of Medicine

Sick pilgrims from all over Greece came to worship at Epidaurus, and seek a cure from the doctor-priests of Asclepius, god of healing. Different parts of Greece, from Messenia in the south to Thessaly in the north, claimed that Asclepius had been born on their territory, in the hope of drawing in the lucrative pilgrim trade. The Epidaurians' story was that Asclepius was born at the shrine of Apollo in Epidaurus, and the centaur Chiron came down from Mount Pilion and taught Apollo's son the secrets of medicinal herbs. Asclepius became so skilled in the arts of surgery and healing that he was revered as the founder of medicine—his symbolic serpents, entwined around his staff, is still the emblem of doctors world-wide. The reputation of Epidaurus began to take off after 430 BC, when Athenians suffering the ravages of plague began to arrive in droves.

While it may not have cured the plague, the Epidaurus regime was certainly health-improving. The medicinal herbs and ritual baths, and the positive atmosphere of the sanctuary's ceremonial process had a beneficial effect, particularly on nervous disorders and psychological complaints. The great theatre, like the band-stands and casinos of the modern spas at Baden-Baden, Vichy and Montecatini, was intended to provide a little therapeutic entertainment. There was also a stadium for remedial athletics. At the peak of its popularity in the 4th century BC, Epidaurus financed the building of its temples and theatre largely from the donations of the grateful patients.

Acrocorinth

South of the ancient town, the citadel sits atop a solid limestone crag 575 m (1,886 ft) high. It was practically impregnable to invaders, and continues to resist all but the hardiest tourists, but you will find the view from the top easily repays your effort.

Many feel this must have been the hill up which Corinth's first king, Sisyphus, was condemned to push his huge rock for eternity, only to see it roll back down each time he got close to the top. This natural fortress served a succession of Greeks, Romans, Crusaders, Byzantines and Turks.

Of the three massive fortified gates you will pass on your way to the top, the first is Turkish, the second Franco-Venetian, while the innermost with the two square towers is part Byzantine, part ancient Greek, and dates back to the 4th century BC. Beyond the third gate, pick your way among the ruined mosques, Turkish houses, cisterns and Byzantine chapels.

A **keep** dominates a 13th-century stronghold built by Guillaume de Villehardouin. A path to the right leads to the **Upper Peirene Fountain**. The water still flows, clean and fresh, but alas is not drinkable—bring your own refreshments.

Double back to climb to the summit where a column marks the site of a Temple of Aphrodite that was famous for its religious harlots. From here there's a magnificent view over to Mount Parnassus, and south across the mountains of the Peloponnese.

Argolid

In this north-east corner of the Peloponnese, the charming town of Nafplio makes a perfect base for exploring the great archaeological sites of Mycenae, Epidaurus and Tiryns. Dominated by the city of Argos in classical times, the region was a constant political and military rival to Sparta.

Nafplio

Nafplio, or Nauplia, or Napoli to the Venetians, this cheerful, low-key, flower-bedecked resort was for a brief moment in the 19th century the capital of a newly independent Greece. The presidency of Ioannis Kapodistrias and the brief stay of King Otto before he moved to Athens in 1834 left a legacy of elegant neoclassical houses to complement the prevalent Venetian style. The city stands on a rocky promontory overlooking a large bay, with the formidable 18th-century Venetian **Fort Palamidi** looming to the south. Drive up to the fort before the heat of the day for the view from its ramparts.

The waterfront is lively, with the best quayside seafood restaurants along Boubouina Street. Out in the bay is the fortified islet of **Bourdzi**, which was built by the Venetians in 1471 and

The pleasant waterfront town of Nafplio provides a convenient "base camp" for exploring the ancient cities of Epidaurus and Mycenae.

served later as a prison and a home for the city's hangman.

In the centre of the old town, Platia Syntagma is an amalgam of the city's history: a stone Venetian lion; behind it a Turkish mosque used for modern Greece's first parliament, now a meeting-hall and cinema; a Venetian arsenal converted into an **Archaeological Museum** exhibiting a splendid suit of Mycenaean armour, sculpted gravestones and ancient jewellery.

But perhaps the town's most attractive museum is the **Peloponnesian**

Folklore Foundation, housed in a handsome neoclassical building in Ipsilantou Street between Syntagma and the port. It displays regional jewellery, costumes, fabrics and working looms.

At the little Venetian church of **Agios Spiridon**, the wall beside the portal is scarred by bullet holes. It was here, in 1831, that President Kapodistrias (see p. 298) was assassinated on his way to worship. His killers were members of the Mavromikhalis family, feudal lords of the Mani in the southern Peloponnese (see p. 146). According to their bloody code of honour, they were avenging Kapodistrias's arrest of their patriarch, Petrobey. The **President's statue** stands on Platia Dikasterion near the bus station.

Epidaurus

It's hard to believe that what might justly be claimed as the most beautiful theatre in the world was in its day little more than a side-show. Nestling between two hills in the tranquil pine-scented Argolid plain, 30 km (19 miles) east of Nafplio, **Epidaurus** was ancient Greece's most prestigious sanctuary of Asclepius, the god of healing. It was part health spa, part grotto of Lourdes.

Roman and Visigoth plunderers reduced the sanctuary, north-west of the museum, to barely discernible ruins. But the **theatre** is one of the country's best preserved monuments, generally attributed to Polyclitus the Younger in the 4th century BC.

Entrance to the stage and auditorium is through one of two reconstructed *parodoi*, double-columned stone doorways. The circular orchestra, where the chorus sang and danced, is 20 m (66 ft) in diameter with the base of an altar at its centre. Behind it are the surviving foundations of the stone *skene* (scene), forerunner of the modern backdrop. The auditorium had 34 rows of seats, and added 21 more with artificial earth-fill in the 2nd century BC to bring the audience capacity to 12,000.

Dignitaries were—and still are, during the Annual Festival of Greek Drama (see p. 332)—seated in reddish stone thrones in the front-row. The acoustics are so good that if you stand in the gods at the top, you *can* hear a pin drop down in the orchestra. But more than the wonderful acoustics, it is the theatre's grandiose natural setting between Mount Velanidhia to the north and Mount Kharani to the south that really impresses.

The little **museum** is worth a visit on the way out for its model of the original sanctuary, and exhibits of sculpture from the temples. Most remarkable are the floral sculptures and rosettes from the coffered ceiling of a Tholos rotunda, and the superbly carved Corinthian capital of one of its columns.

If you need to cool off, take a dip at the nearby beach of **Palea Epidavros.**

Mycenae

Even those who know nothing of the plays of Aeschylus, Sophocles and Euripides can feel the atmosphere of tragedy that haunts the ancient site of **Mycenae**. Even today, long after the dust has settled on scholarly arguments and laboratory tests trying to prove or disprove that this or that group of stones was Queen Clytemnestra's bath-chamber, or King Agamemnon's tomb, you just *know* that something terrible and magnificent happened here. In Greece, legend and reality are inseparable. Nowhere is this truer than at Mycenae,

*S*cholars consider the auditorium at Epidaurus to be the ancient world's greatest achievement in theatrical architecture. Polyclitus used intricate mathematical formulae to develop an auditorium in which ideal sight-lines would be combined with almost perfect acoustics. In order to achieve these objectives, the curve of the terraced seating flattens out slightly and is not completely concentric with the circular stage.

Thirty minutes' drive north of Naf-plio, a visit to Mycenae begins rather mundanely in the site's vast car park just beyond the little town of Mykines. Pocketing a flashlight for exploring the site's darker corners, ignore for the moment the excavations bordering the approach road and head for the **citadel** at the top of the hill. Built between 1350 and 1200 BC, the ramparts of massive untrimmed blocks were known to classi-cal Greeks 800 years later as "Cyclo-pean walls". They could not imagine anyone but the gods' giant one-eyed labourers being able to haul these mas-sive boulders into place. (The possibility that mere mortal slaves had accom-plished such work was conveniently overlooked.)

The entrance at the north-west corner of the hill is through the splendid **Lion Gate**, Europe's earliest known monu-mental sculpture. Above a colossal limestone lintel, two now headless beasts stand with their front paws on small altars on either side of a palace column, the whole forming a coat-of-arms proclaiming Mycenaean power.

Just inside the gate to the right is a **granary** in which earthenware storage-jars were found containing grains of car-bonized wheat. Beyond it is the **Grave Circle A**. This circular stone parapet enclosed six royal shaft graves—large rectangular family mausoleums—and several smaller graves for commoners. The great archaeologist Heinrich Schlie-mann discovered 19 skeletons here—eight men, nine women and two children—accompanied by treasures which are now in Athens' National Archaeological Museum.

A stairway and cobbled ramp lead up to the **Palace**. Cross the courtyard

the citadel of the kings who dominated the Peloponnese from 1400 to 1200 BC (see p. 49). The sky bears down on a grim fortress atop a windswept crag sur-rounded by rolling hills of olive groves; it could only be from here that Agamemnon marched to lead the Greek armada against Troy. And the dark ram-parts enclosing the royal tombs and palace are the obvious setting for the acts of passion, betrayal, murder and revenge that followed his return.

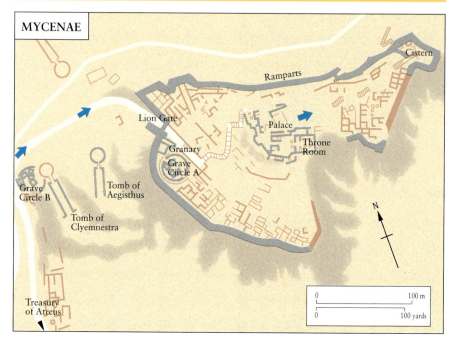

MYCENAE

Cistern
Ramparts
Lion Gate
Palace
Throne Room
Granary
Grave Circle A
Grave Circle B
Tomb of Aegisthus
Tomb of Clyemnestra
Treasury of Atreus

N

0   100 m
0   100 yards

between the remains of a two-columned porch into the **Throne Room** *(megaron)*. Notice the bases of four pillars that surrounded a central hearth. The room was decorated with frescoes now exhibited in Athens. Romantics identify an area off to the left as part of the bathroom where Agamemnon was murdered—though the traces of red plaster found on the floor have not been subjected to forensic study.

In Hellenistic times a small shrine to Athena was built on the upper terrace, and private houses lay to the east of the main palace. Beyond them, at the far end of the fortress, the adventurous can explore the pitch-black depths of the palace **cistern**, with 99 slippery steps leading down into the darkness.

Outside the fortress, coming back downhill from the Lion Gate, visit the two monumental **tombs of Clytemnestra and Aegisthus.** The archaeologists'

*T*he Lion Gate leading to the Palace of Mycenae bears eloquent testimony to the power of the ruling House of Atreus. Notice the downwards-tapering pillar between the two lions, like those in Crete's Palace of Knossos.

dates of 1250 and 1500 BC respectively make it unlikely that the queen and her lover were both buried here, but these "beehive" constructions were typical of Mycenaean royal mausoleums. Tall, vaulted burial chambers stand at the end of long stone passageways dug into the hillside. The entrance's weight-relieving triangular lintel was originally covered by a sculpted frieze.

Closer to the car park, excavations are continuing on **Grave Circle B**, a grouping of 14 royal shaft graves and 12 commoners' graves.

136

On your way back, just down the road on the right, stop off at the greatest of the Mycenaean beehive tombs, known as the **Treasury of Atreus**. The main burial vault of this monumental mausoleum is 13.4 m (44 ft) high and 14.6 m (48 ft) in diameter. Off to the right is a smaller chamber that housed either the treasury or perhaps the remains of the king himself.

Argos
Visible from afar, perched on a high rock, Argos was once the region's dominant city (Homer spoke of its inhabitants, the Argives, as being synonymous with Greeks). The modern town has little interest beyond its open-air market, a good place to stock up for your picnics. The **museum** has some good Mycenaean and Geometric pottery, and an impressive bronze helmet and breastplate from the 7th century BC.

Tiryns
Rising proudly from the Argolid plain 5 km (3 miles) from Nafplio, this ancient citadel served as a satellite fortress for the Mycenaeans in the 13th century BC. The mighty Heracles, who is said to have been born here, may have been needed to help build the massive **cyclopean walls** that make Tiryns' fortifications even more imposing than those of Mycenae. Some of the huge boulders weigh as much as 20 tons, forming ramparts up to 11 m (36 ft) thick. At the top of a chariot ramp, you pass through inner and outer gateways. Built into the eastern fortifications are huge "Gothic" vaulted galleries with chambers that served as artillery positions and storage.

Only the foundations remain of the **Royal Palace** and its entrance hall, the Propylaea. The western bastion protects a well-preserved staircase leading out of the fortress, a terrible trap for invaders. Turn right at the bottom and skirt the outer wall to secret underground galleries that lead to two underground cisterns—only discovered in 1962. Double back and cross through the lower citadel to exit at the chariot ramp.

The South

The coast road south from the Argolid takes you into the heartland of the Peloponnese. The austerely beautiful lunar landscapes of the interior alternate rugged mountains with the plains of Spartan Laconia and Messenia. The peninsula culminates in three prongs with the offbeat resort of Monemvasia to the east, Venetian Methoni to the west, and the dramatic Mani country in the middle.

Arcadian Coast
The winding corniche mountain road gives you splendid views out over the southern Aegean, with occasional cutoffs descending to sand or shingle coves that offer a refreshing bathe. Buy some peaches at the market town of **Astros**, and feast on them down on the beach at nearby **Paralion Astros**.

Perched on the mountainside among terraced olive groves, **Tyros** is a pleasant little village overlooking the resort of **Paralia Tyrou**. An old watchtower stands guard over the beach of **Sambatiki**, with its harbourside tavernas.

As the road turns inland, stop off in **Leonidio** to stroll among its old balconied houses and wood-panelled cafés with marble tables. The locally baked

bread is excellent. From here a rough road climbs up past the Elona monastery into the magnificent scenery of **Mount Parnon**.

The cool hill town of **Kosmas** is a good place to stop for a refreshing coffee on the tree-shaded square.

On the other side of the mountain, **Geraki** has a 13th-century fortress built by a dynasty of French Crusaders, with several Byzantine churches hidden within its fortifications. In **Agios Georgios**, there are some noteworthy frescoes; English visitors might like to light a candle for the icon of their patron, Saint George.

*R*ugged limestone mountains rise above an olive grove in Arcadia, in the central Peloponnese. The pastoral beauty of Arcadia led Greek and Roman poets to idealise the region as a sort of bucolic paradise. This connotation persists to the present day, and the name Arcadia is still used to describe an ideal of pastoral perfection.

Sparta

Even if it were not a convenient stop on the way to the marvels of Mistra, a pilgrimage to this characterless modern town would provide a chastening lesson in history. Once the focus of an omnipotent city-state, founded on military might and disdaining the culture of the "soft" Athenians and other rivals, *Spárta* has not a single remaining monument to show for its past greatness.

Thucydides, the great historian of the Peloponnesian Wars, wrote: "If some day Sparta were devastated, leaving only its sanctuaries and the foundations of the public buildings, the posterity of a distant future would find it hard to believe that its power was equal to its renown."

Today, scarcely a stone or two remain of its sanctuaries and public buildings. The town slumbers in the Evrotas valley with the brooding Taygetos mountains to the west, where Spartan soldiers hardened their bodies, and hurled weakling children into the ravines. Maybe for old time's sake, the Greek army has installed a garrison on the southern edge of town. But these days, those who fail basic training are sent home alive.

In the **museum**, east of the town's central square, Spartan soldiers are depicted on Archaic vases. A bas-relief (6th century BC) shows those two unhappy couples, Helen and Menelaus, and Clytemnestra and Agamemnon. A powerful marble torso is said to be that of Leonidas, the hero of Thermopylae. Sadly, the "Tomb of Leonidas" in the nearby ruins is in fact merely a small Hellenistic temple.

Similarly, all that is to be seen of "Ancient Sparta" are the remains of a theatre (2nd century BC), a temple (1st

The Spiral of Defeat

Sparta lost its supremacy in the 4th century BC to Epaminondas of Thebes and his Peloponnesian allies, and the Macedonians reduced it to a mere vassal-state.

In AD 396 the Visigoths razed the city, and in the 9th century, a Slav invasion drove the last Spartan landowners and peasants into the strongholds of the Mani peninsula. It was not until 1834 that King Otto built a new town on the site of ancient Sparta.

century AD), and a 10th-century Byzantine monastery standing among the pine trees and eucalyptus.

Mistra

The glories of this great medieval Byzantine city are best enjoyed by taking them in easy stages. A short drive west from Sparta into the Taygetos mountains, the town grew out of a 13th-century fortress built by French stragglers from the Crusades, and is set on a hillside that can be tough to tackle in hot weather. The splendid tile-domed monasteries have been beautifully restored, but even the ruined mansions and palace, set amongst enchanting wilderness, provide a vivid insight into Mistra's golden era.

Nearby, the pleasant little new town of **Nea Mistra** has several restaurants and hotels. With car parks located near the top and bottom of Mistra's hill, you can divide your visit into two halves: the monasteries and museum of Lower Mistra, and the palace, Agia Sofia church, and fortress of Upper Mistra.

Lower Mistra

Enter through a gatehouse in the fortifications, and turn right (north) into the **Metropolis**, the 13th-century church of

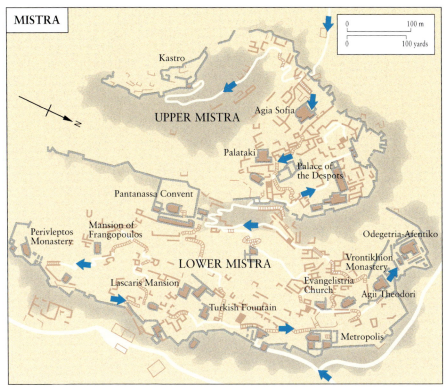

MISTRA

Kastro

UPPER MISTRA

Agia Sofia

Palataki

Palace of
the Despots

Pantanassa Convent

Perivleptos
Monastery

Mansion of
Frangopoulos

Odegetria-Afentiko

LOWER MISTRA

Vrontikhion
Monastery

Lascaris Mansion

Evangelistria
Church

Agii Theodori

Turkish Fountain

Metropolis

0   100 m
0   100 yards

St Demetrios. The main church's paintings of scenes from Christ's life have been "beheaded" by structural transformations, but in the narthex there are some good frescoes of the *Last Judgement* and the *Second Coming*.

In the church courtyard, the upstairs **museum** has among its icons and frescoes a striking 15th-century portrait on gilded metal of *Christ Enthroned*. Its piercing expression suggests the new humanist influence of Mistra's philosopher Gemistus.

Continue north past the cruciform 14th-century **Evangelistria Church**, a gem of finely cut masonry and tile-framed windows. Just beyond it is the **Vrontochion Monastery**, which is Mistra's wealthiest. Of its two churches, the smaller, **Agii Theodori,** was built in

1290 and restored in the 20th century with a multiple-windowed lantern dome. The **Odigitria** (1310), also known as Afentiko, is Mistra's finest architectural achievement. The harmonious blend of rose-tiled domes, vaults, side chapels and belfry blends magnificently into the hillside setting of vines, wild olives and cypresses.

Climb up behind the church to see its roofs overlooking the sprawling Laconian plain to the east. Odigitria artfully combines a lower, three-aisled basilica with a five-domed, cruciform upper church. Among the frescoes are an exquisite *Procession of the Martyrs* in the chapel to the right of the entrance, and *Christ's Miracles* in the narthex.

Take the long climb slowly southwards which leads to the 15th-century

141

*T*he ruins of Mistra have some of the finest examples of 14th-15th-century Byzantine architecture.

Pantanassa Convent, the last to be built here and the only one still active. Nuns tend to the flowers and offer embroidery for sale. The church is noted for its frescoes, that are filled with the new life, joy and deep spirituality that characterized Mistra's late Byzantine art. Most impressive are the *Entry into Jerusalem* west of the apse and the dramatic *Raising of Lazarus*.

Wind your way down past the impressive shell of the balconied **mansion of Frangopoulos**, founder of Pantanassa. Beyond, through a stone gateway, is the 14th-century **Perivleptos Monastery**. Clinging to the rocky hillside, its church

Paris and Helen
Spartan propaganda encouraged the idea that Helen had been abducted against her will from the palace of her husband, King Menelaus of Sparta. She was certainly ardently wooed by Paris, but she was not an unwilling subject.

Back home in Troy, Paris had revealed to the court that he was not just a common herdsman (see p. 123) but King Priam's long-lost son. The priests of Apollo prophesied that Paris must die, or else Troy would perish, but the overjoyed Priam declared "Better that Troy should fall, than that my wonderful son should die!". Soon after, Menelaus arrived on a visit to the Trojan court, and invited Paris to stay with him in Sparta, where he wined and dined him for nine days. Paris, obsessed by Aphrodite's promise that the beautiful Helen would be his, heaped gifts on Menelaus' wife. He stared at her dewy-eyed, heaved great sighs, and flirted outrageously. He ostentatiously drank from her goblet at the very spot where her lips had touched, and even traced "I love you, Helen" in wine on the table top. Helen was bowled over, but terrified that Menelaus would notice. But the king remained oblivious, and even left them alone together when he went off to Crete for his grandfather's funeral. Helen promptly eloped with Paris, and they spent their first night of love on the little island of Cranaë before setting sail from Githio towards Troy.

has on its vaults the best preserved frescoes in Mistra—lively, intimate scenes from the New Testament.

As you make your way back towards the entrance-gatehouse, take a look to the left at the **Laskares mansion**. This is typical of Byzantine houses of the 14th century; it has a ground-floor stable and large upper-storey windows and terrace, and beyond the mansion is a Turkish fountain.

Upper Mistra

The major reward for the precipitous climb to the hilltop **kastro**, the 13th-century castle of Guillaume de Villehardouin, ruler of the Frankish province of Morea (the Peloponnese), are the views over the whole town and the Laconian plain. From the towers at either end of the ramparts, you can gaze into the formidable ravines of the Taygetos mountains.

Downhill, the 14th-century palace church of **Agia Sofia** has an elegant bell tower. Its only notable surviving frescoes are a *Christ Enthroned* in the apse and a *Birth of the Virgin* in one of the chapels to the right.

Continue down past the fortress-like mansion known as Palataki (Little Palace) to the ruins of the **Palace of the Despots**. The right wing may have been built by Villehardouin and turned by his Byzantine successors into a guard house when they built the larger wing to the left. The upstairs gallery and throne room are distinguished by their eight massive Gothic bays.

Githio

With pretty beaches in the town and nearby, this delightful fishing village, the port of ancient Sparta, makes an ideal base for visiting both Mistra and the Mani. Behind the harbour, explore the charming wooden fishermen's cottages with their wrought-iron balconies hugging the lower slopes of Mount Koumaros.

A short causeway crosses to the pine-clad islet of **Marathonisi**, known in antiquity as Cranaë. It was here that Helen and Paris spent their first night after the famous elopement from Sparta.

Monemvasia

Accessible from the mainland by causeway and bridge—its name means "single entrance"—this medieval town built on a craggy promontory has the relaxed charm and atmosphere of an Aegean island. The quickest direct access is by boat from Piraeus, but if you are driving through the Peloponnese, the road from Githio passes through some dramatic, though rather arid countryside.

Byzantium's Jewel of the Peloponnese

Captured from the Frankish prince Guillaume de Villehardouin in 1262, Mistra was a shining centre of Byzantine culture until its surrender to the Turks in 1460. Constantinople at this time was a beleaguered capital, and architects, painters and thinkers sought refuge at the court of the Despot of Mistra (Despot in Greek means "lord", not necessarily a tyrant.)

A Greek cultural revival, with the re-introduction of classical learning, was led by the neo-Platonist Georgios Gemistus Plethon (1355–1452). He had a considerable influence on Renaissance philosophy in Italy after travelling to Florence in 1438, when he carried with him many ancient Greek texts that the Italians had never seen before. At Mistra itself, Gemistus's humanism had a strong impact on the later schools of Byzantine painting. The frescoes and icons in the monasteries show the introduction of more personal touches and a certain psychological subtlety into the hitherto rigidly formal treatment of religious subjects.

After 1460, the Turkish pashas moved into the despots' palace, and the churches were converted into mosques. But a flourishing silk industry continued the city's prosperity well into the 17th century. In 1769, the Russians backed an ill-fated Greek attempt to recapture Mistra. The Turks sent in an Albanian army which crushed the rebellion and set Mistra on fire. It was sacked again in 1825 and the few remaining citizens moved out when the new town of Sparta was built nine years later.

Like the Mani, Monemvasia's remote fortified rock on the south-east coast was a refuge for Greeks fleeing the 9th-century invasion of the Slavs. The Venetians fortified the top of the promontory and the Turks added mosques and a bath house. In 1821, Monemvasia was the first bastion to fall to the Greek national-

ists, but the surrendering Turkish garrison inflicted a terrible massacre before retreating.

The town was progressively abandoned in the 20th century, but elegant little buff stone terraced houses are being tastefully renovated as restaurants, hotels and holiday apartments. Daytime visitors can find accommodation across the causeway at the small mainland resort of **Gefira**. (Like the Aegean islands, this exposed promontory is buffeted by the *meltemi* winds in July and August.)

Park outside the gate of Monemvasia's fortifications—one of the town's great attractions is the absence of traffic—and walk up the narrow stone-paved main street to the village square, **Platia Dzamiou**. The Venetian bell-

*T*he fortified mediaeval town of Monemvasia is sometimes known as the "Greek Gibraltar", as it is built on a steep rocky promontory joined to the mainland by a narrow stone causeway. Its maze of narrow streets is devoid of traffic and bedecked with flowers, a perfect place to explore on foot.

tower here is a convenient landmark for navigating your way around town. The main church, **Elkomenos Christos** (Christ in Chains), was rebuilt by the Venetians in the 17th century, retaining a Byzantine bas-relief of peacocks over

145

the porch. Opposite is a Turkish mosque *(Paléo Dzamí)* being converted for use as the town museum.

The promontory is dotted with the domes of churches and chapels, but only a few are still in use. Take a look at the charming 16th-century Venetian **Panagia Chrisafitissa** down by the seafront ramparts. As you wander among the handsome Byzantine and Venetian houses, look out for traces of ancient marble blocks, columns and pediment fragments filched long ago from the nearby temple ruins at Epidaurus Limera. Due south of the village square, a gateway through the fortifications leads to a rocky beach for swimming.

Walk up to the clifftop **kastro** where the old upper town lies in romantic ruins among a wilderness of flowers, shrubs, olives and fig trees. The 12th-century church of **Agia Sofia** has a handsome brick and stone exterior and a 16-sided drum supporting its dome. Some fine fresco fragments include a *Christ Pantocrator* (Christ Omnipotent). Climbing west of the church to the promontory's highest point, the **citadel**, you can enjoy a view that on clear days, it is said, extends as far as Crete.

Kythira

Campers and hikers fleeing the crowds can take a boat from Monemvasia, Neapoli or Githio to the little island of Kythira. The sweetest thing about this rather arid island is its delicious honey. There is a beach on the north-east coast at **Agia Pelagia.** The capital, **Chora**, on the south coast, has some Venetian houses and a fortress out on the promontory. The prettiest village, which has an old water mill, is over to the west at **Milopotamos**.

> **Sweet Death**
> The English once had quite a taste for "malmsey", a sweet, Madeira-type dessert wine still made in Tinos, Cyprus and Spain. The name is a corruption of Monemvasia, the port from which the grapes used in making the wine were shipped. The wine appears in Shakespeare's *Richard the Third,* where the king's enemy, the Duke of Clarence, is stabbed and then drowned in a butt of malmsey.

Mani

Castles, ghost towns and wild, unspoiled landscapes characterize this windswept peninsula. The Maniotes have maintained a reputation for being independent-minded, though the blood vendettas of old now appear to belong in the past. They can claim to be the last descendants of the ancient Spartans, having fled from the Laconian plain in the wake of the Slav invasions.

The earliest settlers clung to paganism until the 9th century. Many became pirates and adventurers who moved on to Corsica. The rest stayed to build formidable forts and tower houses in the mountains or on cliffs overlooking the sea. The toughest individuals became village chieftains commanding a feudal allegiance that lasted till modern times. Petrobey Mavromikhalis, the most famous of them, was a prominent figure in the fight for Greek independence.

From Githio, a circular tour of the Mani, about 160 km (100 miles), can be managed comfortably in a day. Heading across the neck of the peninsula towards

*A*ll walks around the town of Monemvasia seem to start or finish with the Venetian bell tower at the entrance to Dzamiou Square.

*V*athia is little more than a ghost town now, but its tower-houses are typical of the sturdy defences erected by the Maniotes to protect their independence, not only from the Turks but from the rest of Greece, too. The view extends south to Cape Matapan (or Tenaron), whose coves have for centuries provided havens for pirate vessels. In one of them is the cave from which Hercules is said to have pulled the three-headed dog Cerberus from the gates of hell.

the west coast, you pass the restored 13th-century **Passava Castle** of Jean de Neuilly, Marshal of the Morea (as the Peloponnese was then known). A turnoff 12 km (7.5 miles) further on takes you north to the remains of **Kelefa Castle**, a sprawling Turkish fort of the 17th century.

In **Areopoli**, the small local capital, you will see good examples of the region's characteristic sturdy tower houses. In keeping with the Mani's belligerent history, notice that soldier saints are the preferred motif of the stone reliefs in the 18th-century **Taxiarchi Church**. The town is also known for its good bread.

From the cliffs of **Pirgos Dirou** drive down to the cave entrance of a fascinating **underground lake**. Take the half-hour tour by flatboat among the artfully illuminated limestone stalagmites and stalactites that have been growing drip by drip for tens of thousands of years. A few steps from the entrance to the grotto, you can swim at the small white-rock beach.

The road going south passes through increasingly rugged countryside where the villages thin out, many of them lying in ghostly ruin. The view from the fortified village of **Nomia** is splendid, and take a look at the deserted tower houses in **Koeta**.

Nestling in a bay under soaring rocky cliffs, **Gerolimin** is an attractive little fishing village built at the end of the 19th century. Further along the coast,

Vathia is the best of the tower-house ghost towns.

It is an hour's brisk walk from Porto Kagio to the lighthouse at **Cape Matapan**, the southernmost point of the Greek mainland (there's nothing special to see). The British won a naval battle here against the Italians in 1941.

If you do not want to double back past Gerolimin, the wild, deserted eastern route is on the sunless side of the hills in the late afternoon. But the views are still rewarding, especially from **Kokkala**, whose pretty little creek invites a quiet swim, and **Kotrona**, further north.

If you are heading west to Kalamata, you pass through the splendid rugged landscapes of **Outer Mani** *(Exo Máni)*—ravines and craggy green and brown hills with flashing views of the sea below. Make a stop at the 13th-century church of Agios Dimitrios set amidst lovely greenery overlooking the Gulf of Messenia, outside **Kardamili**, a pretty fishing village. Its old mansions are being turned into guest houses, and there's another fine church, the 18th-century Agios Spiridon.

Kalamata

Capital of Messenia, this industrial town was badly hit by an earthquake in 1986. The old **Turkish quarter** remains the best part of town to visit, and the **market**, although modernized, is still colourful. Kalamata takes pride in being the first city to revolt in the nationalist uprising of 1821.

Messene

The archaeological site of this ancient city lies in a magnificent pastoral setting at the foot of Mount Ithomi, 25 km (16 miles) north of modern Messini.

Messene was a victorious ally of Epaminondas in the fight to end Spartan hegemony in the Peloponnese in 371 BC. The fortified city, rebuilt by the Theban general, spreads around the little country village of **Mavromati**. Ancient ruins poke out of gardens and orchards among the houses, but the best preserved **fortifications**, for which the town was famous, lie to the north of Mavromati. The grand **Arcadia Gate** is protected by a system of towers around its double entrance. Notice the chariot-wheel ruts in the paved road leading to the gate. The walls extended 9 km (5.5 miles) around the city, enclosing farmland too. There are vestiges of a semicircular temple and a small theatre from the city's **Sanctuary of Asclepius**, which offered some modest competition for the ancient medical centre at Epidaurus (see p. 133).

Pylos

Messenia's major west-coast seaport is a lively town on the south shore of the magnificent natural harbour of **Navarino**. It was here that Greek freedom was at last guaranteed when an allied force of British, French and Russian ships annihilated the Turkish fleet in 1827. The town's quayside **Platia Trion Navarkhon** (Three Admirals Square) honours the victors with a pleasant tree-shaded plaza from which to watch the yachts sail in, and the local citizens stroll by on their evening *vólta*. Walk up to the restored Turkish fortress of **Neokastro** for a view over the bay from the outer bastion.

But for a closer look, a harbour cruise is recommended. Out in the centre of the harbour on Tortoise Rock *(Chelonáki)* is a **British Memorial** to the great battle.

On Sfaktiria island, closing off the bay to the west, are French and Greek monuments. The boat also visits **Paleokastro**, a rocky promontory (inaccessible by road) where a 30-minute walk brings you to the ruined battlements and towers of a castle dating back to the 13th century. Beyond it to the north is the **Grotto of Nestor**, a cave with strange animal-shaped stalagmites which encouraged the legend that the old sage King Nestor sheltered his cows here.

Methoni

Just 20 minutes' drive south of Pylos, a golden sandy beach is the main attraction of this old Venetian stronghold. The view over a group of small green islands is one of the prettiest seaside vistas in the Peloponnese. There is good fishing to be had from the islands of **Sapiendza** and **Schiza**.

Methoni was a vital position from which the Venetians controlled the passage of ships heading for the Adriatic. The Turks made repeated efforts to capture it and finally succeeded in doing so in the 18th century. Dominating the town's promontory is the Venetians' great **citadel** with monumental gateways and two large bastions used as arsenals. At the southern end of the fortress over a wooden bridge is the hexagonal **Bourdzi Tower**, a handsome backdrop for scenic photographs.

Nestor's Palace

This intriguing archaeological site on **Englianos Hill**, 14 km (9 miles) north of Pylos, is avoided by the package tours because its "picturesque" quality is marred by a corrugated iron shelter. But it is still well worth a visit. Old Nestor, the garrulous but dignified king

of ancient Pylos, was Agamemnon's most trusted advisor on the Trojan campaign. His contingent of 90 ships was second only to Agamemnon's in the Greek fleet.

His palace, built in 1300 BC, is as big as contemporaneous Mycenae, and traces of frescoes suggest it was just as richly decorated. But it suffered greater damage in a conflagration in 1200 BC. Luckily, the fire baked solid the palace accountants' clay tablets, which a Cambridge scholar was able to decipher— the famous Linear B script, which provided the first evidence that the Peloponnesians of the Mycenaean era spoke a form of Greek (see p. 60).

In the palace's **royal apartments**, you can see the throne room with a round clay hearth surrounded by four columns, similar to the arrangement at Mycenae. In the **queen's chambers** is a bathroom with a terracotta tub still intact, along with jars and pitchers for pouring in the hot water.

Olympia and the West

The western region of the Peloponnese provides contrasting landscapes for the settings of its two great classical shrines. The sanctuary of Olympia lies in the luxuriant green Alfios valley, while Bassae's temple to Apollo stands in the bleak grandeur of Mount Lycaeon's werewolf-haunted peaks. The seaside resort of Killini offers a relaxing coastal retreat.

Olympia

The short drive east from Pyrgos should convince you that Heracles was not just a muscle-bound brute. It was he,

Olympian Zeus

Inside the Temple of Zeus sat Phidias's colossal image of the supreme god. The statue was clad in ivory and gold, and was seated on a throne of ebony and ivory, with an eagle-crested sceptre in one hand and a winged victory in the other. Regarded by the ancients as one of the Seven Wonders of the World, it was over 12 m (40 ft) high and would have knocked the roof off had it come to life and stood up.

In the 1st century AD, the Roman general Agrippa sought the favour of Augustus by erecting a similarly huge effigy of the emperor outside the temple, for everyone to see.

The mad emperor Caligula wanted to take the Olympian Zeus back to Rome, and have its head replaced with a likeness of his own, but legend has it that whenever his lackeys came close to the statue it let out a peal of mocking laughter.

according to the ancients, who chose this magnificent setting, at once serene and grandiose, for the sacred games that for a brief moment every four years united the belligerent Greek world.

At the foot of Mount Kronos, near the confluence of the Alfios and Kladeos rivers, he hedged in a sacred grove *(altis)* of planes, wild olives, poplars, oaks and pines. With votive offerings hanging from their branches, the sacred trees remained as important as the altars and temples that were subsequently built among them.

From the 10th century BC, altars were erected to Hera and then Zeus. However, the temples and treasury shrines that followed were toppled by a shattering earthquake in the 6th century AD. But the tumbled ruins, basking in the golden glow of the late afternoon sun, still offer eloquent testimony to the sanctuary's grandeur.

Sanctuary and Precincts

The main path from the entrance leads through the **Gymnasium** (3rd century BC), a long practice area for the discus, javelin and foot races. There are column bases of porticoes along the east and south sides. Beyond it is the **Palaestra**, a training school for wrestling and boxing. The practice ring was in the central courtyard, surrounded by changing rooms, baths and massage chambers— notice the lipped receptacles for the masseur's oil.

Make your way south through the debris of later Roman houses and the brick walls of a Byzantine church to the stone rectangle of **Phidias's Workshop**. It was here, after his ostracism from Athens (see p. 112), that the great sculptor worked on the statue of Zeus that was to grace the god's temple. The artist's tools, clay moulds, and a cup inscribed with his name are displayed in the site's museum.

Further south is the **Leonidaion** (330 BC), a hostelry for officials with rooms facing in to a square peristyle court.

The **Processional Road** east passes on the right the **Bouleuterion** hall for games officials, where judges and athletes both took an oath of fair play.

Turn left into the sanctuary proper where a ramp leads to the **Temple of Zeus**. Built between 470 and 456 BC, it now lies in total ruin, but the tumbled capitals and drums of the Doric columns are an impressive sight. It was 64 m (210 ft) long and 28 m (90 ft) wide, similar to the dimensions of the Parthenon. Above the columns at either end were sculpted pediments of King Pelops' chariot race and Lapith hunters fighting with Centaurs, now displayed in the museum.

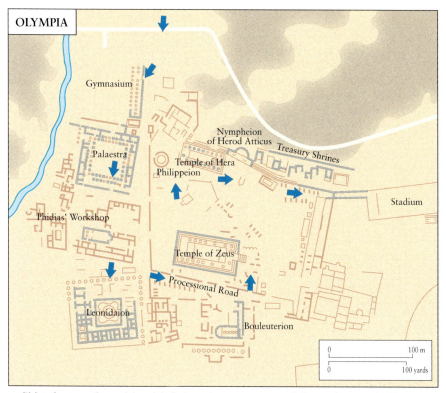

OLYMPIA

Gymnasium

Nympheion
of Herod Atticus

Treasury Shrines

Palaestra

Temple of Hera

Philippeion

Phidias' Workshop

Stadium

Temple of Zeus

Processional Road

Leonidaion

Bouleuterion

| 0 | 100 m |
| 0 | 100 yards |

Skirt the temple and head left (west) to the half-concealed remains of the **Philippeion**, a rotunda built by Philip of Macedonia (and completed by his son Alexander) to commemorate himself and his family. Beside it is the long and narrow **Temple of Hera**, built around 600 BC. Some of its Doric columns have been resurrected. The head from Hera's statue is now in the museum. The goddess was originally Olympia's principal deity, the continuation of a pre-Hellenic cult of the Earth Mother. But the Greeks put an end to such matriarchal leanings by installing a statue of Zeus to accompany his wife, along with Praxiteles' superb sculpture of Hermes (on view in the museum).

Continue east past the semi-circular **Nympheion of Herod Atticus**. This monumental fountain was built by the rich Athenian patron of the arts in AD 160 to capture spring water from Mount Kronos. Beyond, on the way to the Stadium, is a terrace of 12 **Treasury Shrines** erected by cities and colonies for votive offerings to the gods. Below the terrace is a row of bases from bronze statues of Zeus financed by fines levied on athletes for cheating.

Stadium

This is in fact the third Olympic stadium. The other two were located within the sanctuary, but the last was placed outside in the late 5th century BC as the games began to lose their religious significance. Just as in the modern era, professionalism and political prestige gained the upper hand.

The Olympic Games

The games began as a one-day contest of foot-racing, a purely local affair for the Olympian region of Elis. The valley was fine horse-breeding country, and the games soon added horse-racing and chariot-racing. One of the myths surrounding the origin of the games is that the first chariot-race was the famous contest in which Pelops defeated the Elians' rival, Oinomaus.

Eventually boxing, wrestling, discus, javelin and jumping were also included, attracting athletes from further afield. In 776 BC, the games were formally inaugurated as a Panhellenic event, and by the second half of the 7th century BC athletes would gather from all over the Greek world, including the colonies in Asia Minor and Italy. As might have been expected, Sparta dominated the early competitions, but in time they were overtaken by the Sicilians and other Italians.

From 472 BC, the games became a five-day event. The first day was taken up with sacrifices, dedications and general festivities in the sanctuary, while the athletes and judges took an oath of fair play. The games began on the second day with chariot races and the pentathlon. In the latter event, the champion was the winner of a wrestling play-off among the finalists of the running, jumping, discus and javelin events. The third day was boys' day. The sporting climax came on the fourth day with running, naked and in full armour, jumping, wrestling, boxing and pankration, a combination of boxing and wrestling which provided a rather doubtful demonstration of the Olympic spirit. Strangling, kicking in the stomach, twisting the opponent's foot out of its socket and breaking his fingers were all permitted. But biting and gouging were for some reason forbidden.

On the fifth day, the victors celebrated with sacrifices and a banquet, and were crowned with wreaths of wild olives.

The main entrance is through a stone passageway covered now by a Roman arch. The finishing line for the runners is clearly marked at the entrance end, 600 ancient Greek feet—one *stade*—from the other end. Only a few dignitaries and judges had stone seats. Otherwise, the capacity crowd of 40,000—men only, as athletes performed naked—sat on the ground or on wooden benches. The Hippodrome for horse and chariot races was situated to the south of the stadium, but all trace has been washed away by river floods.

Museum

Take a look at the model of the sanctuary in the entrance hall—it helps to give you an idea of what Olympia looked like in its heyday. The central exhibit is the **Pediments Gallery**, displaying the carved friezes from the Temple of Zeus. The East Pediment presents the legendary chariot race in which King Pelops of Lydia in Asia Minor won from King Oinomaus control of the peninsula that was to bear his name. Zeus (headless) stands in the centre. On his right are Pelops and his bride-to-be, Hippodameia. On Zeus's left are Oinomaus and his wife. Beside the kings are soothsayers and servants, kneeling beside horses and chariots (missing). The reclining figures are symbols of Olympia's rivers, Alfios and Kladeos. The West Pediment presents a livelier scene of Centaurs Fighting with Lapiths, with Apollo standing between them. The monstrous sensuality of the Centaurs contrasts with the physical beauty of the Lapiths (Thessalian hunters). The scene was a frequently used theme of the Hellenic ideal (epitomized at Olympia) triumphing over barbarity.

Fragments of the Labours of Heracles from the temple's metope friezes show the hero conquering a lion, and shovelling away in the Augean Stables.

Beyond the central hall, in **Gallery 4**, is a fine terracotta statue of Zeus and Ganymede (470 BC), showing the god well satisfied with his pretty prey, who for his part seems blithely unaware of his privileged destiny. Be sure to see nearby the tools of Phidias, found in the sculptor's workshop, including a bronze goldsmith's hammer, clay moulds and his wine cup with the words "I belong to Phidias" embossed on the base. Off to the right, in **Gallery 6**, is Praxiteles' exquisite statue of Hermes (340 BC) from the Temple of Hera. The head of Hera (6th century BC) from her colossal statue is in Gallery 2 to the left of the entrance.

Bassae

A 2-hour drive south-east from Olympia leads to this magnificent but fragile temple. The closest town is **Andritsena**, a mountain community of ramshackle gabled wooden houses, where carpenters, weavers and ironsmiths share the streets with the farmers' pigs and goats.

 The road continues 14 km (9 miles) south from the town past some formidable ravines to a site of splendid rocky desolation 1,132 m (3,714 ft) up on Mount Kotilion. The **Temple of Apollo** was built by Ictinus from 450 to 425 BC before he went to Athens to work on the Parthenon. The grey limestone edifice has several particularities: it departs from the golden length-width proportions of 9:4 to an exceptionally narrow 15 columns long and only 6 wide; its orientation is north-south rather than east-west; it combines all three architectural orders for its construction—Doric on the outside, Ionic and Corinthian within. One of the Corinthian columns is still standing on the south side—it is the earliest surviving example of a Corinthian capital. The marble metope friezes are in the British Museum.

Killini

Over on the north-west coast, the hillsides ripple silver and green with olive and fruit trees, sweeping clear down to the sea. But the real attraction for the weary traveller is the long stretch of golden sand in the lazy beach resort of **Killini**. You don't have to stray far from the sunbathers to see shepherds and their flocks in the greenery just above. The resort makes a good base for excursions around the western Peloponnese. Down the coast at **Loutra Killinis** are some mineral springs built on the site of old Roman baths, but again it is the beach that provides the real attraction.

North Coast

The ferry service at Patras makes it a necessary stop for many travellers, but the only other reason to dally on this overcrowded stretch of coast is the delightful little detour up the Bouraikos valley to Kalavryta, and beyond to the historic Agia Lavra monastery.

Patras

The largest city in the Peloponnese, with a population of 160,000, Patras is the main Greek port on the Ionian Sea. It has some pleasant green squares around the waterfront. West of the seaport, the large, modern neo-Byzantine church of **Agios Andreas** is said to be built on the spot where the patron saint of Scotland, Saint Andrew, was crucified on an X-shaped cross (represented in the white cross of the Scottish flag). The church's prize relic is the Saint Andrew's silver-mounted skull, retrieved from the Vatican in 1964.

Kalavrita

To get to this breezy town in the Aroania mountains, you have to take the hair-raising but exhilarating 90-minute train ride along the Vouraikos river. The train starts out from the coastal town of **Diakofto**, surrounded by orchards and producing delicious honey. The **narrow-gauge railway** built in the late 19th century labours up beautiful gorges, in and out of tunnels and across striated escarpments.

After one stop at Mega Spileo, you reach cheerful Kalavryta with its central square full of refreshing greenery and lively cafés.

It has recovered from the reprisal raid of 13 December 1943, when German troops killed 1,436 of the male citizens and burned down the town. In remembrance of this atrocity, the hands of the metropolitan clock have been halted at 2.34—the hour of the massacre.

From here, you can hire a taxi to **Agia Lavra monastery**, celebrated as the site where the proclamation of Archbishop Germanos of Patras launched a nation-wide revolt against the Turks on 25 March 1821.

Saronic Islands

Apart from Aegina, which inevitably bears the boisterous mark of its proximity to Athens, the islands' easy-going simplicity makes them a good destination for a pleasant day trip—or perhaps a longer stay. They are all within easy reach of the ports of Ermioni, Galatas and Methana.

Aegina

Rather too close for comfort to Athens, the island's capital, **Aegina Town**, has a lively quayside scene, with more of an Athenian feel than a "touristy" atmosphere, but its a far cry from the laid-back ambience of the Cyclades. The crowded beach at **Agia Marina** is best avoided, but the well-preserved **Temple of Aphaia**, dating from 5th century BC, is worth a look.

Poros

Galatas' 5-minute ferry crossing to the island is just a 2-hour drive from Nafplio. Poros is a favourite holiday spot for the Greeks themselves. Behind its pretty little port, the town's white-washed, blue-shuttered houses cling to pine-covered hills.

Visit the ruined **Temple of Poseidon** where the Athenian orator Demosthenes took poison in 322 BC rather than submit to his Macedonian enemies. Of the beaches, **Askeli** gets a little crowded, but **Neori** is fine, especially at sunset.

Hydra

This island is little more than an 18-kilometre ridge of bare rock. However, it is enormously popular with artists. **Hydra Town** has a spectacular harbour, some good seafood restaurants, and handsome sea-captains' houses for the painters to paint.

Overlooking the port, one of the finest houses, the **Tombazi mansion**, is the island's branch of the Athenian School of Fine Arts. **Mandraki beach** is the most popular, but **Kamini** and **Vlichos** are quieter.

Spetses

The charm of this island's Aleppo pines, cypresses and oleander trees has attracted a mixture of the Athens' jet set (who speed in by hydrofoil) and British package tours. The liveliest spot in **Spetses Town** is the café-lined square overlooking the harbour. In the courtyards and little squares of the town's back streets, look out for the grey, white and black pebble mosaics of marine and mythological scenes. The beaches of **Agii Anargiri** and **Agia Paraskevi** are fine, but if you want something quieter, take a boat over to the pebble beaches on the island's north-west coast.

T he spectacular harbour of Hydra Town, apart from supplying the good seafood restaurants, is a favourite subject of artists and photographers; overlooking the port is the island's branch of the Athenian School of Fine Arts.

A Ring of Sparkling Islands Set in a Sapphire Sea

The Cyclades lie scattered across the heart of the Aegean Sea, like a handful of jewels carelessly flung by the hands of the gods. These are the archetypal Greek islands—rough nuggets of limestone inset with dazzling whitewashed villages, blue-painted chapel domes mirroring the sky, sandy coves lapped by clear turquoise waters, and terraced hillsides of vines and olives. There is something here for every taste, from the secluded valleys of Tinos to the night-clubs of Ios and Mykonos, from the archaeological sites of Delos and Thera to the beaches of Paros. The keen island-hopper could easily spend a whole summer exploring the varied delights of these Aegean gems.

The name of the group comes from the circle *(kyklos)* formed by a dozen islands around the sanctuary of Delos, the legendary birthplace of Apollo. In

T he thatch-roofed wind-mills above the harbour of Mykonos are one of the Cyclades' most famous landmarks. Although the mills no longer work for a living, the one nearest the steps up from the town is occasionally set in motion for the benefit of tourists.

modern times, the archipelago's name has extended to include another 20 islands as far south as Santorini (now officially reclaiming its ancient name of Thera). The modern administrative capital is Syros, an industrialized island to the west of Mykonos.

Cypresses and olive groves, and orange and lemon trees blossoming beautifully in spring lend their colour to the largely arid brown landscapes. Man has added his castles, dovecotes, windmills and his brilliantly whitewashed houses.

A Potted History of the Archipelago

The Aegean's first island-hoppers were farmers and fishermen who came from Asia Minor and settled in the Cyclades around 4000 BC.

The island of Milos attracted a lively Mediterranean trade in its much sought-after glassy obsidian stone, which was vital in the Bronze Age for the manufacture of knives, scrapers and other tools. These cosmopolitan contacts and its inhabitants' prolific skills in stone and clay sculpture made the Cyclades more civilized than the mainland.

With a leading role in Crete's Minoan empire, the island of Thera sustained a society that was probably as rich and sophisticated as Knossos itself, until the great volcanic eruptions and earthquakes of 1500 BC buried both of them beneath layers of lava and cinders.

During the rise of Athens and Sparta, Naxos was the dominant political and economic force in the Cyclades, a major target of the Persian invasion. But Apollo's sacred island of Delos was the symbolic centre of Athens' Aegean empire. As a sanctuary commanding the allegiance of the surrounding islands and protecting their war treasury, it was the "Brussels" of a NATO-like alliance, and became one of the wealthiest trading posts in the eastern Mediterranean.

In the post-classical era, the Cyclades were up for grabs, abandoned by the Byzantines first to the Arabs and then to the Venetians, who set up a Duchy of the Archipelago under Marco Sanudo, Duke of Naxos.

In the 17th century, English aristocrats looted the islands' sculpture for the rival collections of Charles I and the Duke of Buckingham (with much of it ending up in the Ashmolean Museum in Oxford).

In the 19th century. the Cyclades became the first of the islands to be included in the independent Greece of King Otto.

Their all too obvious attractions have made many of the Cyclades easy prey to the package-tour trade. But secluded corners remain for the adventurous traveller to discover, and the charms of the most popular islands, like Mykonos and Santorini, are powerful enough to withstand the commercial onslaught—even despite the summer *meltemi*, which blows at its fiercest here in the southwest corner of the Aegean.

Some of the Cyclades, like Mykonos, Paros and Santorini, have direct air links with Athens and other islands. The main ferry services start out from Piraeus or Rafina. For details of air and sea transportation from the mainland, see the GETTING AROUND IN GREECE section in the FACTS AND FIGURES chapter, p. 18.

Mykonos

The miracle of Mykonos is that it still manages to live up to the expectations of those who come seeking the perfect hedonistic holiday. It attracts everyone from the yachting fraternity to budget backpackers, and is home to the liveliest gay scene in the islands. Lovers of classical Greece come here to the visit the sanctuary of Apollo on the neighbouring island of Delos.

The canny visitor can find escapes from the island's many superficial symptoms of package-tour overkill. For every overcrowded beach within easy access of Mykonos Town, there's another off the beaten track offering peace and quiet and perfect swimming, accessible to any enterprising visitor by boat or motor-scooter. (If you rent a car here, make sure it has four-wheel-drive for the many unpaved roads down to the

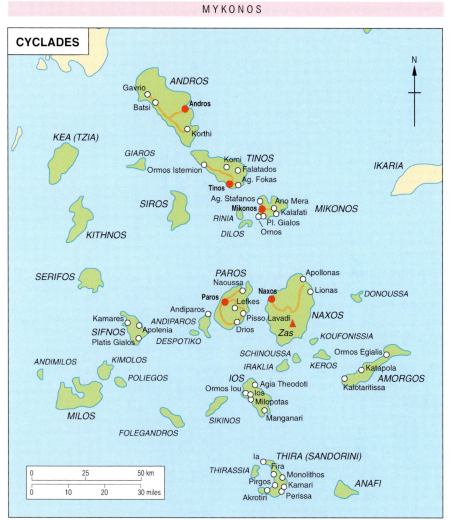

CYCLADES

N

KEA (TZIA)

ANDROS
Gavrio
Batsi
Andros
Korthi

GIAROS
Ormos Isternion
Komi
Falatados
Ag. Fokas
Tinos
TINOS

IKARIA

SIROS
Ag. Stafanos
Mikonos
Ano Mera
Kalafati
MIKONOS
RINIA
Pl. Gialos
KITHNOS
DILOS
Ornos

SERIFOS

PAROS
Naoussa
Paros
Lefkes
Andiparos
Naxos
Lionas
DONOUSSA

Kamares
SIFNOS
Platis Gialos
ANDIPAROS
Apolenia
DESPOTIKO
Pisso Lavadi
Drios
Zas
NAXOS
KOUFONISSIA
Apollonas

ANDIMILOS
KIMOLOS
SCHINOUSSA
IRAKLIA
KEROS
Ormos Egialis
Katapola
AMORGOS
Kalotaritissa

POLIEGOS
IOS
Ormos Iou
Agia Theodoti
Ios
Milopotas

MILOS
SIKINOS
Manganari

FOLEGANDROS

| 0 | 25 | 50 km |
| 0 | 10 | 20 | 30 miles |

Ia
THIRASSIA
Fira
Pirgos
Akrotiri
THIRA (SANDORINI)
Monolithos
Kamari
Perissa
ANAFI

beaches.) Although the main town centre is chock-a-block with boutiques, bars and restaurants, they are bright and not at all tawdry, with good quality merchandise, especially the locally hand-woven linen. With tourists from cruise-ships in mind, the tone is definitely "upmarket". The island's great achievement has been to avoid hideous jerry-built buildings by following a policy of traditional architecture, so that even its newest hotels can resemble a terrace of fishermen's cottages.

Mykonos Town

Surrounded by low hills on the west side of the island, the town hugs its harbour with narrow winding lanes and alleys, deliberately laid out in a labyrinth to confuse mediaeval pirates.

A row of famous windmills looms above the port, at its best in the early morning and late afternoon, outside the hours of the cruise-passengers' daily invasion. Small boats handling the Delos excursion traffic are moored along the natural jetty of the harbour's

161

north arm. Bigger boats dock round to the east.

The quay is shared by cafés, fishermen and an occasional tame pelican; these languid birds have been adopted as an island mascot. The balconied houses of the Alefkándra quarter, with the sea lapping below their harbourside windows, have earned it the nickname of "Little Venice".

Above the port, the spotlessly white-washed **Paraportiani church**, seems these days to be more revered by pagan photographers than devout Christians.

The little **Archaeological Museum** out on Agios Stefanos is devoted principally to tomb-sculpture and ceramics from the Rhenia cemetery, where the dead of Delos were re-buried after the sanctuary's purification in the 5th century BC. Most notable are a statue of Heracles and a *pithos* or jar (7th century BC) decorated with scenes from the Trojan War.

Beaches

The island boasts more than a dozen magnificent beaches. Unless you enjoy the bustle of a crowded beach, the best are the remotest on the north coast and at the east end of the island.

As you hunt down your ideal location, remember that on an island where strong winds blow up in the summer without a moment's notice, fine sand beaches can prove more troublesome than pebbles or coarse-grained sand.

Closest to town and accessible by road are **Ornos**, **Tourlos** and **Agios Stefanos**. Almost as convenient, just an inexpensive 15-minute taxi or bus ride from town, are **Psarou** and **Platis Gialos**. These have a more restrained atmosphere than the secluded coves and

beaches further along the coast, where people begin to ignore the Greek-English sign: "Is forbidden for the undressed people in order of the police."

Paranga and the sandy cove of **Agia Anna** are relatively tranquil spots with pleasant shaded tavernas. There are two designated nudist beaches: **Paradise**, a long, curving arc of coarse, tan-coloured sand backed by gentle rocks and scrub covered hills, and its companion in Karkinagri Bay, **Super Paradise**.

*T*he waterfront at
*Mykonos is frequented by numerous
tame pelicans, which have become
something of an island mascot.
They are so approachable that it is
common for visitors to pose for
photographs beside them.*

You will need a boat or a four-wheel-drive vehicle to get to **Elia** beach with its fashionable tavernas. But a taxi can take you over to the long, curved **Kalafatis** beach at the eastern end of the island. Little caïques sail out to the isle of **Dragonisi**, which is famous for its seals and caves.

On the north shore, **Panormos Bay** is a favourite with wind-surfers, with the remote **Agios Sostis** the best of its beaches.

*M*ykonos harbour at dusk, with the sun sinking in the west behind the neighbouring island of Rhenia and, in the farthest distance, Syros.

Ano Mera

Standing proudly aloof from the coastal resorts, this inland village is worth a bus trip just to pay a visit to the quiet little **Tourlianí monastery** and its 16th-century open-work steeple. The monastery is one of some 360 churches and chapels dotted around the island.

only the spiritual focus of the ancient Greeks' ethnic identity, but also a highly prosperous grain port and slave market. At its height, the latter had a "turnover" of 10,000 slaves a day. The annual religious festival grew into a veritable trade fair, and the Delos of antiquity was as cosmopolitan a port as Piraeus is today.

To honour the birthplace of Apollo, pilgrims from the surrounding islands and city-states of the mainland built great monuments and brought rich gifts and treasures. Their rulers and warriors consulted its sacred oracle, said to be second only to Delphi in importance. The island was twice "purified" on the orders of Athens: no births or deaths were permitted there, and all graves were exhumed and their contents transported to neighbouring Rhenia. The purification is likely to remain in force for some time to come as accommodation on the island is minimal—one hotel of only seven beds.

Those with queasy stomachs should be prepared for a frequently choppy sea on the 30- to 40-minute motor launch ride from Mykonos (longer excursions arrive from Tinos, Naxos and Paros). Take good walking shoes for the hike up Mount Kynthos.

Sanctuary of Apollo

If poor weather does not force a detour around Cape Kako to land at Gourna on the north-east coast, the average three-hour morning visit begins at the jetty immediately beside the old **Sacred Harbour**, long since silted up. Follow the pilgrims' path left along the paved Sacred Way to the shrines dedicated to Apollo. On the north side of the **House of the Naxians** is the huge base on which Apollo's colossal statue was

Delos

This island sanctuary was revered as the birthplace of Apollo and his twin sister Artemis. Its vast archaeological site has revealed grand temples, and the most complete residential quarter surviving from ancient Greece. Situated at the centre of the Cyclades, Delos was not

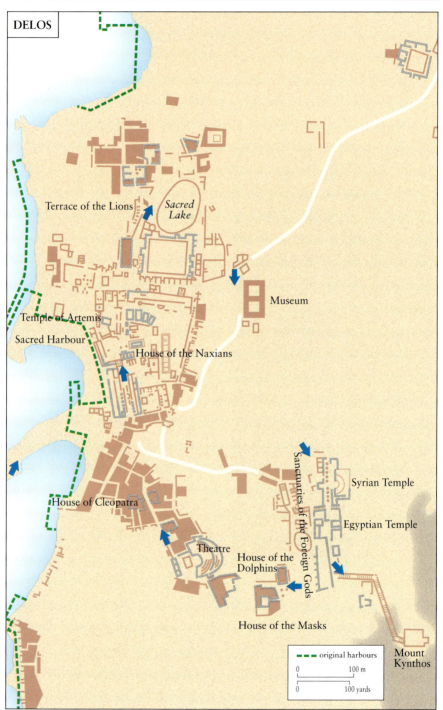

DELOS

Terrace of the Lions

Sacred Lake

Museum

Temple of Artemis

Sacred Harbour

House of the Naxians

House of Cleopatra

Sanctuaries of the Foreign Gods

Syrian Temple

Egyptian Temple

Theatre

House of the Dolphins

House of the Masks

Mount Kynthos

- - - original harbours

0   100 m

0   100 yards

erected in the 7th century BC. An inscription tells that the base and statue were constructed from one solid block, with graffiti added by Venetians and some 17th-century tourists. The statue proved too big for the Venetians to carry off in 1422, and you will find some of the pieces they dropped—fragments of the thighs and trunk—over to the left behind the **Temple of Artemis** (2nd century BC). A hand is displayed in the local museum, and a foot ended up in London's British Museum.

Terrace of the Lions

These majestic lions carved from Naxian marble have become the sanctuary's most celebrated symbol. Five of the original nine lions sit up on their haunches, mouths open to roar, guarding the **Sacred Lake.** Until it was drained in 1926 (because of malarial mosquitoes), the lake was the home of swans and geese, descendants of the shrine's sacred birds. Now a grove of palms has been planted in the middle to symbolize the place of Apollo's birth.

Museum

On a hot day, the museum's airy pavilion provides a cool and pleasant haven before tackling Mount Kynthos and the rest of your tour of the archaeological site. The best of the Delos sculpture is in Athens' National Archaeological Museum, but the seven rooms here include a fine sphinx, a lion's body with woman's head from Paros (6th century BC), Aegean Geometric vases and Mycenaean figurines. Particularly fascinating are objects of everyday life from the days when Delos was a commercial port: medical instruments, utensils, knives, jewellery, keys, combs, anchors and weights.

*T*he famous Terrace of the Lions guards the approach to the Sacred Lake. Only five of the original nine remain. At least one was plundered in the 17th century and now adorns the Arsenal in Venice.

Sanctuaries of the Foreign Gods

Along the stone mountain-path, you pass shrines built by overseas merchants living around the port. The **Syrian temple** (128 BC), honouring the weather god Adad, giver and destroyer of life, was the scene of violent orgiastic rituals, until these practices were banned by an Athenian high priest. The **Egyptian temples** were dedicated to Serapis, the god of healing, Isis, the goddess of fertility, and Anubis, the jackal-headed lord of the dead.

Mount Kynthos

The highest point on Delos (112 m, 367 ft) bears traces of a small temple to Hera, but the climb is well worth the effort for the magnificent views alone. From a platform halfway up, you can take in the whole sanctuary and the ancient town, and at the summit, you can look out over the many islands of the Cyclades that paid ancient allegiance to Delos. The mountain was inhabited during the Stone Age, and shrines were built here for Athena and Zeus in the 3rd century BC. It was from here that the supreme god watched Leto give birth to his son, Apollo.

Ariadne Abandoned

Ariadne, daughter of King Minos of Crete, succumbed to the embraces of Theseus as he emerged from the Labyrinth after slaying the hideous Minotaur (see p. 49). On their way back to Athens, she asked him to take her ashore at Naxos because she was pregnant and very seasick, and worried she might miscarry.

But Theseus sailed the next morning without her, abandoning poor Ariadne who had helped him accomplish his task, and deserted her home and parents for love of him. The god of wine, Dionysus, who was born on Naxos from the thigh of Zeus, found the distraught Ariadne and married her so that her bastard son Oenopion could have a proper upbringing. Ariadne stopped trying to live up to a name that meant "most pure" and became a fertility goddess. She bore Dionysus half a dozen children. Theseus later married her sister, the hot-blooded Phaedra.

*T*he Sanctuary of Apollo on Delos, seen from the top of the ancient theatre. Boats from Mykonos bring day trippers to the landing stage visible in the background.

Theatre District

Coming back down the mountain, turn left towards the sea to the port town's main residential quarter, surrounding the ancient theatre. On your right as you enter the town is the **House of the Dolphins**, so called for its charming mosaic of dolphins with Erotes riding on their backs. Across the street, the **House of Masks** has mosaics of theatrical masks, and a splendid Dionysus riding on a panther. Best viewed from the top overlooking the stage, the fine marble **theatre** (3rd century BC) held an audience of 5500 in its 43 rows of seats. Beyond the theatre, follow the signs over to the left to the **House of Cleopatra**, an Athenian lady whose headless statue, standing beside the image of her husband, welcomes you into their courtyard whose 2200-year-old well is still in working order.

Andros

Quietest and greenest of the Cyclades, and first stop on the ferry-route from Rafina to Mykonos, Andros is a favourite summer holiday retreat of Athenians. Shipping magnates have built luxurious villas along the east coast. Others have houses with delightful gardens in the hills, hidden among pine groves and looking down on the vineyards and olive trees. Like neighbouring Tinos, the island is dotted with the square towers of Venetian dovecotes. Gourmets delight in the local omelettes, grilled octopus, and a crushed-almond dessert, *amygdalotá*.

*A*ndros Town backstreet.

Batsi and the Beaches

The ferry docks on the west coast at **Gavrion**, but the main resort is just to the south at Batsi, built around a charming fishing and sailing harbour with some good hotels and pleasant beaches. Over on the cooler east coast, the best beaches are at **Nimborio** and **Korthion.**

Andros Town

Also known as Chora ("the town"), like many island capitals, Andros Town is built along the ridge of an east-coast promontory. Attractive 19th-century neoclassical houses line the main marble-paved street, joined by a bridge to the ruins of a Venetian castle perched out on a rock. The Goulandris shipping magnates have endowed the town with three new art institutions: a **Museum of Modern Art**, dedicated mainly to home-grown talent; an **art gallery** for temporary exhibitions; and an **Archaeology Museum** housing finds from the excavations of the ancient settlement of Zagora at the southern end of the island. They include ceramics, household objects and sculpture, notably a statue of Hermes.

*L*acking the sandy beaches and nightlife that attract the crowds to Mykonos and Ios, Andros is an island for travellers who want to get away from it all. The Greek middle classes have long sought it out as a haven of peace away from the bustle of the mainland and the foreign tourist traps. From the harbour town of Gavrion you can explore a verdant interior that contrasts sharply with the dazzling but arid landscapes of the other Cyclades islands.

the port capital of Tinos to benefit from the curative powers attributed to an icon discovered in 1823. Ruled by Venice from 1207 to 1714, Tinos has always been the most Roman Catholic island of the Cyclades.

Tinos Town

The capital's pretty **harbour** describes an almost complete circle, and its waters are clean enough to attract some fine big fish right up to the dockside, where local boys with fishing rods try to tempt them to bite. The island caters much more to Greek visitors than to foreigners, but the pilgrimage trade has created an abundance of hotels and a bustling bazaar. The restaurants and cafés are pleasantly unsophisticated, but with the small problem that the menus, like the street-signs, are all in Greek. In the cobbled back streets, the old iron-balconied houses recall centuries of Venetian rule.

The object of the pilgrimage is the vast Panagia Evangelistria church, reached via a broad street sweeping directly up from the harbour. The church stands behind high walls in a marble and tile courtyard, with nine cypresses and a lone palm tree. A monumental staircase leads to its porch, which commands a grand view over the harbour and across the water to Mykonos, Delos and Syros.

Greek Orthodox tastes have clearly influenced the modern church's highly ornate interior. The ceiling is hung with over 100 silver candelabra. Dominating everything is the **icon of the Virgin Mary**, gold-framed and ablaze with jewels. Scores of pilgrims' offerings are placed around it to help summon up its curative powers.

Down the main boulevard from the church, an attractive **Archaeological**

Tinos

The great charm of this mountainous island is in its sparkling white villages, medieval dovecotes, picturesque wind-mills and terraced hillsides. Its serenity is occasionally disturbed, not by hordes of foreign holiday-makers, but by thousands of Roman Catholic pilgrims. Around the times of Annunciation Day (March 25) and Assumption (August 15), devout invalids make their way to

171

Museum exhibits Geometric vases of the 10th century BC, huge amphorae from the 8th and 7th centuries BC, and an ancient sun dial.

Interior

Many of the islands' fifty-odd villages are reachable only by rough roads and donkey-paths—though the local buses seem quite happy to tackle the bumpy tracks. An excursion into the interior is something of an adventure. Take, for instance, the afternoon bus from Tinos to **Komi**. Within minutes you are sweeping up, over and around spectacular mountain ridges, past carefully cultivated terraced fields. The rough narrow road takes you past dozens of the island's characteristic landmarks, the tall stone **dovecotes** built by the Venetians, over 800 of them on Tinos alone.

The bus stops at the hill of **Exombourgo**, well worth the 90-minute hike to the summit (565 m, 1,853 ft) with its ruined Venetian castle and a fine view over the Cyclades.

Other pretty villages are **Loutra**, **Pirgos** and **Falatados**, where you can see nuns of the Kehrovouníou Convent making traditional lace and embroidery.

Beaches

The closest to town and most popular is the long strand of **Agios Fokas**, an easy walk east from Tinos harbour. To get away from the crowds, head north of Komi (rough road and donkey-path) to Kolimbithra, an attractive, secluded sandy beach with a pleasant restaurant up on the hill behind. Even further away, practically at the end of the bus route, is **Ormos Isternion**.

*T*inos Town (below), and one of the hundreds of Venetian dovecotes scattered over the island (right).

Sifnos

For long a haven of calm, away from the main ferry-routes, this sparsely populated island has attracted increasing numbers of visitors to its well organized resorts and beach villages.

In ancient times, the island was famous for its gold and silver mines, and in 526 BC built the most opulent treasury at the sanctuary of Delphi (see p. 277). Now, it is more famous for its churches; the conscientious Christian can worship each day of the year in a different place, touring the island's 365 churches and chapels.

Ferries dock at **Kamares**, the main port and a centre for the island's thriving pottery trade. A bus will take you inland around Mount Profitis Ilias to the inland capital of **Apollonia**. Its classically whitewashed island houses sprawl across the slopes of three terraced hills. On the north coast, **Kastro** is a gently decaying medieval village on the site of what was probably the island's ancient capital. A little museum displays finds from Mycenaean and Archaic-era excavations, including a few clay horses of Geometric design.

On the south-east coast, **Platis Gialos** and **Faros Bay** are the best known of the beach resorts. For more secluded bathing, the long, sandy beach of the almost land-locked **Vathi Bay** is accessible by caïque or a 60-minute walk.

Paros

One of the loveliest of the Aegean islands, Paros also has the reputation of being the friendliest. This and its excellent facilities for water sports have made

it very popular with tourists. Gently rolling hills conceal the famous Parian marble quarries, and slope down to the wide coastal plain. The ferry docks in the bay of Paros Town on the west coast; its position at the hub of the Cyclades ferry network makes Paros an ideal base for island hopping.

Paros Town (Parikia)

A short stroll from the harbour lies a delightful village of narrow stone walkways—shops, archways, churches and houses are all the traditional dazzling white, with shutters painted blue and green, and courtyards of sweet jasmine and basil, with honeysuckle and lemon trees, and canaries twittering in the vine arbour. A particularly lovely corner of town is the sleepy little quarter around the hilltop Kastro, a 13th-century Venetian citadel. Enjoy the view from the church of Saints Constantine and Helen overlooking the bay, with Antiparos and other islets close offshore, and Sifnos looming on the western horizon.

The town's cathedral, **Panagia Ekatontapiliani**, or the "Church of 100 Doors", owes its name to its complex structure—there are nowhere near 100 doors. It is said to stand over a 4th-century shrine founded by St Helen, the mother of Constantine the Great, on her quest for the True Cross in Jerusalem. Earthquakes and modern restoration have subjected it to many changes, most recently from Venetian Baroque back to a hybrid version of its early Byzantine form. In the outer courtyard, notice the five church bells hanging from a tall cypress tree that has served as belfry ever since the original tower tumbled down in an earthquake in the 18th century. Inside, to the left of the choir, the

6th-century chapel of **Agios Nikolaos** is built on Doric columns from an ancient Roman building. A fine bishop's throne stands in the apse of the central Temple of the Virgin. The baptistery, to the right of the main church, has a sunken font.

The little **Archaeological Museum** nearby houses an engraved marble slab that is part of the mysterious Parian Chronicle *(Marmor Parium)*, found in Paros in 1897. A larger fragment, discovered in Smyrna, is now in Oxford's Ashmolean Museum. The whole purported to narrate the history of Greece from Cecrops, first king of Athens, down to 264 BC, with a strange mixture of political, military, religious and literary events. Fifth-century sculpture in Parian marble includes a large lion and calf relief, a Victory, and a winged medusa with snakes. A Roman mosaic in mauve, yellow and blue depicts the labours of Heracles.

*R*estaurant tables crowd the quayside in the tiny fishing harbour of Naousa. The boats here can also be hired for trips to the neighbouring beaches.

Villages and Beaches

Take a bus over to the fishing port of **Naousa**, where the gaily coloured cottage-doors on the quayside complement the yellow and russet fishing-nets, and blue, white and orange boats cram into the tiny harbour.

Motor launches take bathers across the broad bay to the sandy beaches and carved rocks of **Kolibithres**. Naousa boats also sail further around the island's north-east peninsula, to the fine beaches of **Langeri**, **Agia Maria** and **Platis Ammos**.Start out from the village

175

of **Marathi** to explore the ancient marble quarries. These were briefly revived in 1844 to furnish the stone for the tomb of Napoleon in Paris.

The bus for Marathi continues to the pretty mountain village of **Lefkes**, singled out by the twin-towered, orange-roofed marble cathedral, and reputed for its fine ceramics.

At the top of **Kefalos Hill** is a gleaming white monastery with splendid views around the island. Down on the east coast, the beach of **Piso Livadi** is popular with wind-surfers. Further south, long sandy beaches stretch out on either side of **Dryos**.

The snorkelling is good almost everywhere, but best of all over on **Antiparos** (a 40-minute boat-trip from Parikia). The main island's little sister is also noted for its vast cave with stalactites. This is a half-hour walk (slightly faster by donkey or bus) up the slope of Mount Agios Ilias.

Naxos

The largest and most beautiful of the Cyclades has all you need to live the good life: groves of orange and lemon trees, figs and pomegranates, sweet honey, tangy cheeses, and a wine that made the island famous for its ancient Dionysian orgies. Naxos also boasts the highest peak in the Cyclades, Mount Zas (1,001 m, 3,284 ft).

If Naxians are a little cooler in manner than their neighbours on Paros, could it derive from a natural pride in their illustrious history? It was here that Theseus abandoned Ariadne on his journey home from Crete after slaying the Minotaur. The island was famed for its

The town of Naxos climbs up the hill above its harbour. Naxos is the largest and highest of the all the islands in the Cyclades, famed for its wine and its beautiful marble.

fine white marble, and was a leader in early monumental sculpture and Ionic architecture. It was the dominant island power in the Aegean until its destruction by the Persians in 490 BC. It returned to prominence centuries later as the capital of the medieval Venetian Duchy of the Archipelago.

Naxos Town

Looming over the harbour is the town's imposing landmark, the giant **gateway** to the 6th-century BC Temple of Apollo, long since destroyed by the Persians. It stands 5.5 m (18 ft) tall among gleaming white marble ruins, on an islet joined to the port by a causeway.

Ignore the port's dull modern surroundings, and head up to the old **citadel** *(kástro)*. You climb easily through a delightful warren of white-washed cobbled lanes, arches, and tunnels, with cheerful boutiques sandwiched between vegetable shops, butchers, and tavernas. Inside the citadel, coats of arms above the doorways bear witness to the island's Venetian heyday. The church of **Panagia Theoskepastos** has a fine 14th-century icon of the Crucifixion. The **Catholic Cathedral** boasts an even older icon from the 10th century, a rare full-length portrait of the Virgin Mary and Child.

Nikos Kazantzakis, author of *Zorba the Greek* and *The Last Temptation of Christ*, was a pupil in the school that is now the town's **Archaeological Museum.** Among its prize exhibits are early Cycladic figurines, bowls and pitchers excavated from nearby 4,500-year-old tombs. Look, too, for the Mycenaean vases and gold leaf jewellery, as well as Geometric and Archaic pottery.

Climb **Aplomata hill,** just north of town, site of ancient cliff-edge tombs and a memorial to a World War II resistance hero, to share with the goats a magnificent view of Paros, Delos and Mykonos.

Excursions and Beaches

The peaceful Tragea Valley in the middle of the island is the best of the inland excursions. Stop off at the village of Chalki with its old Italian tower-houses. In front of the fine 17th-century Grazia palace, the church of Protothronis has some notable wall-paintings. From here, stroll out into a serene countryside of olive groves, cypresses and lemon trees and, nestling among them, small white Byzantine chapels.

The road through the mountains to the north takes you to the remote little fishing village of **Apollon**. Up on the hill a colossal 10 m (33 ft) statue of Apollo (some claim it's Dionysus) lies where its sculptors left it 2,600 years ago, unfinished because of faults in the marble which caused it to split.

Many of the island's best beaches are south of the capital. Closest to town is Agios Georgios. You will find the best sand and more solitude further out at Agios Prokopios, the tiny port of Agia Anna, and coves around the Mikri Vigla promontory. On windy days, head over to the north coast where the beautiful marble pebbles of **Lionas** beach will not blow in your eyes and ruin your picnic.

Amorgos

This narrow island, just 18 km (11 miles.) long, attracts travellers seeking the quiet life, and is also popular as an excursion from Naxos. Sailing around the south coast, you will see some of the most spectacular cliffs in the Aegean.

The charming island capital of Chora with its little white houses nestling against a Venetian fort, is a 45-minute drive inland. North-east of the capital, on a cliff overlooking the Aegean, is the 11th-century Chozoviotissa monastery, boasting a celebrated icon from Cyprus.

The most accessible beaches are on the north-west coast—**Ormos Egiali** and **Katapola** with its harbour. Others like **Kalotaritissa** and **Pharos** are accessible only on foot or by caïque.

Santorini (Thera)

Earthquakes and volcanic eruptions have made this island one of the most spectacular in all the Aegean. The biggest volcanic explosion, in 1500 BC, blew a great hole in the originally circular island and turned it into the crescent you see today. The central bay is the volcano's collapsed crater, a gigantic caldera 11 km (7 miles) long.

Sailing into the caldera is a memorable experience. Sheer cliffs exposing starkly etched volcanic layers rise over 300 m (1,000 ft) above the sea, and plunge an equal distance down beneath the waves. Two formidable black islets jut out in the middle of the bay, forced to the surface by modern eruptions, most recently in 1950 (an earthquake devastated the west coast six years later). The nearly deserted Thirasia, part of the original volcano, now blocks off most of the western horizon as you reach the port of Fira. The gleaming white buildings of the island's capital are strung out along the top of the dark cliffs like an ivory crown.

Fira and Ia

From the tiny landing stage, on foot or donkey-back, it is a long, sweaty climb up the 587 stone-paved, zigzagging steps to the top, but fortunately only a 2-

minute ride by cable-car. (You might like to take the donkey back down to the boat-excursions around the bay.)

Fira has been well rebuilt since the 1956 earthquake, and the boutiques, especially the jewellery shops, are often crowded with visiting cruise passengers. A small **museum** houses early Cycladic figurines, some Geometric and Archaic pottery and statuettes from the site of Ancient Thera (see p. 181). There are also some finds from the local Akrotiri excavations, kept here until the completion of a new museum down at the site.

Further up the coast, above its tiny fishing harbour, the clifftop village of Ia has done an exquisite job of rebuilding. Highly regarded for its hand-woven fabrics, it is a much quieter place in which to stay, or at least to visit for a grand café-terrace view of the sunset.

Interior

Much of the island is covered with layers of pumice and lava, over 40 m (140 ft) deep in places, but the plain sloping east away from the cliffs is unexpectedly green. Tomatoes and grapes thrive in the volcanic soil. Quiet inland villages like **Pirgos** make a pleasant change from the main tourist haunts. Set on a hillside, its cobbled streets, white houses and green-doored chapels cluster around an old Venetian fortress.

The best vantage point, overlooking the whole island, and with grand views south to Crete, is the summit of **Profitis Ilias** (566 m, 1,857 ft). Try to ignore the towering TV and radio antennae, and visit the **monastery** with its notable 15th-century icon of the prophet Elijah (*Ilias*), set to the right of the main church altar. A little **museum** displays icons, illuminated manuscripts and other

illustrations of monastic life (with explanations in English and German). If you have a taste for such things, you can peek at the ossuary of monks' bones. Others prefer the sweets and the *tsikoudiá* liqueur made from the island's grape leaves.

Akrotiri

The intensive excavations at the southwest end of the island are gradually revealing a remarkably intact city founded by settlers from Minoan Crete. Take a bus, bike, motor scooter or organized tour for a rare view of a momentous dig in progress.

Protected now under the archaeologists' vast corrugated iron roof, the site lay under a crust of volcanic pumice for 3,400 years. Buried by the 1500 BC eruption, and later ravaged by earthquakes, traces of the city first emerged in the 19th century during the mining of pumice as construction material for the Suez Canal. But proper excavations began only in 1967, and revealed a civilization as flourishing and accomplished as that found at Knossos in Crete. The works of art uncovered include the great frescoes presently on view in Athens' National Archaeological Museum, currently awaiting transfer back to a new museum on the island.

But as you take the signposted tour of the site, its major appeal is the vivid sense it gives of the town as a place that was once lived in: houses built of massive ashlar stone, many of them with walls still standing up to the third storey; fireplaces, handsome door and window frames, stone stairways, toilets and drainage pipes. Greek archaeologists wryly acknowledge that the system of winter heating is better than that

179

*A*s ancient Thera, the volcanic island of Santorini was an important bridgehead for the Minoan civilization of Crete during its commercial
and cultural conquest of the Aegean. Today, with its capital town at Fira on
the west coast (viewed here from the north end of its crescent-shaped bay),
Santorini challenges Mykonos for the position of most popular island in the
Cyclades.

found in most Greek houses today. Among the artefacts left in place are some massive millstones and, in the pantry of the tall House of the Ladies, some huge decorated storage vessels.

Ancient Thera

Without the benefit of a protective layer of volcanic deposits, the old hilltop capital of Thera is less easily imagined than the much more ancient Akrotiri, but the site remains evocative and is worth a visit. Let the local guides show you around.

Though some of the tombs are 600 years older, the ruins date mostly from the 3rd century BC, when it was a garrison town for the Ptolemies, the Macedonian rulers of Egypt. Beyond the Byzantine chapel of Agios Stefanos is the Artemidorus Shrine, erected in honour of the Ptolemaic admiral. (Following Alexander, many Macedonian leaders raised themselves to quasi-divine status.) As you tour the site, the guides delight in pointing out the sculpted relief of a phallus bearing the inscription: "To my friends".

Make your way up to the **Festival Terrace**, used as a dance-floor for the rites of Apollo, with a fine view over the southern tip of the island to Akrotiri. At the far south end of the site is the **Gymnasium**, adorned with interesting examples of ancient graffiti.

Beaches

You will quickly grow accustomed to the black volcanic sand and pebbles of Santorini's east coast beaches. The pebbles, when polished, make handsome substitutes for worry beads. Renowned for its good snorkelling, **Kamari** has a pebble beach at the foot of steep rocky cliffs. **Perissa** has the best sand and **Monolithos**, the least accessible by bus, is for that reason less crowded.

Ios

This island is known as Nio by the natives, who are outnumbered 14 to 1 by the hordes of 18 to 30 clubbers who descend each summer to enjoy the day-long, night-long parties on the beach, and in the bars, clubs and cafés. Ios was a hippy paradise in the sixties, and it has retained a reputation as a lively and laid-back playground for party animals. On a clear night, it is rumoured, you can hear Ios from Santorini.

After dancing the night away in the streets of the island capital, **Ios Town**, you can sleep until lunch time in the rented rooms and campsites around the west coast harbour of **Ormos Iou**, with its nearby Gialos beach. The big, beautiful, and very popular sandy beach of **Milopotamos** is a 30-minute walk down the coast; this is where the partying continues through the day. But there are beaches in nearly every cove, mostly accessible by boat—**Manganari Bay** at the southern end of the island, and the remoter **Agios Theodotis** on the east coast, are both good.

The closest the island gets to anything cultural is the claim of the 18th-century Dutch traveller Paasch von Krienen to have discovered Homer's grave in Plakotos Creek at the northern end of the island. But the grave dates from prehistoric times, well before Homer's day. The creek is a two-hour walk from the road, and is an attractive spot for swimming and picnicking. The island is also noted for its many beautiful chapels—nearly 400 of them in all.

*S*antorini, named after the Byzantine Saint Irene.

Thera or Santorini?

Greek place-names are never easy to get right, but Santorini is a case apart. The government, Olympic Airways and some, but by no means all, ferry-operators are gradually reverting to the use of the island's ancient name of *Thíra* (or Thera), which came from a Spartan colonizer of the 8th century BC. Thera is the name, too, of the ancient capital in the south of the island, while *Firá* or *Thíra* is the modern capital on the west coast. The name Santorini comes from the Byzantine Saint Irene.

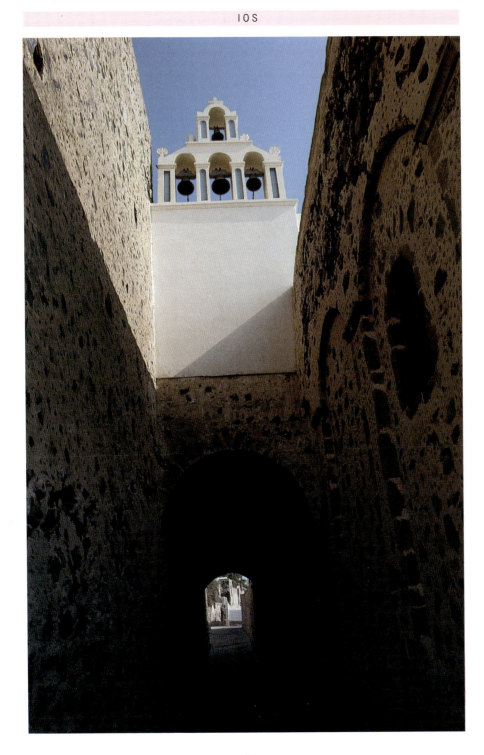

A Mountainous Stronghold Where Independent Islanders Resisted Centuries of Occupation

Crete is almost a country in itself. Sitting at a maritime cross-roads between the Middle East, North Africa, the Aegean and the western Mediterranean, its fertile slopes and balmy climate nurtured the Minoan civilization—the oldest in Europe—which produced the magnificent palaces of Knossos, and bequeathed to us the legend of the Labyrinth. Isolated at the southern edge of the Aegean, the island has long been a bastion of Greek patriotism, and endured centuries of conflict under foreign occupation before final union with Greece in 1913.

*M*alia, one of the many *beautiful beaches that place Crete among the most popular holiday destinations in Greece.*

As a holiday destination, this richly varied island is as self-contained as its people are self-assured. It is not unusual to hear the proud islanders refer to their beloved Crete as a "continent".

Nowhere is it easier to combine lazing on a beach with cultural enrichment, or to indulge yourself with the best of Greek seafood, cheese and wine, and then work them off with a bracing hike through the lovely meadows and mountains of the interior. So you may well be happy to spend your whole holiday on Crete, though good sea and air connections with Santorini, Paros or Mykonos enable you easily to get a taste of the very different Cyclades, too.

Crete rounds off the southern edge of the Aegean Sea. Its mountains are a continuation of the south-eastern sweep of the Taygetos range in the Peloponnese, the biggest of the stepping stones that

185

continue through Karpathos and Rhodes to the coast of Asia Minor. Don't be surprised to see subtropical flora—this island is closer to the equator than Tunis or Algiers. Libya is only 320 km (200 miles) from Crete's south coast.

Crete is a long, narrow island—250 km (155 miles) from west to east but only 60 km (37 miles) across at its widest point—divided lengthways by a series of mountain ranges: to the west, the Lefka or White Mountains, in the centre, the sacred peaks of Ida and Dikti. The population of more than half a million is concentrated mainly along the plains and gentler mountain slopes of the north coast, with only a sparse scattering of villages on the south coast where the mountains drop abruptly into the sea. As a result, most of the tourist facilities are clustered along the north coast, around Chania and Rethymnon, outside Iraklion (the capital), and in Agios Nikolaos, all linked by the island's only major highway. On the south coast, with Ierapetra the only substantial town, you will find secluded fishing villages like Paleochora and Chora Sfakion, and the developing resorts of Matala and Agia Galini.

Nature-lovers will be in their element on Crete. For amateur botanists, the island boasts some 130 unique species of plant life. Ask at the main tourist offices about guided botanical tours. In early spring, you will find orchids and listera, and fields of crocus and anemone; later, narcissus and wild tulips, and whole carpets of buttercup brighten the upland meadows of the Ida and White Mountains. Oleander blossom heralds the summer. Oranges, figs, apricots, almonds, pomegranates and olives—you can find all of them growing wild in the hills and valleys.

Bird-watchers come for the spring migration: egrets, golden orioles, kingfishers and falcons stop off on their way north. Eagles, buzzards, lammergeiers (bearded vultures), blue rock thrush and several species of owl are among the permanent residents.

Iraklion

With its busy airport only 4 km (2.5 miles) from the city, the island capital is a lively but also noisy centre of commerce and industry. Its population of 115,000 places it fifth in size among Greek cities, but first in terms of per capita income. Though it does not invite a prolonged stay, it certainly has plenty to offer for a brief visit: the Venetian legacy of harbour, castle and ramparts; the church of Agia Ekaterini with its great icons by Michaïl Damaskinos; above all, the Minoan treasures in the Archaeological Museum, second only to the National Museum in Athens. The best way to enjoy these attractions is to make excursions into the town from a coastal resort. Plan on one day for the museum and other cultural sights, and perhaps a second day to shop for jewellery and ceramics, or visit the market to make up a picnic for the mountains.

T he impressive Venetian battlements of Rocca al Mare were built to defend the harbour at Iraklion, once the site of a major 17th-century Venetian shipbuilding yard.

The fellows you may see wearing traditional Cretan costume—black scarf around the head, blouse and cummerbund over breeches tucked into knee-high boots—are the real thing, not a tourist-office gimmick.

The Town

The city centre's charm has not been enhanced by centuries of earthquakes (the last major one in 1926), World War II bombardment, and unimaginative modern buildings in reinforced concrete. So start out at the **port**.

The new outer harbour bustles with ferries and freighters, while the inner Venetian harbour is reserved for fishing boats, yachts and caïques. Towering above, out on the jetty, is the grand **Venetian Fort** (Rocca al Mare to the Italians, Koules to the Turks). Built between 1523 and 1549, its massive, buff stone walls provided the main bul-

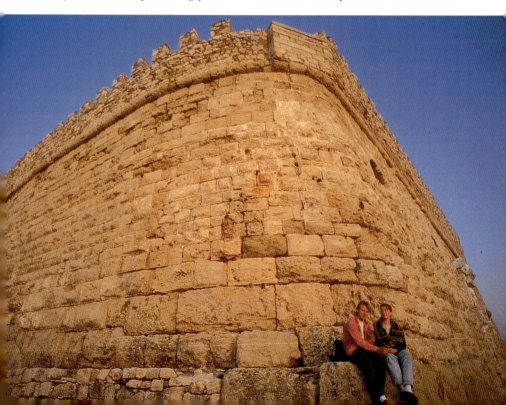

wark of the Venetians' heroic resistance to the Turks' prolonged 17th-century assault. Climb up to the battlements for a fine view over the harbour and the Aegean.

Emblazoned on a fortress wall facing the sea is the best preserved of three sculptured lions of St Mark, the proud emblem of Venice. On the quay across the street from the harbour authority are the lofty arcades and storerooms of the 16th-century **Arsenali**, where ships were repaired and fitted out for battle on the high seas.

From behind the harbour bus station, the well-preserved Venetian ramparts run south past a pleasant public park to the **Martinengo Bastion**, the burial place of Crete's great novelist Nikos Kazantzakis (1885–1957). Born in Iraklion, the author of *Zorba the Greek and The Last Temptation of Christ* wrote his own epitaph for the gravestone: "I hope for nothing. I fear nothing. I am free."

The busy **Platia Venizelou** (Venizelos Square) is a good place to shop for souvenirs, or linger over a newspaper at one of the many cafés. In the centre, four lions support the ornate **Morosini Fountain** (1628), named after a former Venetian governor, father of the man who blew up the Parthenon in Athens (see p. 65).

The Turks destroyed the fountain's Neptune statue, but nymphs, bulls, dolphins and musicians still frolic around the bas-reliefs on the basins. Walk north along Odos 25 Avgoustou towards the church of Agios Titos, dedicated to the island's patron saint, a disciple of the apostle Paul. His skull is kept in the church reliquary.

Down on the other side of Odos 25 Avgoustou, kids (and their parents!) are given the chance to relax at the children's playground in **El Greco Park**.

Moving away from the harbour at Platia Venizelou, take the main shopping thoroughfare of Leoforos Kalokerinou towards the three churches on Platia Agias Ekaterinis. On the west side of the square, the 19th-century cathedral and the charming little church next to it are both dedicated to St Minas. However, the main attraction is the 16th-century Agía Ekateríni, the **church of St Catherine**. Linked to St Catherine's desert monastery at Mount Sinai, the church and its seminary provided a haven for artists and theologians fleeing the Turks in Constantinople. The church is now a museum, with six icons painted by Michaïl Damaskinos, a true master of the genre. Profiting from five years in Venice (1577–1582), the painter infused his traditional Byzantine art with the Venetian school's renowned energy and bold use of colour. In the central nave you will find his Adoration of the Magi; The Last Supper; The Virgin with Moses' Burning Bush; Christ with the Holy Women; Constantine with the Bishops; and Christ Celebrating Mass with the Angels.

The **Central Market**—and, logically enough, the city's best restaurants—are located on and around Odos 1866. Here you will find stalls of fruit and vegetables, exotic spices, and the island's delicious honey and fresh yoghurt, succeeded by meat and fish stalls of astonishing variety.

At the top of the market street, on Platia Kornarou, take a rest at the café whose centrepiece is a kiosk formed from an old Turkish fountain. Behind is the 16th-century **Bembo Fountain** with its headless Roman statue.

A Long and Bitter Struggle Towards Freedom

Following the brilliant Minoan civilization's period of Aegean domination (see p. 47), invasion and earthquake removed Crete from Greek history's centre stage. Some coastal dwellers migrated into remote mountain refuges, while others embarked on an overseas exodus that took them as far as Palestine, where the Israelites referred to them as Philistines. The island stayed out of the Persian and Peloponnesian Wars, but attracted Alexander's attention as a source of brave and energetic mercenaries.

The Romans made the inland city of Gortys their provincial capital. In AD 59, Paul the Apostle arrived with his disciple Titus, Crete's first bishop, and was most unkind.

"One of themselves," he noted, "even a prophet of their own, said: 'The Cretans are always liars, evil beasts, slow bellies.' This witness is true."

But the Byzantine Empire found the Cretans to be enthusiastic supporters, remaining loyal to the Orthodox Church throughout the Arab occupation of the island from 824 to 961. The Arabs systematically destroyed the churches, and turned the island into a pirate base and one of the Mediterranean's major slave markets. Their fortified capital was at Rabd-el-Kandek (Candia, now Iraklion). While recapturing the island, the Byzantine general was no more tender-hearted than his foes. To impress the Arabs holding out in the fort, he catapulted his prisoners' severed heads over the wall.

When Byzantium fell to the Crusaders, Crete was given to Boniface of Montferrat who sold it for cash—1,000 silver marks—to Venice. Crete thrived during the 465 years of Venetian occupation (1204–1669). The ports and fortifications of Chania, Rethymnon and Iraklion bear witness to the Venetians' ambitious public building programme. Crete became a refuge for Byzantine artists fleeing the Turkish conquest of Constantinople in 1453. In the 16th century, one of the most accomplished of Greek icon-painters, Michaïl Damaskinos, combined Byzantine convention with a more audacious technique he had studied in Venice. Another local boy, Dominikos Theotokopoulos, began as an icon-painter, before leaving for Italy, and eventually Spain, to make his name as El Greco.

The Turks waged a titanic struggle to wrest Crete from the Venetians. The latter had strengthened the fortifications of what they saw as the last Christian bastion against Turkey's advance on the western Mediterranean. But Chania and Rethymnon fell in 1645. Three years later, the Turks began an assault and siege of the capital, Candia, that was to last 21 years. After the first 15 years, the Turkish commander, Hussein Pasha, was summoned back to Constantinople and publicly strangled for his failure to take the city. In the end, Candia's capture cost the lives of 30,000 Venetians and 118,000 Turks. As the conquerors entered the city gates, the Venetians fled with the relics of St Titus, the island's patron saint (which were returned only in 1966).

Turkish rule (1669–1898) was a period of cultural and economic stagnation. The darkness was broken only by outbursts of revolt, culminating in the 19th-century struggle for union with Greece (énosis). Violent insurrection provoked equally ferocious massacres in retaliation. In 1898, Britain, France, Russia and Italy forced the Turks to grant the island autonomy within the Ottoman Empire. But it was only in 1913, under the leadership of its great statesman, Eleftherios Venizelos, that énosis was achieved, with a final Turkish evacuation of the island ten years later.

But Crete's suffering was not at an end. In 1941, the retreating Allies staged a desperate effort to fight off German bombardments that devastated the island. With a centuries-old tradition of resistance to foreign invaders, the Cretans maintained constant guerrilla warfare to make the German occupation costly and uncomfortable.

189

If the fountain makes you long for a swim, the closest beach is the popular Karteros (Florida Beach) out at Amnissos, convenient but noisy—it's too near the airport for comfort. Better to head out to one of the resorts.

Archaeological Museum

Many people prefer to tour an archaeological site before visiting the museum displaying its excavated artworks. However, in the case of Knossos, Phaistos, Agia Triada and Crete's other Minoan sites, you will more easily appreciate their significance if you first visit Iraklion's magnificent Archaeological Museum (off the noisy Platia Eleftherias opposite the tourist office). The elegance and vitality of Cretan culture in the days of King Minos will seem more real after you have seen the beautifully exhibited Minoan treasures, along with the scale-models of what the palaces probably looked in their heyday. In fact, for a complete appreciation of the sites, you might like to make a quick preliminary tour of the museum on your first day, and then a second, more leisurely tour at the end of your stay, having visited the excavations in between.

More concerned with resisting earthquakes than appealing to the eye, the museum building is an uninspired concrete blockhouse. But its collection of Minoan art is the most complete in the world—Athens has nothing to match it. Here are the highlights:

Gallery 1: ceramics, figurines, jewellery and weapons from the first 3,000 years of Cretan settlement (5000–2000 BC) until the period immediately before the building of the first palaces.

Gallery 2: works from the early palaces (1900–1700 BC); look for the **town mosaics**, small earthenware plaques from Knossos bearing models of Minoan houses of up to three storeys—similar to those you can see at Akrotiri on the island of Santorini (see p. 178).

Gallery 3: also from the period of the early palaces is the famous **Phaistos Disk** from the south Cretan palace. The clay disk, 16 cm in diameter, is covered on both sides with an as yet undeciphered hieroglyphic inscription spiralling into the centre. Its 241 miniature figures include vases, animals, birds, fish, insects and ships, as well as men, women and children. What may have been a religious hymn or magical incantation can now be seen reproduced in souvenir shops as earrings, key chains or cocktail coasters.

The ceramics include red-and-white patterned Kamares vases and the first eggshell ware from Knossos, so called because of its exceptional thinness.

Gallery 4: from Knossos's golden "Neopalatial" age (1700–1450 BC), two polychrome faïence figures of **snake goddesses** or priestesses, perhaps mother and daughter. As was the Minoan fashion, the dresses leave the breasts bare. Snakes coil around mother's tiara, breasts and waist, while daughter has a small leopard on her cap and brandishes a snake in each hand.

The ivory statue of a **bull-leaping acrobat** shows him in full flight, performing a dangerous athletic ritual involving a bull, the central figure of Minoan culture. The bull, symbol of virility, is represented also in the striking black serpentine **Bull's Head Chalice**, or rhyton, used for sacred libations. The gilded wooden horns have been reconstructed from a sketch, but the eyes and nose are formed by original encrustations of rock crystal, jasper and mother-of-pearl.

Gallery 7: also Neopalatial. The stone vases from Agia Triada are remarkable for their vivid carving. The tall **Boxer Vase** of dark green serpentine is decorated with four scenes depicting boxers wearing helmets, and a bull-leaper. The **Chieftain Cup** shows a chief receiving a gift of animal hides from a hunt or sacrifice. Liveliest of all is the **Harvester Vase**, shaped like an ostrich egg, which has a rustic scene of peasants laughing and singing behind a priest and musicians in a ritual harvest procession.

Gallery 14: the **Hall of Frescoes**, among the most significant of which is the series decorating the **Sarcophagus of Agia Triada**, cut from a single limestone block. One side shows, to the right, a funeral procession in which an image of the deceased receives offerings of calves and a model boat, probably for his voyage to the Land of the Dead; to the left, women perform a purification rite between two pillars topped by the sacred Minoan double-headed axe, while a musician plays the lyre. Along the opposite side is a bull-sacrifice performed by women, accompanied by a flute player. At each end, in poorer condition, are scenes of goddesses with chariots.

From the frescoes found at Knossos, a priestess or goddess has been nicknamed by archaeologists La Parisienne, no doubt because of her elaborate coiffure, big eyes and sensual red mouth. More demure are the pretty Ladies in Blue. The delicate Prince of the Lilies with peacock feathers in his hat does not look as if he would do very well in the bull-leaping depicted in the Toreador Fresco. Whereas men are shown suntanned, women, who also participated in this rough, tough sport, dressed in male attire, apparently kept their complexion milky white.

Historical Museum

On the other side of town, across from the Xenia Hotel, the Historical Museum continues the story of Crete beyond the Minoan civilization. The collections include Early Christian sculpture from Gortys; Byzantine icons, frescoes and bronze liturgical instruments; sculpture from the 17th-century Venetian loggia, and the coat of arms of a Venetian Jewish family with a motto in Hebrew; Turkish tombstones; a typical Cretan peasant dwelling, with traditional costumes and fabrics; and a reconstruction of the novelist Kazantzakis' study, with his desk, library, photographs and personal memorabilia.

Central Crete

In the valleys between the Ida and Lasithi mountains, the Minoan nobility built their earliest road, linking their summer residence at Knossos with winter homes at Phaistos and Agia Triada. Roughly the same route is followed today to the island's principal archaeological sites, including the old Roman capital of Gortys—and beyond to the seaside resorts on the south coast.

Knossos needs a full day to itself. The others can be comfortably combined in one excursion (tourist agencies run guided tours), with the bonus of a swim at Matala or Agia Galini at the end of the day.

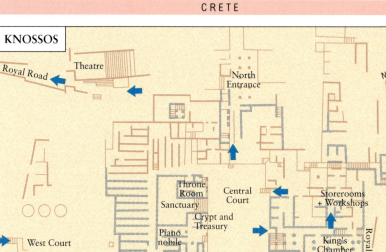

KNOSSOS

Royal Road
Theatre
North Entrance
N

Throne Room
Sanctuary
Central Court
Storerooms + Workshops
Crypt and Treasury
Piano nobile
West Court
King's Chamber
Queen's Chamber
Royal Chambers
Corridor of Processions
South Propylaeum

0   50 m
0   50 yards

Knossos

Just 5 km (3 miles) south of Iraklion, you enter the excavated palace of King Minos through an arcade of magenta bougainvillaea blossom. There on the **West Court** is a bronze bust of Sir Arthur Evans, the man who uncovered and reconstructed—some say excessively—the Minoan world of Knossos. On the left of the court are three well-like walled pits that in fact served as sunken granaries. Notice how the stone blocks of the palace's western façade are blackened by the fire that destroyed it, probably following an earthquake around 1500 BC.

Within minutes, tourists entering the palace precincts arrive at a conclusion that students of antiquity took years to reach. The palace of Knossos is itself laid out like the labyrinth in which King Minos is supposed to have imprisoned the Minotaur. Broad corridors, narrow zigzagging passages, stairways with L-shaped, T-shaped and X-shaped landings, leading up and down and in and out of courtyards and vestibules among the palace's approximately 1,200 rooms. Just when you think you have got to the heart of the palace, the great central court, the corridor deviates away from it. Once you have arrived, you will find that a stairway leading out will just double back, and you will swear that you can hear the ghost of Minos snicker in the shadows. Various theories have suggested that the intricate layout was a deliberate plan to foil invading enemies or evil spirits. Some gloomy scholars have suggested that Knossos was not a palace at all, but a giant mausoleum like the Egyptian pyramids, in which following the complicated pattern was part of a sacred ritual. Or perhaps the maze is simply a natural result of the Minoans' sense of play, so wonderfully depicted in their art.

Adopting the last theory as the most attractive, the game, then, is to get to the central court. It can be done. Leaving Sir Arthur behind you, turn right to the south and take the **Corridor of Processions**. The frescoes here, like others on the site, are "recreations" by the Gilliérons, a Swiss father and son, of originals preserved in Iraklion's Archaeological Museum. Some feel that the paintings, like Evans' reconstructions of columns and other masonry, have been overdone and detract from the ancient palace's mystery. But they do serve to clarify the functions and settings of what would otherwise be rather anonymous, unadorned stones. Here, two curly-haired, dark-skinned Minoans in loin cloths are shown carrying vessels towards the centre of the palace.

Turn left (east) towards the columned vestibule of the **South Propylaeum**. Note the characteristic downward taper of the reconstructed columns. A grand staircase leads north up to what Evans called the **piano nobile**, borrowing a term from the Italian Renaissance for the lofty reception rooms of the upper storey. A balcony here gives you your first view of the central court.

The earthquake has left several paths down, but we suggest continuing north via the palace's **Sanctuary**. In keeping with the intimate, human scale of their lives, the Minoans did not have monumental temples for their worship but preferred the small shrines and chapels

you can see here. Immediately north (to the left) of a stairway leading into the central court is the entrance, via an antechamber with a marble basin, to the **Throne Room**. Frescoes of griffins guard a small gypsum throne, probably not the royal seat of Minos but the ritual chair of the high priestess known as the Lady of the Labyrinth. In front is a sunken area for purification rites. On the other side of the sanctuary's staircase is a columned **crypt and treasury** where various cult objects were excavated, including the snake-goddesses now in Iraklion's museum. It is believed that the sacred snakes had their home here.

Time now to stroll around the grand **Central Court**, 53 m (174 ft) long and 26.5 m (87 ft) wide, and imagine the scenes witnessed here 4,000 years ago. This is where the Minoans held the athletic contests and bull-leaping rituals so vividly depicted in the frescoes and sculpture. Picture the buildings surrounding the court topped by symbolic bull-horns. Tiers of spectators gather in open-air galleries supported on blood-red, gold-banded columns. Festive throngs of women spectators fan themselves with white ostrich plumes, their doe-eyes outlined and shadowed with green malachite, their reddened lips highlighted against white face paint. In their elaborately curled hair, jewels and pendants sparkle in the sunlight. Long, brightly coloured dresses conceal their legs but leave their breasts bare. The Minoan men are relaxed and casual— not stiff and formal like the later Greeks—their coiffures equally elaborate, their eyes also accentuated by make-up. Deeply tanned, their lithe, muscular bodies are covered only by loincloths with tasselled codpieces.

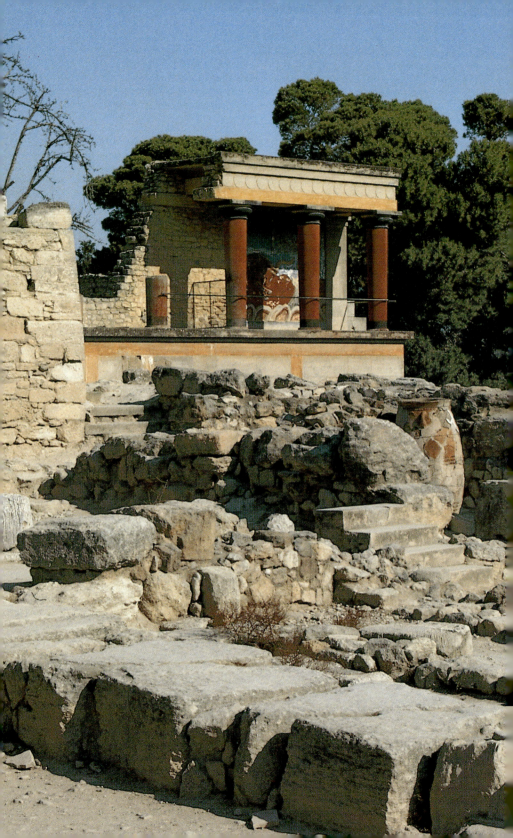

*B*efore the onslaught of earthquakes and Dorian invaders around 1400 BC, life at the Palace of Knossos was comfortable. Energy was devoted to sport, not warfare, and the good things of life–especially food and wine–were plentiful.

Music spills across the courtyard to accompany the dancers and cartwheeling acrobats. Leather-helmeted boxers fight in the blazing sun. Fans toss flowers into the ring for the victor.

A hush falls over the spectators. Across the courtyard, the doors of the sanctuary open and a wide-eyed priestess emerges with writhing snakes in each hand. She intones an incantation, a blessing for the day's main event: the bull-leaping. The priestess withdraws, and athletes enter the arena with the first bull. The nervous creature is steadied by two female athletes standing at the head and tail. Hoisting himself up by grasping the bull's horns, the first acrobat leaps headlong over the beast's back and then propels himself off its haunches for a final somersault onto the ground. The crowd roars its appreciation as one after another lands on his feet. Then, suddenly, a chorus of gasps as the bull balks and tosses his head and an acrobat is impaled on his horns, a terrible, but honourable death. Others triumph, others are sacrificed. The bulls themselves are sacrificed. Later, by torchlight, the divine beasts are roasted for the evening feast, honouring the quick and the dead.

On the east side of the court, opposite the sanctuary, a staircase leads down to what Evans identified as the **Royal Chambers**. These are the palace's best-preserved rooms. Set into the slope of the hill, the quarters were built on four floors, two above and two below the level of the central court. Lighting was channelled down to rooms on lower floors through an ingenious system of spacious light-wells.

Shields in figure-eight shape and signs of the Minoan double axe mark the walls of what was probably the guardroom adjacent to the **King's Chamber**, where Evans found a wooden throne. A narrow passage leads across to the **Queen's Chamber**, decorated with a lively fresco of dolphins and flying fish. Next to it is a room with a clay bathtub, but scholars now feel this was the queen's bedroom, the bathroom probably being located down a dark spiral-frescoed corridor next to her dressing room. The toilet was originally equipped with a wooden seat and a still-visible flushing system much admired by modern plumbers.

North of the royal quarters are the **Storerooms and Workshops** of the palace's tailors, goldsmiths, potters and stone-masons. Notice the enormous earthenware jars (*pithoi*) for storing grain, honey, oil and wine, and big enough for a man to hide in—or drown in, as Minos's son Glaucus found out to his cost when trying to help himself to some honey.

Leave the main palace-grounds through the **North Entrance**. Northwest of the palace is a **theatre** seating some 500 spectators, used for ritual dances and perhaps boxing and wrestling matches. Leading away from it, probably to link up with a main road to Knossos's port at Katsambas, is an impressively well-built **Royal Road** with rain gutters running along the central paving. Imagine the road bordered

*T*he decorative arts of the Minoans extended even to mundane storage containers like these giant pithoi.

with two- and three-storey houses like those depicted in the Town Mosaics in Iraklion's museum (see p. 190).

Gortys

Make an early start if you are combining this old Roman capital with Phaistos and Agia Triada in one excursion, a round trip of 160 km (100 miles) from Iraklion if you include a swim at Matala. Leave Iraklion from the western gate (Chanióporta).

The well-marked road passes through valleys of olive groves, cypresses and vineyards—the town of Daphnes produces some of the island's best wine. The landscape is dotted with rock outcrops and small rounds of rock known locally as "wheels of cheese". After the Pass of Vourvouliti, the rich farmland of the Plain of Messara opens up before you, with the Asterousia mountain to the south-east and the Libyan Sea gleaming in the distance. In spring, nature-lovers will be so entranced by the display of wild flowers here that they may never get to Gortys. In the village of **Agia Deka**—"Ten Saints"—the 13th-century church is built in part with fragments of Gortys's Roman ruins.

The **archaeological site** of Gortys is scattered over a large area. The Italian excavators have chosen not to try the kind of imaginative reconstruction carried out by Evans at Knossos, so the columns and statues of the capital established on an ancient Dorian settlement by the Romans in 67 BC now lie scattered amid a charming wilderness of trees and flowers. The site's major find, near the Roman Odeon, dates from around 500 BC, when Dorian settlers carved their Code of Laws on massive blocks of stone. In 17,000 characters, in rows to be read alternately from left to right and right to left, the code lays down the laws for adultery, seduction, rape, divorce, inheritance, property mortgage and the treatment of slaves. You can also see the Praetorium, residence of the Roman governor, built of marble- and stone-faced concrete. There is a Temple of Isis and Serapis, Egyptian gods that were popular with the Romans. The Temple of Apollo has an interesting pyramidal altar.

From the post-Roman city, a centre of early Christianity, you can see the shell of the 7th-century basilica of **Agios Titos**, built in the form of a Greek cross and destroyed by Arab invaders in the 9th century.

Phaistos

Of all the Minoan sites in Crete, the kings' winter palace and retreat of the priesthood at Phaistos enjoys the most enchanting setting. From the ruins, it commands a magnificent view over the long sweep of Messara, flecked with olive groves and vineyards, to the Libyan Sea. It is framed by Zeus's childhood playgrounds, Mount Dikti and Mount Ida, still snow-capped in spring.

The palace was built and abandoned at the same time as Knossos. It was excavated by Italian archaeologists and, like Gortys, has not undergone Knossos's elaborate modern reconstruction of brightly painted columns and frescoes. As a result, the site's pristine ruins, resurrected but bearing all the marks of time and the elements, evoke more readily the palace-sanctuary's mystic qualities. Cretan monarchs, remember, were both king and priest.

Phaistos has the same labyrinthine layout of corridors and stairways as Knossos, with a similar central court,

but all on a less massive scale. Start from a stairway down from the **North Court**, leaving on your right, outside the main palace grounds, a **theatre** with an elongated narrowing shape like a grand piano, and similar to the one at Knossos.

Another, grander staircase leads left up to the **Propylaeum**, the monumental entrance to the palace proper. Left again, and across a hall where you can see the bases of its peristyle colonnade, are the **Royal Chambers**. What was probably the queen's suite has retained its alabaster paving. East of the royal quarters are commoners' dwellings where the Phaistos Disk was found. From the queen's rooms, a small courtyard and corridor lead back south to the long **Central Court**. It had porticoes along its east and west sides. Most of the eastern part of the court has collapsed down the hill-side, but the column bases of the western portico are all still visible. Walk to the far end to see the **well** and then double back past what was the **Sanctuary** where you will see a two-pillared crypt and a hall with stone benches around its walls. Beyond the sanctuary, turn left down the **Corridor of Storehouses and Workshops** used for metal smelting and pottery. The last house on the right has some huge earthenware **storage jars** (*pithoi*) that were used to hold oil or wine—a receptacle is set in the ground to catch spillage. Notice the jars' many handles through which ropes were passed to haul the gigantic vessels around.

The palace originally covered far more ground, probably including a Minoan village. Now farms and houses stand over the area where Minoan structures are suspected to lie.

Agia Triada

The Minoan **Royal Villa**, with a later Mycenaean-age village below it, is a 45-minute walk or 3-km drive from the palace of Phaistos. Its Minoan name remains a mystery, so it is known by that of a nearby Venetian church (not to be confused with the 14th-century Byzantine church of Agios Georgios directly above the excavations).

Scholars have suggested that the site was the residence of the king's relatives, or a summer hideaway for the king himself. With a splendid view out over Messara Bay, the villa is spacious but more intimate than the palaces, without a central court or monumental staircases. Its elegance is hinted at by fine alabaster paving.

It was here that Italian archaeologists unearthed, among several of the most valuable examples of everyday Minoan objects, the great stone vases with their Boxer, Chieftain and Harvester motifs now on display in the Iraklion museum.

Of the later town (14th–12th century BC), you can see the main square (*agora*) bordered by what were originally arcades of shops.

Beaches

Exploring archaeological sites can be hot and sticky work—after all that hiking you may feel that you deserve a good swim. The expanding resort of **Matala** offers a refreshing, though sometimes crowded, bathe in the Libyan Sea just 10 km (6 miles) south of Phaistos. The beach has fine, white sand and the sea is green and gentle. You may also want to visit the famous **Matala caves** (Spiliés Matálon). They have had a varied history. Originally hewn out of the cliff by the Romans for use as cata-combs, they were subsequently inhabited by early Christians. After the Germans set up artillery positions there in World War II, peace and love prevailed once more when hippie troglodytes moved in in the 1960s.

Agia Galini, 18 km (11 miles) northwest of Phaistos, is a booming tourist resort. A steep, winding road leads down to the resort, situated in a narrow crevice between high cliffs. Camping facilities are available, and it offers good fishing and excellent seafood restaurants.

Eastern Crete

Moving away from the centre of the ancient Minoan civilization, the island's attractions for the foreign visitor are more straightforwardly hedonistic. You will find first-rate beach resorts along the north-east coast—the tourist industry has dubbed the winding corniche coast road the "Cretan Riviera".

Barely an hour's drive east of Iraklion airport, Agios Nikolaos is the main resort, but there are smaller, less-crowded spots on either side. Inland, you can explore caves, hike in the Lasithi mountains, and shop for local handicrafts in the villages. The south coast's main town, Ierapetra, is becoming increasingly popular as a resort. Indefatigable archaeology buffs can visit the Minoan village of Gournia and the palaces of Malia and Kato Zakros.

Agios Nikolaos

Nestling at the heart of the splendid bay of Mirabello, this undoubtedly beautiful resort fights gamely to maintain its natural charm against the onslaught of the

package tour. The climate is dry and sunny, the winters mild, and the sports facilities excellent.

You must avoid July and August if you want to enjoy the relaxed atmosphere of the fishing harbour. Elegant boutiques border the town's main (but short) street, Leoforos Koundourou, climbing from the harbour to the traffic circle of Platia Venizelos.

A man-made channel connects the harbour to **Lake Voulismeni**, once reputed to be bottomless, but in fact 64 m (210 ft) deep, still deep enough to worry anyone casually dropping in. From its landward cliff, which has an aviary, you get a great view of lake and harbour. A *vólta* or evening promenade along the lake's quayside—the equivalent of the Italians' *passeggiata*—is a local institution.

Away from the lake on Odos Paleologou is the **Archaeological Museum**. It

T he harbour at Agios Nikolaos, one of the most popular resorts on Crete.

boasts an admirable collection of Minoan ceramics and gold jewellery from the regional sites. Most notable are the so-called "teapot" and "frying pan" vases, and a distinctive libation vase with two orifices, known as the Goddess of Myrtos.

The **beaches** lie north of the harbour. Further along, the smarter hotels hiding among bougainvillaea, olive and palm trees command a lovely rocky promontory. Occasional international exhibitions of modern art are held at the Minos Beach.

These graceful windmills on the Lasithi Plains should be known as wind pumps. Their sails draw subterranean water to the surface to irrigate the fields of cereals, potatoes, and apple orchards. This upland plateau in the Dikti mountains, remote and difficult of access, made an ideal redoubt through the centuries for rebels fighting Turkish, Venetian and German invaders.

Mirabello Bay

The best way to explore this loveliest of Cretan bays is on a boat excursion from Agios Nikolaos; alternatively, take a tortuous drive along the spectacular coast road. **Elounda** is a charming little fishing village on the bay's western shore. On the adjacent Spinalonga peninsula is **Olous**, a Greco-Roman settlement that is mostly submerged, making a fascinating target for scuba divers. On dry land an Early Christian church has been excavated to reveal a 4th-century dolphin mosaic. The nearby island of **Spinalonga** has an impressive 16th-century Venetian fort that was captured by the Turks and used briefly at the beginning of this century as a leper colony (no health risk today).

On the east side of the bay, you will see the ruins of Minoan settlements on the tiny islands of **Psira** and **Mochlos**, the latter opposite a very pleasant resort village of the same name.

Commanding a fine natural harbour, **Gournia**, 18 km (11 miles) from Agios Nikolaos, is the island's best preserved Minoan town. Excavated by the American archaeologist Harriet Boyd Hawes, it reveals a clear ground plan of multi-storey houses and shops around an Agora leading to the palace. The construction of modern Cretan villages is not so very different from the designs of 3,000 years ago.

Lasithi Plains

This fertile plateau some 850 m (2,800 ft) up in the **Dikti** mountains offers pleasant excursions from Agios Nikolaos. The plains are dotted with orchards of apple and almond trees, and a few remaining white-sailed windmills drive the irrigation system where they have not yet been replaced by oil-powered pumps.

Perched on a mountainside 12 km (7.5 miles) from Agios Nikolaos, the almost excruciatingly picturesque town of **Kritsa** is celebrated for its weaving. Along the steeply sloping streets, villagers sit in their doorways selling their shawls, rugs and table-linen.

In an olive grove on the edge of the village, the small white church of the **Most Holy Virgin** (Panagiá Kerá) is a treasury of 14th- and 15th-century frescoes that are among the most beautiful in Crete. The dome is decorated with four scenes from the gospel: The Presentation of Jesus at the Temple; The Baptism; The Resurrection of Lazarus; and Christ's Entry into Jerusalem. On the vault of the nave you can see The Last Supper. Frescoes in the south aisle depict scenes from the life of the Virgin and her mother Anna, while those of the north aisle show the rivers and gardens of Paradise, St Peter at the gate, and Abraham, Isaac and Jacob beside the enthroned Virgin.

If your car can take the rough road, follow the signs below Kritsa leading up to **Lato**, a Doric settlement founded in the 7th century BC Its spectacular site up in the mountains overlooking the Aegean is in any case worth a 45-minute walk. Students of antiquity will be interested to identify the city gate at the western end of the site, the agora in the centre, and a temple and theatre to the east. Others will be content to sit among the olive and almond groves and dream antique dreams.

Take your best walking shoes and a pocket torch for your visit to the **Diktaean Cave** (Diktéon Ántron). The entrance to Zeus's old home, beyond the village of Psychro 75 km (47 miles) from Agios Nikolaos, is a steep and tricky descent and the cave is damp, slippery and dimly lit—just the way caves should be. There are some impressive stalactites. Bronze votive offerings and stone altars found here, and now in Iraklion's museum, revealed that the cave was a sanctuary during the Minoan era. (Note—the cave is currently closed to the public because archaeological excavations are in progress.)

Malia and Limin Chersonisos

These resorts owe their popularity to their long sandy beaches, among the finest in Crete, a wide range of accommodation and easy access to Minoan sites on or near the north coast.

The **Minoan palace** on the eastern outskirts of Malia dates from the same era as Knossos and Phaistos. The French excavators did little restoration, and you can ramble around the evocative ruins while enjoying a superb view over the sea. Next to the ceremonial staircase just off the south-west corner of the Central Court is a remarkable circular **kernos** or ritual table. Set in the limestone slab are 34 small depressions around a central hollow. One theory is that fruit seeds or grain were placed in the limestone hollows as offerings for a good harvest. Another suggests it was used for gambling, similar to some board games found in Africa.

A short walk north of the palace is the **Chrysolakos** (pit of gold), a royal burial chamber where clay idols and an

H igh mountains rise above the Lasithi Plains, themselves already 850 m (2,800 ft) above sea level. An easy day trip from Agios Nikolaos, the plains offer pleasant walks and the opportunity to visit the town of Kritsa and the Diktaean Cave.

winter when the crowds have gone. It has a good beach, and a **Venetian fort** dating back to the 13th century adds character to the fishing harbour. A Turkish fountain and minaret still stand in the town centre. In summer, boats go out to the little island of **Chrysi** for a quiet swim and a meal in the taverna.

East Coast

The drive from Agios Nikolaos to the eastern end of the island winds along a mountain road with plunging views over the sea. This is the corniche they call the Cretan Riviera. Between orchards and olive groves, it passes white villages perched precariously on steep slopes, ready to topple into the ravine at the first hint of an earthquake. This was the frequent fate of **Sitia**, a Venetian port much plundered by Turkish pirates and now an attractive port of call for boats from Rhodes and Santorini. The beaches are good and the restaurants very good. Visit the **Archaeological Museum** if you plan to visit the Minoan palace of Kato Zakros; its exhibits include many of the most recent finds from the site.

East of Sitia, a short, rough road after a turn-off leads to the 14th-century **Toplou Monastery**. Its icon, Lord, Thou Art Great (1770) by Ioannis Kornaros, is a hallowed masterpiece of Byzantine art.

exquisite gold honey-bee pendant were found, now deposited in Iraklion's Archaeological Museum.

Ierapetra

East of Gournia, the road cuts across the island at its narrowest point, just 14 km (9 miles) wide, to a resort proclaimed as Europe's southernmost town. Certainly it is the only large town on Crete's south coast, and its mild climate and year-round fresh fruit and vegetables make it an attractive spot, even (or especially) in

Further north, cool off after your strenuous mountain drive with a dip in the sea at the fine sandy beach of Vai. The name means "palm" in Greek—the (very popular) beach is surrounded by groves of palm trees said to have grown from date stones spat out by Arab invaders.

At the far eastern end of the island is the fourth of the great Minoan palaces: **Kato Zakros**. The road crosses a high plateau with views across a vast gorge and Karoubes Bay before winding down through banana plantations to the sea, and a delightful little beach with pleasant tavernas. The **Minoan palace** was enriched by its flourishing port trade with Egypt and the Middle East. Its ceramics and stone vases, and ivory and bronze artefacts (now displayed in Iraklion and Sitia) are among the finest found in Crete. The palace layout is similar to those at Knossos, Phaistos and Malia, but with the rare distinction of a well-defined kitchen area north of the Central Court. Climb up to the ancient town above the palace for a good view over the whole site.

Western Crete

This quieter end of the island affords a great opportunity to explore small inland villages, sleepy fishing ports and the secluded beaches of the south-west coast. But in Rethymnon and Chania it also has two popular resorts with good water sports facilities and colourful reminders of the Venetian and Turkish past. Ramblers with a taste for the great outdoors can head for Zeus's cave on Mount Ida, and the Samaria and Imbros gorges in the White Mountains.

Rethymnon

The town's well-established tourist facilities are now being enhanced by a steady programme of restoration in the attractive old Venetian and Turkish quarters of the town.

Down on the seafront a long sandy beach curves lazily around the bay. The Venizelou promenade is lined with outdoor cafés, restaurants and shops, the natural venue for Rethymnon's evening stroll, the *vólta*.

But to enjoy the historic ambience of the old town, park your car by the public gardens (scene of the July Wine Festival) and pass under the arched Venetian gateway, **Porta Cuora**, to enter the narrow streets meandering down to the harbour. Shops installed in the old houses offer an enchanting combination of Venetian façades with overhanging Turkish wooden balconies. A minaret and domes have turned the church of Santa Maria into the **Mosque of Neranzies** (Djamí ton Neranzíon). You get a fine view of the city from the balcony where the muezzin once called the faithful to prayer. Nearby, the lion-headed **Arimondi Fountain** is the strange product of a similar involuntary collaboration between Venetian and Turkish craftsmen.

The town's small **Archaeological Museum**, housed in a 16th-century Venetian loggia, displays prehistoric clay sarcophagi, stone and clay figurines, bone and obsidian tools, Bronze Age jewellery, and ritual artefacts from Zeus's Idaian Cave (see p. 205).

Dominating the town's western promontory is the imposing Venetian **Fortetza** (1574), reached by an ancient stairway from Odos Melissinou. The outer wall, worth the visit for its fine view over the harbour, once enclosed warehouses, the garrison, artillery placements, a church and hospital. Near the main gate, only part of the governor's residence remains standing today.

Monastery of Arkadi

A 45-minute drive south-east of Rethymnon (via Platanias) takes you up along a spectacular gorge to one of the most revered sites of Crete's resistance to the Turkish occupation. Perched on a rugged mountainside, the monastery became in 1866 an armed bastion of revolt, with hundreds of villagers taking refuge within its walls. Rather than surrender to the besieging Turkish troops, Abbot Gabriel waited for them to break into the monastery and then blew up the gunpowder magazine, killing hundreds of enemy soldiers and nearly 1,000 villagers.

The 16th-century monastery has been restored to something of its former ornate Venetian glory. You will notice that the refectory is still pockmarked with bullet holes. A **museum** preserves relics of the suicidal massacre, with an ossuary displaying the victims' bones, as is the Orthodox custom. Every year on November 9 in Rethymnon and Arkadi, solemn memorial services and festive fireworks, music and dancing celebrate the anniversary of this supreme demonstration of the Cretan creed: "Freedom or Death".

Idaian Cave

It was easy for Zeus—he was whisked up here on a cloud. For us mere mortals, the mountain road to his childhood home is a rough but manageable drive—remember that Pythagoras made the pilgrimage on foot. But the scenery alone

makes the trip worthwhile. (Before you set out, check with Rethymnon's tourist office, as the cave is sometimes closed because of archaeological excavations.)

From Rethymnon, drive 52 km (33 miles) east via Perama to the little hill village of **Anogia**, where the residents like to put on a traditional dance or two, and sell their brightly woven fabrics— save the local wine for later, it is a bit of a hike from the car park to the cave.

Just beyond the village the mountain road turns off south up to **Mount Ida**, known locally as Psilorítis, "the high one", in fact Crete's highest—2,456 m (8,058 ft). It is snow-capped till late spring, but in May and June, the wild flowers along your route are a sheer joy, with a veritable explosion of colour when you get to the **Plain of Nida**, at 1,400 m (4,593 ft). The road forks left to a café and car park, and the famous cave is a further 20-minute walk.

Whatever the competing claims of the Diktaean Cave (see p.201), the Greeks certainly treated the **Idaian Cave** as a sanctuary. Italian excavators found votive offerings, jewellery, ceremonial bronze shields and a bronze drum, now on display in Iraklion's museum.

Chania

The buildings of this resort cover the post-Minoan city of Kydonia, and display an agreeable mixture of Venetian and Turkish influences. To keep the charm intact, though, you'll have to make a conscious effort to ignore the garish modern neighbourhoods.

The town's outstanding feature is the grand loop of the **Venetian Harbour**. At night, viewed from the lighthouse at the end of the long breakwater of golden stone, the lights of the shops, cafés and

taverns can be pure enchantment. At the west end of the loop is the Firkas, a restored section of the Venetian ramparts, housing the **Naval Museum** (Naftikó Mousío), with ship models and scenes of key episodes in Greek naval history. Facing it is the Mosque of the Janissaries (1645), now a tourist information centre.

The heart of ancient Kydonia is buried beneath the **Kastelli quarter** behind the mosque. Some of it came to light after the bombardments of World War II and, as you will see in an occasional trench or pit, archaeologists ever since have been pottering around until they get chased away by new builders.

The neighbouring **Splanzia quarter** to the east is dominated on the waterfront by the Arsenals, where the Venetians built and repaired their ships. Behind them you can walk back to the Orthodox church of **Agios Nikolaos**, ecumenically sporting a Venetian Catholic bell-tower and a Turkish Muslim minaret.

*S*trolling along the colourful, relaxed harbourfront of Chania, you would scarcely guess at the violent past of what was once one of the most fiercely defended of Venice's trading posts in the southeastern Mediterranean. Only a fragment remains of the ramparts stormed by the Turks in 1645. The harbour suffered further heavy bombardment in World War II.

Birthplace of Zeus

Cretan tour-operators and scholars of Greek mythology argue about whether the Diktaean Cave or the one on Mount Ida (see p. 205) was the true birthplace of Zeus. Another version of the story, equally authoritative and popular with Peloponnesian tour-operators, suggests that Zeus was in fact born on Mount Lycaeon, in the heart of the Peloponnese. His mother, Rhea, sent him to Crete to save him from his father's plan to eat him. Cronos, Lord of the Titans, had already devoured his other five children, because of a prophesy that he would be dethroned by one of his offspring. When he came looking for Zeus, Rhea fooled him with a stone wrapped in swaddling clothes, which he promptly swallowed. Zeus, spared, grew up in the Diktaean Cave, weaned on goat's milk and good Cretan honey. When he was grown he sought out his father and slipped him an emetic potion, which made him disgorge Zeus's siblings—Hestia, Demeter, Hera, Hades and Poseidon. Later, after a ten year war against the Titans, Hades stole Cronos's weapons, and Poseidon goaded him with his trident, until finally Zeus struck him down with a thunderbolt.

In the **Topana quarter** behind the Firkas, explore the narrow lanes where the houses have Venetian stone façades with wooden upper storeys that were added by the Turks. Stroll along Odos Theotokopoulou for good local handicrafts.

For a wide range of leather goods, including handmade shoes and boots, head for Odos Skridlof in the old Jewish quarter, Evreika. Housed in the Venetian monastery church of St Francis in Evreika, the **Archaeological Museum** has interesting Minoan clay coffins and tomb sculpture.

A covered **market** (Dimotikí Agorá) dominates the centre of town. Bustling but clean and efficient, the stalls, overflowing with Cretan fruit and vegetables, show just how fertile an island it is. This is the place to buy the olives, tomatoes, bread and goat's cheese for your picnic.

Away from the city centre, at Odos Sfakianaki 20, the **Historical Museum** is interesting to anyone curious about the pungent flavour of modern Greek, and more especially Cretan, patriotism. It exhibits the earnest, flashing-eyed portraits of rebel chiefs during the struggles for independence, and documents the resistance to the occupations of the Turks and the Germans.

A special room is given over to the career of Chania's most illustrious son, Eleftherios Venizelos (1864–1936) (Greek prime minister, see p. 67).

Akrotiri

The peninsula east of Chania makes an easy excursion. First stop is a hill, **Profitis Ilias**, scene of the Cretan insurgents' heroic resistance to the Turks in 1897. Beside the impressive **tomb of Eleftherios Venizelos**, you get a panoramic view over the Gulf of Chania.

Drive through the peninsula's cheerful countryside, bright with wild flowers in springtime, to visit three monasteries. The fine 17th-century **Agia Triada** (Holy Trinity) with its nest of domes is a major pilgrimage centre. Just a few kilometres further (an hour's hike) is the older and more isolated **Moni Gouvernetou.** It's another bracing one-hour hike down to the abandoned monastery of Katholiko built beside a bridge at the foot of the cliffs. The caves were inhabited by pagan and Christian hermits.

Samaria Gorge

For a truly indelible impression of the natural beauty of Crete, take one or both of the excursions described here, to the gorges of the Lefka Mountains south of Chania.

The landscape possesses an awe-inspiring, meditative quality—the gentle orange groves in the valleys give way to pine trees overhanging sheer ravines, wild flowers sparkling in dramatic plays of sun and shadow, colours changing from the silvery morning haze to brilliant gold at noon, and softening to pink and purple at the end of the afternoon.

There are two approaches to the more popular, 18 km (11 miles) long **Samaria Gorge**. One way is to take a taxi or bus to Omalos, 42 km (26 miles) from Chania, then hike down through the gorge to the sea at Agia Roumeli, where a boat will take you to the bus (or a pre-arranged taxi) at Chora Sfakion. Or drive directly to Chora Sfakion for the boat to Agia Roumeli to explore just the bottom of the gorge in the early morning before the day-hikers arrive from above.

If you are hiking right through the gorge, **Omalos** is a good place to enjoy breakfast at a café and stock up with picnic goods. You will find springs, drinking troughs and a couple of toilets in the gorge. Take a bottle of water, all the same, and a hat, as the sun beats down strongly and there's little shade. You'll also need good walking shoes.

The descent to the gorge begins on a wooden staircase (*xylóskala*—which is also the name of the bus terminus). Park wardens give you a ticket (no charge) to be surrendered at the other end. This is a means of checking that no one is left stranded in the gorge at the end of the day.

With the huge rock wall of Mount Gingilos towering on your right, the staircase dwindles into a path, dropping sharply 1,000 m (3,280 ft) to the upper gorge bed in the first few kilometres. Take it easy and keep to the designated path. The route is considerably less steep once you reach the chapel of **Agios Nikolaos** tucked away among some majestic cypresses and pines on your right. Among the blues, greens and greys of the rocks, the pools are invitingly cool and clear, but swimming is strictly forbidden. However, nobody will stop you scrumping the fig trees.

The hamlet of **Samaria** and the little Venetian church of Ossia Maria (Mary's Bones) mark the halfway point. Beyond is the gorge's narrowest point, the famous **Iron Gates** (Sideróportes) hemmed in on either side by rock walls 300 m (1,000 ft) high. From here, the gorge opens up as it approaches the sea. Paddle across the shallow Tarraios River and you are almost there. At last, **Agia Roumeli**, where the Libyan Sea invites you for a relaxing swim.

If you are fresh enough, you may like to visit the church of the **Panagia** built over an ancient temple to Apollo whose black, white and red mosaic floor can be seen in the forecourt.

Imbros Gorge

A 90-minute bus ride on the deliciously hair-raising Chania-Chora Sfakion road brings you to the village of Imbros, the start of an 11-km (7-mile) hike through the **Imbros Gorge** almost to the sea, an easy 5 to 6 hours' walk. If you are taking a taxi, ask your driver to stop for a moment at **Vryses** to sample what connoisseurs consider to be the best yoghurt and honey on the island.

The Diggers

The Director of Oxford's Ashmolean Museum, Sir Arthur Evans (1851–1941), began scratching around Knossos in 1894. Hoping to solve the linguistic riddles of Greece's earliest settlements, he was looking for clay tablets with pictographic inscriptions and engraved seal stones like those found on Mycenaean sites in the Peloponnese.

Some 16 years earlier, a local amateur archaeologist with the appropriate name of Minos Kalokairinos had unearthed what Evans later identified as the Minoan palace's storerooms. The Turkish authorities stopped the excavations, but the discovery attracted the attention of the eccentric German archaeologist Heinrich Schliemann, the man who had excavated Troy and Mycenae (see p. 133). Like some latterday Agamemnon avid to cling to the spoils of past battles, he haggled over the price of the land, even the number of olive trees, and abandoned the site in high dudgeon in 1886.

Evans arrived with money, energy, vision and a little more diplomatic skill than was shown by Schliemann. He had pleased the Greeks with his anti-Turkish articles in the *Manchester Guardian* and after Crete won its autonomy was given a free hand to dig at his leisure. From 1900 to 1940 he toiled away on the hillside he had bought in the Kairatos Valley. He turned up relatively few clay tablets and seal stones, but was rewarded with the stupendous treasure trove of King Minos's palace.

Start the hike at the far end of the village of Imbros, and take a sharp left down to the dried-up river bed, then turn right towards the sea. This hike offers a gentler descent than Samaria but offers equally spectacular scenery, notable for its wild flowers, including the lovely purple blooms of Jerusalem sage.

The gorge ends at the village of Kommitades, where a bus takes you down to **Chora Sfakion**, with its beach for swimming and seafood restaurants bordering the harbour.

Some 15 km (9.5 miles) to the east is the stark silhouette of the massive 14th-century Venetian fortress of **Frangokastello**. Its fine sandy beach is accessible by boat or road. At dawn in mid-May, climatic conditions create an eerie mist around the castle's four great towers, and Cretans see the ghosts of Sfakiots who died defending the fort against the Turks.

Western Beaches

West of Chania, the facilities for water sports or sunbathing vary from the sophisticated to the very simple. On the north coast are the elaborate modern resort complex of **Maleme** and the long, sandy beaches of **Kastelli Kissamou**. On the west coast is the splendid curving bay of Falasarna, an important trade port in the 4th century BC. Down the coast, visit the delightful little fishing village of **Sfinari** and bathe at its pebble beach.

On the south coast, **Paleochora** is a busy little port with plenty of accommodation and lively taverns. It is a good base from which to take sea excursions out to the coral-pink beaches of the **Elafonisi islands** or further south to **Gavdos**, where Odysseus dallied with fair Calypso while his poor wife Penelope was patiently weaving and unravelling her tapestry.

*H*ikers pass through the Iron Gates, the narrowest point of the famous Samaria Gorge.

Art in Ancient Greece

Influenced by both southern Mediterranean and northern European cultures, the artistic pendulum of ancient Greece swung back and forth between the warm hedonism of the south and the cool, orderly sobriety of the north.

Minoan Civilization (1600–1400 BC)

Light and colour are the dominant features of art in Minoan Crete, as we can see at the palace of Knossos and in the museum collection at Iraklion, and also in the frescoes of the Minoan settlement on Santorini (currently displayed in Athens). The overall tone is of warm-blooded sensuality drawing inspiration from the island's Egyptian and other Middle Eastern neighbours.

The convivial architecture reflects the Minoans' taste for easy living: no massive fortifications to fend off invaders, and palaces and villas that emphasize the human scale—small decorative rooms, brightly lit, terraces and verandas from which to enjoy a sunset and the landscape.

Palace frescoes are vibrant, depicting plants, animals and people, with a great sense of movement, humour and individuality that sets Minoan art apart from the later more formal and intellectual art of classical Greece.

The intimate scale of Cretan palace life did not lend itself to monumental statuary, and sculpture takes the form of elegant polychrome figurines, most notably the bare-breasted snake-goddesses of Knossos. Wheel-turned ceramics produced eggshell-thin pottery glazed in high-temperature kilns and delicately painted with motifs similar to those of the frescoes. As the Cretan civilization declined, human and animal forms became more stylized without losing their finesse. Jewellery was also highly sophisticated, using gold, silver and ivory encrusted with gems.

Mycenae (1400–1200 BC)

The early art of the Peloponnese shows a clear Minoan influence, but with a tougher, more "masculine" edge to it, brought into Greece by the first wave of northern invaders. This is apparent in the earliest Greek monumental sculpture, the powerful Lion Gate at Agamemnon's palace in Mycenae. Other art of this period can best be seen in Athens' National Archaeological Museum.

Picking up on the late Minoan stylized figures, Mycenaean frescoes disdained naturalism but preferred manly themes of war and the hunt to Minoan dances and butterfly-chasing. Ceramics were less delicate and ornate, but the Mycenaeans proved themselves masterful goldsmiths. With subtle techniques of etched and inlaid damascene, embossing and chasing, they produced splendid goblets, vases, seals, swords, and the kings' famous funerary death masks.

From Geometric to Archaic (900–500 BC)

Archaeologists define Greek art between the fall of Mycenae and the dawn of the classical era by its most visible forms, the styles of painted ceramics. Highly stylized late-Mycenaean figures of animals and humans gradually evolved into zigzagging, wavy or swastika-like geometric patterns. Simple, even crude in Boeotia and the Cyclades, the Geometric pottery of Attica and Athens is ornate and elegant, reflecting the wealth of Athenian aristocrats and already suggesting an intellectualized sense of beauty.

In architecture, the first temples appeared between 850 and 750 BC in the Peloponnese at Perachora (near Corinth) and Argos as simple hairpin-shaped or rectangular wooden shelters for the god's statue. A temple was the house of a god, not of his worshippers; they observed from afar and left their offerings on the altar erected outside. The stone edifices that followed in the 7th century BC derived their structural elements from the wooden temples. The fluted stone columns imitated the old pillars of trimmed tree trunks. Beam ends for the roof became triple-grooved blocks (triglyphs) between the carved panels of the metope. The latter were originally just terracotta slabs blocking gaps between the roof-beams so as to keep birds out of the temple.

Two basic styles of Greek architecture emerged. The Doric order of the Peloponnese was marked by power, sobriety and rigour. More graceful, ornate and fanciful, the slightly later Ionic order spread through the Aegean islands in the 6th century BC from the coast of Asia Minor. Athens achieved a synthesis of the two, using Ionic suppleness to modify Doric severity. The differences are most easily seen in temple columns. The robust Doric column, inspired by the sturdy oaks of the Peloponnese, has sharp-edged fluting, no base and a simple, slightly curved capital to support the entablature. The more slender Ionic column usually has less pronounced fluting, but its most distinctive feature is the elegantly scrolled capital. Beneath the roof, Ionic entablatures have ornate detail framing a continuous sculpted frieze rather than the individual metope panels of Doric entablatures.

Among the major Doric edifices of the Archaic period are the Temple of the

Archaic Sphynx
(Keramikos Museum, Athens)

Artemis at Corfu (a Corinthian colony) and the treasury shrines of Olympia. Ionian temples like the Heraion on Samos are often more colossal, on the Oriental model.

With the evolution of the temple, sculpture developed to monumental

Agamemnon's Death Mask from
Mycenae (National Museum, Athens)

size. Female caryatid statues doubled as pillars. Life-size male *kouros* and female *kore* figures represented deities, priests and priestesses. In all the major museums you usually find examples of these males (naked) and females (in light tunics), most often standing upright with the left leg forward, almond-shaped eyes and rather thick lips set in the famous enigmatic "archaic" smile. At the end of the Archaic period, you find more realism in the muscles, knee joints and pubic hair. The smile has faded into a more serious–even frowning–expression.

Again there are Doric and Ionic distinctions. Doric figures tend to be massive, rigid and severe. Females have a solid stability, with heavy long robes draped over scarcely delineated breasts to fall in folds resembling Doric columns. Ionic sculpture is more voluptuous. There is a taste for animals and mythical creatures, like the lithe lions of Delos. The *kouros* is less athletic, more decorative; clothed and even frankly corpulent, he is often seated and apparently enjoying the good life. The *kore* is more lively and sensuous, her robe coquettishly emphasizing the curves of her body. Firmly muscled in Naxos, softer near to the Asian coast, cheerful in Paros, and positively merry in Chios.

Though early sculpture in Athens was less adventurous, a real style emerged at the end of the 6th century BC. Beginnings of the Athenian synthesis can be seen in the greater psychological depth of a melancholy youth and his sulking sister, both on view in the Acropolis museum.

Ceramics flourished with the growing luxury trade in perfumes, wines and oils. Oriental influence is apparent in the bright colours and animal and plant motifs, most notably on Rhodes and the adjacent coast. Dominant in the 7th century BC, Corinthian pottery, pale yellow with animal and human figures in black varnish, gradually lost its markets to the more sophisticated red and black ware of Athens.

The Classical Era (500–400 BC)

In the arts, the period of the Persian Wars (499–478 BC) should more properly be called pre-classical when, in the struggle for national survival, the prevalent tone is one of severity. The sculpture of this period is stern, stiff-upper-lip stuff, four square in the austere Doric tradition. The mood of Ionic figures is subdued rather than serene.

Under Pericles, Athens fulfilled the classical ideal of combining Ionic harmony and grace with Doric order and discipline. Phidias, the great sculptor and Pericles' "Minister of Culture", achieved the synthesis in overseeing the new architecture of the Acropolis. The Parthenon of Callicrates and Ictinus combined strong Doric columns and heroic metopes on the exterior, with more ornate Ionic friezes on the interior peristyle. And we should not forget that the temple was originally completed by Phidias's own gold and ivory colossus of Athena. The Propylaea gatehouse is in the grandest Doric tradition, while the caryatid columns of the Erechtheion, completed in the Peloponnesian Wars, add a more gracious Ionic touch.

Classical sculpture perfected the athletic figure. Myron produced his famous *Discus Thrower*, known to us only in Roman marble copies of the bronze original.

Polyclitus was the master of the ideally proportioned figure, surviving in copies of his *Doryphoros* (Youth Holding a Spear). But we can better judge the refinement of classical technique in the National Archaeological Museum's *Poseidon* (and the great Riace bronzes of two soldiers, probably by Phidias himself, in Reggio di Calabria). As the sculptor of gods and of men on a divine scale, Phidias gave his statues a new suppleness and freedom of line, and a facial expression infused with a calm, very human spirituality, much the classical ideal.

The humanism of the age influenced ceramics too, refining the decoration and producing more psychological portrayals of its figures. The later motifs show a more relaxed Ionic ambience, with more florid, indolent reclining figures in shimmering colours.

The 4th Century BC

The collapse of the Athenian empire ushered in an era of anguish. Socratic inquiry imposed an intense realism. In sculpture, the serenity of Phidias was replaced by the sensual languor of Praxiteles. Scopas of Paros is renowned for the passion and pathos of his hunting and battle scenes. The gods are portrayed with less exaltation, more of a sense of humanity and understanding of suffering. Lysippus, whose athletes are more elongated than those of Polyclitus, became court sculptor to Alexander, who liked his leonine but gentle portraits.

In architecture, the major development was the Corinthian column with the acanthus leaf motif on its capital. It first appeared on interior columns of the tholos (rotundas) at Delphi and Epidaurus and the Philippeion at Olympia. The theatre at Epidaurus is significant for its strict application of mathematical principles to the achievement of beauty and harmony.

The art of ceramics declined rapidly in a spate of tasteless facility. Athenian red-figure motifs disappeared by the end of the century. Thereafter, with the advent of the Roman Empire, Greece was no longer master of its own art. But its legacy is eternal.

Corinthian columns, Temple of Olympian Zeus, Athens

Aegean Archipelago
Where the Ghosts of the
Crusaders Rub Shoulders with
Today's Sun-Seeking Tourists

The island of Rhodes was the mediaeval stronghold of the Crusader Knights of St John. But long before, in ancient times, it was a trading community under the divine protection of Helios, the sun god, whose colossal statue gazed down upon the harbour, one the Seven Wonders of the ancient world. Today, the sun still gazes down on the attractive islands of the Dodecanese—300 days a year, on average—drawing crowds of holiday-makers to their beautiful beaches.

If you are seeking an essentially peaceful holiday in this south-east corner of the Aegean, your best bet is to visit Rhodes as a side trip from a base on one of the smaller islands. There is no getting around the fact that Rhodes is a major destination for mass tourism. Despite new policies designed to spread people more evenly across the island,

O dos Ippoton — "Street of the Knights"—forms the historic centre of Rhodes Town.

most of the beaches remain very crowded—although with a little perseverance you can hunt down the more secluded spots off the beaten track. Nonetheless, the flowery gardens and historical sites, particularly in the old quarters of Rhodes Town itself, and in the village and ancient acropolis of Lindos, are still enormously rewarding. You just have to be an early enough bird to beat the mob. Similarly, the island of Kos, green and pleasant out of season, is in summer a place for visitors who like their holidays loud and boisterous.

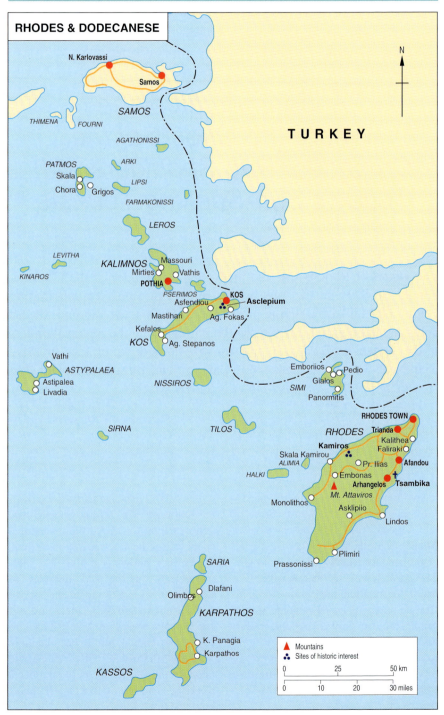

RHODES & DODECANESE

N. Karlovassi
Samos

SAMOS

THIMENA
FOURNI

TURKEY

AGATHONISSI

PATMOS
Skala
Chora
Grigos

ARKI

LIPSI

FARMAKONISSI

LEROS

LEVITHA

KINAROS

KALIMNOS
POTHIA

Massouri
Mirties
Vathis

PSERIMOS
Asfendiou
Mastihari
Kefalos
KOS
Ag. Stepanos

KOS
Asclepium
Ag. Fokas

Vathi
ASTYPALAEA
Astipalea
Livadia

NISSIROS

Emboriios
Gialos
SIMI
Panormitis

Pedio

SIRNA

TILOS

RHODES TOWN
Trianda
Kalithea
Faliraki

RHODES
Kamiros
Skala Kamirou
ALIMIA
HALKI
Embonas
Arhangelos
Mt. Attaviros
Monolithos
Asklipiio

Pr. Ilias
Afandou
Tsambika

Lindos

Plimiri
Prassonissi

SARIA
Dlafani
Olimbos

KARPATHOS

K. Panagia
Karpathos

KASSOS

▲ Mountains
• Sites of historic interest

0   25   50 km

0   10   20   30 miles

N

218

The quieter islands in this group are rugged Patmos, something of an aristocrat, with its handsome coastal villas and private houses up in the capital around the hallowed monastery of St John the Divine; Kalymnos, proud home of the sponge divers and a Mecca for underwater enthusiasts; Astypalaea, remote and still sedate, cultivating a rough chic; Karpathos, where the villagers wear traditional costume for their own comfort rather than for tourist postcards; and closer to Rhodes, the charming little isles of Symi and Chalki, which have so far avoided the masses simply by not catering to them—yet.

The Dodecanese, (the Greek name *dodeka nisi* means "twelve islands"), consists of a dozen islands, united in 1908 against discriminatory Turkish legislation, and subsequently joined by Rhodes and Kos. The islands came under Italian rule from the Italo-Turkish War of 1912 until 1947, when they formed a Greek administrative region covering some 200 islands of which only 14 have any sizeable population. For details of air and sea transportation from mainland ports, see the GETTING AROUND IN GREECE section in the FACTS AND FIGURES chapter, p. 18.

Rhodes

The joy of Rhodes is its smiling climate. More than living up to its name of "the rose" (*rhódon*), the island charms its visitors with the many flowers that adorn its courtyards: besides the rock rose, you will breathe in the scent of jasmine, hibiscus, bougainvillaea and honeysuckle. The hills, which culminate in the peak of Mount Attaviros (1,215 m,

3,986 ft), are fragrant with lavender, sage and marjoram. Its butterflies are so numerous that a whole valley is named after them. And if you come across the Rhodes Dragon, try to discourage your little boy from playing St George and slaying the poor creature—it is only a green lizard measuring at best 45 cm (18 inches) long.

With the prevailing summer winds blowing from the north-west—most often merely hair-ruffling, but occasionally quite fresh—the most sheltered beaches are those on the east side of the island.

Rhodes is just 20 km (12 miles) from the Turkish mainland, and the Turkish heritage is still apparent in the Rhodes Town at the north end of the island, where half of the 90,000 inhabitants are concentrated. But the strongest cultural influence there—and elsewhere in the Dodecanese—remains that of its medieval masters, the Crusader Knights of St John. Of the island's three ancient Greek trading ports, Lindos and Kamiros retain interesting archaeological sites, while Ialyssos is now a beach and hill resort (modern Trianda and Filerimos). Island-hoppers should set aside three or four days to "do" Rhodes.

Rhodes Town

The island's capital is actually two towns, the old and the new. The New Town, with the exception of the harbour area, is rather lacking in charm—modern hotels, restaurants and shops. The true heart of the capital, in all senses of the word, lies behind the fortifications in a maze of narrow streets where the wily wanderer can always duck away from the crowds and find a piece of authenticity and calm. The Old Town itself is

RHODES

Aquarium

A e g é o n   P é l a g o s

PLATIA VASILEOS PAVLOU

Nautical Club

Mosque of Murad Reis

National Theatre

Governor's Palace

Fort St. Nicholas

Town Hall

Church of St John

Post Office

PLATIA AKADIMIAS

PLATIA ARCH. CHRISTANTHOU

M a n d r a k i

Tourist Police

New Market-place

PLATIA NEORION

Son et Lumière Show

Palace of the Grand Masters

KNIGHTS QUARTER

5

Temple of Aphrodite

1

2

3

IPPOTON

4

E m b o r i ó

6

7

8

9

10

11

TURKISH QUARTER

JEWISH QUARTER

1 Píli Eleftherías (Freedom Gate)
2 Museum of Decorative Arts
3 Byzantine Museum
4 Knights Hospital
5 Palace of the Grand Masters
6 Mosque of Suleiman
7 Turkish Library
8 Mosque of the Agha
9 Castellania
10 Episcopal Palace
11 Mosque of Ibrahim Pasha

divided in two: the Knights' Quarter with its medieval monuments, and the Turkish Quarter with its bazaar and mosques and old Jewish enclave.

Fortifications

To get an overall view of the Old Town, it is a good idea to start with a walk along the top of the **ramparts**. The section open to the public (usually Monday and Saturday afternoons, tickets in the courtyard of the Grand Masters' Palace) covers about a mile, one-third of the perimeter.

Quite apart from the historical interest, the walk along the walls, starting from the monumental Amboise Gate, is attractive for the wild flowers that border the path and the lush vegetation in the moats.

The massive fortifications are themselves a major work of military technology, evolving over the centuries as weapons changed from arrow and spear to cannon and gunpowder. The walls became more and more massive, often over 12 m (40 ft) thick, and were curved to deflect cannonballs.

The southern section of ramparts, allotted to the English and Spanish knights, was particularly difficult to defend because the land rises outside the walls, making them more vulnerable to attack. The fortifications here are noticeably more extensive, with extra towers and a double moat.

The moat between inner and outer walls never contained water, but served to discourage invaders from putting up siege towers. You will see cannonballs down there serving as goal posts for schoolboys' football games, as well as others around the old town, neatly piled in pyramids. The iron ones were fired by the Turkish cannons, while those of limestone and marble, more handsome but less deadly, were catapulted over in an earlier epoch.

Knights' Quarter

Start your tour at the north-east corner of the Old Town, at the **Freedom Gate** *(Píli Eleftherías),* so named by the Ital-

ians who saw themselves as liberators of the island from Turkish oppression. The name remained valid for the Greeks when they took over after World War II. On Platia Simis, the little square just inside the gate, are some of the rare vestiges of the ancient Greek city, shafts of columns and fragments of entablature from the 3rd-century BC Temple of Aphrodite.

Up the slope to the south, on Platia Argirokastrou, the curious **fountain** is a Byzantine baptismal font brought here by the Italians from a church in the south of the island. To the left, housed in the Knights' Arsenal, is the **Museum of Decorative Arts**, exhibiting local costumes, embroidery and ceramics, and the reconstructed interior of a traditional Rhodian house.

Also facing onto the square is the **Inn of Auvergne**, built in 1507, with a fine Gothic doorway at its main entrance and now, like many of the other inns, housing administrative offices.

Continuing south past a shopping arcade, you come to the **Panagia tou Kastrou** (Virgin of the Fort). Originally the Knights' cathedral, it had its steeple transformed into a minaret and became a mosque during the Turkish occupation (known to Rhodians as the "red mosque" because of the Christians executed here in 1523), and is now the Byzantine Museum.

Bypass for the moment the famous Odos Ippoton (Street of the Knights) to visit the august **Knights' Hospital** on Platia Nosokomiou (Hospital Square), the noble pretext for the island's massive defences and indeed the order's *raison d'être*. It was built on Roman ruins in the 15th century. Above the grand Gothic doorway of the main entrance,

with its bas-relief coat-of-arms of the Order of St John, was the hospital's chapel. Other ground-floor arches around the courtyard lead to storerooms now used by local merchants.

Among the stone missiles piled in pyramids are some said to have been used in the siege of Rhodes by Demetrius in 305 BC. A marble lion of the 1st century AD sits in the centre.

The infirmary along the upstairs gallery had canopied beds and isolation cells for a hundred patients. Surgeons tended pilgrims, often quarantined from recurring plagues. But in a bizarre vicious circle, most of the patients were the knights themselves, wounded in the defence of the hospital.

T he Amboise Gate gives access to the massive fortifications that defend the Old Town in Rhodes. The 4 km walls are a masterpiece of military architecture.

kneeling Aphrodite of Rhodes (1st century BC), a more graceful piece, holds out her long wavy hair to dry in the sun after emerging from the sea. Other sculpture includes a tombstone bas-relief (5th century BC) of a daughter taking leave of her mother, and a striking head of the island's sun god, Helios (2nd century BC).

Across Hospital Square stands the **Inn of England**, reduced to rubble by earthquake and the 1856 gunpowder explosion (see p. 238), and restored a century later by the British. But the English had left the Order long before, in 1533, following the Pope's excommunication of Henry VIII, and three years after their fellow knights had found a new home on Malta.

Now stroll up the narrow cobble-stoned **Odos Ippoton**, one of the most remarkable medieval thoroughfares in Europe, for which we must thank the Italians' meticulous restoration work, completed in 1916. On the right opposite the hospital, the **Inn of Italy** is the first you come to, with the arms of 16th-century grand master Fabrizio del Carretto sculpted over the doorway. Next door is the mansion of Villiers de l'Isle-Adam, who as Carretto's French successor had the sad task of surrendering to Sultan Suleiman in 1522.

Opposite the mansion, the hospital's original main gate led directly to the

The hospital now houses the **Archaeological Museum** with its fine collection of ancient sculpture, Mycenaean vases and jewellery. The marble Aphrodite of the 3rd century BC, popularly known as the Marine Venus on which writer Lawrence Durrell wrote his *Reflections*, was netted by fishermen off the coast of Rhodes in 1929. The

infirmary. Just beyond the hospital, behind a wrought-iron gate, is a charming shady garden with a Turkish fountain and the museum's marble relics stored among the palm trees and shrubs.

Facing the garden, with the royal fleur-de-lis among the coats of arms, are the splendid late-Gothic façades of the **Inn of France**, its chapel and the chaplain's residence. The doorway inscription dates the inn to 1492, but the chapel, with Virgin and Child in a niche, is much older, bearing the escutcheon of one of the earliest grand masters, Raymond Béranger (1365–73).

Linked by the first of two arches spanning the street, the simpler **Inn of Provence** stands to the right, and the **Inn of Spain** to the left (divided in two after the knights of Spain split into those of Aragon and of Castile). The Church of St John, originally on the left just beyond the street's second archway, was blown to smithereens by the gunpowder explosion of 1856.

From the top of Ippoton, look back down the street to appreciate the orderly arrangement of its perspective. The Italian restorers did a marvellous job of removing the colourful but clumsy clutter of ramshackle wooden balconies added when the Turks billeted their troops in the inns.

The reconstruction of the **Palace of the Grand Masters** on the long tree-lined esplanade of Platia Kleovoulou is more controversial. Admittedly it looks better than the prison to which it had been reduced by Sultan Suleiman, before it was finally gutted by the great explosion. But Greek scholars would have liked the ruins razed in order to dig for the ancient temple they believed to be lying underneath.

As it was, Mussolini ordered the palace to be rebuilt in the 1930s as a summer residence, but World War II interrupted his vacation plans. His legacy looks nothing like the original medieval palace, but presents instead an intriguing hodge-podge of Roman and Byzantine columns, Italian Renaissance wood-panelling, and floors that have been paved with Roman and early Christian mosaics that he had transported from the island of Kos. Among the

statuary in the courtyard, notice the bronze she-wolf, mother of Rome's Romulus and Remus. This statue originally guarded the entrance to Mandraki harbour, and it has now been replaced by a Rhodian deer (see p. 229).

In keeping with this symbolic "change of management" from German to Greek at the end of World War II, notice the two inscriptions near the palace courtyard entrance. One is dated 1940, "the 18th year of the Fascist era".

The Palace of the Grandmasters, restored after a gunpowder explosion in 1856, and lavish home of the leaders of the Crusades.

The other, carved in Greek in 1947, honours the "unconquered Dodecanese people" for preserving "under all foreign occupation that inexhaustible fount of eternal Greek civilization: the ideal of freedom".

*T*he Turkish cemetery in Rhodes' New Town is one of the few monuments of the Ottoman Empire left relatively unchanged by the Greek authorities. It was the burial place of the Turkish élite. Murad Reis was interred here in 1522, after rising from humble beginnings as a pirate to become admiral of the Turkish fleet. Other notables buried here include a Shah of Persia.

today. It stands on the site of a Church of the Apostles from which it is believed the handsome Venetian Renaissance portal was taken. The mosque is spacious and peaceful, quite the best-preserved on the island; unfortunately its elegant minaret collapsed and is awaiting restoration. Opposite is the **Turkish Library**, possessing many valuable Arabic and Persian manuscripts, including two exquisitely illuminated Korans of the 15th and 16th centuries.

Double back to **Odos Sokratous**, where the bustle of tourists and merchants captures much of the boisterous atmosphere of the old **bazaar** of which it was always the main focus. Among the ceramics, icons, daggers, pots, jewellery and junk, you will find as many fakes and bargains as there ever were.

South of the bazaar, make your way to the pleasant Platia Arionos and relax at one of the cafés. Better still, drop in at the **Turkish baths** to steam away the aches and pains of sightseeing (bring your own soap and towel; closed on Sundays). The 1765 building, bombed in World War II, has been rebuilt to something of its old marble-floored splendour.

Back on Sokratous, head down to Platia Ippokratous (noting some good seafood restaurants to return to in the evening). On the far side of the square beyond the Turkish fountain is the **Castellania**, the medieval courthouse and stock exchange. The sockets in the façade once held banners to proclaim the court in session.

Facing the harbour, turn right on Aristotelous along the northern edge of what was the old **Jewish Quarter**. From the earliest centuries, Rhodes' Jewish community played an important role in the

Turkish Quarter

From Platia Kleovoulou, walk south beneath the plane trees of Odos Orfeos down to a clock tower on your left. It replaces a Turkish watchtower from which an inner rampart once ran east to the port, separating the Knights' Quarter from the rest of the fortified town.

Continue down to the **Mosque of Suleiman**, built in honour of the sultan soon after his conquest of 1522, renovated 300 years later and still in use

An Island of Merchants and Knights

In one of his famous odes, the Greek poet Pindar tells how Rhodes was born out of an affair between Helios, the sun god, and the nymph Rhoda. The island's destiny was marked by its proximity to Asia Minor and the Middle East. Carians from Anatolia and Phoenicians from Lebanon were its earliest settlers. Driven from Crete by earthquakes and invaders from the Greek mainland, Minoan merchants set up shop in the ports of Lindos, Kamiros and Ialyssos to continue at closer quarters their lucrative trade with Egypt and the Levant.

For the Greeks accompanying Agamemnon, Rhodes was a stepping stone between Crete and the coast of Asia Minor where they were to conquer Troy. According to Homer, nine Rhodian ships sailed with the fleet.

By 700 BC, Rhodes' three cities set up a trading league with the island of Kos and the Asia Minor ports Halicarnassus (now Bodrum) and Knidos. Looking westward, their merchants colonized the Costa Brava in Spain, Gela in Sicily, and Naples.

In the ancient conflicts, these inveterate navigators trimmed their sails according to the winds of their trading interests, but with varying success. Siding with the Persians, they went down to defeat at Marathon, and ten years later lost 40 ships at Salamis. They supported Athens, then Persia again, against Macedonia, before seeing their advantage on Alexander's side in the trading concessions with Egypt. Turning against Alexander's Ptolemaic successors, they had to face and courageously withstand the brutal assault of Demetrius the Besieger in 305 BC. From the huge amount of battle equipment he left behind him, they amassed the bronze to build the port's famous Colossus (see p. 239).

Under the Romans, they showed disastrous political judgement, backing Macedonia against Rome, and Pompey against Julius Caesar. Even when they resisted demands for support from Caesar's assassins, it cost them the plunder of 3,000 statues, with the lean and hungry Cassius leaving them "nothing but the sun".

But their scholarship commanded Rome's respect. Rhodian law inspired both Augustus and Justinian. Students at Rhodes' School of Rhetoric included Cicero, Julius Caesar and Mark Antony, who acquired what Latin scholars describe as a florid Asian style, well captured by Shakespeare's "Friends, Romans, countrymen, lend me your ears".

With the fall of Rome, Rhodes was constantly plundered by barbarians and pirates. Among the many Crusaders stopping off on their way to Palestine, Philippe Auguste of France and Richard the Lion-Heart recruited mercenaries here in 1191.

A century later, Genoese pirates sold the island to the equally ferocious Knights of the Order of St John, retreating from their role as defenders of pilgrims in the Holy Land. For the next 200 years, they turned Rhodes and its neighbouring islands into a maritime fortress to fight off Muslim assaults, occasionally sallying forth to carry the battle to the Turkish mainland. They also ran a hospital for sick and wounded knights and pilgrims.

Sultan Suleiman the Magnificent seized the island in 1522, and under Turkish rule the island sank into four centuries of stagnant neglect.

Things picked up under the Italians, who occupied Rhodes when the Dodecanese was ceded to them after their victory over the Turks in 1912. Ancient Greek sites were excavated, mediaeval buildings and monuments restored, new roads, homes and public buildings constructed. Mussolini's Fascists tried to suppress the Greek language and the Orthodox Church, but they also made Rhodes a more accessible island to promote the development of tourism.

After German occupation in World War II, the island was liberated by the British and it was united with Greece in 1947.

island's commercial life. Its neighbourhood east of Pithagora was notoriously noisier than the somnolent streets of the adjoining Turkish quarter. Of the 6,000 Jews living in the Old Town in the 1930s, two-thirds of them had emigrated at the outbreak of World War II. When the Germans occupied the island in July 1943, the remaining 2,000 were assembled in what is now **Platia Evreon Martiron** (Square of the Jewish Martyrs). From this square, quiet now and adorned by a cheerfully kitschy modern fountain of bronze seahorses, the Jews were deported to the Third Reich's extermination camps. Only 50 survived, and a mere half-dozen Jewish families remain on the island today. The crumbling **synagogue** with its rusty, barely distinguishable Hebrew plaque above the gate can be found on nearby Odos Dosiadou.

New Town

Under Turkish rule, the Greeks moved outside the walled city into what came to be called the Nea Chora, or New Town. The area surrounding the Old Town was first settled in ancient times and building works today still unearth remains of older civilizations. But the commercial section at the northern tip of the island—hotels, shops, administrative buildings, banks, cafés and restaurants—is less than 100 years old.

Mandraki Harbour, Rhodes' historic port where the knights moored their galleys and modern tour-operators dock their excursion boats, is a natural link between the Old and New towns. (Emborio, the commercial harbour at the foot of Old Town, is used for larger ships.) Derived from its shape, the name Mandraki means "sheep fold", but its

"gates" are guarded by bronze statues of a stag and a hind. The latter, on the harbour's seaward arm, has replaced the she-wolf that symbolized Italian rule, now in the courtyard of the Grand Masters' Palace.

Deer have long been a feature of Rhodes. They were introduced in ancient times at the prompting of the Delphic oracle to combat the island's snakes, said to be repelled by their odour. In the modern era, the deer died out but the island was re-stocked by the Italians, who had read the classics. But despite the deer, snakes are still to be found on the island.

The three drum-shaped stone **windmills** were built during the Middle Ages to mill grain for departing cargo boats. Sea breezes still turn their jib-like sails, but the millstones have long since ground to a halt. Go to the end of the pier for the view from the 15th-century **St Nicholas Fort**, now a lighthouse with a chapel inside. St Nicholas is the Orthodox patron saint of sailors.

The dull administrative buildings along the harbour—courthouse, harbour-master's office and post office— are the rather pompous contributions of the Italian regime. Opposite, and equally uninspired, is the Italian attempt to reproduce the **Church of St John** destroyed in the Old Town. It is the seat of the archbishop of the Dodecanese. Just beyond it, the **Governor's Palace** is a pastiche of the Doge's Palace in Venice.

South of these sad errors in Italian taste, and much more lively, is the **New Market** (*Néa Agorá*), a Turkish-style seven-sided building. Its arcades surround an inner courtyard with stands of fresh fruit, vegetables, meat and fish.

The cafés and restaurants make good vantage-points from which to watch the hustle and bustle.

North of the harbour, past the chic but private Nautical Club, the public **beach** stretches around the tip of the island and down the western shore. The Elli Club charges a small admission fee for its changing facilities.

Inland from the beach club along Odos G. Papanikolaou, a slim white minaret marks the **Mosque of Murad Reis** and the **Turkish cemetery**. The Turks' chief buccaneer, Murad Reis died in the victorious assault of 1522 and is buried in a circular mausoleum next to the mosque. In a peaceful setting of fragrant eucalyptus and pine trees, the cemetery's graves are marked by sharp-angled stones for women, while the men's headstones are topped by carved turbans. Dignitaries are buried beneath ornate porticoes.

Standing alone at the northern end of the island, the **Aquarium** *(Enidrio)* displays its octopus, spotted moray, triggerfish and other exotica in an underground room designed to look like the seabed.

Monte Smith

On the west side of town, the hill where British Admiral Sydney Smith monitored the movements of the Napoleonic fleet makes a pleasant excursion at the end of the day. The view of the Turkish coast and the island of Symi in the late afternoon sun is a sheer delight. Amid the olive groves, Rhodes' hilltop acropolis is crowned by the Doric **Temple of Apollo**. It was destroyed by the same earthquake that toppled the Colossus around 225 BC (see p. 239), and three columns have been somewhat haphaz-

ardly resurrected by Italian archaeologists. Below the temple is the rebuilt theatre, in which only the three bottom rows of marble seats are 3rd-century originals, together with a partially restored stadium.

Rodini Park

The Italians landscaped a beautifully wooded park on the southern outskirts of the capital where scholars believe Rhodes' famous School of Rhetoric once stood. Today, the setting inspires meditation rather than oratory. Streams meander among oleander bushes, cypress, maple and plane trees. A rock-carved **Hellenistic tomb** with Doric half-columns is inaccurately known as the Tomb of the Ptolemies.

East Coast to Lindos

Sheltered from the island's blustery winds, the east coast offers pleasant excursions among the beach resorts and orchards. A high point is Lindos, a historic trading port of ancient Greece and still one of the most beautiful villages in the Aegean, with the bonus of a splendid beach in its bay.

First stop, less than 10 km (6 miles) south of the capital, is **Kallithea**, where the small bay offers excellent swimming and skin-diving. The Italians tried to promote it as a spa for rheumatism, gout, and kidney and liver ailments. Even the claim that Hippocrates, the Greek father of all physicians, came over from Kos to take the waters, failed to draw the crowds, and the buildings have fallen into disrepair.

Rheumatism and gout are not major concerns for the young holiday-makers who crowd the long sandy beach at the booming resort of **Faliraki**. Even the older visitors look pretty limber, driving and putting on the 18-hole golf course overlooking the Bay of Afandou. The village of **Afandou** makes a living from its apricot orchards and carpet weaving.

At Kolimbia, an artificial waterfall pours down as part of the local irrigation system. Turn inland here for **Efta Piges** (Seven Springs), the source of the waterfall. Its pine-shaded restaurant has tables perched on rocks in the middle of the stream.

Back on the coast road, there is a turn-off leading to the relatively quiet sandy beach at **Tsambika.** Stretch your legs with a climb to the town's white hilltop monastery, with fine views across to Rhodes' highest peak, Mount Attaviros. In early September, the local women make this pilgrimage to pray for fertility.

Archangelos lies at the heart of the fruit-growing country amid groves of oranges, lemons, figs, olives and vines. Towering above the lush vegetation is a 15th-century fortress, one of the many defences which the Knights of St John built along the coast to fend off the Turks. The town is famed for its splendid hand-made leather boots, knee-length but traditionally worn folded down to the ankle. The peasants have worn them since ancient times to protect against snakes. You can have boots made to measure if you have the time.

Lindos

This ancient port-city possesses the island's only natural harbour. Its population, estimated at 17,000 in antiquity, has dwindled now to 700—though it can look like 17,000 when the tour buses roll in. The golden rule, as always, is: get there early. It really is worth getting up at dawn for that first view over the wonderful sweep of the bay and the gleaming white village hugging the hillside, crowned by its dark medieval ramparts.

Most of the winding streets are just wide enough for donkeys. (You can hire one for the uphill climb on the main square.) From the bus terminal, footsloggers take the one main street towards the acropolis. You pass first the 15th-century Byzantine **Church of St Mary** *(Panagía)*. It has some fine 18th-

*T*he beach at Lindos enjoys the impressive backdrop of a Crusader fortress atop the rocky acropolis hill, with the whitewashed village scattered below.

century frescoes. Its black-and-white pebble mosaic floor, known as *chochláki*, is a characteristic feature of the Aegean, and you will see it in houses and courtyards throughout the village.

But save your stroll around the village until after tackling the **acropolis**. The ancient sanctuary is built on a triangular rock outcrop above the village. Hewn in the rock at the foot of a long stairway is the carved relief of a Greek warship (2nd century BC). At the top of the stairs is the main gate to the fortress, originally built in the Byzantine era and reinforced by the Crusader knights. Their Commander's Palace and the ruins of a Byzantine church precede a Doric portico leading to the acropolis proper. Take in the view from the portico over the main harbour. At the top of

*T*he three cities of Lindos climb the hill to its acropolis: modern, mediaeval and ancient. Facing the rich markets of the Middle East, this was the most prosperous of Rhodes' three ancient trading posts. The ornamental Lindos pottery is in fact of Asian origin; the town served only as a distribution centre. Today, however, it is manufactured in Rhodes Town. Merchants from Lindos sailed across the Mediterranean to found an Italian colony that eventually became the city of Naples.

Asklipiio. Visit its ruined fortress, and then seek out the local priest—try the café. He'll be happy to give you a guided tour of his 11th-century church, which is adorned with some notable frescoes.

The beaches along this south-east coast are fewer than further north, but blessedly uncrowded. The best are along the wide cove running from **Plimiri** to the tip of **Cape Viglos**. For extra peace and quiet, trundle on down to the perfect tranquillity of **Cape Prassonisi**, where a lighthouse marks the island's southernmost point.

*T**he temple of Athena overlooks the cove where St Paul is said to have landed in AD 51.***

the sanctuary's broad monumental stairway, the terrace of the entrance hall, or *Propylaea*, opens out to a forecourt and the little **Temple of Athena**, standing at the edge of a precipitous cliff. It was rebuilt after a fire in the 4th century BC. From the cliff, look down on the rocky harbour where St Paul is said to have moored in AD 51 on his way to Syria. A small white church marks the spot.

Your tour of the charming village will take you through a maze of beautifully refurbished patrician houses, many with Gothic-arched doorways and windows. Peek in at the flowery courtyards and fine staircases. On top of some of the houses are "captains' rooms" with lookouts for watching passing ships.

South of Lindos

Continue south along the coast road from Lindos to Metamorfosi and turn inland to the lovely old hilltop village of

West Coast

With fewer beaches on this, the more exposed side of the island, the most attractive excursions are inland, up in the hills.

The ancient Minoan settlement of **Trianda** is now a booming beach resort. Above it, on the plateau of **Filerimos**, only a few temple fragments and a Doric fountain of the 4th century BC remain of the great trading city of Ialyssos. The Knights of St John exploited its strategic position above the coast to launch their assault on the island in 1309, before making the Genoese pirates an offer they could not refuse (see p. 228).

The **Church of Our Lady of Filerimos**, originally built in the 14th century, has been many times restored. Behind it, the cloisters of the monastery beautifully set amongst the cypresses invite a moment of meditation. Visit the underground chapel of St George to see its 14th- and 15th-century frescoes.

Continuing along the coast road through Kremasti, notice the American colonial style of the schoolhouse, donated by the town's emigrants to the United States. Hurry past the airport to turn inland to the **Valley of the Butterflies** *(Petaloúdes)*. Besides being used for church incense, the vanilla-scented resin of the valley's storax trees attracts hundreds of thousands of Quadrina butterflies *(Callimorpha quadripunctaria)*. They come to the valley between June and the end of September. to mate. Their undersides bear a camouflage of dark brown to blend with the rocks or storax bark, but in flight their wings open out in a flutter of black, brown, white and red. They earn their name Quadrina from four spots and a Roman numeral IV on each wing. A word of warning: they are a nocturnal species and, like any self-respecting Greek, do not appreciate being awoken from their daytime siesta. To protect their declining numbers, clapping hands or blowing whistles to see them in flight is strictly forbidden.

To get away from the heat of the coastal plain, take the inland fork at Kalavarda up to the cool pine-shaded resort on **Profitis Ilias** (798 m, 2,618 ft). Its two mountain lodges, Elafos ("stag") and Elafina ("hind"), are entirely surrounded by forest.

Kamiros, the third of Rhodes' ancient city-states, was probably founded by Cretans fleeing their devastated island in the wake of earthquakes and falls of volcanic ash from the eruption of Santorini. It prospered from eastern Mediterranean trade well into the classical era in apparent serenity, judging by the absence of any fortifications on the site, excavated by the Italians in 1929. With the dig interrupted by World War II, the surrounding hills still conceal a much vaster city.

Preceding the entrance to town is a **Doric sanctuary** of the 3rd century BC. Footprints on the empty pedestals were left by statues, probably carried off by Cassius in 42 BC (see p. 228). But begin your visit to the town itself by walking up and around the peripheral ridge to take in a view of the whole settlement sloping gently towards the sea. Viewed from above, the residential area is situated to the right of the main street running through the middle of town. The Hellenistic houses have inner courtyards with peristyle colonnades. On the agora (marketplace), six Doric columns have been resurrected from the portico that once shaded the shops.

The town's modern fishing port, **Kamiros Skala**, has some good quayside seafood restaurants. If you prefer a hike and a picnic, turn west off the main road up to the knights' 16th-century hillside fortress, **Kamiros Kastello**, for a delightful view of the sea and the small islands off the coast.

For a more ambitious hike, take the loop road around **Mount Attaviros**, at 1,215 m (3,986 ft) the island's only real mountain. From the village of **Embonas**, surrounded by vineyards and tobacco fields, and famous for its women folk-dancers, the mountain path to the summit takes two hours, passing the remains of an ancient temple to Zeus on the way.

The main road from Kamiros continues south to the 15th-century castle of **Monolithos**, named after the soaring monolith on which it is precariously perched, 236 m (775 ft) above the valley. Inside the battlements are two cisterns and a chapel, but the view alone, along the coast and out to Chalki island, makes the climb well worth while.

RHODES

Aegéon Pélagos

N

RHODES TOWN
Akrotírio Koúmbournou
Kólpos Triánda
Triánda
Rodíni Park
Kremastí
Asgouroú
Koskinoú
Paradísion
Filérimos
Thérme Kallithéas
Theológos (Thólos)
Maritsá
Soroní
Dipótama
Fáne
Kallithié
Faliráki
Kalamón
Psínthos
Kámiros
Petaloudes
Afándou
Psínthos
Loutáni
Eleoússa
Archípolis
Kolímbia
Platánia
Mandríkon
Tsambiki
N. Alimniá
Kámiros Skala
Apóllona
Archángelos
N. Mákri
Akr. Archangélou
Kritinía
Malóna
Makkáris
N. Strongilí
Embonas
Gadourás
Amartos
Attáviros
Assourí
Feraklós
N. Tragoússia
Charáki
Ag. Issídoros
Laérma
Kálathos
Akrotírio Milanós
Akr. Armenistís
Siánna
Inko
Akramítis
Lárdos
Líndos
Monólithos
Istrios
Profília
Kontári
Akr. Mirtiás
Asklipiíon
Kólpos Lárdou
Kólpos Apolakkiás
Vátion
Apolakkiá
Koukouliári
Gennádion
Messanagrós
Skiádi
N. Kténia
Lachaniá
Kattaviá
Chóchlakas
Agios Pávlos
Plimíri
N. Karavólas
Akr. Víglos
Akrotírio Prassonísi

▲ Mountains
✝ Church

0 — 10 km
0 — 5 miles

Symi and Chalki

An easy day-excursion from Rhodes (there is a daily ferry from Mandraki harbour and Kamiros Skala), the two rocky islands of Symi and Chalki offer a charming escape from the crowds on their bigger neighbour.

Although not as famous as the sponge divers of Kalymnos (see p. 241), the Symiotes are recognized in the trade as the most skilful.

Chalki

If this little snippet of an island, just 16 km (10 miles) west of Rhodes, is so peaceful, it is because its sponge divers emigrated to the United States to work in the shallow waters of Tarpon Springs, Florida. There they earned enough money to pay for the paving of Chalki's only real road, from the port to the almost abandoned hill town of **Chorio**, and named, of course, Tarpon Springs Boulevard. **Pontamos** has a sandy beach, but all the sponges are in the souvenir shops.

Symi

The island's pretty harbour of **Gialos** lies at the end of a narrow inlet. Some of its elegant pastel yellow and white neoclassical houses have been converted into stylish hotels. A 15-minute walk takes you up to the hilltop capital, **Ano Symi**, with its castle, dated 1507, bearing the French Aubusson coat-of-arms on the gate.

On either side of Gialos are the seaside resorts of **Emborio** and **Pedi**, a fishing village with a shingle beach. At the southern end of the island, **Panormitis Monastery** has some fine frescoes and icons.

The Knights of St John

Also known as Hospitallers, the Knights of St John were originally attached to a Catholic hostel and hospital founded in the 11th century by Italian merchants in Jerusalem. In their Rhodes bastion, they never numbered more than 600, all members of the noblest families in Europe. They took monastic vows of chastity, obedience and poverty, but their thirst for Muslim blood was decidedly un-Christian.

They were divided into eight groups, according to "tongues": English, French, German, Italian, Aragonese Spanish, Castilian Spanish, Provençal French and Auvergnat French. Each group lived within a compound called an "inn" under an appointed prior. The security-conscious knights walked in pairs and left their walled domain only on horseback. About 5,000 Rhodian Christians staffed the forts and hospital.

Supported by Auvergne and Provence, the French outnumbered the other tongues when it came to electing the lifelong post of grand master. Thus, 14 of the 19 grand masters were French, and French was the order's spoken language (Latin for official documents). The Italians' natural maritime talents made them the obvious choice to command the knights' fleet, while other tongues each defended a section of the city walls, known as a "curtain".

Outside the city, the knights extended their system of defences with some 30 fortresses strung across the island and yet more on outlying islands. They were linked by an elaborate communications network of bonfires, smoke signals and homing pigeons.

After the Turkish invasion, the knights found a home on Malta until Napoleon drove them away to seek the Tsar's protection in St Petersburg, and then the Pope's in Italy, ending up with "branches" of charitable, unbelligerent associations in the United States and Britain.

Karpathos

The island's population is concentrated in the fertile southern end around **Pigadia**, the modern capital, surrounded by orchards and vegetable fields. **Kyra Panagia Bay** has a monastery and a pleasant beach. The real charm of the island, however, is to be found in the more isolated northern part, a broad elongated promontory separated from the south by two mountains.

Boats will take you along the dramatic coastline, with cliffs topped by stunted pine trees, to the little port of **Diafani**. From there, you can continue by donkey past dozens of windmills on the slopes of Profitis Ilias (1,140 m, 3,740 ft), to **Olimbos**, the oldest and most enchanting village on the island.

Continuing age-old folk crafts, the women dress in traditional costume to please themselves, and not the tourists (not that there are that many).

The Big Bang

Shortly after capturing Rhodes, the army of Suleiman the Magnificent hid a stockpile of gunpowder somewhere under the Palace of the Grand Masters and the Church of St John, then forgot all about it. Then, one night in 1856, lightning struck a turret of the palace and fire broke out. Flames spread through passageways and tunnels joining the palace to the church.

Suddenly, an enormous explosion rocked the entire island. Fire spread all the way to the harbour, leaving about 800 dead.

Among the many medieval treasures destroyed, the Church of St John and the Inn of England were levelled and the Grand Masters' Palace was left a burnt-out shell. As for the Inn of Germany, it vanished completely; today, nobody even knows where it used to be.

The Revelation of St John

Patmos is not much easier to get to now than when the Romans chose it as a penal colony for political prisoners sentenced to hard labour. Among them, in AD 95, was John the Divine (or the Theologian), a Christian activist in Asia Minor. He was condemned, as he wrote, "for the word of God and for the testimony of Jesus Christ", in opposition to Rome's enforcement of emperor-worship. Between shifts of quarrying stone on the mountainside, John had his mystic visions of the Apocalypse, "a great voice as of a trumpet" foretelling Christianity's terrible trials and ultimate triumph. His powerful, enigmatic poetry composed in a cave on Patmos became the last book of the New Testament, the Book of Revelation.

Kos

A magnet for mass-market package tours, this island is either Paradise or Hades, depending on your point of view. Even if the crowds, packed like sardines along the beaches, or pouring into and stumbling out of the harbourside cafés, are not really your glass of lager, you may be tempted to visit for a brief moment of anthropological observation.

Greener than most of the Dodecanese, Kos is actually a very pleasant island if you can get away from the crowds. Its fishermen boast of the best catch in the Aegean, and it produces fine wines—Glafkos white and Apelles red—delicious table grapes, and a well known lettuce.

The local hot springs are strong in iron for all that ails you, and the same were heartily recommended by the island's ancient physician, Hippocrates; the "Father of Medicine" was born here in 460 BC.

Kos Town

The island's Italian-style capital is pleasantly tree-shaded. Overlooking Mandraki harbour, the grounds of the 15th-century **Knights' Castle**, built with masonry from the Asclepium, are littered with the flotsam of the island's ancient and medieval history—marble statuary, vases and rusty cannons.

Near a Turkish mosque of the 18th century there is a huge plane tree propped up on crutches, and in need of a tree-doctor. It is very old—but not old enough to justify the tour guide's claims that Hippocrates taught in its shade 2,500 years ago. Life and death meet at the fountain, whose basin is an ancient sarcophagus. The doctor is of course also prominent, in sculpture and mosaic, in the town's little **museum** on the main square.

Between Mandraki harbour and the ancient acropolis, the colourful **Turkish quarter** reminds you that half the town's population is Muslim, close to 5,000.

Excursions

The **Asclepium**, a terraced sanctuary and medical school founded in the 4th century BC after Hippocrates' death, is 4 km (2.5 miles) out of town at the end of an avenue of cypresses. At the lower level are the remains of a Roman bath (1st century AD) exploiting the island's sulphur- and iron-rich springs. You will see some fine Ionian column-capitals on the middle terrace, but the principal Doric Temple of Asclepius is on the upper terrace. From here you have a good view of the Turkish mainland, the Knidos peninsula to the south and Bodrum (ancient Halicarnassus) to the north. Further west, high on the north

slopes of Mount Dikeos, **Asfendiou** is a charming commune of white stone houses where the bread is baked in stone ovens out in the courtyard among the fig trees.

Beaches

The most popular beaches are along the north coast at **Tigaki** and the fishing village of **Mastichari**. The distinctive feature of **Agios Fokas** on the south-east coast is its black sand. At the west end of the island, Club Med has planted its flags on **Agios Stefanos Bay**. Nearby **Kefalos** has good sandy beaches, lively tavernas and a working windmill.

Bronze Colossus

The Colossus of Rhodes, one of the Seven Wonders of the ancient world, did not bestride the harbour entrance as is popularly believed. Its 20 tons of bronze would have sunk immediately into the seabed. The huge statue of Rhodes' protector, the sungod Helios, 32 m (105 ft) high, probably stood near the site of an ancient sanctuary, where the Palace of the Grand Masters is today.

Sculptor Chares of Lindos took 12 years to cast the Colossus. Extracting bronze from the battle-machines and tools left after Demetrius's abortive siege (see p. 228), he finished the work around 290 BC. He committed suicide after discovering a mistake in his calculations. An assistant tried to correct it, but to no avail. During an earthquake around 225 BC, the Colossus cracked at the knees and crashed to the ground.

The Delphic oracle warned the Rhodians not to restore the statue, and the crumpled bronze lay where it had fallen for nearly 900 years. Arab pirates eventually shipped it to the Lebanon and sold it as scrap to Jewish merchants, who needed 90 camels to carry it away.

Kalymnos

Diving and underwater fishing are the major attractions on Kalymnos, an island that still maintains its ancient profession of sponge diving. Largely arid and mountainous in the interior, the island has a dramatic coastline of coves, cliffs and caves.

Set against a dark mountain backdrop, the shuttered houses of **Pothia** make a colourful splash of white, green, blue and yellow. During the last years of Italian occupation, when the Fascists tried to suppress the Greek language and Orthodox worship, Kalymnotes turned their house-painting into an act of political resistance by restricting the colours to patriotic blue and white. A green mermaid sits on the breakwater to comfort the departing sponge divers.

Further up the east coast away from the bustle of the island's capital, the lovely inlet of **Vathi** protects in its transparent blue waters the ghostly remains of an Italian warship sunk by British aircraft in World War II. A fertile oasis in an otherwise barren interior, the valley behind the tiny port makes delightful picnic country. The volcanic soil nurtures vineyards and rich groves of mandarins and oranges, figs and olives. Among the ancient remains on the hillsides are a throne cut out of the rock at **Rhina**, and sturdy walls of rough-hewn stone at **Platanos**.

The best of the easily accessible beaches are over on the west coast. **Kantouni** is a good family beach, while

*T*he harbour of Kalymnos is the starting point for the island sponge-divers' annual expedition.

the narrow strands of **Mirties** and **Masouri** are more popular with the singles crowd. A quick ferry takes you out to good swimming, snorkelling and nudist beaches on **Telendos**. When an earthquake split this islet off from Kalymnos in AD 535, it submerged an ancient town, still visible under the water.

Patmos

The island where St John the Divine had his apocalyptic vision of the struggle of good against evil is these days a haven of peace. Its rugged coastline and sheltered bays, elegant clifftop villas and immaculate white houses nestling against the fortified monastery at Chora, make it a picturesque little island.

Skala and Chora

Sheltered from the open sea on an isthmus in the middle of the island, the ferry harbour of Skala is also an easygoing commercial centre serving the island

---

Sponge Divers of Kalymnos

Each spring, carrying on a 3,000-year-old tradition, some 200 Kalymnotes sail around the Mediterranean and along the North African coast, to scour the seabed for that luxurious marine animal the sponge. The departure from Pothia harbour for five or six months is blessed by an impressive quayside religious ceremony, and the return of the fleet, decks laden down with sponges, is received with great festivities. There is a veritable explosion of joy and relief that the men have survived the considerable risks of death or injury. Shallow-water sponges have been over-fished, but among the deep-sea varieties, the most desirable is Venus's flower basket.

---

capital, Chora, up on the mountain. Hotels, cafés and restaurants line the quayside.

Behind the port, a road winds up the mountainside past the **Convent of the Apocalypse**. Here, below three chapels of the 17th and 18th centuries and a theological college, is the **Cave of St Anne** where St John is said to have had his revelation. A stone ledge is pointed out as his desk.

Three windmills line the ridge leading into Chora, with its immaculate 300- to 400 -year-old white houses.

Crowning the mountain, the **Monastery of St John** has all the foreboding towers, battlements and ramparts of the fortress it was obliged to be, considering the treasures it had to protect from marauding pirates. The monastery was founded in 1088 by the powerful Abbot Christodoulos from Asia Minor,

and subsequently amassed its riches from commercial shipping plus a small cut from piracy, too. A stairway zigzags up to the pebble-paved central court-yard, with the monastery church off to the left, built over a temple to Artemis. To start construction off on the proper footing, Christodoulos smashed the pagan goddess's statue. His marble sarcophagus is in the **Founder's Chapel** to the right of the church entrance. North of the nave, over the door to the outer treasury, is an icon of the Apocalypse (1625). The 12th-century **Chapel of the**

*T*he quiet streets of Patmos offer a tranquil alternative to the crowded beaches and noisy bars of Kos and Rhodes.

*T*he faces of the islanders defy classification as "Greek", "Turkish" or "Slavonic". Etched into every feature are elements from the whole of the Mediterranean, the sum of the country's turbulent history.

Virgin, opposite, has an exquisite wooden icon-screen (1607). On the east wall are austere, profoundly solemn icons painted around 1190, fine examples of the unadorned early Byzantine style. Note the superb Virgin and Child, flanked by the archangels Michael and Gabriel. Above them is Abraham serving three holy guests, symbolic of the Holy Trinity.

Behind the chapel and left across the inner courtyard, the 11th-century refec-tory has long marble-faced stone tables with hollows for the monks' cutlery and pewter. The 13th-century frescoes are in a livelier, more emotionally involving style than the chapel paintings. Just beyond, the kitchen has some splendid high-domed ovens.

Climb up to the roof terrace for the view of Samos to the north, and on a clear day, Mykonos in the west.

In what is one of the wealthiest monasteries in Greece, the **library** has a magnificent collection of illuminated early Christian and Byzantine manu-scripts. Among the most precious are a 6th-century codex of St Mark's gospel, with silver letters on purple parchment and the titles and sacred names in gold, and an 8th-century Book of Job. In the equally impressive **treasury** are 200 icons from the 11th century to the modern day, 300 pieces of silverwork, amulets and gold medallions given by Peter the Great and Catherine II of Russia, bejewelled bishop's staffs and richly embroidered liturgical vestments.

Beaches

The best sandy beach on the island, some say in the whole Aegean, is on the east coast at **Psili Ammos**. Unless you are sailing, you must bike or hike to get there. **Grikos Bay** is an easily accessi-

ble beach resort, with ancient cave dwellings to visit. **Meli** and **Lampis** are good for windsurfing and water-skiing.

Astypalaea

Still hard to get to and as yet untouched by the tour-operators, this island is particularly beloved of the French. Many of the sharply indented coves at the foot of the tall cliffs are accessible only by boat,

waiting for each new traveller to discover them anew. The handsomely restored white houses of the island's only town spill down the hillside from **Kastello**, with its 13th-century Venetian citadel, past a row of windmills to the little harbour of **Perigialo**. Down the coast, the charming seaside hamlet of **Livadia** has a nudist beach, and the French clientele keeps up the quality of the tavernas. At the northern tip of the island, you can explore the caves of **Vathi**.

Hippocrates and his Oath

Local tradition, understandably seeking to promote the qualities of the island's spa waters, claims that the great physician born in Kos in 460 BC lived for at least 100 years. In fact, all we know for sure is that he was a contemporary of Socrates, active in the late 5th century BC, that he was short in stature, and that he travelled a lot and died at Larissa on the Greek mainland.

In his medical teaching, we know that he broke away from the old belief in magic towards more modern therapies based on empirical reasoning. He examined the effects of climate and environment on man's psyche and physiology, rejecting, for example, the "divine" explanation of epilepsy, known then as the sacred disease. His treatise on the dislocation of bones was still in use in the 19th century.

His name is remembered in the Hippocratic Oath, an ethical code which in one form or another has been used by doctors for the last 2,000 years. It began: "I swear by Apollo the physician, and Asclepius, to reckon him who taught me this Art equally dear to me as my parents…" and continues with pledges to teach his Art to his sons, to act only for the benefit of his patients, not to administer poison, even if asked to, nor to procure abortion, to abstain from mischief and corruption, and from seducing male or female patients, and to observe professional confidentiality.

A peaceful bay with fishing boats bobbing at their moorings, whitewashed houses lining the waterfront, a good book, and the shade of a tamarisk tree as the sun sinks slowly in the west— the pleasures of a quiet corner of the Dodecanese.

From Athos to Olympus — the Macedonian Homeland of Alexander the Great

The lands of Northern Greece, fringing the Balkans, have always had an identity quite separate from the rest of Greece. Indeed, scholars have argued that Macedonia, the kingdom of Philip and Alexander, was never truly Greek. Frequently fought over, and influenced by the proximity of old enemies Bulgaria and Turkey, Macedonia, Thrace and the scatter of islands from Thasos to Samos have an intriguingly different flavour from the rest of the country.

*D*usk falls on the calm, reed-lined waters of Lake Kastoria.

Far from the national capital, with slow train and ferry connections, the north has long remained a tourist backwater. But now the number of direct flights to the northern capital of Thessaloniki from major European cities has increased, the package tour companies are beginning to exploit the resort potential of the Chalkidiki peninsula and the islands of Thasos, Limnos, Lesbos, Chios and Samos.

Even if the old Byzantine districts of Thessaloniki itself have practically disappeared in the aftermath of war, earthquake and fire, Greece's second city is a busy modern centre of commerce, well worth an excursion from your resort for its fine museum of Macedonian treasures, and some of the best restaurants in Greece.The north is a region of religious mysticism. The ecstatic cults of Dionysus and the gods of the underworld have left their mark on the sanctuaries of Thasos and Samothrace. Zeus's Mount Olympus straddles Macedonia's southern boundary with Thessaly. After years of decline, the Orthodox Church is

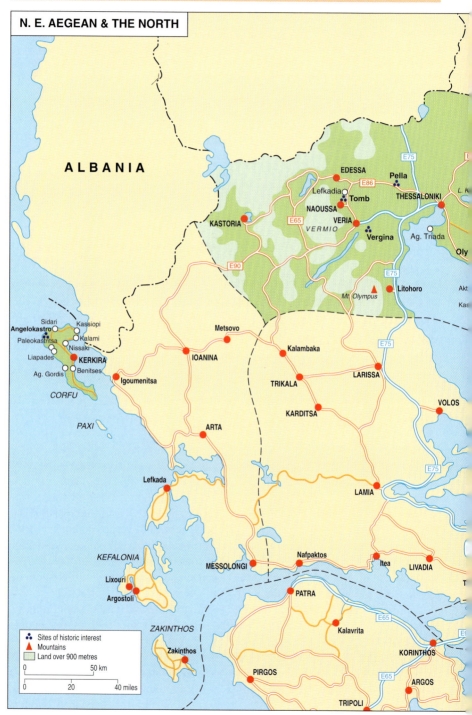

N. E. AEGEAN & THE NORTH

ALBANIA

EDESSA
Pella
E75
E86
Lefkadia
Tomb
THESSALONIKI
L. K
NAOUSSA
E65
VERIA
KASTORIA
VERMIO
Vergina
Ag. Triada
Oly
E90
E75
Mt. Olympus
Litohoro
Akt
Kas
Sidari
Kassiopi
Metsovo
E75
Angelokastro
Kalami
Paleokastritsa
Nissaki
Kalambaka
Liapades
IOANINA
Ag. Gordis
KERKIRA
Benitses
LARISSA
Igoumenitsa
TRIKALA
CORFU
VOLOS
PAXI
KARDITSA
ARTA
E75
Lefkada
LAMIA
KEFALONIA
Nafpaktos
Itea
LIVADIA
MESSOLONGI
T
Lixouri
PATRA
Argostoli
E65
ZAKINTHOS
Kalavrita
E
Zakinthos
KORINTHOS
PIRGOS
E65
ARGOS
TRIPOLI

Sites of historic interest
Mountains
Land over 900 metres

0   50 km

0   20   40 miles

N

BULGARIA

TURKEY

XANTHI
KOMOTINI
Filippi
E90
KAVALA
Fanari
E85
nfipolis
E90
Kalamitsa
ALEXANDROUPOLI
Nea Peramos
Thassos (Limin)
Makriamos
Hrissi Amoudia
Kinira
THASSOS
Aliki
ollonia
Stagira
Paleopoli
Therma
Lerissos
Kamariotissa
Samothraki
N. Roda
ni
M. Hiliandariou
SAMOTHRAKI
Tripiti
M. Vatopediou
Ouranopoli
M. Stavronikita
fossi
Ormos
M. Iviron
Panagias
Dafni
M. Simona Petras
Paradissos
Mt. Athos
Neos Marmaras
M. Agiou Dionissiou
igi
Porto Carras
Toroni
aniotis
Kalamitsi
Koufos
Mirina
NDRA
SITHONIA
Plati
Moudros
SULA
PENINSULA
Thanos
LIMNOS

TURKEY

AG. EFSTRATIOS

Mithimna
Sigri
Eressos
nos
MITILINI
Skopelos
Skala Eressou
Agiassos
SKOPELOS
SKIROS
LESVOS
Vatera
Skiros
Plomari

PSARA

Marmaro
Kardamila
Vrondados
HALKIDA
Anavatos
CHIOS
Nea Moni
HIOS
Mesta
Pirgi
Karfas
E75
Emborios
FSINA
ANDROS
Andros
SAMOS
N. Karlovassi
Avlakia
Lavrio
Marathokambos
Samos
KEA
Kokari
TINOS
IKARIA
Ormos
Tinos
Pithagorio

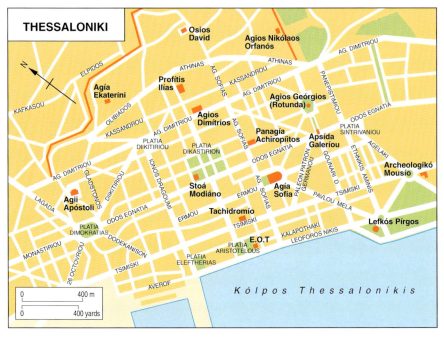

reaffirming the monastic tradition and scholarship of Mount Athos, its peninsula accessible only to male visitors.

Inland, forbidding mountain ranges form natural barriers with Greece's Balkan neighbours, but the fertile plains of Macedonia and Thrace produce fields of grain and tobacco. In springtime, birds and bird-watchers flock to the eastern marshlands of Thrace.

The northern mainland is subject to a Balkan continental, rather than Mediterranean, climate, so winters are colder, and summers more torrid, with more rain in autumn and early spring.

Thessaloniki

Named after Alexander's sister Thessalonikeia, the bustling business capital of the north has gone through many changes since it was founded by the

great conqueror's general, Cassander, in 316 BC. Its importance in the Byzantine Empire, second only to that of Constantinople, is attested to by the many monumental Orthodox churches still being painstakingly restored after recent earthquakes. Under Ottoman rule, the city's population became predominantly Jewish in the 16th century, after Jews expelled from Spain joined those from Bavaria already settled here. In World War II, nearly all the city's 60,000 Jews were deported to German concentration camps. Today, underlined by an interna-

Patience, Men at Work
Thessaloniki still has the most extensive collection of Byzantine monuments outside Istanbul. Unfortunately, the damage caused by the 1978 earthquakes necessitates reconstruction which may make much of the artwork described here temporarily inaccessible. Contact the tourist information centre for up-to-date information.

tional trade fair each September, the city is again prospering from its focal position at the centre of the old Byzantine maritime triangle of the Black Sea, the Aegean and the Adriatic.

The City

The natural, and indeed most attractive place to start a tour of the town is at the waterfront. It is there on the broad, airy square of **Platia Aristotelous** that the bourgeoisie of Thessaloniki congregates in tree-shaded cafés to conduct its business deals, romantic liaisons and political intrigues. The square is also the starting point for the ritual evening stroll—the *vólta*—along the promenade to the **White Tower** (*Lefkós Pírgos*). The Venetians built this massive, battlemented landmark for the Ottoman rulers as part of the harbour fortifications in the 15th century. Executions performed here earned it the title of "Tower of Blood". It now houses a **museum** documenting local history from early Christian to late Byzantine times.

Back on Platia Aristotelous, walk north to the small brick church of **Panagia Chalkeon** set amid pleasant gardens at the south-west corner of Platia Dikastirion. Its name, "Our Lady of the Coppersmiths", refers to the trade still practised in the surrounding streets, their doorways aglow with the red heat of the forges. The 11th-century frescoes inside are worth a look.

Opposite the church on the same square is a 15th-century **Turkish bathhouse**, now serving the Greeks under the evocative name of *Loutrá Parádeisos*.

Work your way east along Odos Egnatia, named after the great Roman road running from the Adriatic to Neapolis (modern Kavala), which passes the north-west corner of the city. North on Odos Agia Sofias, **Panagia Achiropiitos** is one of the city's oldest churches, probably completed in the 5th century. The name, "Not Made by Human Hand", refers to an icon believed to be of divine origin. Note the fine Theodosian capitals of its columns, so called because of the wind-blown acanthus leaf motif which was popular under the Byzantine Emperor Theodosius II. In the south aisle are 13th-century frescoes of church martyrs.

Egnatia continues east, past little shops still practising the ancient art of icon painting, to the Roman **Arch of Galerius** *(Apsída Galériou)*. This commemorates the victory over the Persians in AD 297 of Galerius Maximianus, military commander of the Eastern Empire. On a rise above the arch, the **Rotunda of St George** (*Agios Georgios*) was built in the 4th century as a mausoleum for Galerius, but it was converted into a church, and later a mosque. After its restoration as a museum of Christian art, you will be able to admire the magnificent mosaics of angels and martyrs in the eight recesses of the peripheral wall.

Make your way back west again to the city's largest Byzantine church, **Agios Dimitrios**, with the best preserved (and currently most accessible) mosaics. Dedicated to Saint Demetrius, a noble executed by Galerius, its crypt (entrance in the south transept) contains remains of the shrine built over the martyr's tomb, and the Roman baths where he was detained and killed. The main structure is a good reproduction of the 5th-century basilica destroyed in the great fire of 1917. It houses five superb

8th-century mosaics of Demetrius with church benefactors mounted on pillars flanking the iconostasis (icon-screen).

South of the church is the **Bezesteni,** a bazaar-style street market of clothes and household goods. Adjoining it, the covered arcades of the **Central Food Markets** *(Stoá Modiáno)* are the town's liveliest daytime spot.

One more church worthy of your attention, a short taxi-ride to the west, is the 14th-century **Agii Apostoli.** The complex patterns of its brick façades have the intricacy of mosaic work. Inside, in the barrel vaults, are some splendid Nativity mosaics showing a handmaiden preparing the baby's bath, and the midwife carefully testing the water while Jesus shies away in his nursemaid's arms.

Archaeological Museum (Archeologiko Mousio)

Even if you have no time for a thorough tour of the city, spare a half a day for the astounding riches in the tombs of the kings of Macedonia.

Just up the road from the White Tower, near the main entrance of the International Trade Fairgrounds, the Archaeological Museum houses ancient and prehistoric finds from all over northern Greece. Stone Age vases from Thrace, elegant Geometric vases, jewellery, delicate spectacle-frames, and swords and knives from Macedonia are among the many enthralling exhibits.

Even the most seasoned museum-visitor will be dazzled by the **Treasures of Vergina** excavated from the Macedonian royal tombs some 80 km (50 miles) west of Thessaloniki (see p. 259). Highlights include the exquisitely wrought gold laurel-wreaths worn as necklaces by the kings and queens; the king's armour of bronze helmet, iron cuirass with gold lion's head, and bronze greaves for the shins; a massive gold and ivory shield with its bronze casing; small carved ivory reliefs that decorated a wooden bed—including a bearded man, perhaps Philip himself holding forth to a reclining Alexander. But the most chillingly exciting exhibit comes from one of the two magnificent gold funerary chests, embossed with a 16-point star, emblem of the Macedonian dynasty. It contained the slightly charred skull and bones of Philip, displayed nearby in almost complete skeletal form. Traces of a terrible eye wound sustained in battle have persuaded scholars that these are unquestionably the remains of Alexander's father.

Chalkidiki

This centrally located region has plenty of new beach resorts that make ideal bases from which to explore the northern mainland and the nearby islands. Around its mountainous interior, fertile plains form a rich grain belt, with fine beaches lining much of the coastline.

To the south, there are three peninsulas which jut out into the Aegean like the prongs of Poseidon's trident—from west to east they are Kassandra, Sithonia and Mount Athos.

Just 29 km (18 miles) around the coast from Thessaloniki, **Agia Triada** remains a traditional Macedonian village, while still offering a holiday resort's fine sands, camping facilities, and good hotels along **Thermaikou beach.** Hugging the coast road to Kassandra Bay, you pass the archaeological site of **Olynthos**, one of the region's most important ancient cities, rebuilt by Greek colonists in the 5th century BC. Its allegiance to Athens brought about its destruction by Philip of Macedonia. Built on two table-top mounds, the town's ruins follow the classical grid plan laid down by Pericles' town planner, Hippodamus of Miletus. Its artefacts and mosaics are on show in Thessaloniki's Archaeological Museum. Nearby is the beach bungalow resort of **Gerakini** in a refreshing setting of lawns, flower gardens and olive groves.

Explore the interior mountain country via the regional capital of **Poligiros**, with its little archaeological museum (a fine sculpted head of Dionysus) and a hilltop view from Profitis Ilias over all three of Chalkidiki's peninsulas. The road to the east winds up through pine forests to the hill town of **Arnea**, where the women spin and weave handsome rustic tapestries, carpets and long-pile flokati rugs. You will see the natural wool hanging out to dry on the balconies of the houses. You can buy either direct from the loom, or from one of the small shops around the main square.

En route to the east coast, philosophically inclined travellers can visit a little garden on the outskirts of **Stagira**, the birthplace of Aristotle, who is "honoured" by a dreadful modern statue looking understandably disgusted with his sculptor. Sympathize with the ancient sage, who said, "Misfortune unites men when the same thing is harmful to both." The road leads on through the rolling hills to the fishing and boat-building village of **Ierissos**. Just 7 km (4 miles) down the coast, the road from Nea Roda to Trypiti marks the narrowest point of the isthmus lead-

ing to Mount Athos. This follows the course of **Xerxes' Canal** of 480 BC, of which mounds, depressions and other infrastructures are still discernible. The Persian king cut through the isthmus to avoid the treacherous sea route around the peninsula which had devastated the Persian fleet 11 years earlier. (You will understand why if you try to cruise south around Cape Akrathos today.)

The gateway to Mount Athos, **Ouranopolis** is of growing importance as a smart beach resort with fine hotels and first class sandy beaches. The waterfront **watchtower** was built in the 12th century to guard against pirates, but the town itself was founded in 1922 by refugees from Turkey. Another recent innovation is local hand-knotted Byzantine-patterned rugs, introduced by a Grecophile Australian with an eye to the tourist trade.

Kassandra

The long, sweeping beaches of the western peninsula have been developed into large-scale holiday centres by the Greek National Tourist Organization. The resorts of **Sani**, **Kalithea**, **Kriopigi**, **Chanioti** and **Paliouri** are ideal for family vacations. Facilities include protected swimming areas and swimming pools, bars, restaurants, discotheques, boutiques, tennis and volley ball courts, mini-golf and horse riding. Sports equipment can be hired on the spot. Non-residents can use the facilities for a small fee. Smaller hotels and rooms in private houses are also available. The government-run camping grounds are impeccably clean and well organized. Trees and hedges lend privacy to the individual grassy sites.

Named after Alexander's general, Kassandra was settled in ancient times,

A Boyhood in Macedonia

Alexander had as simple a boyhood as could be imagined for someone destined to conquer the greatest empire the world had seen. Much of his childhood is obscured by the embellishments of legend—understandable for a man who convinced himself as well as his followers and enemies that he was a god. He was born in Pella (see p. 258) in 356 BC, son of King Philip of Macedonia and Olympias, princess of Epirus. The Persians explained their astounding defeat at his hands by claiming he was in fact of Persian blood, his mother having been secretly seduced by the king of Persia and then sent back to Macedonia.

As a 10-year-old, he played the lyre and recited poetry at Philip's banquet for Greek ambassadors who were warned to curb their amorous interest in the pretty fellow. But he also developed an early taste for hunting birds and foxes. At the age of 12 he was given Bucephalus, the legendary black horse he rode for the next 20 years. The stallion bucked, reared and refused all commands until young Alexander, realizing he was shying away from his own shadow, turned him to face the sun. He quickly soothed and mounted Bucephalus, and his father Philip wept for joy.

The next year, at a time when the rough-and-tumble Macedonian court was eager to acquire some of the polish and culture of Athens, Philip sent for Aristotle, then a research fellow at Plato's Academy, to become Alexander's tutor. For two years, the philosopher, himself a Macedonian from Chalkidiki, kindled in Alexander an undying passion for Homer. Identifying himself with Achilles (whom his mother claimed as an ancestor), Alexander carried Aristotle's annotated edition of the *Iliad* throughout his travels. Efforts to teach him some politics were less successful—"young men," the tutor wrote later, "are not a proper audience for political science, they have no experience of life." Alexander was more responsive to Aristotle's interests in zoology and botany, later sending him back rare animals and plants from all over his empire.

largely by cattle farmers, until the Turkish Pasha of Thessaloniki massacred the inhabitants and destroyed their houses in the struggle for independence. The peninsula was resettled with refugees from Turkey during the great population exchange of the 1920s, but full-scale development is a recent phenomenon.

Sithonia

This is undoubtedly the prettiest and most cheerful of Chalkidiki's three peninsulas. A corniche coast road winds along the bays and creeks past occasional fishing ports, amid sea pines, olive trees and newly developed vineyards. Tiny beaches afford absolute privacy and perfect calm. Inland, the fragrant pine forests of **Mount Longos** are dark and cool with streams and springs.

You will find fine beaches from **Metamorfosis** down to **Toroni**, and a superb natural harbour further south at **Koufos**. From **Kalamitsi**, look east to the dramatic pyramidal silhouette of Mount Athos. There are first class camping facilities at **Paradissos** and **Neos Marmaras** on the west coast. Near the latter, Sithonia boasts one of the country's best resort complexes, **Porto Carras**. It comprises two hotels and a village inn, two theatres, an 18-hole golf course, an excellent beach and a marina for luxury yachts and smaller craft. The complex is backed by a large estate run as a model farm, producing fruit, olives, almonds and an honourable wine drawing on vine-cuttings and wine-growing experts from Bordeaux. It is the brainchild of shipping magnate

John Carras, whose other contribution to upgrading Greek tourism was to promote the renovation of Athens' Plaka district.

Mount Athos

 Although our only access to the world of ancient Greece is through the stones of its ruined cities, sanctuaries, palaces and tombs, Mount Athos provides a surviving example of the spiritual world of Byzantium. The Holy Mountain *(Ágion Óros)*, as Athos is known to the Orthodox Church, is a world apart. Within the Greek state, the monks of Mount Athos rule over an autonomous theocratic republic, and control all access to the peninsula.

Many women feel slighted at not being allowed to visit this totally male preserve. Yet even male visitors should remember that however hospitably they are received, they are in essence intruders into the natural rhythm and spirit of the monastic life. Nobody can visit as a mere tourist. A letter of introduction from one's consul is required of all foreign visitors, as a guarantee of their seriousness of purpose. Even then, a stay on Athos is usually limited to a maximum of four days. For those fortunate enough to be permitted entry, the peninsula's wild, unspoiled beauty, and the art treasures contained in the churches are memorable enough, but it is the fascinating insight into monastic life, and the peninsula's all-pervasive spirituality that make the greatest impact.

Applications for an individual or group permit must be made to the Ministry of Foreign Affairs, Directorate of Churches, Zalokosta 2, Athens, tel. (01) 36.26.894, or to the Ministry for Northern Greece, Directorate for Cultur-al Affairs, Platia Dioikitiriou, Thessaloniki, tel. (031) 270.092. Apply three to four months in advance. Women are forbidden access, and visitors are not allowed to stay overnight unless they can show proof of a religious or scientific interest, and are over 18 years of age. A maximum of ten visitors are allowed to stay on any one night.

For those who have obtained a permit, the Mount Athos boat leaves early in the morning from Ouranopolis. Travel light, with a small backpack, walking shoes, a sweater for cool evenings on the mountain, and a pocket flashlight—the monasteries have little or no electricity after dark. The boat itself is an exclusive community of men—Greek locals delivering monastery supplies, visiting priests or resident monks, and only a sprinkling of foreign visitors. On the quayside, the women wave goodbye with a bemused smile.

They and others without residence permits can at least enjoy a sea view of the Holy Mountain's west coast monasteries on a **boat cruise** (from Ouranopolis or Ormos Panagias on Sithonia). The cruises follow the same route as the regular Athos launch, but at a more respectful distance from the coast. The launch pulls in to drop supplies and passengers at the monasteries' ports—simple landing-stages with old watchtowers and little warehouses. The first monastery you pass is **Docheiariou**, a cluster of russet-roofed houses dominated by an 18th-century watch-tower lying snugly against a green hillside. Its church has some splendid 16th-century frescoes in the decorative Cretan style. Further down the coast, amber onion-domes behind tall tenement-like shorefront houses announce the Russian monastery

Athos, the Holy Mountain
The first religious men to seek refuge on Mount Athos were hermits who sought refuge in caves during the persecutions of the iconoclasm controversy in the 8th century (see p. 63). The monks' cells were organized into communities by Athanasius, counsellor to Emperor Nicephorus Phocas, and founder of the Great Lavra monastery in 963. In its 15th-century heyday, the Holy Mountain numbered 40 monasteries, each with up to 1,000 monks. Good relations with the Sultan after the Turkish conquest meant that while Constantinople remained the "political" capital of the Orthodox Church, Mount Athos was its spiritual centre. But support for Greek independence brought Turkish oppression in the 19th century and the number of monks dwindled drastically. In 1926, Mount Athos was made a theocratic republic under Greek suzerainty.

Of the 20 monasteries left today, 17 are Greek and the other three Russian, Bulgarian and Serbian. Each has a deputy on the Holy Council, led by the First of Athos, ruling in the village capital, Karyes. The monastic communities are either *cenobite*, the monks "living in common", observing strict discipline and an austere diet; or *idiorrhythmic*, each monk "going his own way", less rigid in discipline. The day is dominated by the liturgy, most of it after dark. Worship begins with twilight *hesperinón*, vespers; then *apódipnon*, after dinner; *nykterinós*, and the main nocturnal service; *agry*

of **Agios Panteleimon**, a 12th-century foundation locally known as the *Rossikón*. Visitors will find a gaily coloured church built in 1812, with green lantern-domes and white, blood-red and ochre walls inspired by the Baroque architecture of St Petersburg. The halls have heavy Russian furniture, monumental samovars, and portraits of

the Tsars. Other monasteries on the west coast visible from cruise boats include **Simonopetra** and **Dionysiou**, both perched on rocks high above the sea.

All visitors pass through the main port of **Dafni** to take a bus to administrative headquarters for the issuing of residence permits *(diamonitírion)*. In **Karyes**, the peninsula's capital and only town, try to hitch a ride with monks visiting from outlying monasteries. They may appear to live in a Byzantine time-warp, but they know how to handle jeeps, lorries, and caïques with outboard motors. But you may also be able to travel on mule-back, or join up with a fellow hiker.

Before setting off, visit the town's **Protaton** church, built in the 10th century but much restored since. It has a fine 16th-century iconostasis (icon-screen), but is most admired for the frescoes (1300) by the great Byzantine painter, Manuel Panseleinos. *The Nativity, The Presentation at the Temple, The Washing of the Feet*, and *The Baptism* are depicted in his own very personal style, angular and forceful.

North of Karyes is the most modern of the monasteries, **Vatopedi**, with telephone and electricity. Built around a triangular courtyard, the refectory and accommodation overlook some smart little motor boats in the harbour. The 15th-century bronze doors on its basilica come from Thessaloniki's Agia Sofia. There are fine icons of Saints Peter and Paul in the northern chapel of St Demetrius. This relaxed community is the only one on the peninsula to use the standard European clock and calendar—the rest of Athos still observes the Julian calendar, 13 days behind our own, and the day is divided into flexible Byzan-

256

*A*ll women, even locals, are forbidden to set foot within the monastic enclave of Mount Athos.

tine hours, so that the sun always sets at 12 o'clock.

Further north, the Serbian monastery of **Chiliandari** lies hidden from the coast in a beautiful green valley surrounded by wooded hills. Visit the church, built in splendid multi-coloured brick in 1197, the year of the monastery's foundation, when there were 1,000 monks in residence. A beautiful 30-minute walk among chestnut, oak, maple and eucalyptus leads to the pretty little pebble **beach**.

Down the east coast, **Stavronikita** is a battlemented fortress-monastery dramatically positioned on a rock overlooking the sea—it was under constant pirate attack in the 13th century. Its prize treasure, in the church, is a mosaic icon of Greece's patron saint, Nicholas.

Iviron or Iberia (meaning Russian Georgia, not Spain and Portugal) is now a fully Greek monastery. This hamlet by the sea serves as a hospitable port of call

for travellers between Karyes and the Holy Mountain's oldest and biggest monastery, the **Grand Lavra** *(Megísti Lávra)*. At the foot of Mount Athos itself, this fortified village has alone escaped unscathed from the peninsula's countless fires. Its diligent monks work away in the carpentry shops, gardens, fields and vineyards, each planted with a red wooden cross to bless the crop. Tradition insists that the gnarled and split, but unbent cypresses in the spacious courtyard were planted in the year of Lavra's foundation, 963. The **church** possesses in its nave the Holy Mountain's finest frescoes, executed by the Cretan artist Theophanes in 1535. In front of the church is an elegant 17th-century Holy Fountain *(Phiale)*, a basin of porphyry stone and sculpted bronze under a domed canopy decorated with the baptism of Christ. The refectory with superb semi-circular stone tables is graced by more Theophanes frescoes, most notably *The Last Supper.*

Of Lavra's numerous dependencies to the south, perhaps the most forbidding is **Karoulia** at the south-west tip of the peninsula. This group of flimsy wooden dwellings clinging to the cliff-face is accessible only by ropes and ladders, but visible from the sea—when weather permits.

Mount Athos, 2,033 m (6,670 ft) bears the name of a rebellious giant buried here by Poseidon. Alexander's architect-sculptor Deinocrates once proposed to carve the whole white limestone mass into a statue of the great conqueror. Alexander declined. From the south-east, via the *skíti* of Kerassia, the summit, with its little chapel and magnificent view, is a perfectly manageable day's hike.

*T*he last ferry of the day
slips quietly into harbour.

Western Macedonia

This mountainous region was the stronghold of the ancient kings of Macedonia. Their palaces and tombs make a good one-day round trip from Thessaloniki. **Pella**, Philip's capital and the birthplace of Alexander lies some 40 km (25 miles) north-west of Thessaloniki. It was the home of Macedonian kings from about 400 to 167 BC.

Excavations have not yet located the palace, but the city is re-emerging among the columns of a classical temple, traces of the theatre where Euripi-

des saw the première of his tragedy *The Bacchae*, and the wide streets where Aristotle walked in the shade of the colonnaded buildings.

The **House of the Lion Hunt** (300 BC) still has its patterned pebble mosaic floors, but the great pictorial mosaic that gave the house its name is now displayed in the site's **museum**. The scene is believed to show Alexander in Sidon (Lebanon) being rescued from the clutches of a lion by his faithful officer, Craterus. Other museum mosaics depict *Dionysus Riding a Panther,* a *Gryphon Attacking a Deer* and a *Battle of Amazons*. North of the main road, in a house at the western end of the site, two mosaics have been replaced in their original setting: the *Rape of Helen* and a *Stag Hunt*.

Cool off with a 40-minute drive west to the foothills of Mount Vermion. Several bubbling streams run through

Edessa, a town of refreshing parks and greenery. The waters converge into a grand **cascade** dropping 24 m (80 ft) down cliffs thick with fig trees, pomegranates and almond trees.

Turn south 18 km (11 miles) to the site of an ancient Macedonian cemetery, near **Lefkadia**. Most impressive of the three monumental mausoleums is the **Great Tomb** or Tomb of Judgement (3rd century BC). Sheltered by a hangar, the limestone mausoleum comprises two rooms of two storeys with frescoes of the dead man's judgement in the Underworld. Sculpted battle friezes on the tomb suggest he participated in the Macedonian campaigns in Asia.

Continuing south, you pass through the peach orchards and vineyards of prosperous **Naousa** to the ski resort of **Veria** on the eastern slopes of **Mount Vermion**, which offers pleasant summer rambles in the woods of chestnut, hazel, oak and beech. Just 11 km (7 miles) south-east of Veria are the **Royal Tombs of Vergina** unearthed by Professor Andronikos in 1977. The treasures of Philip and other Macedonian kings have been transported to Thessaloniki's museum (see p. 251), but frescoes decorating the tomb walls are being prepared for public display.

Kastoria

This charming lakeside town, the capital of Greece's fur industry, is off the beaten track but well worth a detour. Prettily located on a promontory jutting out into Kastoria Lake, it is served by direct flights from Athens, and reliable bus and train services from Thessaloniki. If you are in the market for a fur coat, stole or hat, the price savings will go a long way to repaying the fare. In any case, you should see the grand 17th- and 18th-century **patrician mansions** (*archontiká*) with their ground floors, once stables, converted now to furriers' workshops. Resisting creeping modernization, many of the best houses are in the old cobble-stoned Kariadi neighbourhood around the southern lakefront. Beneath an overhanging roof, the corbelled upper storeys have handsome casement windows with dark wood shutters. Inside are wooden ceilings, carved wall panelling and imposing fireplaces. One of them, the **Nerandzis house**, is now a folklore museum. Most of the fur shops are on the main street, Mitropoleos.

"Kastoria" derives from the Greek word for beaver, a species that populated the lake until the 19th century. Started by Jewish furriers from eastern Europe, the fur trade continues to flourish using imported mink, fox, squirrel and stone marten. The pelts are worked into garments and sold worldwide, promoted by an annual fur fair in March.

Most of the town's 70 churches, more than 50 of them still in use, were originally the patrician families' private chapels. But take a walk around the south shore of the lake to visit 11th-century **Panagia Mavriotissa**, one of the more attractive, with frescoes both outside and inside. The fine *archontiká* house opposite is also worth a look.

Notice on the lake the strange snub-nosed, flat-bottomed fishing boats, an ancient form unchanged for centuries.

Mount Olympus

Tackling the home of the gods is strictly for seasoned mountain-climbers. Anyone driving from Thessaloniki to Athens can get a close-up view of the country's

The beavers that gave Lake Kastoria its name have long since disappeared. However, the town's fur trade survives by using imported pelts.

highest mountain by turning off south of Katerini to the climbers' base-camp village of **Litochori**. The summit, 2,917 m (9,570 ft) high, is named Mitikas (the Needle) and Zeus's Throne stands 8 m (26 ft) lower.

Eastern Macedonia

The drive east from Thessaloniki around the **Koronia** and **Volvi lakes** leads through orchards and tobacco plantations. North of Koronia from April to June, you may see nesting herons rising from the plane trees in the red-earthed landscape. Attractively surrounded by hills, Volvi Lake offers a hot springs resort at **Nea Apolonia**, good for rheumatism.

If you prefer cool sea water, head down to the beach resort of **Asprovalta**. Where the Strymon river reaches the sea from the Bulgarian mountains, the great **Lion of Amfipolis** (4th century BC) guards the bridge. This stone burial monument was washed downriver from the nearby Athenian colony.

The scenic coast road passes several fine beaches, the best located between **Nea Peramos** and **Kalamitsa**. The camping at **Batis** is excellent.

Kavala

Macedonia's second-largest city and centre of the Greek tobacco industry, rises in tiers from the waterfront up the slopes of Mount Symvolon. The fishing boats and the houses behind share a taste for bright reds, yellows and blues. This was the port of Neapolis where St Paul landed on his way to Philippi to bring Christianity to Europe (see p. 67).

The town's dominant feature is a huge Roman-style Turkish **aqueduct** built in the 16th century to carry water to the old citadel (*acropolis*) out on the eastern promontory. Walk along the Byzantine ramparts for superb views over the har-

bour and city. Down past the Imaret, a 19th-century enclosure of domes, courtyards, and terraces, established as an almshouse by Mohammed Ali, founder of the modern Egyptian dynasty that ended with King Farouk. Close by is **Mohammed Ali's house** with his swash-buckling equestrian statue in front. The monarch, son of a rich Albanian tobacco merchant, was born here in 1769. A caretaker will show you the Pasha's quarters, the lattice-shuttered harem, and an attractive garden. A belvedere nearby looks out over the island of Thasos.

The **Archaeological Museum** has interesting local finds, notably a stone frieze of fighting soldiers carved in the 5th century BC

Philippi

Conquered and renamed by Philip of Macedonia, the town's **ruins** are of Roman and early Christian interest. It was here that Julius Caesar's assassins, Cassius and Brutus, were each defeated by Octavius and Antony in two famous battles that ended the Roman Republic in 42 BC. The town was promptly elevated to the status of a Roman colony. On the north side of the modern road, you can see the excavated Greek theatre (4th century BC) where Roman gladiators fought and where classical tragedies are again performed today. Nearby are the ruins of a sanctuary dedicated to the Egyptian deities Isis and Serapis. Beside the road is Basilica A, a 5th-century church near where Paul made his first European conversions. Opposite is the forum, its outline still clearly visible. Much of its masonry went into the building of the adjacent Basilica B, a 6th-century church left unfinished when its dome collapsed. Equally impressive in its own way is the neighbouring ancient public lavatory, reached via a portal and a flight of steps down to its splendid marble seats.

Thrace

Bounded on the north by the Rhodope mountains, what is really only western Thrace (Thrace in its entirety extends east to Istanbul) stretches from the Nestos River to the Evros, on the frontier with Turkey. The climate is more Balkan than Mediterranean, with hot summers, cold winters and considerable rainfall. The atmosphere and architecture of the towns are noticeably more oriental here, ethnically more Bulgarian and Turkish than Greek. The town of **Xanthi**, centre of the region's finest tobacco-growing country, has some delightful traditional houses and little shops on a hill north of the modern quarter. The university town of **Komotini** has a distinctly oriental bazaar, but also an impressive modern **Archaeological Museum**, boasting a gold bust (2nd century AD) of emperor-philosopher Marcus Aurelius.

There is pleasant swimming down at the pebble beach of **Fanari** backed by its tree-shaded campsites. Birdwatchers should head for the eastern **Evros Wetlands** to spot herons, wild swans, storks and cormorants among the tamarisk, poplars and willows. **Alexandroupolis**, the region's capital, has a wine festival in August, but gourmets come mainly to sample the mussels and caviar, before enjoying a post-prandial stroll along the charming harbourside promenade.

Visitors' Etiquette

If you are approaching a monastery by mule, dismount before you reach the entrance. Present your residence permit at the visitors' hostel (archontária), where the guest-master will receive you with a welcoming glass of ouzo, or some other potent home-made liqueur, and a loukoúm sweetmeat. Lodgings are of monastic simplicity. Do not expect hot water for shaving—this is a land of beards. At the end of the afternoon, a wooden-beam gong is sounded for dinner. The refectories have a handsome austerity; the massive stone tables set into the floor have recesses on top to for receptacles for olives. Served in pewter dishes, a typical meal might be chickpea soup, bread, olives, feta cheese and fruit, with retsina or water. Breakfast, taken very early, may be a spicy vegetable stew, feta, fruit, and again wine or water. The stricter monasteries ask visitors not to enter the church during services, and to dine after the monks have finished their meal. A donation to the monastery funds should be made before you leave.

Thasos

Famous of old for its fine white marble and heady wines, this most northerly of the Aegean islands still cultivates a taste for the good life, though the wine is now imported from the mainland. A good ferry service from Kavala brings you to an island of serenity, green with graceful pines and chestnuts, with a silver filigree of olive groves, and fine sandy beaches. You will find the people here much more friendly and easy-going than on the mainland.

The modern port town of **Limin** is built among the ruins of the classical city, including a rampart of the 5th century BC, complete with towers and gates. The wall rises steeply from the harbour to the ancient theatre, a lovely creation with a proscenium dedicated to Dionysus, where classical drama is performed in summer. Further up, a rock-hewn shrine to Pan has a carved relief of the god piping to his goats.

The **Archaeological Museum** near the old harbour has some fine sculptures of local marble, notably a *kouros* (temple statue, 6th century BC) of Apollo carrying a ram, and a handsome head of Dionysus (3rd century BC).

Just 2 km to the south-west, sandy **Makriamos** is a luxury beach resort providing almost every sport under the sun, but especially scuba-diving, fishing and sailing. **Chrisi Amoudi** is the favourite beach for the snorkelling fraternity, and has some good seafood restaurants too. Head south to **Kinira** for some gentle windsurfing. In the old quarries down at **Aliki**, the marble still bears the scars of ancient picks. During your stay on the island, don't miss the opportunity to taste the Thasian honey, and the preserves (*glyká tou koutalioú*) of green figs or green walnuts, cooked in the gardens in giant cauldrons over glowing wood fires.

Samothrace

It isn't hard to believe that the gods of the nether regions live on here in the deep shadows of the rugged granite mountains, hiding from the blinding sunlight like the island's eternal goats. In days of old, Aristophanes, Plato and monarchs from Philip of Macedonia to Rome's Emperor Hadrian, came here to be initiated into the mysteries of Samothrace's cult of the Underworld. Today, after a short ferry ride from Alexandroupolis via the port of Kamariotisa, you can retrace their pilgrimage to the **Sanctuary of the Great Gods** at Paleopolis.

Ask at the Xenia Hotel for admittance to the archaeological site, set in a wilderness of rocks and olive trees. Leaving the museum till later, take the path left to the Anaktoron (500 BC), an initiation hall with a small adjoining room where novices changed into their sacred robes and later obtained their certificate of initiation. The Arsinoion rotunda was erected in the 3rd century BC by Egyptian Queen Arsinoe. Built of marble from Thasos, and combining all three Greek architectural orders—Doric entablature, Ionic cornices and Corinthian columns—it was the largest circular edifice in ancient Greece, 20 m (64 ft) in diameter. To the south, sacrificial feasts were held in the enclosed courtyard of the Temenos (4th century BC). Several Doric columns have been restored in the porch of the grand Hieron, where the

*P*hoenician merchants are popularly believed to have been the
earliest settlers on the island of Thasos. Their wide-ranging journeys around
the Mediterranean and beyond led to the birth of a thriving boat-building
industry which continues to this day. Many of the techniques have survived
unmodified since the classical age of the war galley and the trireme.

Mysteries of the Underworld
Samothrace's Great Gods of the Underworld were of Balkan and Anatolian origin. First among them was Axieros, a universal Earth Mother worshipped at sacred rocks. Her subordinate male consort was Kadmilos. Two other gods consigned more specifically to the Underworld, Axiokersos and Axiokersa, were the equivalents of the Greek Hades and his wife Persephone. When the sages and nobles of antiquity sought initiation into the dark mysteries of this Underworld, it was for the knowledge of moral judgements that it imparted—the overtones of evil and damnation to which the Christian conception of Hell have accustomed us did not apply. Initiation entailed confession, purification, and the moral resolution to lead a better life. All we know of the actual ritual is that it was performed at night, and was conducted in the Thracian tongue. Unlike Eleusis (see p. 122), the Samothracian mysteries were open to all nationalities, men, women and children, freemen and slaves.

culminating ritual was held. On a hill above the theatre is a fountain marking the original site of the famous statue known as the *Winged Victory of Samothrace* that was carried off in 1863 to Paris, where it is now graces the halls of the Louvre.

In the sanctuary's **museum**, the sculpture collection includes the Temenos frieze of musicians and dancing girls performing for a wedding of the gods.

On the north coast, the spa of **Therma** claims to cure infertility. The women's pool is much hotter than the men's. If a dip does not appeal, then use the spa as base camp for the 5-hour climb up **Mount Fengari** (1,600 m, 5,250 ft). From what Homer described as the "topmost peak of wooded Samothrace", you can gaze across the sea to the battlegrounds of Troy.

Limnos

Facing the Turkish islands of Gökçe and Bozca (Imbros and Tenedos to the Greeks), and the Dardanelles beyond, this island is of obvious strategic importance, and its natural sheltered harbour

265

of **Moudros** is a major military base. It was from here that the British launched their World War I attack on the Dardanelles; 900 British Commonwealth soldiers lie buried in the cemetery.

But the island's charm derives mainly from its tree-shaded capital of **Myrina** on the west coast. It has two harbours, divided by a promontory guarded by a Venetian fortress. Traditional sailors' houses with wooden balconies line the stone-paved streets. The town's well-organized **museum** displays finds from the archaeological sites of Poliochni and Hephaestia. North of town, at the end of the beach, is one of the Aegean's major luxury hotels. The best beaches, none of them overcrowded, are around the south coast at **Ziniatha**, **Thanos** and **Plati**.

Lesbos

Greece's third-largest island (after Crete and Euboea) is bustling and prosperous. Covering 1,632 sq km (630 sq miles), it offers lazy days on good pebble or sand beaches, and delightful rambles through the hilly interior of pine forests and olive groves.

The legendary home of Sappho—along with fellow poets Arion and Alcaeus, and the father of Greek music, Terpander—has an enduring cultural tradition among modern Greek artists, too. From all over the world, pilgrims seek out the island that inspired Sappho's exalted verse about the young women she loved.

The island takes an alternative name from its capital of **Mytilini**. The sophisticated modern port-town has a boisterous bazaar-like shopping street running behind the harbour, with a rather unflat-

> **The Divine Blacksmith**
> Limnos is the island of Hephaistos, the god of volcanoes, patron of smiths and metal workers. The son of Zeus and Hera, he was so ugly and feeble as an infant that his mother dropped him into the sea off Limnos. He was rescued by the sea-nymphs Thetis and Eurynome, who nurtured him in an underwater grotto, and gave him a smithy as a playroom. He began making little pieces of jewellery, and in particular a brooch for Thetis that was so beautiful that Hera was jealous of it. When she discovered that her abandoned son had made it, she took him back to Olympus and set him up in a much finer smithy, with 20 bellows working day and night. But Zeus lost his temper with Hephaistos when his son reproached him for mistreating Hera, and cast the unfortunate smith out of Olympus once more. Hephaistos's fall lasted one whole day, and he hit the rocks of Limnos with such a crack, that from then on he could only walk with the aid of golden leg-irons that he fashioned for himself.

Lesbos, the home of Sappho, can boast its own Mount Olympus, seen here rising above the hill-town of Agiassos. The name occurs in several places apart from Lesbos and western Macedonia. There are other Mounts Olympus in Arcadia, Elis, Euboea, Laconia, Cyprus and Asia Minor, but only the Macedonian peak can truly claim to be the home of the gods.

tering statue of Sappho. For an overall view, head up to the **kastro**, the Genoese-Turkish citadel.

At the **Archaeological Museum**, look out for the 3rd-century Roman villa mosaics portraying the Athenian playwright Menander and scenes from his comedies.

Inland from the capital, **Agiassos** is a lovely hill town on pine-clad Mount Olympus. It is famous for its ceramics and woven fabrics. On the north coast, **Mithymna** (also known as Molyvos) is an increasingly popular fishing port with a maze of tall tower-houses climbing steeply from the harbour to the Genoese castle. It has a great beach.

On the west side of the island, between Sygri and Eressos is a fascinating **petrified forest** of conifers and redwoods that were buried by volcanic ash and solidified by rainwater and underground springs. Sappho's home is believed to have been at the port of **Skala Eressos**, not the more modern inland town. In any case, its sandy beach makes the pilgrimage more rewarding. Only fragments of stone wall remain from ancient times.

Other beaches on Lesbos are on the south coast, at **Vatera** and **Plomari**— famous for its ouzo.

The Tenth Muse

Plato wrote: "Some say the Muses are nine, but how carelessly! Look at the tenth, Sappho from Lesbos." Born in 612 BC, she was forced into exile as a child with her aristocratic family, but returned from Sicily to marry and bear a child, Cleis. At Eressos, on Lesbos, she lived in a commune of women devoted to music, poetry and the worship of Apollo. Her odes and elegies treated love with a simple tenderness and passion, praising her companions' beauty and goodness in a direct and unaffected manner.

That man seems to me on a par with the gods who sits in your company and listens to you so close to him speaking sweetly and laughing sexily, such a thing makes my heart flutter in my breast, for when I see you even for a moment, then the power to speak another word fails me, instead my tongue freezes into silence, and at once a gentle fire has caught throughout my flesh, and I see nothing with my eyes, and there's a drumming in my ears, and sweat pours down me, and trembling seizes all of me, and I become paler than grass, and I seem to fail almost to the point of death in my very self.

of the northern part of the island are in sharp contrast to the lush orange and lemon groves, and almond and olive trees of the south.

Chios

Proud without being aloof, this island's striking personality owes much to its Italian past and its tormented relationship with Turkey (now the object of peaceful day-excursions to Çesme, 30 minutes by ferry). It competes with Turkey's Izmir as the birthplace of Homer. The dramatic, barren landscapes

Chios Town

The busy port capital tingles with excitement when the evening ferry comes in from Piraeus, and local citizens mingle with travellers for the *vólta* along the waterfront. The most rewarding of the town's art collections is in the **Argenti Folklore Museum** on Platonos Street, with its superb display of old costumes and exquisite painted porcelain statuettes of the island's Greek and

Mastic Magic

The people of southern Chios boast that theirs is the only true mastic region in the world—even a few kilometres to the north, the "gum tree" cannot produce the proper kind of resin (Portuguese claims are dismissed as humbug). But what is so great about mastic? Midwives use it as an antiseptic during childbirth. Hunters stuff mastic twigs into gutted hares to preserve them. It was a staple aphrodisiac in the harem of the Turkish Sultan. And it makes good toothpaste, hygienic chewing gum, and a potent alcoholic drink.

Turkish peasants. The **Byzantine Museum**, housed in an old mosque, combines church art with relics of the Venetian and Genoese past. The **Archaeological Museum** (Odos Michalou) has Chian ceramics and terracotta figures from the 7th to the 4th centuries BC.

The beach suburb of **Vrontados** boasts a "master's stone" where people like to imagine that Homer recited his verse. South of Chios Town, **Karfas** has a popular sandy beach.

Nea Moni

Take the exhilarating excursion west of Chios Town to this 11th-century monastery tucked into the mountain side. The few nuns who have taken the place of hundreds of monks that once lived here will show you the church's Byzantine mosaics. See, too, the handsome refectory with its marble table and a grim ossuary containing skeletons of Chians massacred by the Turks in 1822. More than any other, it was this event that roused foreign writers and artists to support Greek independence.

Further into the mountains is the mysterious half-abandoned village of **Anavatos**. Byzantine ruins straggle up to a precipice from which women and children jumped to avoid slaughter in the 1822 massacre. Today the hilltop church is just a shell, but its frescoes are intact. Elderly people occupy a couple of houses, a few fig trees and pomegranates still bear fruit, and the bakery's smoke-begrimed oven stands empty.

North Coast

The island's many prosperous ship-owners live up in the pleasant little village of **Kardamyla**, claiming that Homer preceded them. Their villas look down on the charming port of **Marmaro**. You will find a couple of good pebble beaches nearby at **Nagos** and **Giossonas**.

South of Chios Town

Beyond Chios airport, old mansions with Italian coats of arms on walls enclosing citrus orchards, olive groves and cypress trees, remind the visitor of the island's Genoese and Venetian masters. Thereafter, you begin to see the bush-like lentisk trees from which Chians have tapped since antiquity a resin of wondrous powers called *mastícha*.

Centre of the "mastic country" is the delightful town of **Pyrgi**. Unique grey and white geometric patterns adorn its houses, a subtle touch of colour added by strings of tomatoes and peppers hanging from the balconies to ripen.

To the west, **Mestra** is an equally charming mediaeval village with streets shaded by arches and tunnels linking the houses from one roof-patio to another. **Emborio**, 10 minutes' drive south of Pyrgi, has an attractive black pebble beach. Nearby are (currently off-limit) excavations of a town that occupied the site from Trojan to classical times.

*V*isiting yachts line the
harbour wall in Samos.

Samos

This fertile island just 3 km (2 miles)
from the Turkish mainland is renowned
for its sweet red muscatel wine and a
much admired olive oil. The mathemati-
cian Pythagoras was born here in the 6th
century BC, but fell foul of tyrant Polycrates and went off to southern Italy.
Before him, another great Samian traveller, Colaeus, sailed through the Straits
of Gibraltar—the Pillars of Hercules, as
they were known in ancient times—to
explore Spain's Atlantic coast. Today,
many islanders have gone clear across
to Massachusetts, and not returned.

The sleepy port resort of **Pythagorio**
stands on the site of Polycrates' ancient
capital of Samos. North-west of town,
take a torch to explore the **Tunnel of
Eupalinos** built in the troubled 6th century BC to provide clandestine passage
under the city walls. Along the coast
west of Pythagorio are the ruins of the
Heraion sanctuary, with what was
once the largest temple in the Aegean—
one and a half times the size of the
Parthenon. One column and pillar
stumps defining the ground plan are all
that remain. The nearby beach resort
pays homage with its name **Colonna**.

The modern capital is over on the
north coast. **Samos Town** has a spacious
harbour serving the northern islands. In
the **museum**, sculptures from the
Heraion sanctuary include a giant
kouros (6th century BC), 5 m (16.5 ft)
tall, and a seated female statue, perhaps
of Hera herself. Up on a hill behind the
port is the old Turkish capital of **Vathi**
with charming old houses and a view
across to Turkey. North coast beaches
include **Kokari**, **Avlakia** and
Karlovasi.

On the west side of the island, the
atmospheric hill town of **Marathokam-
pos** preserves its leafy tranquillity
among impossibly steep narrow streets,
overlooking **Ormos**, its little beach
resort.

*T*he distinctive geometric
patterns on the façades of Pyrgi's
buildings are achieved using a technique known as sgraffito. The walls
are covered with a layer of plaster,
parts of which are scraped off to
reveal the contrasting grey beneath.

Omphalos — the Centre of the World, Where Kings and Commoners Sought the Wisdom of the Delphic Oracle

The sanctuary of Delphi was for ancient Greeks the centre of their universe, where Zeus had flung the sacred stone that marked the navel of the world. Here, the Pythian priestesses entered a state of ecstasy, and dispensed the enigmatic prophecies of the divine oracle. Further north, the plains of Thessaly lie between the cool, wooded slopes of Mount Pilion in the east, and the airy retreats of the Meteoran monasteries, perched atop their rocky pinnacles in the hills to the west. Offshore lie the hedonistic delights of the Sporades.

Apart from the sanctuary of Delphi, which attracts as many pilgrims today as it did in antiquity, this region remains pretty much untouched by the tourist crowds. The road that travels north from Athens leads past Mount Parnassus, rising behind the sacred oracle at Delphi. It

*T*he monks of Meteora *have built their monastic retreats on the summits of spectacular, sheer-sided rock towers.*

was once a stronghold of the rebellious klephts, who spearheaded the resistance against the Turkish and German occupations. Today it is the haunt of hikers in summer and skiers in winter.

Since ancient times, Boeotia's mountain barrier has protected north-western approaches to Athens, separating Attica and Thebes from the plains of Thessaly. North of Parnassus is the famous Pass of Thermopylae, that breaches the mountains near Lamia, where Spartans were able to hold back the southward

273

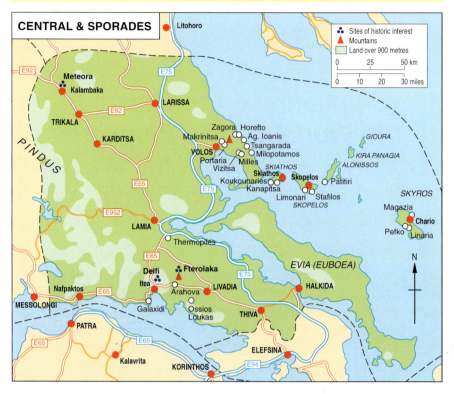

CENTRAL & SPORADES

Litohoro

Sites of historic interest
Mountains
Land over 900 metres

0   25   50 km
0   10   20   30 miles

E92
Meteora
Kalambaka
LARISSA
E75
E92
TRIKALA
KARDITSA
PINDUS
Zagora Horefto
Makrinitsa   Ag. Ioanis   GIOURA
Tsangarada
VOLOS   Milopotamos   KIRA PANAGIA
Portaria / Milles   ALONISSOS
Vizitsa   SKIATHOS
Skiathos   Skopelos
Koukounaries   Patitiri
Kanapitsa   SKYROS
Limonari Stafilos
SKOPELOS   Magazia
E65
E75
E952
LAMIA   Chario
Pefko Linaria
Thermopiles
E65
Delfi Fterolaka
Itea   EVIA (EUBOEA)   N
Nafpaktos   LIVADIA   HALKIDA
Arahova
MESSOLONGI
Galaxidi Ossios THIVA
Loukas
PATRA
E65   E65
ELEFSINA
Kalavrita
KORINTHOS   E94

advance of the Persian army for two vital days in 480 BC.

In the hills west of Thessaly, the inaccessibility of the rock towers of Meteora attracted monks fleeing from Turkish oppression. Their extraordinary monasteries, built precariously atop sheer-sided rock towers, are one of central Greece's most spectacular sights. Mount Pilion, near the port of Volos, is becoming increasingly popular for skiing, but in summer it has the quiet Alpine charm of Switzerland, with the bonus of superb seafood restaurants and good beaches on the nearby coast. Just offshore lie the islands of the Sporades, where you can choose between the lively crowds of Skiathos' modern resorts, and the remoter, more traditional atmosphere of Skopelos, Alonnisos and Skyros.

The Road to Delphi

The spectacular natural location chosen by the ancient Greeks for their most important sanctuary, on the southern slope of Mount Parnassus, is best appreciated by following the land route of the ancient pilgrims coming from Athens.

Thebes

It is purely for history's sake that we make a first stop at Oedipus's Boeotian capital, Thebes—*Thíva* in modern Greek. Here is a city apparently still beset by the king's ancient curses. Two 19th-century earthquakes and an equally devastating bout of building speculation have left the city "reeling like a wreck", as Sophocles put it. Archaeologists haunt new building sites, hoping to

274

scavenge treasures from Mycenaean palaces that have been buried beneath the office buildings.

If you do find yourself downtown for some reason, pay a visit to the **museum** at the north end of Pindarou Street. Relax in the garden and courtyard among fragments of sculpture, mosaics and Turkish tombstones. Inside are some phallic terracotta figures, Mycenaean ceramics and carved gravestones of Boeotian soldiers.

On the drive north, you can mull over the riddle which the Sphinx of Thebes put to all Thebans travelling this route. The punishment for a wrong answer was to be strangled and devoured on the spot. "What being, with only one voice, has sometimes two feet, sometimes three, sometimes four, and is weakest when it has the most?" When the Sphinx put the riddle to Oedipus, who had just killed his father Laius, the Theban king, he guessed correctly: "Man, because he crawls on all fours as an infant, stands firmly on his two feet as a youth, and leans upon a staff in his old age." The Sphinx, thwarted, flung itself to its death. Oedipus became king of Thebes, and unknowingly married his mother.

Levadia

This pleasant town of shady plane trees is renowned for its brightly coloured handspun cotton fabric and succulent roast lamb, especially at Easter. It has two landmarks: a **clock tower** left by Lord Elgin, and a pretty **Turkish bridge** across the Erkina river.

Osios Loukas

After Levadia, turn south via Distomon to this 11th-century **monastery**, a masterpiece of Byzantine architecture with splendid mosaics and icons. Dedicated not to the Apostle Luke but to a local hermit, it stands on a hill commanding a grand view over the Helikon mountain range. Above the refectory, the two adjoining churches, **Katholikon** and smaller **Theotokon** to the north, have

*T*he monastery of Osios Loukas (The Blessed Luke—not the Evangelist, but a beatified hermit), often visited as a side trip on the way to Delphi, is a masterpiece of Byzantine architecture.

*T*he golden mosaics of Osios Loukas are a beautiful testimony to the skills of the 11th-century Byzantine artists who created them.

richly varied exteriors. Brickwork and rough hewn ashlar stone, enhanced by rust-red mortar, frame the elegantly mullioned double and triple windows. In the Katholikon (1022), the narthex vaults have glowing mosaics of *The Washing of the Feet*, *The Crucifixion* and *The Resurrection*. In the apse is a *Virgin and Child* beneath the vault's *Descent of the Holy Ghost*. In the body of the church are 16th-century icons by the Cretan painter Mikhaïl Damaskinos. Inside the Theotokon, notice the columns' fine Corinthian and Islamic-style capitals.

*T*he domed nave of the Katholikon church at Osios Loukas shows the traditional Greek octago-nal plan, with the bema (or chancel) and transepts forming a cross within the octagon.

Mount Parnassus

The home of Apollo and the Muses, shared with Dionysus and his nymphs, has two peaks, *Lyákouri*, "Wolf's Mountain" (2,457 m, 8,061 ft), and *Gerontovráchos*, "Old Man's Rock" (2,435 m, 7,989 ft). Climbers and experienced hikers can make it to the top in the snow-free months of July and August from **Fterolaka**, which functions as a ski-resort from December to April. (Inquire about mountaineering guides at the Alpine Club in Athens.) The view takes in Olympus and Mount Athos to the north, the Sporades and the Cyclades, and the mountains of the Peloponnese to the south.

Arachova

With cool streams running down its narrow streets, this charming terraced mountain village is a good place to stay overnight so that you can, like the pilgrims of old, get a first view of Delphi in the early morning as you arrive from the east. The villagers make excellent flokati rugs and good wines. Try the local fried cheese speciality, *formaéla*.

Otherwise, most hotel accommodation is 1 km west of the archaeological site in the modern town of Delphi. Until excavations began in 1892, the town, then named Kastri, had stood for 12 centuries directly over the sanctuary.

Delphi

Anyone finding it hard to capture the essence of the Greek religious experience among the broken pillars, entablatures and monumental pedestals of ancient sanctuaries may see things more clearly in Delphi. If the sheer beauty of the site of the ancient oracle can inspire awe in the most blasé modern traveller, imagine what it did for the believing pilgrim. Amid cypresses, olives and pines on the southern slopes of Parnassus, a walled enclosure of temples and treasury shrines stands at the foot of two soaring crags, the **Phaedriades**. Some 600 m (2,000 ft) below is the sparkling Gulf of Corinth.

With steep paths to tackle, take the visit in easy stages: in the early morning start by exploring the sanctuary; relax for the view from the theatre; then a slow walk to the stadium, and cool off at the museum; then a visit to the sacred Castalian Spring and Athena's sanctuary at nearby Marmaria. Purists follow in the footsteps of the ancient pilgrims by visiting Athena's temple and the spring *before* the main sanctuary.

For ancient Delphi's magnificent reconstruction by French archaeologists, and our knowledge of lost features such as the statues stolen by Nero and company, thanks are due to the detailed descriptions by Pausanias, a Greek traveller of the 2nd century AD. His 10-volume *Description of Greece* was the world's first real guidebook.

The Sanctuary

Start at the courtyard of the Roman **agora** where pilgrims bought supplies in shops behind the portico or washed in the public baths. No secular buildings were allowed inside the sacred precincts.

Four steps lead up to the beginning of the **Sacred Way.** Inscriptions in the paving come from masonry that the Romans recycled from ruined shrines. The road climbs to Apollo's temple past remains of **votive offerings** donated by the city-states, free-standing statues or elaborate treasury shrines (*thesauroi*). Immediately to the right of the entrance, for instance, is the base of a bronze bull offered by the people of Corfu in gratitude for an exceptional catch of tuna fish. Opposite was a series of 37 statues donated by Sparta to celebrate its destruction of the Athenian fleet in 404 BC. This was considered arrogant and in bad taste because it concerned a victory over fellow Greeks. But, 40 years later, the Arcadians retaliated by commemorating their defeat of Sparta with a bronze monument of nine gods and heroes on the oblong platform next to the Corfu bull.

Just beyond, a well-preserved semicircular wall marks the enclosure of Argos's **Monument of Kings** to honour its alliance with Thebes.

The Sanctuary's treasury shrines cluster around a bend in the Sacred Way. First on the left is the **Treasury of Sicyon** (an ancient city-state west of Corinth), a rotunda of tufa (volcanic stone) built in 500 BC whose friezes of the Argonaut expedition are now in the museum (see p. 283). The neighbouring **Treasury of Sifnos**, financed by the Cycladic island's silver and gold mines, was among the sanctuary's richest. The museum shows splendid remains from its sculpted pediment, and the entablature, supported by two caryatids.

At the road's elbow is the **Omphalos**, the stone navel of the universe that once stood in the temple. Scholars debate whether it is Roman or Hellenistic. Zeus's two golden eagles crowned the original. North of the Omphalos, the **Treasury of the Athenians** was the grandest of Delphi's shrines. Built of white Parian marble, this miniature

Doric temple is also a masterpiece of archaeological reconstruction, pieced together from four-fifths of its original materials. The sculptured friezes are cast copies of originals preserved in the museum. The shrine was erected around 507 BC by the new Athenian Democracy and re-dedicated after the defeat of the Persians in 490 BC. An inscription on the south terrace wall proclaims: "From the Athenians to Apollo: the Persian spoils from the battle of Marathon."

*T*he Temple of Apollo was the heart of the Sanctuary of Delphi,
housing the Oracle itself. Apollo's association with the handing down of
oracular advice derived from the elevated moral position attributed to him.
He prescribed purification and penance for crimes committed, and discouraged acts of vengeance. Criminals hoped for the clemency shown by Apollo
when he defended Orestes against the vindictive Furies.

DELPHI

Stadium

Theatre

Apollo's
High Alter

Temple of Apollo

Athenian Stoa

Sybilline Rock

Treasury of
the Athenians

Sacred Way

Omphalos

Sacred Way

Treasury
of Sifnos

Treasury
of Sicyon

Monument
of Kings

Roman Agora

Votive offerings

0   50 m

0   50 yards

Beyond a rectangular building that was probably an assembly hall for Delphi's administrators is the **Sibylline Rock**, a clump of boulders fallen from the Phaedriades crags marking the site of the pre-Apollonian oracle. To the right is a smaller rock on which the goddess Leto sat, holding her little boy Apollo while he fired off his arrows at the serpent, Python. The column drums strewn around here are part of the monument that supported the Sphinx of Naxos, now in the museum.

Up against the polygonal wall which surrounded Apollo's temple, the **Athenian Stoa** was a seven-column marble portico with a wooden roof to shelter naval trophies captured from the Persians in 478 BC.

The Sacred Way climbs sharply to **Apollo's High Altar** (5th century BC) at the entrance to the temple, donated by the island of Chios. As the inscription explains, the donation gave the people of Chios priority in questioning the Pythia. Before the pilgrim had his goat sacrificed on the altar, the priest sprinkled water over the beast; if it trembled in all its limbs, then the signs were favourable for a good oracle.

The **Temple of Apollo** in its present state dates from 330 BC. Originally there was just a hut of laurel branches (laurel is Apollo's sacred tree) sheltering a wooden cult statue.

You can still see lying around the temple Parian marble column drums from the great edifice of classical times, destroyed by earthquake in 373 BC. The temple now has 6 Doric columns at each end and 15 along the sides. Imagine it housing huge statues of Apollo and Dionysus surrounded by the pilgrims' votive offerings. A bronze relief of Homer bore the inscription of the oracle he received.

Skirt the north side of the temple—where the famous Charioteer statue (see p. 283) was buried by the polygonal wall—and take the stairway up to the **theatre**. Built in the 4th century BC and enlarged by the Romans, it seated an audience of 5,000 on its limestone terraces. From the topmost seats, the view over the ruined temple and shrines, and the dramatic Pleistos ravine beyond, reveals the ancients' genius in marrying their sanctuary with the grandiose beauty of its natural setting.

*T*he theatre at Delphi offers a superb view over the ruins of the sanctuary, and the valley of the Pleistos River far below. The road curving around the ridge on the left leads to Marmaria and the Temple of Athena.

The Delphic Oracle

Zeus discovered the site of the centre of the world by having two eagles fly towards each other from the eastern and western edges of the world, meeting at the middle. There, the world's "belly" or "womb"—Delphi—was marked by a stone omphalos (navel). The sacred flame that burned there became the "common hearth of all Greeks", to which the remotest outposts of Hellenic civilization sent pilgrims to consult the oracle. Athletes too were sent to Delphi to compete in games that were second in importance only to those of Olympia.

The Delphic oracle came into its own in the 8th century BC, when it played a vital role in the colonization of Sicily and southern Italy. Emigrants from islands and city-states began by consulting the oracle on where to go, and which deity to choose as patron of the enterprise. Three sacred wars were fought for control of the sanctuary—and the treasure deposited there by the city-states.

But Delphi was sacred ground long before the arrival of the Dorian Greeks. Earlier inhabitants worshipped a dragon or serpent god guarding a cave entrance to the Underworld. The spot had been discovered by a herdsman whose goat was overcome by the cave's mephitic fumes. Everyone who approached was reduced to weird mumbling. Henceforth a prophetess, or Sibyl, sat at the cave to pass on messages from the Underworld.

The Greeks took over the sanctuary after the infant Apollo, symbol of the conquering Dorians, had arrived from Delos to slay the serpent Python. Deferring to existing tradition, a priestess, Pythia, was kept on to murmur the oracular incantations—these were incoherent to the pilgrims until they were interpreted by a male priest, representing the new power. Originally, Pythia was a young virgin, but because the priests and oracle-seekers took too many sexual liberties, she was replaced by an old hag, dressed as a young virgin and seated on a tripod.

After purification, sacrifice to Apollo and a gift to the Delphic treasury, the pilgrims would question Pythia via the male interpreter—on marriage, childlessness, commercial enterprises or affairs of state. Enveloped in a smoke of burning laurel twigs and barley flour, Pythia worked herself up into a frenzy, chewing bay leaves, sipping holy spring water and babbling away. The priest composed his interpretation in hexameter verse.

Like established religion everywhere, the Delphic oracle was generally conservative. Moral precepts inscribed in Apollo's temple preached: "Know thyself" and "Nothing in excess". But a concession was made in the winter months when the sanctuary was handed over to the ecstatic worship of Dionysus, who shared Mount Parnassus with Apollo.

Political interpretation of Pythia's mumbles sided, often wrongly, with what were considered the most powerful forces of the day. Delphi championed the aristocracy (who were generous donors), discouraged Greek resistance against mighty Persia, defended Sparta against Athens and supported Philip of Macedonia. In doubtful cases, the oracle hedged its bets.

To gain acceptance in the Greek world, King Croesus of Lydia poured gold into the Delphi treasury. Should he attack Persia? If you do, the oracle replied, you will destroy a mighty empire. He attacked, and the empire he destroyed was his own.

After centuries of decadence, Roman Emperor Julian tried to revive its fortunes in AD 360, but Delphi sent its last pathetic oracle:

Tell the king the well-wrought hall has fallen to the ground.
No longer has Pythia a hut or prophetic laurel,
Nor a spring that speaks. Quenched is the speaking water, too.

West of the theatre, the path winds up through a grove of olive trees to the **stadium** where athletes from all over the Greek world gathered for the prestigious Pythian Games. Notice at the east end of the arena the runners' starting blocks, or rather grooves, set in marble slabs and, 178 m (585ft) down the track, the finishing line. On the north side of the stadium is the judges' box, the only place where the seats have backrests. Delphi also had its hooligans: an inscription on the south wall specifies penalties for drunkenness, but warns spectators not to take wine *out* of the stadium.

Museum
Housed in a bright and airy modern building, the sanctuary's surviving statues and superb architectural reliefs have been assembled by the French School of Archaeology.

The marble on the staircase leading to the exhibition halls was found in the temple precincts. Early Roman or Hellenistic, it has a carved relief of the woollen net that was draped over the sanctuary's original stone "navel".

Hall 4, though known as the Sifnian Room, is dominated by the Sphinx of Naxos (560 BC) seated on an Ionian capital that topped a 12-m (40-ft) column. It has a woman's head, with characteristic Archaic smile, bird's chest and wings and lion's haunches. Among the sculpture from the Sifnian Treasury (6th century BC), notice the Homeric frieze. On the right, Trojan heroes Aeneas and Hector fight the Greeks Menelaus and Aeas, watched on the left by the gods, with Zeus in the centre (headless). The shrine's eastern pediment shows Heracles and Apollo fighting for the Delphic tripod on which Pythia was to sit. The

Caryatid, one of two statue-pillars supporting the treasury entablature, was originally decorated with jewels in the holes around her headband.

Hall 5 contains two *kouroi*, monumental Archaic statues (580 BC), perhaps of Argos heroes Cleobis and Biton. The blurred remains of the Sicyon frieze show the adventures of the Argonauts.

In **Hall 6** the wealth of Delphi's treasury is hinted at by fragments of a silver bull (6th century BC) once mounted on gold plate, and by figures of gold, silver and ivory that have been found discarded in storage pits.

Hall 7 is devoted to the Treasury of the Athenians. The sculpture includes eight metope friezes of the *Labours of Heracles*, the best preserved being the first, of the hero fighting a stag. Theseus is shown with Antiope, Queen of the Amazons, and fighting the Minotaur.

Hall 13 boasts the museum's finest treasure, the magnificent bronze **Charioteer**, one of only half a dozen bronzes surviving from the classical era. It was dedicated by Polyzalos, tyrant of Gela in Sicily, in 470 BC, after his man won the chariot race at Delphi's Pythian Games. Portrayed on his victory lap, the charioteer (left arm missing) has a winner's ribbon around his head and a subtle expression of contained triumph. The eyes are of white enamel and brown and black onyx with tiny bronze wires for the lashes. Notice the superbly moulded feet. The body's disproportionate length may be a deliberate effect to correct optical distortion when viewed from below. The statue was part of a group with a four-horse chariot and what was probably a groom. Shown separately are three horse legs, a tail, reins and the groom's arm.

Hall 14 has a particularly elegant example of the countless sculptures of Antinoüs which Emperor Hadrian had made after his beloved companion died in Egypt in 130 AD. They had visited Delphi together to consult the oracle.

The Castalian Spring

Named after the nymph Castalia who drowned escaping from the clutches of Apollo, the ice-cold waters have their source in the ravine dividing the two Phaedriades crags. The large stone-paved basin in which pilgrims purified themselves can be seen at a sharp bend in the road running past the sanctuary. Purification before consulting Apollo's oracle generally meant rinsing the hair, in imitation of Apollo. Murderers had to wash from head to toe.

Marmaria

Still generally known by its pre-excavation name, Maramria, the **Sanctuary of Athena Pronaia** lies just down the mountainside south of the road back to Athens. In ancient times, this was the pilgrims' first stop on their way to the Castalian Spring and the Oracle.

The Doric **Temple of Athena** (6th century BC) stands opposite the entrance to the site. Beyond are the remains of two treasuries, the larger perhaps Athenian and the smaller erected by Greek colonists from Marseilles. But the site's most striking monument, and the most noteworthy work of architecture in Delphi, is the **Tholos**, a marble rotunda of 390 BC. On a raised platform, 20 Doric columns, three of which have been reconstructed and topped with their entablature, encircled an inner shrine that had 10 Corinthian half-columns around the interior wall. Schol-

ars have not yet determined what form of worship was performed in this and two other similar rotundas at Epidaurus and Olympia.

Coast West of Delphi

For a refreshing swim after clambering around the ruins at Delphi, head down to the beach resort of **Itea**. Some 20 km (12.5 miles) along the coast is the old port town of **Galaxidi**, sleepy now but once a thriving shipbuilding centre, as you can see in the local **maritime museum**.

Nafpaktos

The fortified port that the Venetians named Lepanto, the scene of Christian Europe's momentous naval victory over the Turks in 1571, is now little more than a tranquil yachting harbour with a square of pleasant jacaranda trees. To appreciate the port's strategic importance, follow the ramparts up to the old pine-shaded Venetian **citadel** for the view over the entrance to the Gulf of Corinth. The fortifications contain ancient masonry from the 5th century BC, when the port was a major Athenian defence against Sparta in the Peloponnesian War.

The Road to Pilion

The cool mountains of the Thessaly region come as a welcome relief. On the road north from Athens (or from Delphi via Levadia) to Volos, history buffs might like to stop at the **Pass of Thermopylae**. Celebrated as the site of a desperately courageous fight to the death by

the 300 Spartans of King Leonidas (see p. 56), it has been regarded throughout history as the military gateway to Athens and southern Greece. It was the route taken by the invading Goths and the Crusaders, as well as the Persians. The pass is 6.5 km (4 miles) long, narrow at either end and widening out in the middle. The bravery of the Spartans is honoured by a modern white marble monument topped by a bronze statue of Leonidas, opposite the soldiers' grave mound.

Today, the hot springs of Thermopylae ("Hot Gates") are recommended as a cure for sciatica.

The Tholos at the Sanctuary of Athena Pronaia, Delphi.

Volos

Thessaly's chief port is a modern town, ravaged by two earthquakes in 1955, and of little interest to the visitor, but it provides an ideal gateway for tours of the Pilion peninsula, and for ferries to the Sporades islands. It has good hotels and an extremely agreeable harbour promenade. Volos olives are a gourmet favourite, as is the local delicacy of *spetsofái*, a sausage stew with tomatoes

285

*T*he harbour town of Volos is the chief port of Thessaly, and a major jumping-off point for trips to the Sporades.

and red and green peppers. The ancient site of Iolkos, the port from which Jason and his Argonauts set out in search of the Golden Fleece, has turned up some important finds for the local **museum**. They include Stone Age jewellery, fig-urines and Mycenaean vases. From ancient Demetrias, south of Volos, comes a remarkable collection of 300 painted tombstones.

 ## Mount Pilion

Cool summers, luxuriant vegetation and charming alpine villages with good hotels are what make the Pilion peninsula a bracing change from the familiar Greek landscape. The highest peak in

what is in fact a range of mountains rises to 1,651 m (5,417 ft). The hills are green with forests of chestnut, beech and oak, and orchards of apple, cherry and peach. Botanists have catalogued over 2,000 species of plants.

The villages, about 20 in all, hug the slopes and hilltops and nestle in ravines, a few sitting down on the coast by sand or pebble beaches. Plane trees lend a welcome shade to the village squares, and the courtyards are fragrant and bright with basil, gardenias and gerani-ums. Notice the houses' timber-framed, gabled upper storey and beautifully

The Health Food of the Gods

Mount Pilion's invigorating climate was the source of Achilles' strength. Abandoned by his mother, he was brought here to be reared by the centaur Cheiron. At the age of six, he killed his first wild boar and brought it proudly to his foster father, who told him to go away and eat it. To nurture his bravery, Cheiron fed the boy on a special diet of lion's and boar's tripes and bear bone-marrow, supplemented with honey and fawn bone-marrow to give him extra speed.

weathered, grey stone-tiled roofs. The churches have distinctive external galleries and free-standing belfries.

The mountain roads from Volos around the Pilion peninsula are mostly well paved, but give yourself plenty of time to negotiate the hairpin bends. Head north-east to **Anakassia**, where a house has been transformed into an **art museum** of works by the popular 20th-century naïve painter Theophilus.

At **Portaria**, pause in the delightfully shady village square to sample the local wine and cheese. Then take the side road north to **Makrinitsa** up on a green mountainside overlooking the Bay of Volos. Several tall, traditional houses have been turned into comfortable inns around a square with a carved marble fountain.

Notice the sculpted chancel of the little 18th-century **church**, which also has some good icons inside.

Double back to Portaria and continue through chestnut forests to the mountain pass of **Hania**, a ski-resort at 1,350 m (4,429 ft). Further on, at **Zagora**, the old houses are prettily scattered among orchards of pears, peaches and plums. The town also boasts a heady red wine. A swim and a meal can be enjoyed down at the sandy beach of **Chorefto**, a fishing village and resort with good seafood tavernas. You will find another beach resort down the coast at **Agios Ioannis**, framed by green hills.

The houses of **Tsangarada** stand amid majestic oak forests with splendid views over the Aegean. A winding 8-km (5-mile) drive takes you down to a dazzling white beach at **Milopotamos**.

If you are looping back to Volos, stop off at the hill resort of **Milies** with a side trip to the old houses of **Vizitsa**.

Meteora

Unlike those on Mount Athos (see p. 255), Meteora's **monasteries** are open to everyone, man, woman and child—if you can get up there. It's a long, hard climb. The monks' astounding isolation on top of these barren crags in the remote northern reaches of Thessaly epitomizes the fierce eastern spirit of asceticism. *Meteoros* means "high in the air", and these huge pillars of grey rock, creviced, streaked and eroded by the wind and the rain, rise up to about 530 m (1,740 ft) above the Valley of Meteora. After living for years in caverns at the foot of the rocks, the holy men built their monasteries on the pinnacles as refuges from the Turks and Albanians in the 14th century.

By the 16th century, there were 24 monasteries, of which a dozen remain, but only a few are still inhabited. (They no longer provide accommodation for visitors, so you should plan on staying at nearby **Kalambaka**. If you have time, visit the **cathedral** to see its 12th-century frescoes and unusual marble pulpit.)

Monastery opening hours are irregular, so check in Kalambaka before you start your visit. Strict clothing regulations are enforced: skirts for women, long trousers for men, no sleeveless tops. In the old days, monks clambered up rope ladders or were pulled up in a woven basket by a brother monk working a hand winch. Today, there are power winches to haul up supplies, and steep but negotiable stone stairways for people.

For the less adventurous, one of the monasteries, **Agios Stefanos** (now a convent and orphanage) is directly accessible from the road by a footbridge

The Battle of Lepanto

This famous naval battle was a short, bloody rerun of the Crusades, with the forces of Christianity lined up against those of Islam. To halt further westward expansion of the Ottoman Empire, Spain, Venice and the Vatican forgot their differences for long enough to present a common front against a Turkish fleet supported by Egypt and Algeria. At sunrise on 7 October 1571, Don Juan of Austria, half-brother of Spain's Philip II, drew up 208 ships of war to face the Turks west of Lepanto at the entrance to the Gulf of Corinth. The Turks outnumbered the Catholic forces by 22 vessels, but their crews were already exhausted after months of pillaging in Crete and the Adriatic. Massive Venetian galleys in the front ranks proved to be veritable maritime fortresses which, with the aid of Spanish discipline, heavy cannon and long-barrelled arquebuses, overwhelmed a Turkish fleet that still relied in large part on bows and arrows. The Turks escaped with only 30 ships, and the sea did indeed run red. Muslim casualties numbered 30,000 dead and wounded, the Catholic forces 8,000 dead and 21,000 wounded. Among the injured was Miguel de Cervantes, who crippled his left hand but survived to compose Don Quixote 30 years later.

spanning a ravine (turn off south-east of Kalambaka). The fine icons and frescoes in its 14th-century **church** are worth seeing, but you are likely to be more impressed by the sweeping view across the Thessaly plain.

*T*he monasteries of Meteora (previous pages) sit high above the plains of Thessaly, with the snow-capped ridges of the Pindus Mountains rising behind.

Those prepared to climb should set out west from Kalambaka, skirting the village of Kastraki. On the left, you will pass the abandoned ruins of two monasteries perched on the **Doupiani Column**. Three km (2 miles) west of Kalambaka is **Agios Nikolaos Anapafsas.** Partially ruined and uninhabited, it is nevertheless accessible for those hell-bent on climbing up to see the church's well-restored 16th-century frescoes by Theophanes of Crete, notably of *The Last Supper.* To the east, you can admire the needle-like rock of ruined **Agia Moni**, one of the valley's earliest monasteries, built in 1315, but do not even dream of tackling it.

The road continues round to the **Great Meteoron** (*Megísti Meteóron*), crowning the tallest rock in the valley, 534 m (1,752 ft) up. Slowly but surely, climb the 115 stairs to the richly endowed 14th-century monastery. The **Church of the Transfiguration** (*Metamórfosis*), with its impressive 12-sided dome, has a fine iconostasis and austere frescoes of the 15th and 16th centuries. The refectory has been laid out as a museum for the church's treasures. In the library is a collection of rare editions and monastic manuscripts.

At nearby **Varlaam** (1517), the flowers and butterflies of the lovely walled monastery garden are almost reward enough for the 195-stair climb. Notice the winch that once hauled up supplies and visitors. In the two adjoining churches, **All Saints** and the smaller **Three Hierarchs**, see the elaborately ornamental gilded iconostasis and 16th-century frescoes by Frangos Castellanos of Thebes. For many, the monastery's most handsome building is the guest house, sadly no longer in use.

Taking a Pass

In 1941, British officers with too much knowledge of the Classics and not enough knowledge of modern geography thought that they could hold the advancing Germans at the Pass of Thermopylae, just as the Spartans had briefly done against the Persians in 480 BC. The trouble with this plan, as the British realized when they put down their Herodotus for long enough to go and look at the terrain, was that the coastline, which had been close by in ancient times, had silted up, and the sea was now 5 km (3 miles) away, giving a land attack all the room it needed. Fortunately, the British abandoned their indefensible position before the enemy arrived.

The Sporades

The Sporades, literally the "scattered" islands, east of the Pilion peninsula, are an attractive mixture of well-organized (sometimes almost too well organized) beach resorts and traditional, old-fashioned places where the Greeks themselves like to spend their holidays.

Though there are plenty of fine sand beaches, in a region where the *meltemi* can blow quite fiercely, you will quickly appreciate the advantages of the smooth pebble beaches, too.

For details of air and sea transportation from mainland ports, see the GETTING AROUND IN GREECE section in the FACTS AND FIGURES chapter, p. 18.

Skiathos

This is *the* beach resort island. It boasts over 60 beaches, of fine sand and smooth pebbles, and several bays and harbours for yachts and small craft. Dense forest blankets the interior with beech, evergreen oak, chestnut, hazel,

pine and the low arbutus strawberry tree—its berries are pretty but inedible.

Skiathos Town

Surrounded by wooded hills, the island capital has plenty of cheerful cafés and souvenir shops. Cross the causeway to **Bourdzi** islet for its view of the harbour.

Beaches

Buses run west from the capital to the beaches on the **Kalamaki peninsula**, the most popular being **Kanapitsa**. At the west end of the island, the celebrated **Koukounaries** beach has an arc of fine sand stretching for over half a mile between the sea and the lagoon. More secluded, around on the west coast is **Agia Eleni**, facing Mount Pilion. Nearby is the nudist **Banana Beach** (*Krássa*). Further north, amid beautiful pine trees and backed by russet cliffs, are the sand dunes of **Mandraki**. The best of the pebble beaches is on the north side of the island at **Lalaria**.

Kastro

To get away from the crowds, head out to this ghost town, now lying in ruins on its north coast promontory. Islanders built a refuge here in 1538 when the Turkish pirate Barbarossa Khair ed-Din was slaughtering the population of neighbouring Skopelos.

There are guided boat tours, but you can also drive north-west from the capital and take a delightful 30-minute walk through the forest to the coast. The fortified town, with only a drawbridge linking it to the rest of the island, once had 300 houses. Of the 20 churches, two remain. One of them, the **Church of Christ**, still contains icons and a carved wooden altar screen.

The Greek Ark

The Greek story of Deucalion's flood has a familiar ring to it. Zeus decided to destroy humanity because of the impieties of Greece's first inhabitants, the Pelasgians. Warned by his father, Prometheus, that the earth was about to be flooded, Deucalion built an ark and sailed with his wife Pyrrha for nine days. He, too, sent out a dove to reconnoitre and bring back an olive twig as a sign the flood was over. While Noah's Ark ran aground on Ararat, Deucalion ended up on Parnassus. The biblical and Greek stories were apparently both inspired by a Mesopotamian flood in the 3rd millennium BC.

Like Noah, Deucalion invented wine—his name means "new-wine sailor"—but the Greeks transferred the patent to Dionysus, who also held sole rights to Parnassus until Apollo arrived with the Muses.

Skopelos

The islanders here are remarkably friendly, and the women especially proud of their traditional costume—flowered silk skirt, velvet jacket with billowing sleeves, and light silk kerchief on their heads. The capital, **Chora**, is a typical Aegean town of dazzling white houses with blue-slate or grey stone-tile roofs, with a **Venetian castle** at the top of the hill. Its craftsmen produce some fine black pottery. Visit the 17th-century **Church of Christ** to see the icons and altar screen. The island's hilly interior is dotted with monasteries and chapels.

Beaches

The best are on the south and east coasts. **Limonari** has the best reputation, with some good tavernas, too. Nudists can strip off over at **Velanio**. The nearby beach at **Stafilos** is named after the Cretan general believed to have colonized the island after the collapse of Minoan civilization. His grave was found here in 1927, with a gold crown, weapons and burial offerings now displayed in Volos museum.

Alonnisos

This simple little island of herdsmen and fishing folk has great appeal for swimmers and snorkellers, and also for hikers who come to explore its pine-clad, thyme-scented hills. The island's limpid waters have been declared a marine conservation park. The best pebble beaches of the **Kokkinokastro peninsula** are a 30-minute boat excursion from **Patitiri**. The tavernas in the little yachting harbour of **Steni Vala** serve the island's best seafood.

Skyros

Out on its own, further east, the largest of the Sporades splits into two distinct halves on either side of an isthmus. To the south, oak, beech and pine forests cloak rugged mountains, while the north is pleasantly green and fertile with farmland and cattle pastures. The famous Skyrian miniature ponies, descendants of an ancient breed known as Pikermic, are kept in a hillside pasture near the port of **Linaria** from late autumn until late spring.

The island capital, **Chorio**, is an attractive town of white houses, many of them veritable museums of the island's traditional handicrafts. One such house has been turned into the **Faltaitz Museum**, displaying embroidery, furniture, copperware and basketware. The **Archaeological Museum** has some good Mycenaean ceramics. The hilltop **fortress**, part Byzantine, part Venetian, stands on the site of the ancient acropolis from which King Lycomedes is believed to have pushed the Athenian hero Theseus to his death.

Just north of town is the popular **Magazia beach**. Among the best of the others is the sand and pebble cove of **Pefkos** on the west coast.

Lovers of English poetry will find **Rupert Brooke's grave** amid olive trees on Mount Kokhilas above Tris Boukes Bay; the 28-year-old World War I poet died offshore in 1915 on his way to fight in the Dardanelles. His poem for all English soldiers served as his own epitaph:

If I should die, think only this of me:
That there's some corner of a foreign field
That is for ever England.

Achilles Discovered

Achilles was made to look rather silly during his short stay on Skyros. His mother Thetis, apparently feeling guilty about abandoning him in early childhood (see p. 286), decided that he should avoid the Trojan Wars by coming the island disguised as a girl. Under the name of Aïssa, Achilles mingled with the ladies at the court of King Lycomedes. But cunning Odysseus found him out. He brought gifts to the palace, a pile of jewels, robes and other finery for the ladies to rummage about in. Then he ordered a battle trumpet blown outside the palace, along with the clash of arms. One of the ladies immediately stripped to the waist and grabbed a shield and spear which just happened to be in the pile of gifts. Odysseus had his man.

*L*ocally made embroidery is just one of the traditional Greek handicrafts on display in the Faltaitz Museum on the island of Skyros.

"A Greekish Isle, and the Most Pleasant Place That Ever Our Eyes Beheld for the Exercise of a Solitary and Contemplative Life..."

Thus did an early 17th-century traveller describe the island of Corfu. Much has changed since his day, but away from the crowded beaches of the tourist resorts, the wooded hills and rocky bays of Corfu still make it one of the loveliest of Greek islands. The green landscapes and Italian influences of the Ionian archipelago combine to lend these western isles an ambience distinct from the islands of the Aegean. The mainland attractions too, from the beach resort of Parga to the lakeside town of Ioannina, have a different feel from the rest of the country.

Lying closer to western Europe than the rest of Greece, the Ionian islands of Corfu, Lefkas, Ithaca, Kephalonia and

*T*his view from Kanoni has come to symbolize the natural beauty of Corfu. Vlacherna monastery is in the foreground, with Pondikonissi (Mouse Island) beyond.

Zakynthos (formerly Zante) make a convenient target for package-tour companies. The tourist resorts are loud and crowded throughout the high season, but the richly varied countryside and abundant beaches draw large numbers of independent travellers at all times of year, with the spring being a particular favourite for its lush greenery and wildflowers.

*T*he Venetians, the French and the British have come and gone, but the Orthodox priests remain the most influential members of the Corfu community.

Don't be put off by the fact that it rains more in western Greece than elsewhere. Rain is still a marginal phenome-non, leaving more than enough spring and summer sunshine to go round. The advantages are that the landscape is greener, and the climate gentler than in the Aegean. The blustering *meltemi* does not blow in the Ionian Sea.

While Corfu seems to lie outside the seismically sensitive area, other Ionian islands have been frequently ravaged by earthquakes, most recently in 1953. Historical monuments have suffered, and rebuilding has sometimes been more

N. W. GREECE & IONIAN ISLANDS

KASTORIA

ALBANIA

E90

E90

Sidar
Kassiopi
Nissaki
Paleokastritsa
Kalami
Liapades
Ipsos

Perama
E92
Metsovo

IOANNINA

TRIKALA
E92

CORFU TOWN

E90-92

Dodona

KARDITSA

Ag. Gordis
Benitses

Igoumenitsa

CORFU

E951

N

EPIRUS

PAXI
Lakka
Parga

Logos
Gaios

E55

ARTA

ANTIPAXI

Lefkas

LEFKAS

E951

Nidri

Vassiliki

SKORPIOS

Fiskardo
Frikes

Nafpaktos

Assos
Ithaki

E55

MESSOLONGI

KEPHALONIA
ITHACA

Lixouri

E65

Argostoli

PATRA

E55

ZAKYNTHOS

Alikes

Zakynthos

Vassilikos

Laganas

PIRGOS

Sites of historic interest
Mountains
Land over 900 metres

0   25   50 km
0   10   20   30 miles

hurried than tasteful, with the notable exception of Zakynthos. For details of air and sea transportation from mainland ports, see the GETTING AROUND IN GREECE section in the FACTS AND FIGURES chapter, p. 18.

The mainland can be tackled as a two- or three-day excursion from the islands. Cool off in the forests and caves of the Pindus mountains, and visit Dodona's ancient theatre and sanctuary. Romantics may want to make a special pilgrimage to Missolonghi, the last resting place of Lord Byron's heart.

Cosmopolitan Island

Set at the entrance to the Adriatic Sea, and the nearest Greek island to Italy, Corfu's strategic importance has made it a constant target for colonizers. In the 8th century BC, the Corinthians founded a colony here, but relations between the island and the mother-city were always tempestuous. Corfu's sea battle with Corinth was a major cause of the Peloponnesian War, with the island lending its support to the Athenian cause.

In the modern era, the island's stepping-stone position between Italy and the Balkans exposed it regularly to invasion—Norman Crusaders, Venetians, the French during the Napoleonic Wars, and the British in the 19th century (who held on to it as a protectorate for more than 40 years after Greek independence). Typical of the island's cosmopolitan history, Corfu-born Count Giovannni Antonio Capo d'Istria served as the Russian tsar's foreign minister in St Petersburg before returning to become independent Greece's first president in 1827. When he was assassinated by political rivals four years later, he had changed his name to its Greek form, Ioannis Antennas Kapodistrias, and this is how he is remembered on the monument at the south end of the Esplanade.

Corfu (Kerkira or Corcyra)

Corfu is the most popular of all the Ionian Islands, and understandably so. People may curse the crowds at the beach resorts in high season, but the island is big enough for the independent traveller to find more isolated corners and coves for a quiet family picnic or a solitary swim. Certainly the beaches, of fine sand and smooth pebble or shingle, are among the best in the whole of Greece.

The island is rich in literary associations. The final episode of Homer's *Odyssey,* when the shipwrecked Odysseus is washed ashore on the island of the Phaecians, is supposed to have taken place at Paleokastritsa on the north-west coast. Some Shakepearian scholars have argued that Prospero's island, in *The Tempest,* with its "fresh springs, brine-pits, barren place and fertile", is actually Corfu. And the novelist Lawrence Durrell, with his brother, the naturalist Gerald Durrell, and the rest of their family, lived on and wrote about the island in the 1930s.

On the map, Corfu has the curved, tapering shape of a scythe blade— 64 km (40 miles) long but rarely more than 15 km (9 miles) wide except in the north, where the tallest mountain, Pantokrator, 906 m (2,972 ft) dominates the scenery. The rolling hills of the interior are rich in orange and lemon groves and fig trees, and the pointed tops of tall, dark green cypresses prick the horizon. But most impressive of all are the millions of silver-green olive trees, a result of the planting policies of the Venetians who ruled here from 1386 to 1797. They also left the legacy of their language, still widely spoken on the island.

Corfu Town

Known to the Greeks, like the island itself, as Kerkira, the bustling, sophisticated island capital is built on the end of a small peninsula, protected by the Venetian fortifications at the end of the promontory.

The **Esplanade** *(Spianáda)*, the town's main social focus, neatly displays the foreign cultural influences that have shaped the city and indeed the whole island. The broad green expanse was levelled by the Venetians as a parade ground for their garrison.

The **cricket field** on the northern half of the Esplanade is a legacy of British occupation in the 19th century. The outfield is grassy enough, with a few treacherous Greek bumps, but the wicket itself is of coconut matting. The July cricket matches pit the local Corfiotes against visiting Englishmen and a "touring side" from Malta, and are most appropriately enjoyed from a shady table beneath the trees at the edge of the Esplanade, while sipping a glass of that

Relaxing in a sidewalk café in historic Corfu Town.

other British legacy, ginger beer. Across the street, and offering only a distant view of the cricket, the elegant **Liston** arcade was built by the French. Inspired by the arcades that Napoleon constructed along Paris's Rue de Rivoli, this pleasantly cool retreat shelters the town's best cafés (lively in the evening, but perfect for a quiet early morning breakfast).

North of the Esplanade is the neoclassical **Palace of St Michael and St George**. Handed over to the Greek monarchy in 1864 by the departing British High Commissioner, it houses a **Museum of Asian Art**, (Anáktoro Sino/Iaponikó Mousío) exhibiting ancient Chinese, Thai and Khmer ceramics and sculpture .

The Venetians' *Fortezza Vecchia*, the **Old Fort**, stands out on a promontory to

299

CORFU

Sidári
Perouládes
Róda
Karoussádes
Avliótes
Kassiópi
Cape Varvara
Ágios Stéfanos
Strinílas
Períthia
LAKE BUTRINTO
Arílas
Ágios Stéfanos
Mesariá
PANTOKRÁTOR ●576
Afiónas
Ágios Athanásios
Kalámi
Agios Georgios
Kastelláni
Spartílas Nisaki
Kouloúra
Pági
Troubétta
Ágios Markos
Arkadádes
Makrádes
Pirgí
Barbáti
Lákones
ALBANIA
Paleokastritsa
Ípsos
Liapádes
Dasiá
Gulf of
Gouviá
Kérkira
ÍPIROS
Giannádes
Alikés
VÍDOS
Ermónes
Mandouki
CORFU (KÉRKIRA)
Mirtiotissa
Mon Repos
Pélekas
Análipsi
Glifada
Kanóni
Sinarádes
ÁGÎI DÉKA
Ano Garoúna
●576
Benítses
Agios Gordis
Káto Garoúna
Stavrós
I O N I A N
N
S E A
Ágios Matthéos
Moraítika
Mesongí
Boukári
Korission Lagoon
Petretí
Lákka
Argirádes
Loggós
Lefkími
PAXÍ Gáios
ANTÍPAXI
Kávos
Sparterá

| 0 | | 10 km |
| 0 | | 5 miles |

CORFU TOWN

N

OLD TOWN

DONZELOT
ARSENIOU
ZAVITSIANOU
Mitrópoli
Néo Froúrio
SOLOMOU
VELISSARIOU
NIKIFOROU THEOTOKI
PALEOLOGOU
Anáktoro Sino/
Iaponikó Mousío
Tourist
Office
Agios
Spiridon
Agalma
Adam
KAPODISTRIOU
KONSTANTINOU
Mandráki
Palaió
Froúrio
ESPLANADE
VOULGAREOS
DOUSMANI
GEORGIOU THEOTOKI
GILFORDOU
ESPLANADE
VASILEOS
Agios Georgios
PLATIA
GEORGIOU
THEOTOKI
MOUSTOXIDOU
Iónios
Voulí
MANTZAROU
Peristílio
Métland
Ormos Garitsas
ALEXANDRAS
DOUKISSAS
MARIAS
Tachidromío
AKADIMIAS
Agalma
Kapodístria
VRAILA
MEGALIS
Post Office
ROMANOU
British
Cemetery
Archeologikó
Mousio
To Kánoni

*C*olourful horse-drawn carriages provide a leisurely means of touring the streets and waterfront of Corfu Town. Owners strive to outdo each other in the colour and beauty of their decorations.

Upsetting the Natives

Britain's William Gladstone is remembered as a good prime minister, but before that, in 1858, he was a wretchedly inept Lord High Commissioner Extraordinary, sent on an abortive mission to deliver a new constitution to Corfu. He was mistrusted by everyone—the islanders were convinced (wrongly) that he wanted to annex Corfu to the British Empire, while the British military command suspected (rightly) that his major concern was to deepen his knowledge of Homer and The Odyssey. For his part, Gladstone voiced dismay at the islanders' "complete and contented idleness". He then proceeded to turn their indifference into complete and utter rage by making all his speeches to them in Italian.

Odysseus in Corfu

Homer's Odyssey is not all blood and thunder. The episode which Corfiotes believe is set at Paleokastritsa is one of blushing lyricism. Cruelly ship wrecked, Odysseus swam for two days before reaching shore at a rocky cove, where he fell asleep in a thicket. At a river nearby, the beautiful princess Nausicaa and her court ladies were washing their linen. While the laundry dried on the rocks, they bathed in the river, rubbed their bodies with olive oil and played with a ball. Suddenly, the ball soared out of reach into the sea, causing Nausicca to shriek and wake up Odysseus. He leapt up, saw the girls and grabbed a leafy bough to cover his nakedness. The girls fled behind the sand dunes at the approach of this rough fellow begrimed with the salt of the sea. Only Nausicaa stayed, though her legs trembled. She offered to wash the caked salt off his body and rub him with oil. Ah, women! First Calypso, then Circe, now Nausicaa. How was Odysseus ever going to get back to his beloved Penelope? He declined the offer and bathed himself in private.

the east of the Esplanade, separated by a sea-filled moat. Part of it is now a Military Academy, but you can climb up to the rather dilapidated fortifications at the top for a view across to Epirus and the mountains of Albania. In the summer an evening **sound-and-light show** traces the island's history from Odysseus to modern times.

More characteristically Italian is the labyrinth of narrow winding streets and piazzas in the **Old Town**, between the Royal Palace and the ferry port. As you wander around this maze of alleyways, look out for a charming little square with a carved stone Venetian well-head (1699) and a romantic restaurant.

On the south edge of the Old Town is the 16th-century church of **Agios Spiridon**, Bishop of Cyprus in 319 and Corfu's patron saint ever since his remains were smuggled into the island from Constantinople in the 15th century. Kept in a brilliant silver coffin beside the high altar, they are the object of great veneration for the healing powers attributed to them.. The coffin is paraded through the town on major holidays—Orthodox Palm Sunday; Easter Saturday; the saint's day, August 11; and the first Sunday in November.

St Spiridon takes special care of the island's fishermen—many of the boats have a small icon of the saint fixed to the mast—and Corfiote mothers invariably name at least one of their sons after the island's patron. Call out the name "Spiros!", and half the male heads within earshot will turn around in answer.

On an island with few remaining ancient monuments, the **Archaeological Museum** (Archeologiko Mousío) is worth a visit for its mostly pre-classical sculpture and ceramics (at Odos Vraila 5, just off the waterfront south of the Esplanade). The highlight of the collection is the **Gorgon pediment** (590 BC) from the island's Temple of Artemis. The serpent-haired Medusa (one of three Gorgon sisters) beams out her famous petrifying glare from the ancient carving, looking much fiercer than her guardian panthers. The Lion of Menekrates is a splendidly carved tomb sculpture for a warrior of the 6th century BC. (The ancient tomb is south of the museum in the garden of the police station.)

Kanoni

The natural beauty of the peninsula south of Corfu Town has been sadly diminished by the airport and surrounding resort hotels. But tour-operators promote the spot so insistently, you may be curious to know what the excursion offers. It's certainly worth an hour or two's diversion.

The route begins with a side-trip to **Anemomilos** to see the 12th-century Byzantine **Church of Saints Jason and Sosipatros**, who brought Christianity to Corfu 1,800 years ago. They are depicted in icons (16th century) inside the pretty little church. You pass **Mon Repos**, a villa on the site of the ancient city of Corcyra but better known as the place where Britain's Prince Philip, the Duke of Edinburgh, was born in 1921.

Since the villa is not open to the public, here at least is some biographical background: the grandson of Prince William of Denmark, who was crowned King George I of the Hellenes, Philip Schleswig-Holstein-Sonderburg-Glücksburg took his mother's name,

Mountbatten, before he married Princess Elizabeth in 1947. Like his wife, he is a great-great-grandchild of Queen Victoria.

You can look down on the villa and its gardens from nearby **Analipsi**, the hill of the ancient acropolis.

The reward at the end of the peninsula is a picture-postcard view of the two islets of **Vlacherna**, with its red-roofed, white-walled monastery, and the tiny and more distant **Pondikonissi** (Mouse Island), its monastery half hidden amongst cypress trees. You can follow a steep path down to the water's edge, and walk out to Vlacherna along a causeway. Unfortunately the view is regularly shattered by the roar of charter flights taking off from the adjacent airport.

Achillion

A short drive south of Corfu Town is one of those magnificent follies dreamed up from time to time by the idle rich, where the ordinary criteria of beauty or ugliness no longer apply. In this case it was Elizabeth of Austria who, in 1890, built this outlandish, grandiose villa to honour her Greek hero Achilles. Whatever the lapses in architectural taste that may be evident in the main building, the **Italian landscaped gardens** surrounding the mansion are really very attractive. It is interesting to wander among the cypress trees and gloomy Homeric statuary and imagine Sissi walking barefoot through the dewy grass to watch the sunrise. One sculpture at least has some artistic merit— Ernst Herter's famous *Dying Achilles*.

After the Empress's assassination in 1898, Kaiser Wilhelm II of Germany bought the house, spending holidays here each spring from 1908 until the

*L*ush gardens and classical statuary surround the architectural oddity of the Achillion. The terrace at the foot of the gardens provides an excellent view along the eastern coast of the island.

outbreak of World War I in 1914. After a spell as military hospital, it has been restored and converted to a casino by descendants of the famous Red Baron von Richthofen. The villa's ground-floor **museum** has Austrian and German memorabilia, including a portrait of Sissi by Franz Winterhalter, and the Kaiser's saddle-seat from his study.

For a view of the whole of the Achillion and its grounds—and the rest of the island—take the pleasant drive inland up to **Mount Agii Deka** (576 m, 1,890 ft). Directly below on the east coast, you also have as good a view as you need of the hugely popular **Benitses**, once a pretty fishing village and now a major package-holiday resort.

Paleokastritsa

One of the loveliest spots on the island, the west coast resort of Paleokastritsa attracts droves of tourists and day-trippers in high season. But the crowds cannot detract from the beauty of these rocky coves where, according to legend, the lovely Nausicca found Odysseus washed up on the shore.

Swimming, snorkelling and sailing attract the more energetic visitors to the turquoise waters of its coves. Dreamers prefer a clifftop stroll or siesta among the olive, lemon and cypress trees. To take in the full beauty of the scenery, drive or hike up to the precipice to which the village of **Lakones** clings. From the *Bella Vista* café, the **panorama** is truly stupendous. Paleokastritsa's six coves fan out below you. You look out, too, over the town's 16th-century **monastery**, which is worth a visit more for the peace of its gardens and terraces than its icons and old manuscripts. But remember to observe the strictly enforced dress code—no swim suits, shorts or sleeveless tops.

From Lakones, or the nearby village of Krini, you can hike to the ruined 13th-century castle of **Angelokastro**. This is spectacularly situated on a clifftop high above the sea. Turn left as you pass through the gate to see the tiny church built in cave under the castle. The view from the ruins is even better than from Lakones—on a clear day you can even see as far as the Old Fort back in Corfu Town.

Paleokastritsa is frequently identified as the spot where Odysseus swam ashore from the shipwreck on the last lap of his homeward journey. Just off the coast is the faintly ship-shaped **Kolovri** rock. Those familiar with the legend assert it is the ship that was turned to stone by Odysseus's enemy, Poseidon, for having dared to take the hero back to Ithaca.

*O*ne of the beautiful coves that surround the tiny monastery at Paleokastritsa, on the west coast of Corfu.

Beaches

Just below Paleokastritsa, there are boats that will take you to the less crowded beaches of **Liapades Bay**, one of the prettiest being the cypress-fringed **Gefira**. Further south, also accessible only by boat, are the secluded pebble and sand beaches of **Homous** and **Stiliari**, lying at the foot of soaring cliffs. The most popular family beach on the west coast is **Glifada**. To get away from the crowds, though, hike through the woods below the hill village of Pelekas to the bewitching little sandy beach of **Mirtiotissa**, backed by rugged cliffs and romantic greenery. Be warned though— this is the island's only nudist beach.

Above Pelekas is the **Kaiser's Throne**, a lookout point where Wilhelm II sat to watch the sunset, and enjoy the view across the centre of the island to Mount Pantokrator. Modern sunset-watchers gather on the café-terraces at Pelekas and toast the departing day with a glass of wine.

Easier to get to from Corfu Town is the west coast beach of **Agios Gordis**, long and sandy, approached through an attractive landscape of orchards, olive

305

groves and vegetable farms. Snorkelling and spear-fishing are particularly good at the southern end of the beach.

North of Paleokastritsa, the beaches of **Agios Georgios Bay** are worthwhile as much for the trip itself as for the soothing swim at the end. The countryside of this north-west corner of the island is beautifully unspoiled, with scarcely more than the sheep and goats to disturb your contemplation of the olive groves and majestic cypresses. Dressed in traditional blue and white costume, the peasants in the villages of **Arkadades** and **Pagi** are friendly, and refreshingly unpreoccupied by the "tourist trade".

On the north coast, **Sidari** is an attractive beach and cove area notable for its curiously eroded and stratified

T he soft, stratified rocks at Sidari have been eroded into pretty coves and narrow inlets, perfect for swimming and diving. Further along the coast, the rocks rise into tall cliffs, with tiny beaches squeezed beneath.

sandstone cliffs. Once more, the drive is half the pleasure. Between the hamlets of **Mesaria** and **Agios Athanasios**, the road winds through some of the island's most ancient olive groves, with clumps of ferns hugging the contorted trunks. To the east, the little beach of **Agios Spiridon** is especially safe for children, with shallow water stretching far off the shore, it is a favourite with the Greeks who crowd in here at the weekend.

306

North-east Coast

Facing the mysterious mountains of Albania, this stretch of coast was the stamping ground of the famous Durrell family, whose idyllic summers, spent here in the 1930s, are recorded in Gerald Durrell's popular book, *My Family and Other Animals*. Gerald's older brother, the novelist and poet Lawrence Durrell, also produced a book about Corfu—*Prospero's Cell*, a romantic evocation of island life in the days before package holidays came on the scene. Since his day, resorts have sprung up at **Ipsos** (Club Med), **Barbati** and **Nisaki**. The "white house" in the pretty bay at **Kalami**, where the Durrells stayed, is now in part a thriving taverna.

But the coast still makes for a beautiful excursion, either by road along the winding corniche that cuts across the rugged green mountain slopes, or better still, by motorboat from **Kouloura**, coasting along through the limpid blue-green waters around **Cape Varvara** to the lively harbour resort of **Kassiopi**. Be careful not to drift into Albanian waters—the mainland is only a couple of kilometres away, with armed patrol boats there to remind you that visitors are not welcome. In the waters of the Corfu-Albania channel, archaeologists have found amphoras from a ship wrecked in classical times, but unauthorized underwater exploration is strictly forbidden.

T he olive harvest is particularly prolific on Corfu, with much of the crop being gathered in the north-western corner of the island between Paleokastritsa and Sidari.

Paxi and Antipaxi

The perfect refuge from Corfu's crowds, these two tiny islands to the south offer very little hotel accommodation, but there are plenty of private rooms. The major attraction here is snorkelling and scuba-diving, particularly among the caves in the towering cliffs along Paxi's west coast. The sea depth off these sheer rocks plunges from 30 to 100 metres.

Gaios is Paxi's port and main village, with charming old Venetian houses. There are also pleasant tavernas to be found at **Lakka** and **Logos**. The local claim to being part of the Odyssey legend is that Paxi was the island of the enchantress Circe, who turned the hero's crew into pigs.

The tiny neighbouring island of Antipaxi has two excellent beaches, **Vrika** and **Voutoumi**, accessible by boat from Paxi. There are no tavernas at the beaches, so take a picnic. The small hilltop village, which houses the entire island population of around 200, has a taverna and a couple of rooms to let.

Lefkas

The mainland is linked directly by bridge to this mountainous island, making it a convenient pot of call for road travellers on their way from Igoumenitsa to Kephalonia. In recent years archaeologists, much encouraged by local tour operators, have tried to demonstrate that Lefkas, rather than its allegedly misnamed neighbour, is the historic Ithaca, the original homeland of Odysseus.

Although the west coast has more sandy beaches, those on the east are better sheltered from the wind, tucked in at the foot of tall rugged cliffs. The best of the resort towns is **Nidri**, while offshore to the east is the private island of **Skorpios**, where Aristotle Onassis wooed and won Jackie Kennedy. The ferry to Kephalonia leaves from the southern fishing port of **Vassiliki**, which has a pleasant beach where you can enjoy a swim while you are waiting. On the island's south-west cape is the dramatic **Lefkatas cliff**, with a drop of 72 m (236 ft), famous in ancient times as a "lover's leap". Lesbos poetess Sappho (see p. 268) was said to have jumped to her death here when jilted by Phaon, a handsome ferryman. In Roman times, criminals could gain their freedom by surviving the jump. Ponder all this as you snooze on the sand at the fine beach of **Porto Katsiki**, just around the cape.

Ithaca

Is this the true home of Odysseus? The topographical evidence is convincing. Several of the small natural harbours, creeks and coves are exactly the kind of spot where the hero might have landed and hidden the treasures gathered on his voyage. Archaeologists claim to have found the homes of Odysseus, his wife Penelope and son Telemachos. For the modern traveller, Ithaca is a tranquil island of hospitable people. Though relatively barren, the interior is fragrant with aromatic herbs and shrubs. Clumps of myrtle and oleander add their bright splashes of colour. The wines are good and the roast hare excellent. The charming, sleepy, whitewashed capital of **Vathy**, founded only 400 years ago, has been attractively rebuilt since the 1953 earthquake.

In the north of the island, you will find two enchanting little fishing harbours at **Kioni** and **Frikes**, both with good seafood restaurants.

Many scholars and most of the tour-operators locate the famous **Nymphs' Grotto**, where Odysseus was left to recuperate at the end of his long voyage, at **Marmarospilia**, just a few kilometres west of Vathy on the Bay of Dexia. Besides the nymph-like stalactites, the cave meets Homer's specifications of two entrance, one for men and one for the gods. You will find a gap in the rocks wide enough for a man to squeeze through, and a hole in the roof for the gods. In the cave, says Homer, Odysseus hid the gold, fine fabrics and the 13 copper tripods given to him by the Phaeacians as a going-away present. A century ago, British archaeologists found 13 copper tripods in a cave near an ancient villa they were excavating at **Pelikata** in the north of the island, now on view in the site's **museum**. Unfortunately, although the Mycenaean-age villa would fit in chronologically with the Odyssey's Trojan era, scientists put the date of the tripods' manufacture at 400 years later. Tour-operators have not been discouraged, though, and describe the villa as "Odysseus's Palace".

of good roads, a welcome legacy of British 19th-century administration, makes a car a real asset for touring the island.

Kephalonia suffered terrible destruction from the 1953 earthquake, and its two main towns, Argostoli, the capital, and Lixouri, were rebuilt rather heavy-handedly. But the pretty fishing harbour of **Fiskardo**, the port of arrival for the ferry from from Lefkas, escaped unscathed and makes a more pleasant base for your excursions.

Fiskardo is named after Norman crusader Robert Guiscard, who died here in 1085. He apparently stayed long enough to provide work for his own architects, as the ruined church north-east of town has twin towers of distinctly Norman aspect.

Beautifully situated on the west coast of Fiskardo's peninsula, **Assos** is as charming a harbour as you will find anywhere in the Ionian Islands. In the shadow of an imposing ruined Venetian castle, the pretty vine-covered cottages are proof enough that post-earthquake reconstruction can be attractive. Immediately to the south, surrounded by soaring cliffs, is **Myrtos Bay**, the finest beach on the island, with a pounding surf almost worthy of Hawaii. Don't let the children wade too far out.

Kephalonia (Kefallinia)

The largest of the Ionian Islands boasts a landscape of magnificent mountainous scenery and rugged coastlines. Below mountainsides covered in dense forests of dark firs peculiar to Kephalonia, the vineyards produce one of Greece's finest white wines, Robola. The network

Zakynthos (Zante)

One of the reasons the ancient Greek name of Zakynthos (now being officially re-adopted) is proving slow to catch on is the popularity of the Venetian slogan: *Zante, Zante, fior di Levante* ("flower of the Levant"). This pretty island (which is really rather a long way

from the Levant) is indeed blessed with beautiful gardens and wild flowers, a special joy in spring. The heady wines from its vineyards justify a trip at any time of the year.

The island has suffered frequent earthquakes, three in the 19th century and a big one in 1953, but rebuilding has been intelligent and tasteful.

Zakynthos Town

The capital has retained something of its old Italian atmosphere, with the quay-side *campanile* an unmistakable legacy of the lengthy Venetian colonization. Behind the port, the churches have been rebuilt in their original Italian Renaissance or Baroque style. On St Mark's Square, Greek heritage is emphasized by the **Dionysios Solomos museum**, honouring the Zakynthos-born poet who in the 19th century championed modern popular (Demotic) Greek as the nation's literary language. Art treasures that were salvaged from churches damaged by the earthqake are housed in the **Museum of Byzantine Art** on Solomos Square. The **Venetian citadel** affords a fine view down to the Peloponnese.

Beaches

The most peaceful and pleasant beach resort·is **Alikes**, a small fishing village on the north-east coast. The most popular—and crowded—is **Laganas**, with a sandy beach 6.5 km (4 miles) long. With **Geraki** further east, it provides protection for some stoical turtles. On the south-east corner, the fishing port of **Vassilikos** has a good sandy beach.

The Zakynthos coastline is pierced by many lovely rocky coves.

Epirus

Literally "the mainland", Epirus is split between Greece and Albania, with the Pindus mountains to the east separating it from Thessaly. This mountainous land of sheep pastures and dense forests has always been remote from the rest of the country. It is worth a few days' exploration, to shop for jewellery in the Ioannina bazaar, pay homage to Zeus at Dodona, and picnic in the mountains.

The Lion Loses His Head

For most of its history, Epirus was little more than a backwater, until 1787 when the Turks appointed as governor the dashing Albanian brigand, Ali Pasha. The Lion of Ioannina, as he styled himself, fought for and against his Turkish masters, supported and betrayed Napoleon, the British, the Russians, the Greeks, and anyone else who served his purposes. By 1807, he was the undisputed ruler of Epirus, and most of Albania, too. With 500 women in his harem and scores of assassins at his beck and call, his life was an astounding mixture of sensuality and sadistic cruelty—he murdered his son's mistress and 16 of her girl friends—and an enlightened taste for the arts. He fascinated Lord Byron. After years of quiet amusement at his trouble-making, the Turks decided to crush Ali, who was pinning down Turkish troops which were badly needed to deal with the resurgence of the Greek independence movement. In 1822, after their siege of Ioannina had failed, the Turks invited Ali to negotiate at an island monastery in the middle of Ioannina's lake. There, he was ambushed by Turkish troops and finally executed. His body was buried in Ioannina but, with the kind of touch Ali himself would have appreciated, his head was put on show for the citizens of the town, and was then taken to Constantinople.

Igoumenitsa

For those arriving by ferry from Italy, this bustling transit town makes a most unromantic first view of Greece. On the waterfront, refresh yourself at one of the cafés, settle your business at the shipping agencies (return bookings, ferry-routes, currency exchange) and head out of town as soon as possible. Roads run down to Prevesa and the southern Ionian Islands or east over the mountains to Ioannina.

Ioannina

A two-hour drive from Igoumenitsa brings you to the Epirote capital on Lake Ioannina, known in antiquity as Pamvotis. Facing Mount Mitsikeli, it is built on a rocky promontory at a refreshing altitude of 520 m (1,706 ft). Much of the old town was burned down by Ali Pasha during the Turkish siege of 1820, but the **bazaar** retains its colourful atmosphere among shops selling gold, silver, copper, brass and embroidery.

A shepherd guards his flock up in the Epirus Mountain range between Ioannina and the port of Igoumenitsa.

south-west, the **tomb of Ali Pasha** occupies the site of his palace beside the **Fethi Mosque**.

The **Archaeological Museum** has finds from the Dodona sanctuary, notably figurines made of terracotta and inscribed lead oracle tablets.

Take a boat tour out to the **lake island** (*Nissí Ioanína*) and the 16th-century **Agios Pandelemon monastery,** where Ali Pasha made his last stand—note the Turkish bullet holes in his bedroom floor. The 11th-century **Agios Nikolaos Dilios** has some good frescoes of *Judas* and *The Last Judgement*. Not the least of the island's attractions are the restaurants serving lake trout, crayfish, eels and frogs' legs with the good local wine.

T he Ottoman heritage of the inland town of Ioannina survives in the 17th-century Aslan Mosque, which now houses a folk museum.

The centre of town is around the bustling Platia Pirrou and Kentriki.

The Muslim past survives in the maze of streets crowded into the **citadel** where Turks and Jews lived side by side. In the north-east corner, the 17th-century **Aslan Mosque** with its slender minaret now houses a **Folk Museum** exhibiting fierce weaponry and colourful Epirote costumes. Behind it is the old **Synagogue**—Ioannina had 6,000 Jews in the 19th century. Facing the

Perama Caves

Just five minutes' drive north of town is a bewitching wonderland of stalactites and stalagmites in galleries and caverns stretching for over 2 km underground. Discovered in World War II by families seeking refuge from bombardment, they have now been subtly illuminated and can be comfortably visited on a guided tour. Among the traces found of previous inhabitants were the teeth and bones of a family of bears hibernating here 600,000 years ago.

Dodona

Some 20 km (12.5 miles) down the Arta road, south-west of Ioannina, Greece's most ancient oracle stands in an appropriately lovely natural setting, where Mother Earth was worshipped as far back as 1900 BC. Beyond the sanctuary's remains, green meadows dotted with oaks and an occasional silver olive stretch away to the slopes of Mount Tomaros, rising gently in the violet distance to the south.

By 800 BC, the Greeks had taken over the sanctuary to consult the oracle of Zeus. Priests and priestesses interpreted his words from the rustling of leaves in a sacred oak tree, and sounds from the rhythmic beating of a copper vessel. In AD 390, when the Christian Emperor Theodosius ordered all pagan sanctuaries closed, the sacred oak was destroyed.

The most impressive remaining monument is the great **theatre** (3rd century BC), beautifully restored, and now the venue for a classical drama festival each summer. Bigger even than the great theatre at Epidaurus (see p. 133), it was used by the Romans as an arena for gladiators.

To the north, a long wall with a gate and towers enclosed the acropolis. The **sanctuary** lies on a terrace east of the theatre. The first buildings you come to, of which only the foundations remain, was an assembly hall for the shrine elders, a small rectangular Temple of Aphrodite, and beyond that, the Shrine of Zeus which enclosed the sacred oak, sheltered by a temple built in the 3rd century BC.

Metsovo

This delightful village 915 m (3,000 ft) up in the Pindus mountains makes a bracing excursion 50 km (31 miles) east from Ioannina. The sinuous road affords splendid views over the mountains and thick forests clinging to the ravines.

Metsovo was a refuge for wealthy Christians who were fleeing the Turkish capture of Constantinople in 1453. Built on terraces up the mountainside on both sides of a ravine (linked by a bridge), the handsome **patrician mansions** of massive stone with wooden balconies are the imposing legacy of these refugees. Grandest of them all is the house of the Tossitsa family, converted into a **Folk Art Museum** displaying fine local embroidery, woollen textiles and rugs.

Parga

Back on the coast, 48 km (30 miles) south of Igoumenitsa, this resort is prettily situated but often overcrowded. From its **Norman castle** (the Venetian Lion of St Mark is a later addition), you can look down on the harbour, very picturesque with its little islets scattered in the bay, and surrounded by groves of orange and olive trees. Swimmers should head for **Khristogiali beach**.

Arta

Travellers heading for the Gulf of Corinth can stop off at this lively commercial town to admire its elegant 17th-century humpbacked Turkish bridge over the Arachthos River. According to a popular song, the master builder reinforced the structure by walling his wife up in the foundations. If you have business in town, visit the six-domed church of Panagia Parigoritissa, built in the 13th century. In the sombre but imposing interior, notice the Italian style of the sculpture derived from Byzantine Epirus's links with Naples. The iconostasis has a 15th-century *Virgin the Comforter* and a later *Virgin and Child*.

Missolonghi

Once a thriving fishing port, this unprepossessing town in the province of Etolia, south of Epirus, is a pilgrimage strictly for Byron fans. It was here in 1824 that the romantic poet, rallying to the cause of Greece's freedom fighters, died of a fever, probably malaria. The poet's heart is buried beneath his statue in the **Heroes' Garden**, beside the tomb of Markos Botsaris, the commander of the local forces who saw the city razed by the Turks two years after Byron's death. In the centre of town, the **Museum of the Revolution** (Platia Botsaris) displays Byronic memorabilia along with a graphic account of the horrors to which the town was subjected.

Bitter Last Words

Byron was a true philhellene, who worked tirelessly to further the cause of Greek independence. Even in his poetry he did not miss the opportunity to condemn his own country's archaeological bandits, as in this extract from Childe Harold's Pilgrimage:

*Cold is the heart, fair Greece, that looks
    on Thee,*
*Nor feels as Lovers o'er the dust they
    loved;*
Dull is the eye that will not weep to see
*Thy walls defaced, thy mouldering shrines
    removed*
*By British hands, which it had best be
    hoved*
To guard those relics ne'er to be restored.
*Curst be the hour when from their isle
    they roved,*
*And once again thy hapless bosome
    gored,*
*And snatched thy shrinking Gods to
    Northern climes abhorred!*

*F*rench influence in Corfu Town is reflected in the graceful arches of the Liston Arcade

Rogues and Heroes

Outside of the church, the Greeks have never had much time for saintly men. The legendary heroes were magnificently, even hilariously flawed. If Achilles and Odysseus were admired for their strength and courage, it was the former's pouting sulks and the latter's sneaky duplicity that made them more humanly endearing. And the cultural and political glory of the Byzantine Empire was achieved by a bloodthirsty thug who fully earned his title of Basil the Bulgar-Slayer.

It is no accident that the most popular heroes in Greece's fight for independence from the Turks were the klephts (bands of mountain brigands), and merchant seamen who divided their energies between trade and piracy. The seamen's descendants have transferred their techniques into company offices and are now known as shipping magnates. Though Georgios and Andreas Papandreou are acclaimed by their countrymen as champions of democracy, their methods were often just as tough as those of their opponents.

Let's take a closer look at just a few of these heroic rogues and roguish heroes.

Theodoros Kolokotronis (1770–1843)

He was born, say all the Greek textbooks, under a tree in the Peloponnese. For generations, the Kolokotronis clan had led a band of klephts preying mainly on rich Greek landowners known contemptuously as Turkish Christians for their collaboration with the Ottoman authorities. Looking back on his exploits in the War of Independence, Kolokotronis was endowed with the aura of a Robin Hood, but there is no evidence that he ever distributed his booty to the poor. Heroic paintings of him show the great bandit in traditional flowing pantaloons over slippers and gold-bound leggings. On his gold-braided tunic he wore lion-head epaulettes to match his great white mane of hair, fierce moustache and predatory stare.

Inspired by the French Revolution which, he said, "opened the eyes of the world", he concentrated his attacks on the Turks, who drove him to seek refuge in the Ionian Islands. His hero had been the greatest rogue of them all, Napoleon, but on Zante (Zakynthos) he joined the British army of Sir Richard Church.

Back in the Peloponnese after the Napoleonic Wars, he resumed the fight against the Turks. In 1822, he captured the Turkish garrison in Nafplio. But, still more of a bandit than a committed patriot, he refused to let the Greek government hold its national assembly there and kidnapped four of its members to block retaliatory measures against him. Now virtual master of the Peloponnese, he furthered the national cause again with a famous victory over the Turks at Dervenaki Pass (near Argos). He used the 13th-century Crusader castle of Karitaina as his stronghold against the Ottoman armies of Ibrahim Pasha. Proving that he could match the enemy in brutality, his capture of the key town of Tripolis in 1824 resulted in the wholesale massacre of its Turkish civil population.

He finally did hand Nafplio over to the Greek government in 1824, in exchange for half the support funds that Lord Byron had brought from London. He rebelled again and was thrown into jail. In 1832 he broke up the National Assembly in an abortive attempt to impose his choice of the

Admiral Kanaris

Ari Onassis

Russian Admiral Ricord in place of King Otto. His valour is celebrated with equestrian statues in Nafplio and Athens.

KonstantinosKanaris
(1790–1877)

This great Aegean seaman also began life as an outlaw, but mellowed with age into a more statesmanlike character. He was born on the heroic island of Psara, west of Chios, a perpetual thorn in Turkey's side until a massacre wiped out nine-tenths of its population. Before the independence struggle began in earnest, Kanaris plied the Mediterranean in a merchant freighter but made most of his money from smuggling and piracy. He looked like every schoolboy's image of a pirate, kerchief tied around his brow, bristling moustache, dagger at the ready in his cummerbund.

With the outbreak of war—Psara was, with Spetses and Hydra, the first of the islands to revolt—Kanaris wrought havoc among the Ottoman fleet. His most famous victory came in November 1822, when his fireship destroyed the Turkish admiral's flagship off the island of Tenedos (Turkish

Bozca). This action stopped an advance to relieve Nafplio and drove the Ottoman fleet back to its harbours in the Dardanelles. Kanaris became an admiral.

During the equally turbulent years of peace, Kanaris stowed away his dagger and supported the moderate Ioannis Kapodistrias. He was one of the few Greek leaders to obey the new Constitution. As prime minister in the 1860s, he championed democratic reforms, but was not averse to employing the old strongarm tactics when the king resisted. Returning from a tour, Otto was prevented from landing at Piraeus, and Kanaris promoted the enthronement of the more amenable Danish King George I.

Aristotle Onassis
(1906–1975)

This famous shipping magnate's full name was Aristotle Socrates Onassis. More appropriate for this not very philosophical fellow would have been "Odysseus", for his opportunistic cunning, and "Croesus" for his fabled wealth. He was born in Smyrna (now Izmir) in Turkey, from which his family of prosperous tobacco merchants fled after the defeat of the Greek fleet in 1922. Ari became a telephone operator in Buenos Aires. By the age of 19, he had revived the family tobacco business, importing Turkish tobacco. With dual Greek and Argentinian citizenship, he became Greek consul-general in Argentina.

He had made his first million dollars by 1931. A year later, convinced that the Great Depression was a fantastic business opportunity, he bought his first ships, six Canadian freighters, for $120,000—five years earlier they would have cost $2 million *each*. In 1939, he had a similar hunch about World War II, and purchased his first oil tanker. He put his merchant fleet at the disposal of America and its allies, and in return he acquired 23 Liberty ships (wartime cargo vessels) for a song.

Back in Greece in 1946, he married Athina (Tina), the daughter of fellow shipping magnate Stavros Livanos. With Stavros Niarchos as his brother-in-law (married to Tina's sister Eugenie), Onassis belonged to the most powerful shipping clan in the world. But family ties were never as strong as business rivalry and personal vanity. When Onassis acquired the island of Skorpios (off Lefkas), then Niarchos had to have one, too, and bought Spetsopoula (off Spetses). The toys they fought for were yachts and women. Niarchos, divorced, seduced Tina away from Ari, and Onassis retaliated with his biggest coup of all, his marriage to Jackie, the widow of President Kennedy.

Business was not neglected. The money he lost on a fleet of whalers was more than recouped by turning from whale oil to petroleum. Again anticipating crisis, Onassis built the world's first supertanker in 1953. Three years later, he made a cool $115 million out of the diversion of oil shipments when Egypt blocked the Suez Canal. In 1957 he founded Olympic Airways (nationalized in 1975). For many years, he was the principal stockholder in the company that owned the Monte Carlo casino.

He did not like giving money to charities or cultural foundations, but did much to make bouzouki music fashionable by having it played on his yacht and in smart night-clubs. In Greek politics, he played on all sides. He kept in with the colonels' dictatorship of 1967 by agreeing to invest $600 million, then reneged on the deal in time to win the favour of the democrats who overthrew the colonels in 1974. By the time of his death in the Paris suburb of Neuilly a year later, Onassis's wealth was beyond counting, but he left a few more tangible figures: 6 supertankers with a total capacity of 2 million tons, 56 merchant ships totalling 5,586,000 tons, 87 companies in 12 countries, and 217 bank accounts.

Georgios and Andreas Papandreou
As prime ministers of Greece, though their terms were 20 years apart, father and son were both fierce libertarians. Steeled by years of ruthless treatment at the hands of their enemies, these staunch champions of democracy proved equally ruthless in its defence. It was a national tradition that stretched back to Pericles himself.

Georgios Papandreou (1888–1968) founded the Social Democratic party in 1935. With brilliant oratory, this charismatic demagogue (in the true ancient sense of the word) soon posed a threat to the dictatorship of Ioannis Metaxas. His best men were jailed and tortured and he himself was driven into exile in 1938. During World War II he formed a government-in-exile in Cairo, which he brought back to liberated Athens in October 1944. His efforts to disarm resistance fighters ended in confrontation between left-wing partisans and the British army, forcing him to resign.

Back in power in 1963, he was in perpetual conflict with King Constantine II, who as commander-in-chief resisted his purge of right-wing extremists in the army. Exploiting Papandreou's anti-monarchist rallies as part of what they claimed was a Communist threat to the state, army colonels staged a coup in 1967. Georgios Papandreou was jailed, released due to failing health, and died the following year. His funeral, the biggest in modern Greek history, turned into a massive demonstration for democracy against a dictatorship that was to last another six years.

His activist son, Andreas Papandreou (1919–89) followed him into prison on treason charges, but not for the first time. In 1939, he had been jailed by dictator Metaxas before going into exile to study in the United States. In the forties and fifties he taught economics at Harvard, Minnesota, Northwestern (Illinois) and Berkeley.

Andreas resumed his political career in Greece in 1964 as a minister in his father's government. Under the colonels, he was exiled again, but this time to Sweden and Canada, since the United States was the Greek regime's discreet but firm ally.

Andreas returned in 1974 with scores to settle. Electoral campaigns for his socialist party, PASOK, branded his father's old conservative enemies as nothing less than traitors for having handed the country over to the colonels. On similar grounds, he was equally hostile to the US. With fiery rhetoric reminiscent of his father, but an ideology much further to the left, he became prime minister in 1981 on the simple campaign slogan of *Allagi*—Change. He pushed through sweeping social reforms in welfare, education and health. But his party cronies lived too well off the fat of the land, and financial scandals marred the Papandreou crusading image. This was what cost him victory, and his health too, in his 1989 election battle. The fact that he had jilted his 65-year-old American wife Margaret for the sexy 34-year-old air hostess Dimitra upset only a prim and proper minority.

Andreas Papandreou

Beyond the Beach and the Ancient Cities — Shopping, Sports, and Entertainment

The activities we look at here have an uncanny knack of capturing the spirit of Greece both ancient and modern. The best bargains for souvenir hunters are the products of the country's authentic folk arts, and the best jewellery and ceramics borrow from the designs of ancient Greece. While most of the sporting activities are resolutely modern—the ancient Greeks considered the sea as a dangerous place to be avoided whenever possible—sailing in the Aegean or hiking through the island hills can re-create a miniature Odyssey. Entertainment can be found in the traditional bouzouki music of a waterfront taverna, or watching Orestes avenge his father under a full moon in the ancient theatre at Epidaurus. And the year-round festivals in towns and villages maintain a link between the ancient customs of pagan carnivals and the more solemn religious celebrations of the Orthodox Church.

Shopping

*P*ots, pans, trays and tankards in copper, brass and pewter form the glowing centre-piece of a stall in the Monastiraki flea market in Athens.

Go the bazaar with a little bit of knowledge and your eyes open, and you'll soon be able to sort out the wheat from the chaff. Rugs, pottery, lace and embroidery, furs and jewellery, whether moderate or expensive, can be a bargain. But first let's deal with the chaff.

Souvenir Junk

Some of it is so marvellously awful as to demand your immediate attention. To be fair, the shopkeepers go out of their way to warn you by putting up a sign. You can't miss it—"Greek Art," it says, hoping to lift the wares it describes above the ordinary with that ancient seal of aesthetic quality evoked by the word "Greek". Kitschmongery here knows no limits. Miniature white Corinthian columns are actually bottles of ouzo. The Parthenon is a basket for nuts and raisins, the Phaistos Disk a cocktail mat, key ring or earring, the Charioteer of Delphi a bedside lamp, the Athens Poseidon a garden dwarf. True kitsch-collectors buy a statue of an over-endowed satyr just to be able to declare it at customs.

Folk Art

Not all of the craftwork is mass produced in factories. Hand-made creations, the work of traditional artisans, maintain a high standard and a remarkably low price. Styles in wood carving, fabrics, lace and embroidery obviously differ considerably from north to south and from the islands to the mountain villages of the mainland. The major cities have a selection of craftwork from all over the country. It is a good idea to look at the range—and price—of goods in the shops in Athens or Thessaloniki so as to be able to compare them with what you might find in villages like Kritsa or Anogia in Crete (lace and embroidery), and Metsovo in Epirus (wood carving).

In any case, the first stop before you go out to buy anything should be the **folk art museums** where, unhustled by shopkeepers, you can study the cream of

authentic regional handicrafts. Most of the museums also have excellent shops with knowledgeable assistants, though the range of goods may not be as wide as you will find in the bazaars and specialist shops. Among the most important handicrafts museums are—in Athens, the Benaki and the Greek Folk Art Museums; in Iraklion, the Historical Museum; in Thessaloniki, the Macedonian Folklore Museum; on Skyros, the Faltaitz Museum; in Nafplio, the Peloponnesian Folklore Foundation; and in Ioannina, the Epirus Folk Museum.

Rugs

The celebrated shaggy flokati rugs have not changed much since they draped the walls and floors of Mycenaean palaces, or served as winter bedcovers for Helen and Paris. They are priced by the kilo (a square metre weighs about 2.5 kilos). You should soon be able to tell the difference between the machine-made variety and the much more tightly-knotted hand-made rugs. Pure sheep's wool shag is spun from fibres into yarn, and then looped on a loom to create a rug that is straggly on the surface and matted underneath. To give them a finish that is both fluffy and compact, the rugs are soaked for a few days under running water. The industry has flourished in northern Greece where the villages like Metsovo have fast-flowing mountain streams. The rugs may be dyed bright red, a more subdued blue or brown, or left as creamy "natural". The village of Arachova, near Delphi, has given its name to a vividly patterned version that is popular as a wall-hanging.

Tagári, rug-like shoulder bags, once popular with the hippies of the 1960s, are making a comeback.

Pottery

The ancient art of pot-throwing is not dead, and it is worth making a trip out to the Maroussi suburb of Athens to see the variety of local and regional products. The pottery of the Dodecanese, and Rhodes in particular, is admired for its vivid versions of Turkish designs. The famous Lindos pottery, with its designs of tulips and roses on a dark green background, is made now in the town of Rhodes.

Visit factories like the Ikaros to see the patterns being hand-painted on to the pots.

In Crete, most of the major north coast towns produce attractive replicas of Minoan and Geometric-patterned vases. Unglazed pottery from the village of Margaritis is considered the finest handwork produced in the Aegean.

A flash of gold from the grin of a lace maker plying her wares in the Plaka district below the Acropolis in Athens.

Ceramics from the Peloponnese have a distinctive green glaze with pale green and yellow designs. Nafplio has a good selection, and Corinth has revived its ancient tradition. Be a little more wary in the shops around the great archaeological sites of Mycenae, Epidaurus and Olympia, however, where the quality may be suspect.

The highly decorative Epirote pottery you will find at Ioannina and Metsovo goes for bright reds, blues and greens.

*R*ethymnon's shops are good places to check out Crete's reputation for hand-woven fabrics. If you fall in love with the richly textured material but prefer to have the clothes made up back home, buy it by the bolt; most shops will ship it for you. Even with mailing costs, it's still a bargain.

Jewellery

The styling of gold and silver jewellery is dictated more by ancient history than by any more recent regional traditions. Designers have moved beyond the time-honoured fine, lacy, silver filigree to draw inspiration from the great museum collections. It's difficult to improve on the necklaces, bracelets, rings and earrings of the jewellers of King Minos in Crete, or Queen Clytemnestra at Mycenae, or those of Philip and Alexander in Macedonia. Just as timeless are the ancient designs for plates, bowls and chalices. But you will also find modern designs executed with admirable workmanship.

Gold and silver are sold by weight, with a relatively tiny fraction of the cost added for workmanship and creativity. The bazaars at Rhodes and Ioannina remain the most enjoyable places to hunt for treasures.

Athens' best jewellery shops are in the Voukourestiou and Panepistimiou area; in Iraklion, near the museum. Elsewhere, you can be sure that there will be good jewellery shops in major resorts like Agios Nikolaos in Crete or Nafplio in the Peloponnese, and wherever the cruise ships regularly stop—Mykonos, Santorini, and Corfu.

Antiques

Lord Elgin would not be able to loot the Acropolis so easily today. Anything that predates Greek independence (1821) is considered an antique, and an export permit to take it out of the country is practically impossible to get. Customs officials watch out for the big pieces; small smugglable items like coins, terracotta or bronze figurines are probably fake. If you are in the market for Byzantine icons (easily faked, too), you will

find reputable dealers on Athens' Leoforos Amalias, Voukourestiou or around the Monastiraki district.

Good replicas, or modern icons are found in museum-shops, and occasionally in monasteries, notably at Mistra and Mount Athos.

Furs

There are bargains in mink, chinchilla, red fox, squirrel, Persian lamb and stone marten. Hats, coats, stoles, capes and patchwork quilts are made from imported pelts, hand sewn in northern Greek towns like Kastoria. Take a look at the range in Athens (around Syntagma) or Thessaloniki (along Odos Egnatia) before making the trip. Kastoria prices are unbeatable, especially in summer.

Clothes and Leatherware

At best, a fisherman's sweater, a pair of sandals or handmade boots (especially from Archangelos on Rhodes). But the

*T*he warm, clear waters of the Aegean are perfect for swimming and snorkelling, while the reliable afternoon sea breezes make for good sailing and windsurfing. Waterskiing and parascending are available at the more popular resorts.

mediocre workmanship of the leather bags and luggage does not justify the huge displays of the stuff at every resort.

Sports

Ancient Olympic champions returning to see what's going on in Greece these days might be puzzled by the huge numbers of people enjoying themselves in the water. In their day, swimming was something you did to escape a shipwreck, not for fun. Today, on the other hand not many people will be doing much running, jumping, boxing or wrestling—except, perhaps, in the odd hooligan bar in Corfu or Kos.

Still, the Aegean and Ionian seas are magnificent aquatic playgrounds.

Swimming

Choosing the right beach from the hundreds available is not so easy. The ideal beach is not always the one with the finest sand. On the Aegean islands, locate a few pebble beaches for the days when the *meltemi* is blowing. Rock ledge beaches have the considerable advantage of being uncrowded, but you should keep plastic sandals handy if you are going to paddle around on the rocks.

For children, make sure you have some really safe shallow bathing available—lifeguards are rare, and usually non-existent.

Nude bathing is officially forbidden, but in practice, you will find several beaches where people take it all off. The criterion seems to be to choose relatively secluded places not frequented by families, or by the Greeks themselves.

As for pollution, the obvious beaches to avoid are those close to major ports— Piraeus, Patras, Igoumenitsa, Thessaloniki and Iraklion. The European Commission's Blue Flag for top-rated cleanliness has recently been awarded to seven beaches: Vrontados (Chios), Faliraki, Kallithea and Reni (Rhodes), Vai and Elounda (Crete) and Loutraki (near Corinth). The Green Flag for clean waters went to Nisaki, Gouvia and Benitses (Corfu), Sani, Kalithea and Porto Carras (Chalkidiki), Tigaki (Kos) and Chersonisos (Crete). There are no doubt many more, but Greece submitted for inspection only 100 beaches from its 24,000 km (15,000 miles) of coastline.

Water Sports

The seas around the islands and mainland coasts are warm enough for swimming from May to mid-October.

The Aegean is a few degrees warmer than the Ionian Sea in May, but, probably due to the *meltemi* wind, the temperature of the Aegean drops faster in October.

For sports where you need to rent equipment, the major resorts are the obvious places to go. However, even in even the tiniest, secluded fishing harbour you should be able to find a little caïque to hire.

Snorkelling and Scuba Diving

The joy of underwater exploration around the Greek coasts is not just the marine fauna and flora you will see, but the vestiges of ancient ports and cities.

On Crete's Mirabello Bay, for instance, you can swim out from Elounda to see the submerged ruins of Olous, a Greco-Roman settlement. Across the bay, part of the Minoan ruins of Mochlos are also underwater.

But for the most part, you will have to content yourself with glimpses snatched while snorkelling. Like underwater photography, scuba diving is restricted to government-designated sites where you cannot disturb any ancient shipwrecks and archaeological sites. These include Corfu's Paleokastritsa, which has a good diving school, and Chalkidiki in the north.

Windsurfing and Water Skiing

Equipment can be hired at all the major resorts. Water skiing schools for are available at Porto Carras and Gerakini in Chalkidiki, and on the islands of Corfu, Chios, Lesbos and Skiathos. But adepts of both sports are increasingly being shunted away from the popular family beaches. Opportunities for straight surfing are limited. There is nothing on the Hawaiian or Australian scale, but Mykonos' Ormos Bay attracts serious *aficionados* and Myrtos Beach on Kephalonia has possibilities.

Sailing

Even just chugging around in a caïque fitted with an outboard motor, you can face the open sea and imagine yourself as Jason with or without his Argonauts. If you fancy yourself as a full-blown Odysseus, the National Tourist Office can help you charter a yacht at Piraeus. Renting smaller sailing vessels is possible at any fair-sized port in the islands. You can take sailing lessons at the Kalamaria Naval Club in Thessaloniki. For

landlubbers who like boats just enough to watch them race, Thessaloniki has a regatta in Navy Week at the end of June.

Fishing

Fishing from the rocks or from a boat can land you a catch of sea-bass, swordfish, dentex and a host of eastern Mediterranean fish that have no English names. No special licence is needed, though underwater spear fishing is restricted. Ask at the local tourist office. It is sometimes possible to "hitch a ride" with a friendly professional fisherman going out at night to fish with flare lanterns. Another useful friend is the local taverna chef, to cook your catch.

Freshwater fishing is available on the lakes at Ioannina and Kastoria.

Tennis and Golf

Most big resort hotels have hard courts, and there are public courts in the large towns—in Athens, at the Agios Kosmas Sports Centre, and behind the Archaeological Museum in Iraklion. Thessaloniki Sports Club accepts non-members.

Golf is more limited; you can play at Afandou on Rhodes, at Porto Carras in Chalkidiki, and at Athens' Glifada Golf Club, if you do not mind the jumbo jets landing and taking off just beyond the bunker.

Mountain Climbing and Skiing

Contact the GNTO (see TOURIST INFORMATION OFFICES) for information about guides, equipment, and which mountains may be off-limits for reasons of military security. In winter on Mount Parnassus, the villages of Arachova and Delphi turn into winter sports resorts. On Mount Pilion in Thessaly, you will find good skiing facilities at Hania.

In the Peloponnese, skiers head for the slopes of Ostrakina and Vrissopoulos, both near Olympia.

Horse Riding

The Macedonians keep up their ancient horse riding traditions at the Northern Greece Riding Club in Thessaloniki. There are also facilities on Chalkidiki at Porto Carras, Sani and Palini Beach, and at Thermi on the island of Samothrace.

Cricket

Cricket? Yes, the great English game is played in summer on the Esplanade in Corfu Town. The game was introduced to the island by the British in 1864, and it has remained popular.

There are two local clubs, and matches are often arranged against visiting sides from England, the Royal Navy and Malta. Keen cricketers might be able to

*M*otorbikes, scooters and mopeds are available for hire in the major resorts and on most of the islands. They are a fun way of exploring the more remote nooks and crannies. But be warned— motorbikes and even mopeds can be very dangerous in inexperienced hands, especially on winding, pot-holed island roads. Always wear a crash helmet, take things slowly until you get the hang of your machine, and never, ever ride after drinking alcohol. Too many tourists end their holiday in hospital after a motorbike accident.

take part in one of the Saturday afternoon games–you can make arrangements through your hotel.

Entertainment

The entertainment the Greeks most enjoy is their own conversation. The *vólta* (the evening stroll, a local institution) along the harbour promenade, or around the town's main square, followed by an hour or two at a café under the plane trees, is their daily theatre. Who is wooing whom? Is *that* her new fiancé? Will his rich uncle from America buy the supermarket? What about the politician's mistress? The building promoter's "heart attack"? The pleasure is contagious and infects the hitherto most introverted visitor from cooler climes. To execute an authentic *vólta*, you should dress with a casual elegance. No camera, no shopping bag. Arm in arm rather than hand in hand, and you're set to join the gossiping throng. And after the *vólta*, you still have time to take in some more formal musical or theatrical entertainment. Sound-and-light shows, with English-language commentaries, start around 9 p.m. In Athens, the Acropolis show takes place on the Pnyx Hill. On Rhodes, in the town's municipal gardens, they recount the siege of Suleiman the Magnificent. Corfu's history is recounted in the Old Fort.

Music and Dance

Greek music amounts to more than the ubiquitous twangy movie themes from *Never on Sunday* and *Zorba the Greek*, but the power of modern sound-amplifying systems insists that we start there.

Some purists claim that the long-necked mandolin-like **bouzouki**, which

*T*he café—kafeneion in Greek— social hub of village life.

has given its name to the music and to the night-clubs where it is performed, is not even Greek, but Turkish. The *syrtáki* dance popularized by Anthony Quinn's Zorba, is in fact a combination, invented for the film, of several distinct traditional dances. The *zeybékiko*, coming originally from Asia Minor, is an introspective dance of meditation with the man swaying slowly, arms outstretched, eyes half-closed, leaning backwards, bending his knees, occasionally taking long steps sideways or forwards and making a sudden sharp twist or leap before retrieving a more deliberate rhythm. This blossoms into the *khassápikos* or butcher's dance, in which two or three men join arms and find a community of spirit by swaying, dipping and stepping together, the sudden changes signalled by a shout or squeeze of the shoulder from the lead dancer (the one carrying a handkerchief). These dances are in turn linked to the slow, majestic *tsamíko* performed by the mountain klephts; the dragging round-dances, the *syrtós*, of the islands; the faster *kalamationós* of the southern Peloponnese, and the *soústa*, the hop-dance of Crete.

The hybrid *syrtáki* is performed at hosts of resort tavernas and night-clubs in Piraeus, Athens and Thessaloniki. This is where the dancers smash plates or toss gardenias (both are added to the bill). You can, of course, join in. Your best chance of seeing the more traditional dances is at country weddings, festivals or, more formally, the Dora Stratou Theatre on Athens' Mousion hill.

The alternately harsh and plaintive popular music that inspired composer Mikis Theodorakis was the *rembétika*. This was created by the militant urban youth of the tempestuous 1920s after the mass exchange of Turkish and Greek populations.

Symphonic and choral music are performed at Athens' ancient Odeon of Herodes Atticus from mid-June to late September, along with foreign opera and ballet companies. The concerts and recitals are part of the Athens Festival which highlights classical Greek drama (see p. 38). Tickets can be hard to come by unless you book well in advance, but the bigger hotels can sometimes help, at slightly higher prices.

Theatre

Even if you do not understand a word of it, an evening of **classical Greek drama** can be a magical experience. In Athens, the tragedies of Aeschylus, Sophocles and Euripides, or the comedies of Aristophanes, are performed on the slopes of the Acropolis as part of the capital's summer festival. The open-air Odeon of Herodes Atticus (see p. 106), with the Parthenon illuminated behind you, recaptures the atmosphere of these ancient dramas. (Most of the plays received their premières at the nearby Theatre of Dionysus, no longer in use.)

The acoustics are good, but take binoculars if you have to sit at the top of the amphitheatre. You will have a plastic seat on the marble terraces, but you'll be more comfortable if you supplement that with some padding of your own. The plays are performed in modern rather than ancient Greek, which most of today's Athenians would have a hard time following. To get the maximum enjoyment, as you might for an opera, try to read the text, or at least a synopsis of the plot, in English before you go. Tickets are not as difficult to get as for

the festival's concerts and operas, but you will still need to make advance bookings.

For many, the spectacle of Greek drama is even more impressive when staged in the magnificent mountain setting of Epidaurus in the Peloponnese (see p. 133). Performances take place at weekends from mid-June to early September; obtaining tickets is usually easier than in Athens. The productions are nearly all of classical drama performed, as in Athens, by the National Theatre of Greece, but with Europe's cultural frontiers breaking down, you may also see works by Shakespeare, Racine or Goethe.

In the north, classical drama is performed at the ancient amphitheatres of Philippi and Thasos. In October, Thessaloniki holds a flourishing arts festival, the Demetriada, with good theatre and symphony music.

A more recent tradition, from the last years of the Ottoman Empire, is the **shadow puppet theatre**, adored by children and adults alike. As with so many authentic folk arts, its death is regularly reported, only for it to be resuscitated by a new troupe of cultural conservationists—mostly in Patras and Athens, but also in small towns in Epirus and the Peloponnese. It is known to the Greeks as Kharaghiozis, after its principal character, "Black Eyes", an indomitable down-and-out, once the great symbol of Greek resistance. Barba Yorgos is his uncle, a well-meaning but simple-minded fellow from the mountains; Hadjiavatis is the friendly Turk, Morphonios a silly dandy, and Stavrakas a city layabout. Again, if you cannot follow the intricacies of the plot, you will soon be caught up in the boisterous

atmosphere. It helps if you go with children, as they usually catch on much faster than adults.

Cinema

In the summer, films are always shown in the open air. Movie buffs must bow to the custom of a sudden 20-minute break in the middle for refreshment. But since the Greeks do not dub their foreign films, everything is presented in its original version with Greek subtitles. This has the strange effect of the Greeks in the audience often laughing before you do, because the subtitles translate the jokes much faster than they are spoken. But you can get your own back, since they apparently do not always translate *all* the jokes.

*C*ustomers in a back-street café enjoy an impromptu performance by an itinerant accordionist. Such wandering musicians vary in quality from excellent to appalling, but are usually infinitely preferable to the recorded bouzouki music which blasts out incessantly from many of the tourist bars in the major resorts.

The Right Place at the Right Price

Hotels

Hotels are classified by the Greek government according to the size, decor and amenities of the rooms and public areas, and the standards of services and facilities provided by the hotel and its staff. The categories are L (Luxury), A, B, C, D and E. Prices within each category (except L, where the sky's the limit) must fall within limits set by the government, and room rates must, by law, be displayed in the reception area. However, these set rates are open to variation in both directions. In popular areas, prices may increase by up to 20% from July to September, and a 10% surcharge may be added for stays of less than two nights. In winter, rates may drop by up to 40%. All rooms in categories L to C, and many in D, have private bathrooms. A rough guide to the price of a double room is given below:

22,000–55,000 drachmas	
12,000–22,000 drachmas	
6,000–12,000 drachmas	
3,000–6,000 drachmas	

Athens and environs

Achileas
Lekka 21, 105 62 Athens
Tel. (01) 32.33.197
Bright, modern hotel in a quiet street near Syntagma Square. Large rooms, some with garden terraces. Good value. 34 rooms.

Acropolis House
Kodrou 6-8, 10558 Athens.
Tel. (01) 32.22.344;
Fax 32.44.143
Restored 19th-century villa offers good value accommodation with old-world charm, in a quiet corner of Plaka.19 rooms.

Adonis
Voulis 3, Plaka, 105 58 Athens.
Tel. (01) 32.49.737;
Fax 32.31.602
Small new hotel in Plaka. Roof garden with panoramic views of the Acropolis and Mt. Lycattus. 26 rooms.

Alexandros
Timoleontos Vassou 8,
11521 Athens.
Tel. (01) 64.30.464
Pleasant hotel in quiet spot beneath the Lycabettos Hill. Rooms are plain but spacious, clean and comfortable. 96 rooms.

Amalia Hotel
10 Amalias Street,
105 57 Athens.
Tel. (01) 32.37.301;
Fax 32.38.792
Comfortable hotel in central location. Coffee shop, retaurant, bar. 100 rooms.

Aphrodite Hotel
21 Apollonos Street,
105 57 Athens.
Tel. (91) 32.34.357;
Fax 32.25.244
Centrally located hotel, with bar and air-conditioning. 84 rooms.

Athenaeum Inter-Continental
Singrou 89–93, 11745 Athens.
Tel. (01) 90.23.666;
Fax 92.43.000
Huge luxury hotel two miles from centre, with rooftop bar and terrace. Spectacular view of Acropolis. Four restaurants and a night-club. Swimming pool. Fitness centre. 596 rooms.

Athens Chandris
Singrou 385,
17564 Paleo Faliro.
Tel. (01) 94.14.824;
Fax 94.25.082
Conference oriented hotel in a coastal suburb, with free shuttle service to Syntagma. Comfortable rooms. Two restaurants. Swimming pool. 350 rooms.

Athens Hilton
Vas. Sofias 46,
11528 Athens.
Tel. (01) 72.50.201;
Fax 72.53.001.
All you'd expect from a Hilton, with a splendid view of the Acropolis and the sea from the rooftop garden. Four restaurants, four bars. Swimming pool, health club, air-conditioning. Night-club. 453 rooms.

Athinais
Vas. Sofias 99,
11521 Athens.
Tel. (01) 64.31.133;
Fax 64.61.682.
Pleasant hotel in residential area about two miles from city centre. Roof garden. 84 rooms.

Attalos
Athinas 29, 10554 Athens.
Tel. (01) 32.12.801;
Fax 32.43.124.
Set on a lively street in the market area. Roof-garden bar with view of the Acropolis. 80 rooms.

Best Western Coral
Possidonos 35,
Paleon Phaleron,
17561 Athens.
Tel. (01) 98.16.441;
Fax 98.31.207
Waterfront location between city and airport, with balconies overlooking the Saronic Gulf. Pool, beach, roof garden. 160 rooms.

Candia
Deligianni 40,
10438 Athens.
Tel. (01) 52.46.112.
Opposite main railway station, near Omonia Square. Comfortable air-conditioned rooms, and good restaurant. Swimming pool, small roof garden. 142 rooms.

Delphi
Ag. Konstantinou 21,
10437 Athens.
Tel. (01) 52.38.624;
Fax 52.33.645
Old-fashioned hotel on busy main road, five minutes from Omonia Square. Exterior is rather off-putting, but inside is much better. 54 rooms.

Divani
Acropolis Palace
Parthenonos 19–25, Athens.
Tel. (01) 92.22.945;
Fax 92.14.993.
Good hotel in excellent situation, quiet side street behind Acropolis. Five minutes from Plaka. Roof garden, swimming pool. 265 rooms.

Electra Palace
Nikodimou 18,
10557 Athens.
Tel. (01) 32.41.401;
Fax 32.41.875.
Pleasant hotel in rather shabby area, but only five minutes walk from Syntagma Square. Swimming pool and roof garden. Secure parking. 106 rooms.

El Greco
Athinas 65, Omonia.
Tel. (01) 32.44.553;
Fax 32.44.597
Small, modern hotel in central market area (can sometimes be noisy). Dining room, bar and coffee shop; roof garden with view of the Acropolis.

Grande Bretagne
Syntagma, 10563 Athens.
Tel. (01) 32.30.251;
Fax 32.20.211.
Traditional 19th-century British style hotel, built 1862, with marble-lined lobby and wood-panelled bar, and big, old-fashioned rooms. The GB is an Athens institution.Three restaurants. 355 rooms.

Hermes
Apollonos 19, 10557 Athens.
Tel. (01) 32.35.514;
Fax 32.32.073.
Pleasant modern hotel with attractive flower-bedecked balconies, set in a relatively quiet side street, ten minutes walk from Plaka. Roof garden. 45 rooms.

Herodion
Robertou Galli 4,
10402 Athens.
Tel. (01) 92.36.832
Plain but comfortable hotel tucked under the south side of the Acropolis, with rooftop bar, restaurant, and cocktail lounge. Parking available. 90 rooms.

Ilisia
Michalakopoulou 25,
11528 Athens.
Tel. (01) 72.44.051;
Fax 72.41.847.
Set back from the road in a pleasant residential area. 90 rooms.

Imperial
Mitropoleos 46, 10432 Athens
Tel. (01) 32.27.617
Old hotel at edge of Plaka, modest, but clean and inexpensive. 21 rooms.

Keramikos
Keramikou 32, Athens.
Tel. 52.47.631
Ten minutes west of Omonia Square. Rooms are small and plain but bright and clean, all with balconies and private bath. Bar and cafe. 54 rooms.

King Minos
Pireos 1, Omonia Square,
10552 Athens.
Tel. (01) 52.31.111;
Fax 52.31.361.
Large, plush and centrally located, with restaurant and roof garden. In red light district. 287 rooms.

Ledra Marriott
Syngrou 113–115, 11745
Athens.
Tel. (01) 93.47.711;
Fax 93.58.603
*Excellent accommodation, with
rooftop swimming pool and
unusual Polynesian/Japanese
restaurant. Located away from
the centre, about 2 km from
Acropolis. 259 rooms.*

Leto
Missaraliotou 15,
11742 Athens
Tel. (01) 92.31.768
20 rooms.

Lycabette
Valaoritou 6, 10671 Athens.
Tel. (01) 36.33.514
*Good value hotel in Kolonaki at
foot of Lycabettus Hill. No
restaurant, but breakfast is
served in your room. 63 rooms.*

Marathon
Karolou 23, 10437 Athens.
Tel. (01) 52.31.865;
Fax 52.31.218.
*Pleasant tourist hotel on a busy
street close to Omonia Square.
View of the Acropolis and Lyca-
bettus. Roof garden, disco in
summer. 94 rooms.*

La Mirage
Omonia Square.
Tel. (01) 52.34.071;
Fax 52.33.992
*Small modern hotel in central
location, near the metro.*

NJV Meridien
Syntagma Square,
10564 Athens.
Tel. (01) 32.55.301;
Fax 32.35.856
*Luxurious rooms with "ancient
Greek" decor and marble bath-
rooms, fully sound-proofed and
air-conditioned. Gourmet
French restaurant. Within walk-
ing distance of Plaka and
Acropolis. 177 rooms.*

Novotel Mirayia
Michail Voda 4–6,
10439 Athens.
Tel. (01) 82.56.422;
Fax 88.37.816.
*Large hotel geared mainly to
business travellers. Roof gar-
den with swimming pool.
Underground parking. 195
rooms.*

Omonia
Omonia Square,
10431 Athens.
Tel. (01) 52.37.210;
Fax 52.25.779
*Large, modern hotel in noisy
but central location. Good
value rooms with private bathroom and balcony. Rooms overlooking square have view of
Acropolis. 255 rooms.*

Plaka
Kapnikareas 7,
10556 Athens.
Tel. (01) 32.22.096;
Fax 32.22.412.
*Good value accommodation at
edge of Plaka, bright, clean and
quiet. Most rooms have balconies, those at the back with a
view towards the Acropolis.
Roof garden, pleasant cafe. 67
rooms.*

Philippos
Mitseon 3, 117 42Athens.
Tel. (01) 92.23.611;
Fax 92.23.615.
*Quiet hotel with roof garden,
close to the Acropolis.*

President
Kifissias 43,
11523 Athens.
Tel. (01) 69.24.600;
Fax 69.24.900.
*Large conference venue about
three miles out from centre,
comfortable but poorly located
for sightseeing. Roof garden.
Swimming pool, disco. 530
rooms.*

Royal Olympic
28–34 Diakou Street,
117 43 Athens
Tel. (01) 92.26.411
Fax 92.33.317
*Luxury hotel, with bar, restau-
rant, swimming pool, beauty
salon and 24-hour room service. 297 rooms.*

**St George
Lycabettus**
Kleomenous 2,
10675 Athens.
Tel. (01) 72.90.712;
Fax 72.90.439.
*Modern luxury hotel in pleas-
ant residential area, close to
Lycabettus Hill. No public
transport. Swimming pool, roof
garden. Grill room with superb
panoramic view of the Acropolis. 150 rooms.*

Stanley
Odysseos 1, 10437 Athens.
Tel. (01) 52.20.011;
Fax 52.44.611
*Bright, spacious, comfortable
hotel geared to package tours.
Awkward location for those
without transport, about 15
minutes walk west of Omonia
Square. Rooftop pool with
grand views. 400 rooms.*

Titania
Panepistimiou 52,
10678 Athens.
Tel. (01) 36.09.611;
Fax 36.30.497.
*Large, recemtly refurbished
hotel, with comfortable rooms,
good restaurant and cafe, and
central location. Piano bar,
rooftop garden. 396 rooms.*

Zafolia
87–89 Alexandras Avenue,
114 74 Athens.
Tel. (01) 64.49.012;
Fax 64.42.042
*Roof garden, swimming pool,
private garage. 191 rooms.*

Corfu

Akrotiri Beach
Palaeokastritsa, PO Box 28,
49100 Corfu.
Tel. (0663) 41.237; Fax 41.277
On a peninsula between two coves, so both sides have sea views. All rooms have bath and balcony. Gravel beach on one side, secluded rocky shore on other. Swimming pool and terrace restaurant. 250 rooms.

Arkadion
Kapodistriou St, Corfu Town
Tel. (0661) 37.670
Good location on the Esplanade, with fantastic views. Friendly staff, good value. 95 rooms.

Arion
Fiakon 6, 49100 Corfu Town.
Tel. (0661) 37.950
Family-run hotel, two miles from town centre, and five minutes from Mon Repos Lido. Swimming pool, rooftop garden, disco. 105 rooms.

Bella Vanezia
Zambeli 4, 49100 Corfu Town.
Tel. (0661) 46.500; Fax 20.708
Fine old town house, recently renovated, with a view of Corfu Town, only five minutes from centre. Popular patio cafe. 32 rooms.

Bretagne
Kapa Georgaki 27, Garitsa,
49100 Corfu Town.
Tel. (0661) 30.724
Well looked after and cosily furnished, handy for the airport. 44 rooms.

Cavalieri
Kapodistriou 4,
49100 Corfu Town.
Tel. (0661) 39.041; Fax 39.283
Comfortable and cosy, set in grand 17th century Venetian-style house overlooking the Spianada and the sea. 48 rooms.

Chandris Dasia Complex
Dasia Bay, 49083 Corfu.
Tel. (0661) 97.199;
Fax 45.20.715
Bungalows and villas in landscaped garden, with view of sea and mountains. Swimming pool, tennis, private beach. 527 rooms.

Constantinoupolis
Zavitsanou 11,
49100 Corfu Town.
Tel. (0661) 39.826.
Old French-style mansion facing the harbour, offering clean, basic accommodation with good views. 44 rooms.

Corfu Palace
Democratias 2,
49100 Corfu Town.
Tel. (0661) 39.485. Fax 31 749.
Elegant old hotel on seafront, only 10 minutes walk from town centre. Luxurious rooms all have balcony with sea view. Swimming pool and beautiful gardens overlooking the Nautical Club. 110 rooms.

Corfu Hilton
Nafsicas, Kanoni,
PO Box 124, 49100 Corfu.
Tel. (0661) 36.540; Fax 36.551
Set on hillside with panoramic view of the sea and hills. Outdoor and indoor swimming pools, lovely gardens, tennis, private beach, bowling. Part overlooks airport runway, and aircraft noise can be a problem. 255 rooms.

Grand Glifada
Glifada Beach, 49100 Glifada.
Tel. (0661) 94.201
Modern, open plan hotel overlooking glorious sandy beach and open sea. Swimming pool, colourful garden. Dancing most nights. 242 rooms.

Kerkyrka Golf
Alykes, Corfu.
Tel. (0661) 31.785.
Comfortable modern hotel with large, airy rooms, and gardens leading down to the beach, two miles north of Corfu Town. Night-club, watersports, swimming pool. 240 rooms.

Kontokali Bay
Kontokali, 49100 Corfu.
Tel. (0661) 38.736;
Fax 91.901
Deluxe hotel 6km (4 miles) north of Corfu Town. Beautiful gardens by the sea, swimming pool and private beach, restaurant, taverna and beach bar, tennis courts and activities. Most rooms have sea or garden views. 152 rooms, 81 bungalows.

Marina Hotel
Anemomilos,
49100 Corfu Town.
Tel. (0661) 32.783
Set on the headland at the south end of Garitsa Bay, two miles from town centre. Rooms are large, bright and quiet, with balconies overlooking the sea. Swimming pool, restaurant, rooftop garden. 102 rooms.

Palaeokastritsa
Palaeokastritsa, Corfu.
Tel. (0661) 41.207.
Lovely setting high above the beautiful bay, with long flight of steps winding 200 m down to its own beach. Choice of rooms or bungalows. 163 rooms.

Pension Phoenix
H. Smirnis 2,
49100 Corfu Town.
Tel. (0661) 42.290.
Family-run budget hotel, with small rooms and very basic facilities, about a mile out of town on the way to the airport. 23 rooms.

Crete
Aghios Nikolaos

Apollon
Minoos 9,
72100 Aghios Nikolaos, Crete.
Tel. (0841) 23.023
Large rooms with private bath and balcony, spacious lobby and bar. 50 m from town beach. 72 rooms.

Elounda Beach
72053 Elounda, Crete.
Tel. (0841) 41.412
Luxury hotel/bungalow village two miles south of Elounda, built in traditional Cretan style. Two private beaches, excellent pool, beautiful landscaped gardens. 301 rooms.

Elounda Mare
Elounda, PO Box 31,
72100 Aghios Nikolaos, Crete.
Tel. (0841) 41.512
Luxury hotel/bungalow complex on gently sloping terraced hillside above the sea. Studio bungalows with private pool and patio. Restaurant and bar on shaded terrace. Varied sports facilities. 90 rooms.

Hotel du Lac
Oktobriou 28 ,
72100 Aghios Nikolaos, Crete.
Tel. (0841) 22.711.
Average accommodation, but nice setting, with cafe terrace overlooking the "Bottomless Lake". Right in the middle of town, near post office and tourist information. 33 rooms.

Minos Beach
72100 Agios Nikolaos, Crete.
Tel. (0841) 22.345; Fax 23.816
Stylish luxury hotel with lush gardens, on seafront one mile north of town. Good restaurant. 130 rooms.

St Nicholas Bay
72100 Aghios Nikolaos, Crete.
Tel. (0841) 25.041;
Fax 24.556.
Luxury holiday complex two miles north of town, with beautiful gardens above bay. Private beach, covered pool, tennis courts. 120 rooms.

Chania

Porto Veneziano
Enetikos Limin,
73132 Chania, Crete.
Tel. (0821) 59.311; Fax 44.053
Simple, modern hotel in Chania Old Town, near the Venetian harbour, 15 minutes from town centre. 61 rooms.

Xenia
Theotokopolou,
73132 Chania, Crete.
Tel. (0821) 24.561
Set in a beautiful part of town, on top of the Venetian fortifications close to the old harbour. Lounge with traditional Cretan fireplace. Restaurant, snack bar, swimming pool. 44 rooms.

Iraklion

Apollonia Beach
PO Box 1132,
71100 Iraklion, Crete.
Tel. (081) 821.602
Hotel and bungalows, terraces overlooking sandy beach. Six km west of town. Tennis, water sports, minigolf, horse riding. 320 rooms.

Atrion
K. Palaeologou 9,
71202 Iraklion, Crete.
Tel. (081) 229.225;
Fax 223.292
Modern, elegant hotel with bright, tastefully furnished rooms, near centre of town. Restaurant, cafeteria, patio-bar. Parking available. 70 rooms.

Castello
Iraklion. Tel. (081) 251 212;
Fax 25.00.00
Comfortable hotel near city walls in Old Town. Roof garden. 64 rooms.

Creta Maris
Limin Chersonisou,
70014 Iraklion, Crete.
Tel. (0897) 22.115, 22.127
Luxury hotel complex 800 m from centre of Hersonissos. 745 beautiful rooms, terrace gardens with swimming pools.

Cretan Village
Limin Chersonisou,
700 14 Iraklion, Crete
Tel. (0897) 22.295
288 rooms. Built in traditional style of an old Cretan village.

Dedalos
Dedalou 15, Iraklion., Crete
Tel. (081) 22.43.91.
Friendly, cheap and centrally located, basic rooms with balconies. 61 rooms.

Galaxy
Dimokratias 67, 71306 Iraklion.
Tel. (081) 23.88.12;
Fax 21.12.11
Pleasant modern hotel in residential area, one mile from town centre. Restaurant, cafe, rooftop garden. 144 rooms.

Idi
Zaros, 700 02 Iraklion
Tel. (0894) 31.301/2
35 rooms. In the foothills of Psiloreitis. Swimming pool.

Silva Maris
Limin Chersonisou,
70014 Iraklion, Crete.
Tel. (0897) 22.850, 22.205
Village complex on beach; rooms with shutters and balconies overlook pool and terrace. Restaurant, cafe, bar. Tennis, billiards, children's playground. 249 rooms.

Rethymnon

Fortezza
Melissinou 16,
74100 Rethymnon, Crete
Tel. (0831) 23.828; Fax 54.073
In the Old Quarter. 54 large rooms with balconies; swimming pool and terrace.

Grecotel
Creta Palace
Adelianos Kambos,
74100 Rethymnon, Crete
Tel. (0831) 21.181; Fax 20.085
Luxury complex in village style; private grounds and sandy beach, 3½ miles from town. Indoor and outdoor swimming pools, tennis courts, watersports, bikes. 366 rooms.

Grecotel
Rithymna Beach
Adelianos Kambos,
74100 Rethymnon, Crete.
Tel. (0831) 29.491, 71.002; Fax 71.668
Luxury mini-resort on a long, sandy beach. Excellent facilities for children. 568 rooms.

Jo-An
Dimitrakaki 6,
74100 Rethymnon, Crete
Tel. (0831) 24.241
Good hotel near centre of town, 15 min. from beach. Roof-top bar and swimming pool with views of harbour. 65 rooms.

New Alianthos Beach
Plakias, 74060 Myrtios, Crete.
Tel. (0832) 31.227; Fax 31.282
Family hotel with balconies overlooking the cove. Magnificent scenery. 150 rooms.

Palladion
Adelianos Kambos,
74100 Rethymnon, Crete
Tel. (0831) 71.789
Informal family hotel five minutes walk from the beach, with pool and sun terrace. 48 rooms.

Rhodes

Aliki Hotel
Symi, Rhodes
Tel. (0241) 71.665; Fax 71.655
Tastefully restored, waterside townhouse with charming accommodation, relaxed atmosphere and pleasant restaurant.

Constantinos
Amerikis 65,
85100 Rhodes Town
Tel. (0241) 22.971
Close to the beach. All rooms with balcony. 133 rooms.

Faliraki Beach
85100 Faliraki, Rhodes.
Tel. (0241) 85.403
Attractive whitewashed hotel with pleasant gardens, restaurants, bars, sea-water swimming pools, tennis. Open Apr. to Oct. 316 rooms.

Grand Hotel
Astir Palace
G. Papanikolaou,
85100 Rhodes Town
Tel. (0241) 26.284
Luxury hotel, with outdoor and indoor swimming pools, piano bar, health centre, tennis, night club, casino. Two restaurants. Cafeteria. 368 rooms.

Ibiscus
Nissirou 17,
85100 Rhodes Town
Tel. (0241) 24.421; Fax 27.283
Set right on the beach at the north end of town, with balconies overlooking the sea. Restaurant and bar. 205 rooms.

Lindos Bay Hotel
85000 Vliha Bay, Lindos
Tel. (0244) 31.502; Fax 31.500
Superbly situated, A-category hotel on a quiet, sandy bay, 3km (1½miles) north of Lindos. Bars, restaurant, tennis facilities; hotel bus to Lindos.

Pension Massari
Irodotou 42,
85100 Rhodes Town
Tel. (0241) 22.469
Lovely situation at the back of the Old Town, close to the walls.

Pension Steve
Omirou 60,
85100 Rhodes Town
Tel. (0241) 24.357
Quiet, inexpensive pension with charming garden, in an atmospheric street of the old town.

Rodos Bay
Trianton, 85100 Ixia, Rhodes.
Tel. (0241) 23.661
Bright, colourful rooms with balconies, most of them with sea views. Private beach reached by underground passage. Rooftop swimming pool. Open Apr. to Oct. 330 rooms.

Rodos Palace Hotel
85100 Ixia
Tel. (0241) 25.222, 26.222; Fax 25.350
Luxury high-rise hotel complex with bungalows and apartments, overlooking private shingle beach. Restaurants, bars, disco, outdoor and indoor sea water pools, tennis, watersports, health centre. Open March to November. 610 rooms.

S. Nikolis Hotel
Ippondamou 61, 85100 Rhodes
Tel. (0241) 34.561; Fax 32.034
Lovely hotel covered in creepers, in a quiet location. Some rooms have balcony overlooking the garden. Roof-top terrace and ouzeria.

Spartalis Hotel
N. Plastira 2,
85100 Rhodes Town
Tel. (0241) 24.371
Close to Mandraki. 79 rooms.

Thessaloniki and environs

ABC
Angelaki 41,
54621 Thessaloniki
Tel. (031) 265.421
Convenient but noisy location opposite the trade fairgrounds. Cafeteria. Breakfast room with fireplace. 105 rooms.

Astoria
Tsimiski 20,
54624 Thessaloniki
Tel. (031) 527.121
Soundproofed rooms. Roof garden. American breakfast. 90 rooms.

Capitol
Monastiriou 8,
54629 Thessaloniki
Tel. (031) 516.221
Near the station, on the edge of the red-light district. 194 rooms.

Capsis
Monastiriou 18,
54630 Thessaloniki
Tel. (031) 521.421
Swimming pool, sauna. 430 rooms.

City
Komninon 11,
54624 Thessaloniki
Tel. (031) 269.421
Some rooms with veranda. Cafeteria. 104 rooms.

Electra Palace
Pl. Aristotelous 5A,
54624 Thessaloniki
Tel. (031) 232.221
Old hotel in convenient location in the city's shopping and restaurant district. Two restaurants, coffee shop. Shopping arcade. Good service, 131 rooms.

El Greco
Egnatia 23,
54630 Thessaloniki
Tel. (031) 520.620
90 rooms.

Makedonia Palace
Megalou Alexandrou,
54640 Thessaloniki
Tel. (031) 837.520
Waterside luxury hotel in a lovely location on the eastern seafront promenade, with fabulous views. Swimming pool. 294 rooms.

Nefeli
Komninon 1, 55236 Panorama
Tel. (031) 942.002
On the hillside at the western edge of the village of Panorama, with wonderful views of Thessaloniki from its roof garden. Night club. 70 rooms.

Pefka
Panorama, 552 36 Thessaloniki
Tel./Fax (031) 341.153
Quiet and comfortable old hotel.

Olympia
Olimpou 65, Thessaloniki
Tel. (031) 235.421
Well-situated near the Roman agora. 110 rooms.

Sun Beach
54007 Agia Triada
Tel. (0392) 51.245
123 rooms.

Vergina
Monastiriou 19,
54627 Thessaloniki
Tel. (031) 516.021;
Fax 529.308
Large, comfortable rooms with balconies, close to the railway station. Roof garden. 133 rooms.

Restaurants

Outside of Athens, Greek restaurants are usually very informal, and regularly change ownership and name. Gradings and recommendations are difficult, as most places serve similar food, and all depends on the whim of the chef and the quality of the fish that were unloaded at the quay that morning. You can eat well—even on the smallest islands—in modest little tavernas, at very reasonable prices. Needless to say, the cost of a meal will be higher in the popular tourist resorts, and in waterfront seafood restaurants. Your best bet is to follow the locals—they always know where the best food is being served. Athens enjoys a more cosmopolitan dining scene, with a range of international cuisines in addition to the home-grown tavernas and cafés. Below is a list of recommended restaurants in the capital.

Apotso's
Panepistimiou 10, Athens.
Tel. (01) 36.37.046
Wood-panelled traditional taverna, favourite hang-out for journalists & theatrical people. Closes at 5pm each day, and on Sundays.

Athinaios
Eduard Lo & Stadiou, Athens
Tel. (01) 32.38.105
Theatrical decor with mirrors and shining brass. Expensive but good quality, sophisticated food.

Balthazar
Tsocha 27, Athens
Tel. (01) 64.41.215
Fashionable international restaurant with attractive bar, in renovated mansion south of the Hilton.

Boschetto
Alsos Evangelismou, Athens
Tel. (01) 72.10.893
Athens' top Italian restaurant enjoys a beautiful location in leafy Evangelismou Park. Closed Sunday. Very expensive.

Byzantino
Kidathineon 18, Plaka
Tel. (01) 32.37.368
Pleasant modern interior and outside tables in the main square of Plaka. Traditional, good taverna food.

The Cellar
Kidathineon 10, Athens
Tel. (01) 32.24.304
Colourful basement taverna in Plaka, popular with the local Athenians. Inexpensive.

Costoyanis
37 Zaimi St., off Alexandras
Tel. (01) 82.20.624
Very old established taverna near the National Archaeological Museum. Closed Sunday.

Delphi
Nikis 13, Athens
Tel. (01) 32.34.869
Centrally situated near Syntagma, and a popular lunchtime rendezvous. Wide range of Greek dishes and salads. Inexpensive-moderate.

Dionysos
Robertou Galli 43, Athens
Tel. (01) 92.33.182, 92.31.936
Package tour Greek restaurant with patisserie. Outdoor dining with a spectacular view of the Acropolis. Expensive.

Eden Vegetarian Restaurant
12 Lissiou, Plaka.
Tel. (01) 32.38.858
Popular vegetarian restaurant in the heart of Plaka. Generous helpings. Closed Tuesdays.

Everest
Tsakalof, Athens
No tel.
A Greek-style fast food restaurant serving pies, pastries, sandwiches and coffee, located in the Kolonaki district at the corner of Odos Iraklitou. Very inexpensive.

Fatsio's
Efroniou 5, Athens
Tel. (01) 72.17.421
An attractive little restaurant serving Greek and Oriental specialities. Near the US Embassy. Inexpensive.

Hermion
15 Pandrossou, Plaka
Tel. (01) 32.46.725
Good food and courteous service in this restaurant in a quiiet courtyard at the lower end of Plaka. Open all day.

Je Reviens
Xenokratous 49, Athens
Tel. (01) 72.10.535, 72.11.174
Gourmet French and Greek cuisine. Enjoy the garden terrace in summer, or the traditionally decorated dining room in winter. In the Kolonaki district. Expensive.

Kanaris
Mikrolimano Piraeus
Tel. (01) 41.22.533, 41.75.190
The best of the many seafood restaurants in Piraeus, where you can dine on fresh fish beside the harbour where it was landed that morning. Expensive.

Kentriko
Kolokotroni 3, Athens
Tel. (01) 32.32.482
Popular lunch rendezvous for local business people, with tables spilling out onto the terrace. The usual Greek taverna menu, with prompt and attentive service. Moderate.

Gerofinikas
Pindarou 10, Athens
Tel. (01) 36.36.710
Greek cuisine with a Levantine touch, and a cosmopolitan atmosphere. Pleasant indoor courtyard. Moderate.

Ideal
Panepistimiou 46, Athens
Tel. (01) 36.14.604
Pleasant, tastefully decorated restaurant serving unusual Greek specialities like kokoretsi (grilled lamb tripe). Closed Sunday. Moderate.

Kona Kai
Ledra Marriot Hotel, Syngrou 117, Athens
Tel. (01) 93.47.711
An unusual and very popular Polynesian/Japanese restaurant with extravagant tropical decor. Very expensive.

Kostoyannis
Zaïmi 37, Athens
Tel. (01) 82.12.496
Huge open air taverna which serves consistently good food, popular with students and travellers. Closed Sunday. Inexpensive.

Manesis
Markou Mousourou 3, Mets,
Tel. (01) 92.27.684
Traditional taverna in a quiet area near the ancient stadium, restored for the first modern Olympics in 1896. Closed Sunday.

Myrtia
Trivonianou 35, Athens
Tel. (01) 90.23.633
Large, well-known taverna offering a huge choice of mezedes (appetizers). Garden with strolling bouzouki players. In the Pangrati district. Closed Sunday. Expensive.

La Pergola

Athenaeum Inter-continental,
Singrou 89–93.
Tel. (01) 90.23.666
*Poolside restaurant with
relaxed atmosphere, though
expensive. Open a ll day.*

Psaropoulos

Kalanion 2, Paralia Glifada
Tel. (01) 89.45.677
*Waterside fish taverna out on
the coast near Piraeus. Expensive.*

Rosebush

17 Gr. Lambrakis St., Glyfada
Tel. (01) 89.43.107
*Greek taverna close to the sea,
specializing in mezedes, Greek
starters which can make a full
meal.*

Socrate's Prison

20 Mistseon St., Makriyanni.
Tel. (01) 92.23.434
*This friendly restaurant, lying
immediately to the south of the
Acropolis, offers Greek and
international style dishes,
including many house recipes.
Popular with tourists and residents. Closed Sunday.*

Steak Room

Eginitou 6, Athens
Tel. (01) 72.17.445
*If you are feeling tired of moussaka and shashlik, then try a
juicy steak or wiener schnitzel
at this international restaurant,
near the Hilton. Moderate.*

Strofi

Roberto Galli 25, Athens
Tel. (01) 92.14.130
*Traditional taverna with outdoor dining and a spectacular
view of the Acropolis. Closed
Sunday. Moderate.*

Ta Nissia

Athens Hilton, Vas, Sofias 46,
Athens
Tel. (01) 72.20.201
*Popular upmarket taverna-style
restaurant with Greek and
international cuisine. Dinner
only. Expensive.*

Themistokles

Vas. Georgiou B 31, Athens
Tel. (01) 72.19.553
*This pleasant whitewashed taverna in the Pangrati district is
a local landmark. Inexpensive.*

Vladimiros

Aristodimou 12, Athens
Tel. (01) 72.17.407
*Enjoy charcoal-grilled lamb,
veal, pork and beef in this
restaurant's pine-fringed garden in the Kolonaki district.
Dinner only. Moderate to
expensive.*

Xynou

Angelou Geronta 4, Athens
Tel. (01) 32.21.065
*Traditional taverna in Plaka,
very popular with Athenian diners—reservations are recommended. Closed weekends and
July. Moderate.*

Dionysus-Zonar's

Panepistimiou 9, Athens
Tel. (01) 32.30.336
*The best zacharoplastio (pastry
shop/café) in the city. Other
branches on Philopappou Hill
and at the summit of Lycabettus
enjoy magnificent views of the
Acropolis. Moderate-expensive.*

INDEX

For easy reference, names of regions, large towns and all islands have been set in **bold face**. Page numbers in **bold face** refer to the main entry, and those in italics refer to photographs and maps.

049/612 RP